Published by

ATLANTIC

PUBLISHERS & DISTRIBUTORS (P) LTD

7/22, Ansari Road, Darya Ganj,
New Delhi-110002
Phones : +91-11-40775252, 23273880, 23275880, 23280451
Fax : +91-11-23285873
Web : www.atlanticbooks.com
E-mail : orders@atlanticbooks.com

Branch Office
5, Nallathambi Street, Wallajah Road,
Chennai-600002
Phones : +91-44-64611085, 32413319
E-mail : chennai@atlanticbooks.com

Printed in India at Nice Printing Press, A-33/3A, Site-IV, Industrial Area, Sahibabad, Ghaziabad, U.P.

Aknowledgments

First, I wish to thank my wife Usha Sangia, who has given me the full support, in writing this book. Secondly, I wish to thank my sons, Rajesh and Rajeev. Rajeev has edited and reviewed the book, while Rajesh has provided me the required facilities and moral support. Finally, I wish to thank my daughters-in-law Papia and Jailaxmi, who have discussed with me about the subject matter, as they have expertise in software and telecommunication fields.

G.P. Sangia

Preface

Internet technology has spread throughout the world within a short span of time. Network is a powerful tool that has brought the world together. Information can be transferred from one corner of the world to another within no time.

This book has nineteen chapters that provide the basic concepts about networking elements like protocol, media, architecture, and various functions used in networking. OSI model for network communication, which is a conceptual blueprint of networking, is explained in detail.

Protocols like NetBEUI, IPX/SPX, AppleTalk and TCP/IP are explained in detail along with network components like Ethernet cards, modems, routers, switches, bridges, repeaters, gateways and hubs and their connection media.

Configuration of router is explained thoroughly along with various commands that are used for its configuration.

Various types of LAN and WAN maintenance equipments like digital voltmeter, time-domain reflectometer, advanced cable testers, protocol analyzers, network monitors, terminators, etc. are briefly described. LAN and WAN problems and their solutions are also explained.

Internet explorer and outlook express are described in full detail. If you can understand all about the Internet explorer, most of the Internet problems can be solved by yourself.

Network is facing the threat from several types of viruses. Some antiviruses with their characteristics are described along with the software and hardware threat in detail. For security of network, chapter on firewall is included.

The book covers the networking fundamentals that are extremely useful to those who want to seek jobs in various IT organisations as front and back office executives. The technicians, engineers and trainees, who are new to networking, can acquire applicable skills in network design and maintenance. The book is also useful for Internet users to solve their internet problems by themselves. The book contains the certificate course material of various institutions, which will help the students to improve their profile and enhance their job prospects.

G.P. Sangia

Contents

Basic Concept of Networking

1

Networking is the term that is used for Internet. Local Area Network (LAN) is a network of computers, which works for relatively a small area. When two or more LANs are connected with each other, it forms a network. This network can be further expanded by adding more LANs to it. When we made connections with LANs across greater geographical distances, we use WAN technology. This huge network is called Wide Area Network.

The data packets are transferred, from one computer to another and from one network to another network, through wire or wireless connections, with very high speed. Thus network is a .powerful tool that has brought the world together. Information can be transferred from, one corner of the world to another within no time.

Networking has the following basics elements:

1. Protocol
2. Media
3. Architecture
4. Functions
5. Applications
6. Other areas

1. Protocol

Protocol is a basic element of networking. It is, therefore, necessary to understand the protocol.

1. Why are the protocols needed?

2. How are protocol used in the networking?
3. What are the other protocols it relies upon?

There are many operations carried out, before the internet system transmits the data, from one computer to another. The internet system uses network protocols, which are the sets of standards that perform all the activities within a network.

Set of standard defines methods, for all these operations, which are carried out on the network. Protocols contains all information which enable the outside devices, to interact with the network. Protocols define all the basic networking data structures and the higher level application programs.

Many services and utility programs definitions are contained by the protocols which are used at various layers of network model. There are many protocols used in internet technology. Some of the most useful protocols are NetBEUI, TCP/IP, IPX/SPX and AppleTalk. There are some more protocols that support the NetBEUI, TCP/IP, IPX/SPX and AppleTalk.

2. Media

Transmission of data across the network needs some media. Copper cable, fiber optic, or ether are the main medias that enable the network to transmit data from one computer to another.

Copper Cables

Many types of copper cables are commonly used with LANs.

Twisted pair cable is twisted to minimize crosstalk interference. It has two varieties:

1. Shielded twisted pair (STP)
2. Unshielded twisted pair (UTP)

Coaxial Cable

Coaxial cable is another category of cable which is used in networking. Coaxial cable has a single copper conductor at the center of the cable. It is coated with the plastic layer throughout its length. A braided metal shield is provided on the plastic layer.

It is a general practice, to use one type of cable for a network. In some case a network may use a variety of cables.

Network topology, protocol, and size are the basis for choosing different type of cable. For designing a successful network we must know the characteristics of each type of cable.

3. Architecture

Architecture of a network is physical concept (layout) of the network. It is a design, in which we fix the positions of all hardware on the network, along with the physical transmission media like cat-5 wires, coaxial cable or wireless connection. The data access method (OSI Layer 2) is one of the another consideration of design.

Network architectures enable us to move data quickly and efficiently on the network medium. The particular Ethernet is a kind of network architecture that define the topology of the network. Ethernet also defines the working strategy for the network. There are some other network architectures like IBM Token Ring, FDDI and AppleTalk.

4. Functions

Several functions are carried out during transfer of data from one computer to the another on the network. Routing is used to route the message. Firewall is used for security of the system. Many other functions like, documents multicasting, dynamic routing, and network management are used in networking.

5. Applications

Networking application includes ping and traceroute that will cover telnet, Rlogin, and FTP.

How the applications such as ping and traceroute work. Both ping and traceroute are the router command.

Ping

Ping is short name for Packet Internet Groper. Ping command is applied when you are dealing with router on a network. It is used for testing the connection between client computers, servers, or routers.

Ping uses ICMP echo message requests and listens for ICMP echo message reply from its intended host. Using the—R option with ping enables the record route feature. If this option is used, ping will set the record route (RR) in the outgoing ICMP IP datagram.

Traceroute

This program also uses ICMP messaging and the time to live (TTL) field in the IP header. It works by sending a packet to the destined host with a TTL value of 1. The first router will send back the ICMP "time exceeded" message to the source node. Then the traceroute program will send a message with a TTL value of 2, then 3, etc. This way source node will get information about each router using the information received in the ICMP packets. To get information about the receiving host, the message is sent to a port that is not likely to be serviced by that host.

6. Other Areas

These include the following:

1. Installing drivers for modem Ethernet Adapter.
2. Network operating systems and their application.
3. Configuration of modem subnet mask and gateway.
4. Backing up the network.
5. Trouble shooting of the network.

When two or more computers are connected through a media and with the support of hardware and software they communicate with each other. This arrangement, we may call a network. The network may be of two types:

1. Distributed network system
2. Internet network system

1. Distributed Network System

Distributed system is run by a main computer at the center. This computer at the center is called mainframe computer. Distributed system uses only one type of operating system. Many computers are connected with the mainframe computer to share information. Computer at each terminal acts as input or output device. These computers depend upon the mainframe computer and process the data provided by mainframe computer.

Mainframe computer is kept away from WAN for its data security. Areas like process industries, banking, etc. which require a very high reliability, use the distributed system. The application of distributed system generally used for a unique objective.

2. Internet Network System

Many computers of different architectures can be connected in a network. Each computer is autonomous and can access the network independently. Each computer can also share the information with each other. Network system is used for wide area of application, like education, business, entertainment, etc. and various type of files and data can be transferred from one machine to another.

World Wide Web

2

World wide web is sometimes called only web, in information technology. The documents and the link between them, forms a "Web" of information. Files or pages on the web are interconnected. You can access the other pages by clicking the special text or graphics. These text or graphics are called hyperlinks. A page can contain text, images, movie and sound. These pages can be located, on a computer, anywhere in the world. When we are connected to the web, we can access them. Thus anybody has equal access to information worldwide.

Client/Server Model

Server provides service to the client and client utilizes the services. Suppose you enter in a restaurant and take your seat, you are greeted by a menu. You see the menu and order for a cup of tea. You are served with tea but you do not want to know how tea is prepared and what are its gradients. You just order a cup of tea and you are served by the waiter.

Client/server model is also based on the same philosophy. Client places the request or order to the server and server responds to the request and serves the client. Here also after receiving the request from client, server has to go through many operations for preparing the response for the client. The response is exactly prepared, according to the request of the client, to satisfy his requirements.

Let us take an example of chat of clients and server interaction. Suppose a client computer called A and a server computer called B. Client computer A can send a request at any time to Server B. Server computer B can receive the request from A and can respond to the request of A. The condition during this interaction is that in both the cases the server computer must be connected with the client computer.

Now suppose client A wants to chat with client C through server B. Then client A and client C both must be connected through chat program which are provided by the MSN, Yahoo, etc. Suppose client A wants to chat with client C then client A may open chat program and include the client C in his chat program through its email address. Server B will act as a bridge in between client A and client C and sends response to both client A and C on their requests.

When client A wants to chat with client C, client A sends a request to server B and asks for a chat connection with C. If computer C is on line then server B sends message to computer C that client A is online and wants to chat with you. Now client C opens the chat window and types a message to client A. The message is first sent to the server and then server sends this message to client A. Now A gets the message in chat window from C and the chat process starts. The message are sent from client to server and server to client in the form of html pages with the help of hypertext protocol.

The web uses the following two gradients on the internet for transmission of files or data:

1. Hypertext Transfer Protocol (HTTP)
2. Hypertext Markup Language (HTML)

1. Hypertext Transfer Protocol (HTTP)

Hypertext Transfer Protocol has the four main functions:

1. Connection,
2. Request,
3. Response,
4. Close.

2. Hypertext Markup Language (HTML)

1. It is the language to design a web page.

2. It defines the structure and appearance of the web page. Html files are the simple ASCI (plain text) documents, which are saved with an .htm or .html extension.

3. HTML allows inclusion of mainly two types of text/data:

(a) **The Content:** The actual data are to be displayed on the web page (text, pictures, etc.).

(b) **The Markup:** The tags, which are used to specify the format, in which data must be interpreted by the web browser.

Type of Web Page

Web server responds to a web browser request, by returning a HTML page.

The return page can be of three types:

Static html page

Dynamic html page

Directory listing html page.

Static html Page

Static html pages that are prepared in advance according to the request of the client.

The web server returns the html pages to the user, but takes no special action.

The user requests a static page typing an URL as follows in the address strip of the browser.

http://www.company.com/home.htm. and then press enter.

The same operation can be carried out by clicking on the link http://www.company.com/home.htm.

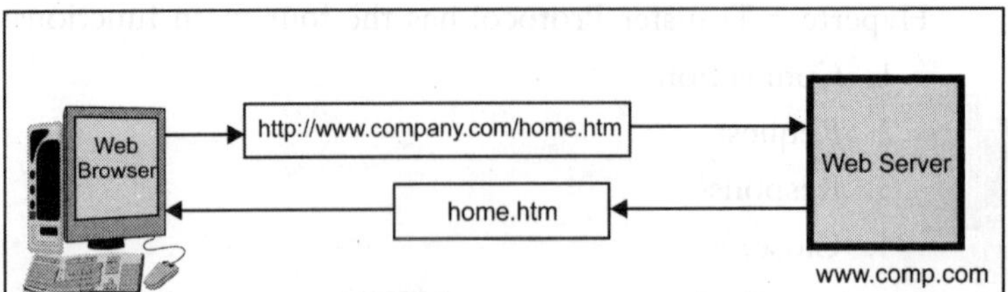

Static HTML Page

Dynamic html Pages

1. Dynamic pages are created in response to a user's request.

2. Web browser collects information by presenting a page with text boxes, menus and check boxes that the user fills or selects.

3. When a user clicks a submit button on a form the data from the form are sent to the web server.

4. The server takes the following actions:

(a) The application is processed and returns the result to the user as html page.

(b) The application is transferred to some other point.

(c) The data may be posted to a database server.

Example 1

Following figure shows that the web browser sends the problem application for calculation of the sum of two digits to the server. Web server received the request and sends a page with the addition of two digits. You fill up the two digits and press the submit button.

The request is again sent to the server by the browser. After reading the requirement of client web server sends the application to the processing unit. After processing the calculation by Add.dll file, it is sent back to web server. Web server finally sends the solution, in the form of html page to the browser.

Example 2

Following figure shows that the web browser sends the order.inc file to the server by writing the http://

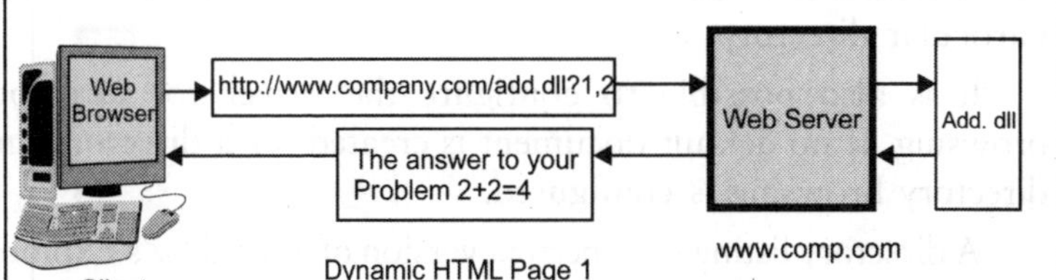

Dynamic HTML Page 1

www.company.com/order.inc in the address bar of the browser and by pressing enter.

Web server received the request and after reading the requirement of client, web server connect it to data base through internet data bank connector.

Data bank processes the application and result is sent back to server. Server sends this response, in the form of order form, to the browser as html page.

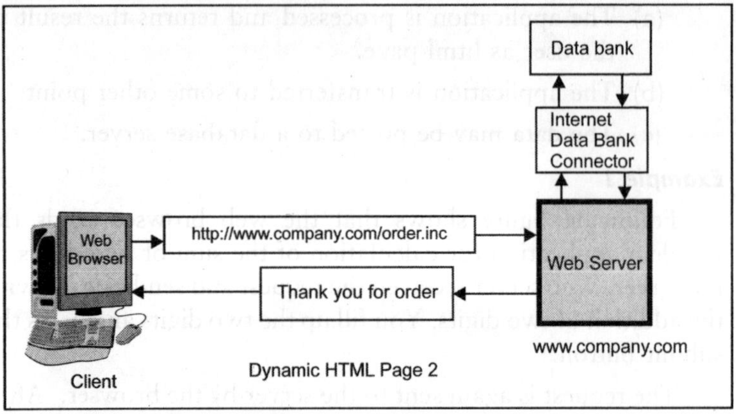

Dynamic HTML Page 2

Browser or client fill up the form and submit the request to the server. If you fill the form correctly. You get the response by thanking you. If there is any mistake, then you are prompted by the server to rectify the entries and resubmit the order again.

Example 3

Dynamic Listing

If the client sends quarries without specifying a particular file, a default document may be created for the web site or for a particular directory.

It is also possible to configure the server for directory browsing. If no default document is created for a directory and directory browsing is configured.

A directory listing (a hypertext version of a window's Explorer or file manager listing) is returned to the user in the form of html page, then client jumped to the appropriate file by clicking in the directory listing.

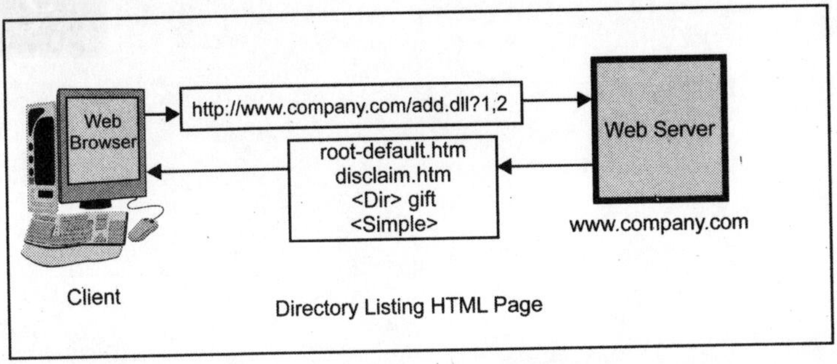

E-mail gateways uses Simple Mail Transfer Protocol (SMTP) or the X.400 standard to deliver messages from source to the destination.

Electronic data interchange (EDI). It is the set of standard that processes the flow of data and enable to perform various activities like accounting, shipping, receiving, inventory tracking between businesses.

Special interest bulletin boards. It has developed the chat rooms where people can communicate with each other either by typing messages or by live conversation.

Internet navigation utilities. It provides the search engines like Google and Yahoo! You can access various type of information with the help of such search engines.

Financial transaction services. Financial transactions such as marketing, trading, currency exchange, etc. becomes easier and faster.

OSI Model

3

Open System Interconnection (OSI) is a theoretical model for network communication. It is a conceptual blueprint that explains the communication, in between transmitter and the receiver. Certain rules have to be followed during sending and receiving of messages on a network.

FEATURES OF OSI MODEL

1. Setting up Connection

It establishes communications, in between the PCs and other devices, on the network. When data are sent from a PC, it supplies a mechanism that applies a communication channel, between sender and receiver.

2. Data Control

After a communications session has been established between computers, it sets the rules to control the data that passes between them.

3. Logical Addressing

Logical addressing of packets is converted to the actual physical addressing, provided by the network. Network uses logical addressing schemes such as IP addresses. There must be a conversion of these logical addresses into the actual hardware addresses, found on the NICs of the computers.

4. Standard Model

Open System Interconnection (OSI) is the standard model for data communication. All the standards for data communication are defined by the International Standards Organization. OSI model is designed as open system that is suitable for data transfer in between the different type of computers and operating systems.

5. Layered Structure

The design of communication system is based on layered architecture. The processes for smooth and effective communication are divided into logical groups which are called layers. It is a seven layers model, where each layer performs a specific task and works in a group.

The seven layers are shown in the following figure.

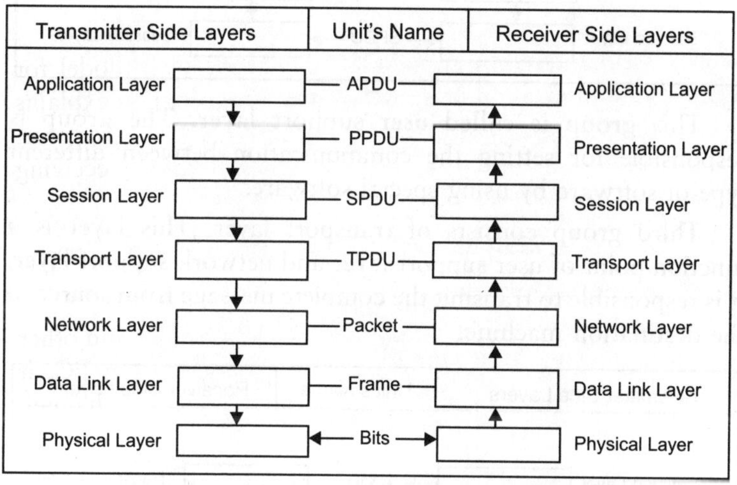

These seven layers may be grouped in three groups.

First group consists of three layers as shown in the following figure.

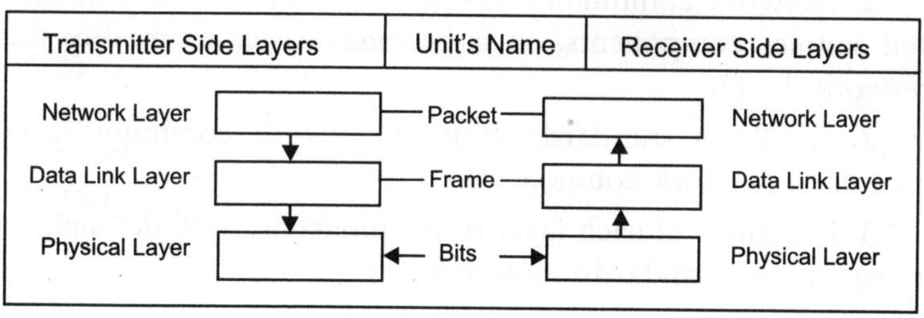

This group is called Network Support Layers. Network support layers are hardware implemented and use the various types of software to manage the different type of network. Network support layers are responsible for physical transportation of data.

Second group consists of another three layers, as shown in the following figure.

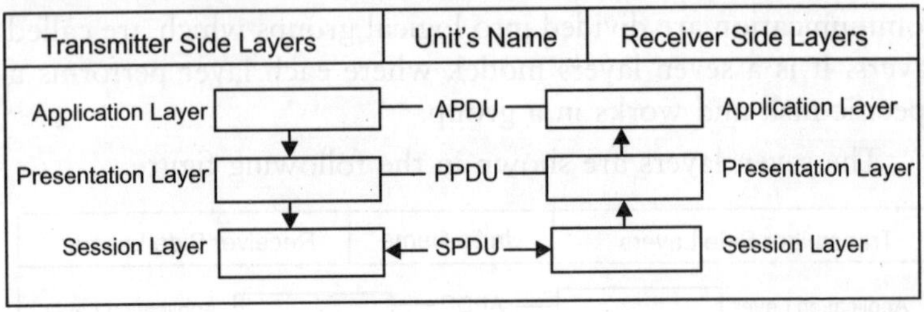

This group is called user support layer. The group is responsible for setting the communication between different type of software by using special software.

Third group consists of transport layer. This layer is a junction point of user support layer and network support layer. It is responsible to transmit the complete message from source to the destination machine.

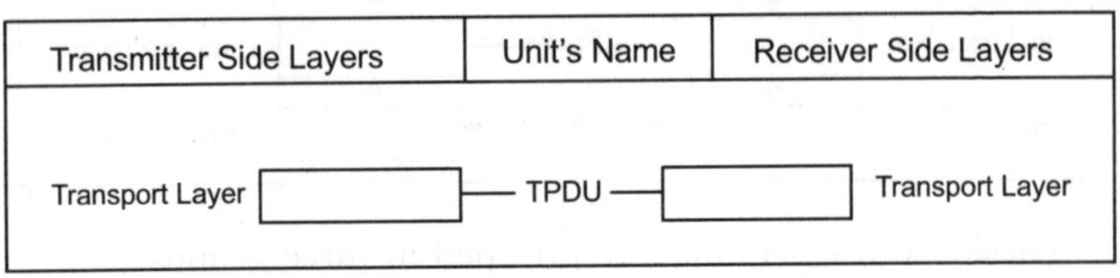

ADVANTAGES OF OSI MODEL

1. Network communication process is broken into smaller and simpler components, so it becomes easier to modify the network design.

2. It allows standardization of network communication process of network components.

3. Functions of each layer of the model are well defined, so it attracts the standardization industry.

4. It enables different types of network hardware and software to communicate.

5. The changes in one layer does not affect the other layers, so it does not come in the way of development.

Functions of the layers are indicated in the following figure.

Layer	Function
Application Layer	File print message database and application service
Presentation Layer	Data encryption, compression and transmission services
Session Layer	Dialog control
Transport Layer	End to end connection
Network Layer	Routing
Data Link Layer	Framing
Physical Layer	Physical topology

OSI MODEL

The seven layer OSI model is described below. Each layer is responsible for an unique type of function to enable the communications on the network. This seven layer design of OSI model is able to accommodate any changes in network technology. The layers are described here from the higher levels starting with the application to the lower levels.

1. Application Layer

Application layer enable the internet user to input data and transfer them to the remote computer.

The message passes through the six layers of OSI model, where various sequence of operation are performed and finally message is transmitted to the destination by physical layer.

Functions of application layer:

1. Network terminal or node
2. Message handling services
3. Remote file access
4. Directory services

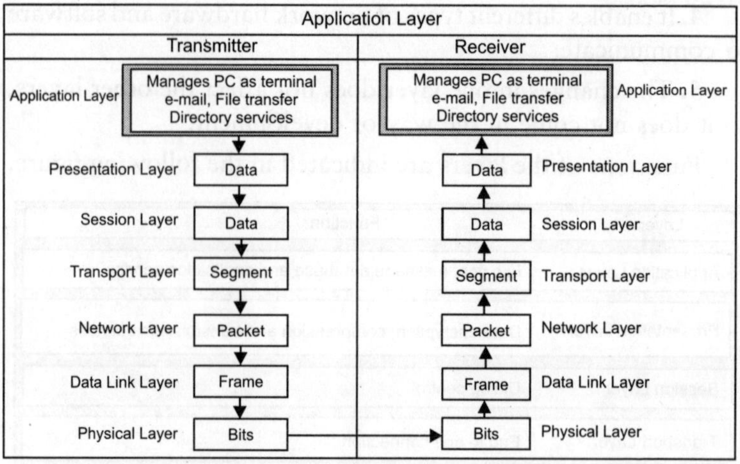

1. Network terminal or node. Application layer is a software program, that establishes a connection of one computer with the another remote computer, and acts as a node. Computers of different architecture are used by a network. For logical flow of information between the two different types of computers, a software is used that is called terminal emulator. The terminal emulator's function is to convert the input data sequence transmitted by the source computer to the data sequence that can be understood by the receiving computer.

2. Message handling services. You can send and receive e-mails by using messaging services. Message is sent from one node to the another node. Each node is provided with a message storing service. When a node receives a message, it is first stored and then transmitted to the next node. The message is routed through various nodes and finally reached to the destination node.

MHS system has three components:

I. User Agent

II. Mail Box

III. MT Agent

I. User Agent. It is a software which enables the user to access the message. It is the editor where you can write your mails and read them. MS mail and CC mail are the example of user agent.

II. **Mail Box.** This is a storage provided for storing the mails. You can use this storage for sending and receiving mails.

III. **MT Agent.** Mail transfer agent access the message at a node and transmits it to the next node.

E-mail Form

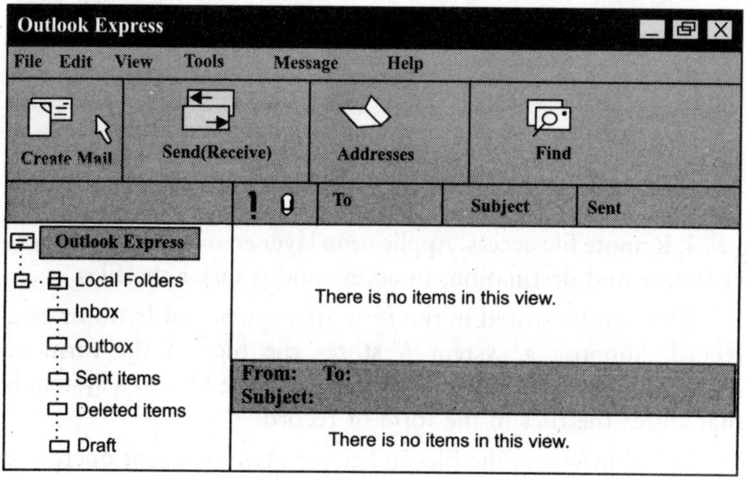

Outlook express is a Microsoft product used for sending receiving e-mail. There is a local folder that contains folders named as Inbox, Outbox, Sent Items, Deleted Items and Draft. Inbox for storing the incoming message, Outbox for sending the message. Sent items are stored in sent item folder. Deleted items are stored in delete folder. Draft folder stores the newly drafted e-mails.

Create e-mail by clicking on Create Mail button.

Following e-mail editor will appear on the screen.

E-mail editor contains the following:

To: This field contains the recipient e-mail address.

CC: It also contains the e-mail address to whom the copy of the message is to be sent.

BCC: It contains the address of the recipient e-mail address whose address is not displayed in the e-mail list. It is called blind copy of e-mail.

Subject: This field contains the subject of the message.

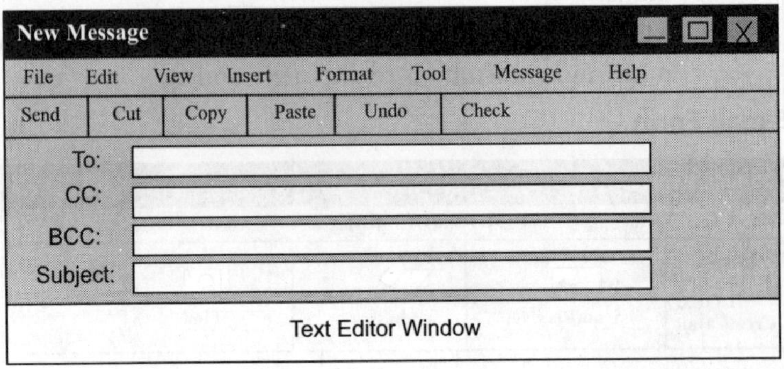

3. Remote file access. Application layer enables the computers at source and destination, to access and transfer the files.

Files can be stored in the form of sequence of bytes or as a record. Suppose a system A stores the files in the form of sequence of bytes and wants to transfer these files to a system B that stores the files in the form of record.

For transferring the files in between two different operating systems, we have to include two hardware devices which are called initiator and responder.

Initiator sends a request to the remote computer to transfer the files from responder store. Responder creates the virtual files from the real file which is requested by the initiator and allow the initiator to access it.

4. Directory services. It enables the user to access the information on various topics. If the client sends quarries without specifying a particular file, a default document may be created for the web site or for a particular directory. It is also possible to configure the server for directory browsing.

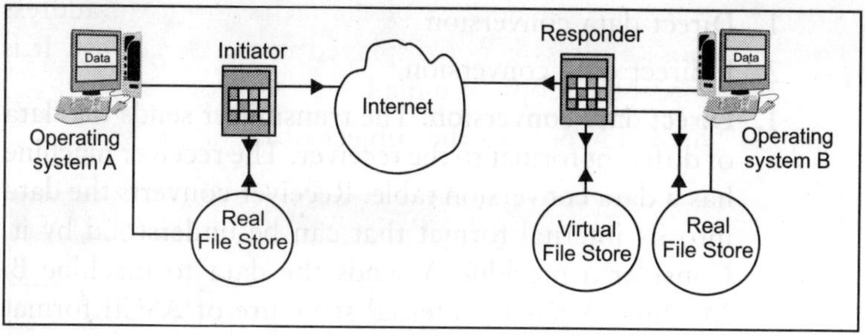

2. Presentation Layer

Presentation Layer presents data to the application layer. It is responsible for data translation and code formatting.

Following are the main functions of presentation layer:

1. Translation
2. Encryption
3. Compression
4. Security

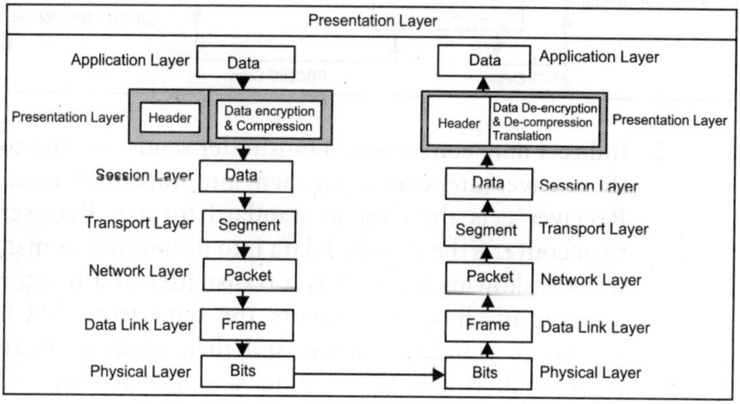

1. Translation. There are computers of different architectures that use different type of operating system. Some computers use ASCII data format and other use EBCDIC data format. Presentation layer works as interpreter to translate the data from ASCII to EBCDIC and *vice versa*. There are two methods adapted for this type of data conversion:

1. Direct data conversion
2. Indirect data conversion

1. **Direct data conversion.** The transmitter sends the data of different format to the receiver. The receiver machine has a data conversion table. Receiver converts the data into its internal format that can be understood by it. Consider a machine A sends the data to machine B. Machine A has its internal structure of ASCII format while machine B has EBCDIC format.

Machine B uses its data conversion table and translates the data of ASCII format to EBCDIC format while machine A translator converts the data from EBCDIC format to ASCII. Thus Machine A and B can communicate with each other.

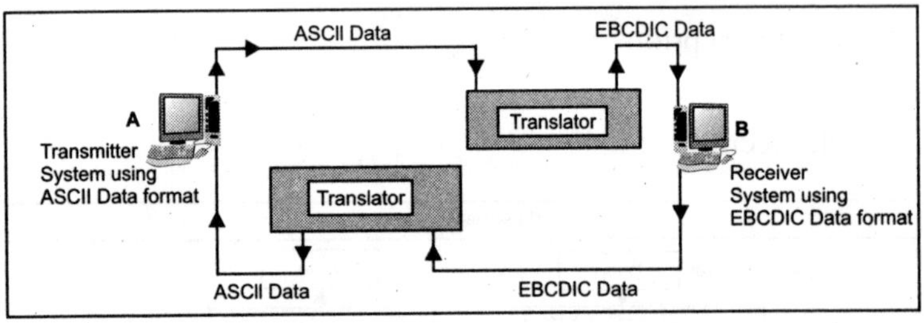

2. **Indirect data conversion.** Transmitter sends the data to the receiver after converting them into standard format. Receiver gets the data in standard format. Receiver then converts the standard data into its internal format. In the following figure A is a transmitter and B is the receiver machine. A converts the data from ASCII format to standard format and then sends them to receiver B. B gets the data in standard format and converts them from standard to EBCDIC format to read and understand the content.

In the reverse process B sends the data after converting them from EBCDIC to standard format. A receives the data in standard format and converts them from standard to ASCII to read and understand the content of the message.

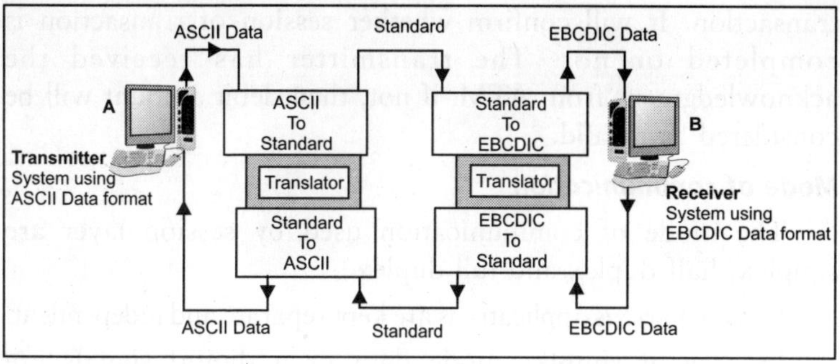

2. Encryption. Data are encrypted by the source and decrypted at the destination at the presentation layer level. This enhances the security of the data.

3. Compression. Data are compressed at this level and then transmitted to the receiver where the presentation layer decompressed the data.

4. Security. To transmit the data safely and accurately presentation layer's standards are used.

3. Session Layer

Session layer is responsible for creating, managing, and terminating sessions between applications. It establishes two ways communication between source and the destination machines. Its functions are to start, control, and end communication, between the transmitter and the receiver. The time between starting and ending of communication between two nodes is called session.

This layer also provides dialogue control between two nodes. Session layer terminates the connection, when complete data are received, by the receiver machine and transmitter gets the acknowledgment. The session layer is equipped with checkpoints that manages the data and minimize the retransmission of data.

Example

Consider the withdrawal of cash from ATM. It fails during transaction without handing the cash. The transaction of money is recorded and debited in saving account, though the receiver did not get any money. The Session layer here control the transaction. It will confirm whether session of transaction is completed or not. The transmitter has received the acknowledgment from ATM, if not, then debit amount will be considered as invalid.

Mode of communication

The mode of communication used by session layer are simplex, half duplex and full duplex.

Data of various applications are kept separate and independent.

In case of simplex mode data or a digital signals are transmitted in only one direction.

In half duplex mode data are transmitted in two directions but only one direction at a time.

In full duplex mode data are transmitted in both directions simultaneously.

Session layer of OSI model is shown in the following figure.

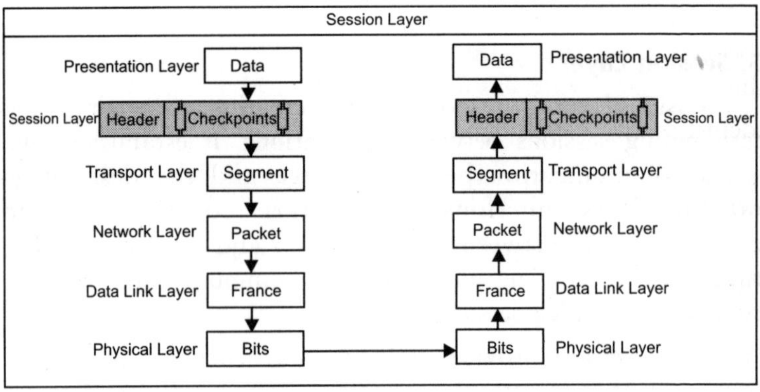

Functions of session layer:

1. Managing session,
2. Managing dialog,
3. Handling error,
4. Security.

1. Managing session. Session layer starts and terminates the connection when complete data are received by the receiver and transmitter gets the acknowledgment. As soon as the message is sent by the transmitter, session layer set up a calculated time of reaching the message to the destination. It includes the acknowledgment time also. The time between, starting of the message from source and getting acknowledgment from the recipient is called session.

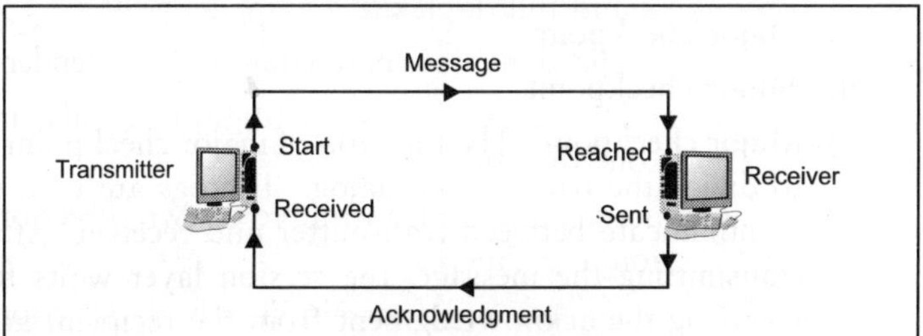

Session for a message

At the session layer level, data are transformed into logical unit that is called dialog. It control the data at this level are specified as session protocol data unit (SPDU). The SPDU has the following fields as shown in the following table:

Identifier	It identifies the types of data to be transmitted.
Length indicator	It indicates the length of the parameter fields.
Parameter fields	It specifies the level of service. It has checkpoints to handle errors.
Data	Data which are transferred from presentation layer to session layer.

2. Managing dialog. Session layer manages the two ways dialog, between the transmitter and the receiver machines. Every time the session layer worked out dialog session and determines who communicates and when. Checkpoints are used in between the dialog, to find any error during communication. In case of error, retransmission takes place, to continue the dialog session and duration of session is increased accordingly.

3. Handling error. There is no reliability of transferring the data at the lower layer level while session layer provides the complete reliability. Session layer set up the checkpoints to handle the error. The advantage of checkpoints is that it orders the source to retransmit only that packet which has the error and not the complete message. This minimize the time of transmission. There are two types of checkpoints used by session layer:

(i) Major checkpoint

(ii) Minor checkpoint

(i) **Major checkpoint.** The function of major checkpoint is to divide the packet into dialogs. Dialogs are used to communicate between transmitter and receiver. After transmitting the message, the session layer waits for receiving the acknowledgment from the recipient at a checkpoint. If any error occurs at this point session layer immediately goes to the previous checkpoint and rollback operation takes place. This rollback provides the errorless message and the dialog with error is discarded. Transmitter retransmits the dialog and the data are recovered.

(ii) **Minor checkpoint.** In between the two major checkpoints minor checkpoints are inserted. These minor checkpoints do not need to get acknowledge from recipient. In case of error, it is checked between the two minor checkpoints and rectified by retransmission. This reduces the retransmission time of the message.

4. Security. Session layer provide the user name and the password to access the server. Before the connection is made with server you have to enter, the user name and the password. The server verifies the user name and the password and if found ok connection is made. The session further moves after this.

4. Transport Layer

Transport layer is the junction of user support layers and the network support layers. The function of the transport layer is to transfer the complete data from originating source to the final destination. It divides the message into segments. The segment contains header. The header contains the addresses of transmitter and the receiver. Each segment is provided sequence number. Sequence number is used for assembling the message at receiver end.

Transport layer transmits the data in the form of transport protocol data unit (TPDU). TPDU has four parts:

1. Length
2. Fixed parameter
3. Variable parameter
4. Data

1. Length. Length field contains the length of the data in the form of bytes. Length field includes all the four parts of TPDU.

2. Fixed parameter. The fixed parameter has four sub-parameters.

(a) Code
(b) Address
(c) Sequence
(d) Credit allocation

(a) Code. Code identifies which types of data are being transmitted. There is a separate code for the following operations:

(i) Connection establishment,
(ii) Sending of data,
(iii) Acknowledgment of connection and disconnection,
(iv) Acknowledgment of data.

(b) Address. This fixed parameter includes the addresses of source and the destination.

(c) Sequence. It contains the sequence number of each segment. Sequencing of segments help in processing the data at the receiver end. It helps in error detection and flow control of data.

(d) **Credit allocation.** This fixed parameter is used for regulating the flow of data. If the rate of processing the data at receiver end is faster than the transmission of data from source, then receiver sends a request to sent more number of segments. Transmitter can regulates the flow of data after receiving such request.

3. Variable parameter. This parameter contains codes, which are used for testing the network system.

4. Data. Data are received by transport layer from the session layer.

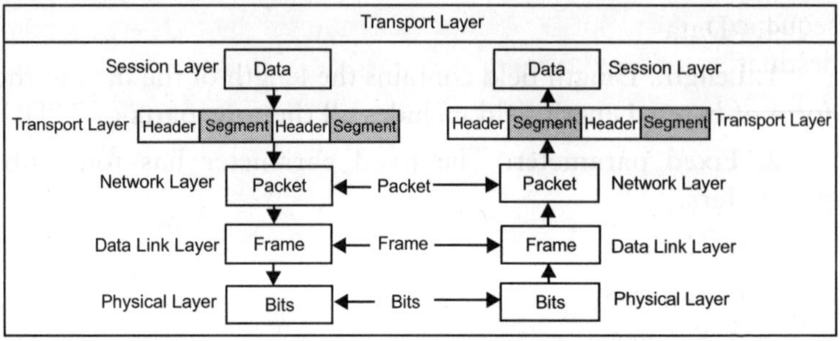

Functions of transport layer

1. Each segment is acknowledged back to the originating transmitter by the end receiver, that confirms the delivery of complete message.

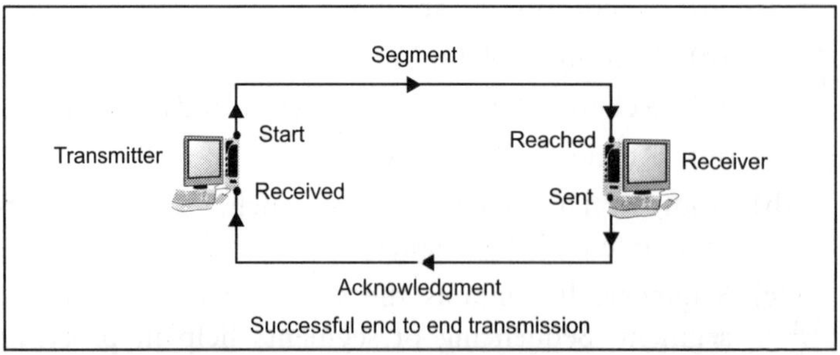

2. If segment is not received by the receiver due to failure of hardware or software, it is retransmitted and acknowledgment is sent to the original transmitter by the end receiver.

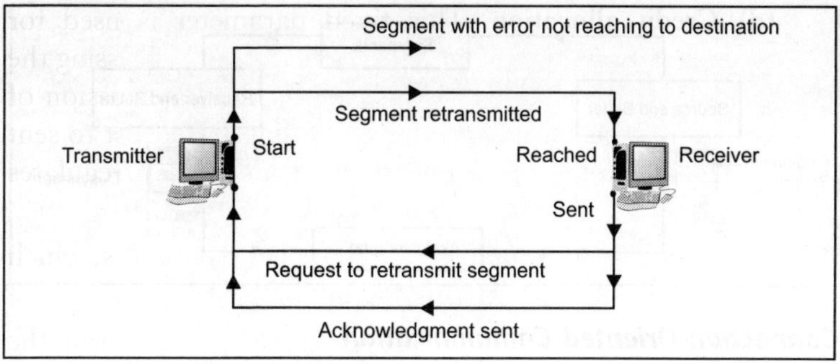

3. Segments are provided with sequence number and sequenced back into original order after arrival at the end destination and complete the end to end delivery of message.

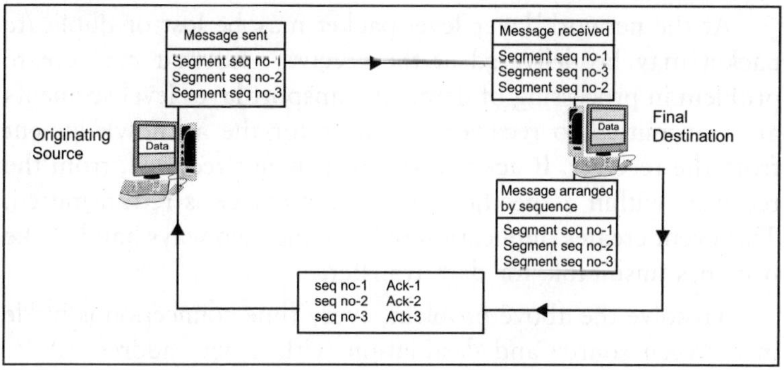

4. Data are managed in order to avoid congestion, overflow or data loss. Data are sent from the source to the receiver at certain rate. In case the speed of data transmitted by the source is more than the speed of data handling at the receiver end, data may be lost. To solve this problem transport layer uses buffers at both the ends to store the data. Source side buffer control the speed of transmission of data and receiver end controls the speed of processing the data, thus flow of data is controlled for smooth transmission of data.

Transport layer controls reliable data flow between systems. Flow control prevents the source to send the data to receiver, when overflowing the buffers takes place at the receiving end. Overflowing of buffer causes the loss of data.

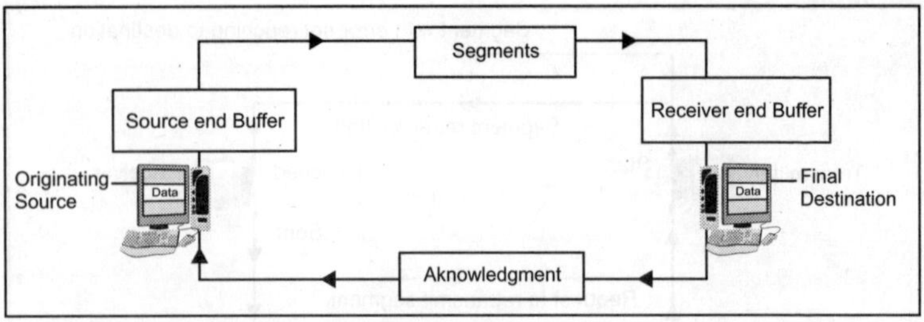

Connection-Oriented Communication

Transport layer set up connection in between originating source and the remote destination. Connecting source machine with the receiver is two ways hand shake. This method is only suitable when no error occurs during transmission of data.

At the network layer level packet may be lost or duplicate packet may be delivered at the receiver end that may create problem in processing of data. At transport layer level segments are transmitted to receiver and wait for the acknowledgment from the receiver. If acknowledgment is not received, from the receiver, within a specified time, the message is retransmitted. This event creates duplication of data and two ways hand shake becomes unsuitable for data transfer.

To solve the above problem, every time connection is made in between source and destination with a new address. After delivery of the message connection and the address are discarded. The process is repeated for every delivery.

Another method is to keep the history of discarded connection by each machine. If the receiver gets the data of discarded connection the data are not processed and sent to garbage store.

Another method where hop count is used. At every pass of message from the router the hop count is increased by one. The hop count is predetermined for the shortest route in between source and the destination. If the hop count is found more than the specified hop count at any node, the message will be discarded.

In a stamping method each message is stamped for a fixed duration to reach the destination. If the message does not reach to the destination within specified stamped time the data are discarded.

The source machine establishes a connection-oriented session with its peer system which is called three-way handshake. Data are then transmitted to receiver and when complete information is received by the receiver, the connection is terminated.

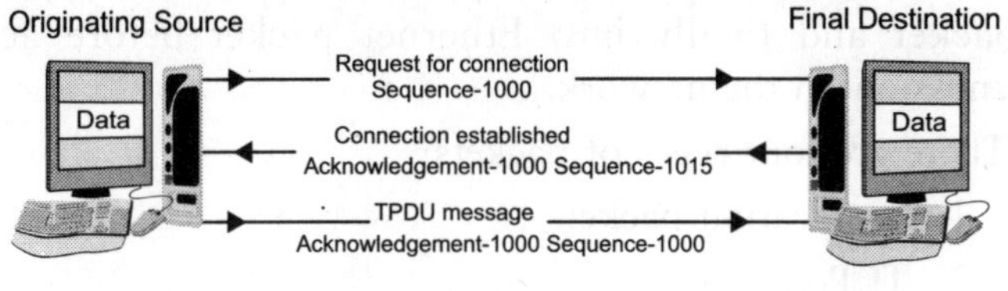

Three-Way Handshake

Three-way handshake is the communication in three steps, in between source and the destination.

Considering the above picture:

1. Source sends a request to receiver for establishment of internet connection with sequence number. In the above picture sequence number is assumed 1000.
2. Receiver in response sends the confirmation that connection has been established. Receiver sends an acknowledge—1000, for the receipt of sequence 1000 and sequence 1015 to the transmitter.
3. The transmitter acknowledged the connection establishment and sends the TPDU message to receiver with sequence 1000. These three steps complete the three-way handshake.

5. Network Layer

Network layer is the packet-oriented layer of OSI model. The data are transferred to it, from the transport layer. Its main function is to transform the data into packet and add header to it. This header contains the addresses of original source and the final destination node.

Packet Concept

Client types an application in a buffer and passes it to a socket. Packet contains an IP header and other data. It may be a complete IP datagram or a fragment of an IP datagram. This application packet is ready for transmission but, cannot be sent directly to the other computer without passing through another four steps.

The data are wrapped into Application packet, TCP packet, IP packet and finally into Ethernet packet before actual transmission on the network.

There are four types of packets:

1. Application packet
2. TCP packet
3. IP packet
4. Ethernet packet.

The structure of packet is illustrated in the following table.

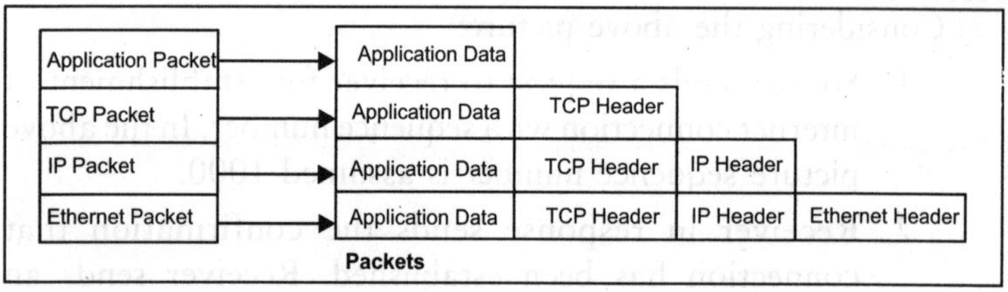

Application Packet = Application Data

An application typed by the client in a buffer and passes it to a socket. This is the application packet ready for transmission, but it cannot be sent directly to the other computer without passing through another four steps.

TCP Packet = TCP Header + Application Data

The application packet is used by the software program, which supports the socket. The complete application and the data are put inside the TCP data packet. In fact the TCP header is added to the application data. TCP header contains source and destination port number along with some other information.

IP Packet = IP Header + TCP Header + Application Data

IP header is included with the TCP packet. In IT terms TCP packet is placed inside IP data packet with source and destination IP addresses along with some other data for network management.

This operation is carried out with the help of some data link library (.dll) files and supporting programs.

Ethernet Packet = Ethernet Header + IP Header + TCP Header + Application Data

Ethernet packet adds the Ethernet header in the IP Packet.

Ethernet header contains destination and the source address of the Network Interface Card.

This is actually the address of hardware which is also called MAC address.

The following picture illustrates the addition of TCP, IP and Ethernet headers to Application.

TCP, IP and Ethernet packets are added to application at the source end and then these headers are removed one by one at the receiver end.

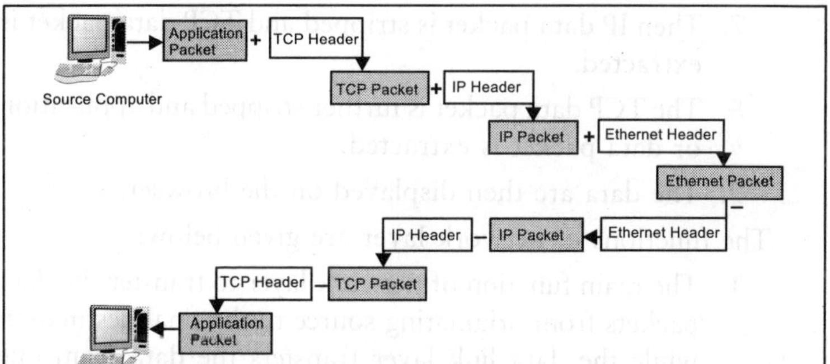

Packet Concept

The following actions take place for sending data on a network from client computer to the destination computer:

1. Application typed in a buffer and placed into the socket. This is called as application packet.
2. This application packet is put inside a TCP data packet. TCP header is added to the application data packet. This TCP header contained a source and destination port number. Some additional information and a checksum is also included in this packet.
3. This TCP packet is further put inside an IP data packet. IP header is added to the TCP data packet. This IP

header contains source and destination IP addresses. Other data are also added for network management.

4. The IP data packet is further placed inside an Ethernet data packet. Ethernet header is added to the IP data packet. This Ethernet data packet contains the destination and source addresses of the network interface cards (NIC) on the two computers. The hardware address of the respective cards is called the MAC address.
5. Finally, the Ethernet packet is transmitted over the network from source computer to the destined computer. The destined network interface card (NIC) on the intended machine, gets the address of the source machine and gets the data.
6. The Ethernet data packet is stripped first and IP data packet is extracted.
7. Then IP data packet is stripped and TCP data packet is extracted.
8. The TCP data packet is further stripped and application or data packet is extracted.
9. The data are then displayed on the browser.

The functions of network layer are given below:

1. The main function of network layer to transfer the data packets from originating source to the final destination while the data link layer transfers the data from one node to the next node. See the following figure.

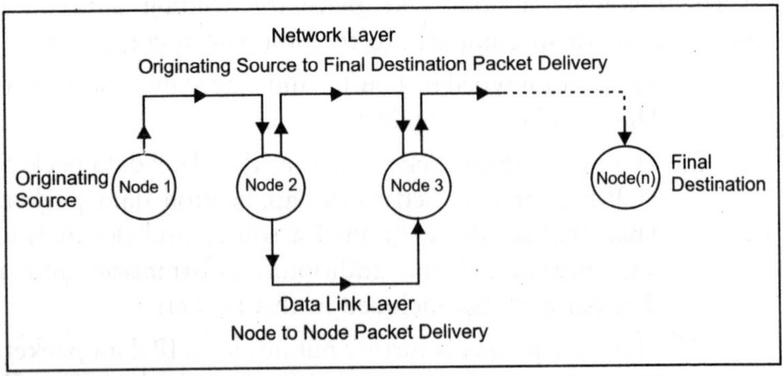

2. Network layer transforms the data into packet and header is added to the packet. The header contains the address of the originating machine and the end receiver. The addresses are different from the addresses which are added by data link layer.

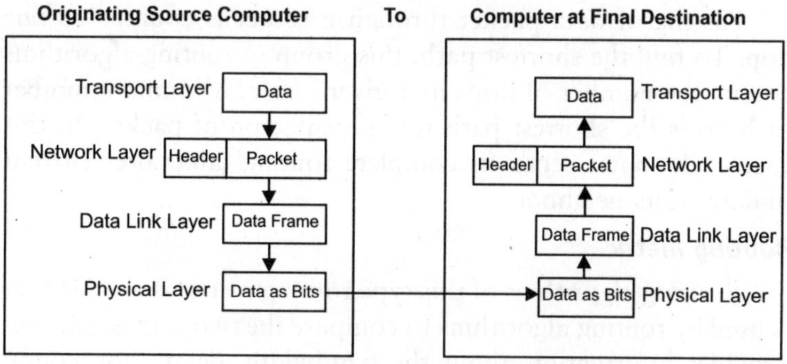

3. Inside information are also controlled by the header.
4. Network layer sends the data packet to data link layer which converts them into frame and sends it to physical layer which converts it into data bits and send to the destination physically.

Routing of data

Routing is a network layer mechanism that may be either software or hardware. This mechanism uses metrics for choosing the most suitable path for transmission of network traffic. Data packets are transferred between the networks by the routers as per the information provided by the network layer.

The main function of network layer is to transfer the data packets from originating source, to the final destination.

Network is consisted of nodes and the data passes through these nodes. For transfer of data from source to the destination, various path are available. Network layer chooses the most suitable route for the transfer of the data packets. This is called routing.

Distance-vector protocols

The distance-vector protocols detects the best path to a remote network by calculating the distance. The path with the least number of hops to the network is determined to be the best suitable path. Beside this, distance-vector protocol uses a composite metric of bandwidth and delay of the line to determine the best path to a remote network.

Distance-vector routing algorithm

Passing of data packet through a router is counted as one hop. To find the shortest path, this group of routing algorithms counts the number of hops in a given route. Minimum number of hops is the shortest path for transmission of packet. In this case each router sends its complete routing table after current update to its neighbors.

Routing metric

Routing algorithms of this type routing metric is a value that is used by routing algorithms to compare the two routes. Metrics provides information about the bandwidth, delay, hop count, path cost, load, MTU, reliability, and communication cost. Only the best possible paths are stored in the routing table, while all other information may be stored in link-state.

Routing table

It is a table kept in a router that maintains a record of only the best possible paths of a particular network destinations and the metrics associated with those routes.

There are two types of routing:

1. Adaptive routing
2. Non-adaptive routing

1. Adaptive routing. Network layer chooses the path considering the traffic condition and sends the data from source to the destination. Distance-vector routing is the example of adaptive routing.

Distance-vector routing. Each and every active router on the network keeps information about the distance of its neighbor router. At a fixed interval of time a router sends a vector table to another that rectify the exiting vector table and passes on to the other router. This way each and every active router updates its vector table. Suppose router A has a neighbor B at a distance of Xab. Now router B has a neighbor C at a distance of Xbc. Router B sends the vector table to router A, that contains the information about the distance of the router C form B. Router A updates its vector table and include the distance from Router A to C as Xac = Xab + Xbc as shown in the following figure.

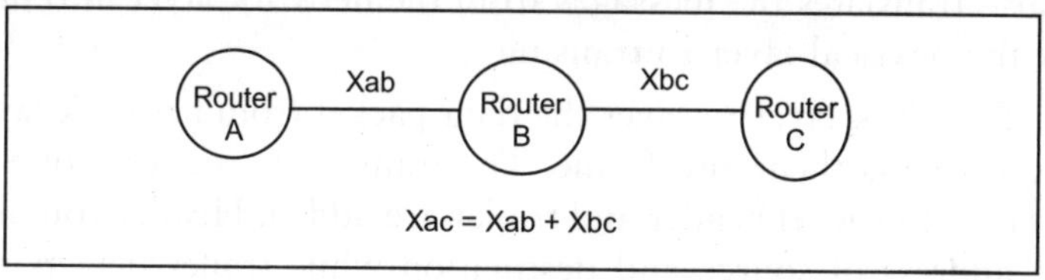

2. Non-adaptive routing. Network layer does not consider the traffic on the route and sends the data from source to the destination. Shortest path routing is the example of non-adaptive routing.

Shortest path routing. This non-adaptive routing works on the basis of the graphical distance between two nodes. Shortest graphical distance between the source and the destination is the best route for transmission of data. Other considerations for choosing the best suitable path are:

1. Distance between the source and destination is a physical distance between them.
2. Actual time taken by the message to reach from source to the destination.
3. Traffic conditions and queue at a machine.
4. Cost of communication.

When a router sends data by choosing shortest path above four points are taken into account. It considers the shortest physical distance and shortest time to reach the message to the destination. It also considers the line traffic. It may choose longer path with lesser traffic, if the time required in reaching the message to the destination is lesser than the shorter path. Next it considers the cost of communication. It compares the cost of transmission of data with the durations. If the faster data transfer is too costlier then, it will choose the path of longer duration than less costlier data transfer.

6. Data Link Layer

The Data link layer that transmits the data from node to node and notifies the error. It controls the flow of data and handles network topology. Data link layer ensures the delivery of message to the appropriate device, using hardware addresses. It also translates the messages from the network layer into bits, for the physical layer to transmit.

Data link layer receives the data packet from network layer and converts them into frame. The frame is a smaller group of data. At this level header and trailer are added. Header contains the address of source and destination while trailer detects the error of the data packet. This data frame is translated into bits. These bits are transferred to physical layer for transmitting the message to the destination. On the receiving end data link layer gets the data from physical layer and passes it to network layer.

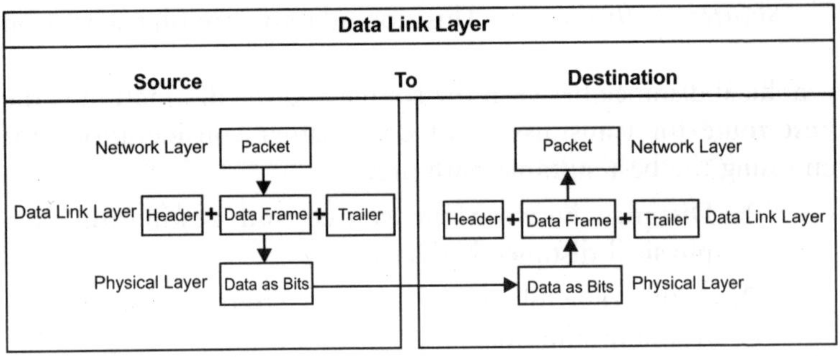

It is important to know that routers, which work at the network layer, don't take care of about location of particular host. They are only concerned about where and at what logical distance the networks node are located, and always use the most suitable path to reach the node, including the remote ones.

Functions of data link layer:

1. Transmission of the data from node to node.
2. Addressing the nodes.
3. Access control.
4. Flow control.
5. Handling error.

1. Transmission of the data from node to node. Network is a group of several nodes. Data link layer uses address of the hardware and delivers the message from one node to the next node. In other words packet is sent from router to router. Information is stripped off at the receiving router and only the original packet is left fully intact. The conversion of packet into frame continues, for each hop, until the packet is delivered to final destination machine.

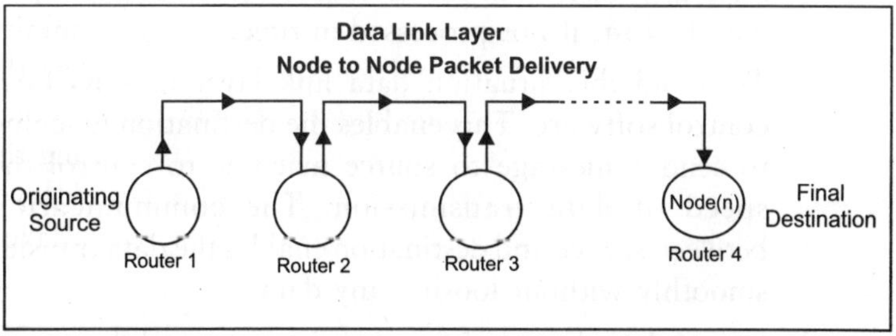

2. Addressing the nodes. Data link layer converts the packet into frame. The addresses of source node and destination node are added into the frame. This inclusion of address of source node and destination node is called addressing of nodes.

A data link layer address uniquely identifies, each physical network connection, of a network device. These addresses are referred as physical or hardware addresses. Data link addresses generally exist in a flat address space and have a pre established fixed relationship to a specific machine.

3. Access control. Two or more network interface cards send frames simultaneously, on a single channel. These frames meet on the physical media simultaneously. They collide with each other. When such collision occurs the frames are damaged and data are lost. Data link layer defines the protocol for controlling the channel. In case of any collision the source machine is informed about it and asked to wait for retransmission of the data frame. The source machine waits for certain amount of time and then retransmits the data.

4. Flow control. Flow control deals with data considering the following:

1. Speed of data transmission.
2. Size of data.

1. **Speed of data transmission.** The best speed of data transmission is when, speed of transmission of data by the source = Speed of data processing by the destination. If the destination machine is not able to process the data at the speed at which source transmits them, then a queue is formed at the destination point and the data may be lost, if not processed in time.

   To avoid this situation data link layer uses its flow control software. This enables the destination machine to send a message to source machine to control the speed of data transmission. The communication between source and destination enables the data transfer smoothly without loosing any data.

2. **Size of data.** Speed of data transmission and the size of the data are two important aspects related with data flow. When the data reached to the destination they are not necessary be in the same order in which they are transmitted from the source. Data link layer provide the sequence to each frame so the destination machine can assemble the message in readable order.

5. Handling error. It may happen that the data may be lost or corrupted during passing through the physical medium. The error may occur due to various reasons. Interference in the signals, faulty hardware and associated connectors may be the reason for such error.

Error Detection and rectification

1. Destination machine acknowledges the receipt of frame.
2. Destination machine does not acknowledge the receipt of frame.

1. **Destination machine acknowledges the receipt of frame.** Data link layer adds trailer to the frame for error free transfer of data. This trailer contains the error detecting software. If the destination machine detects any error, it informs the source machine to retransmit the message.

This type of error detection and its rectification, can be performed only when the destination machine receives the frame.

2. **Destination machine does not acknowledge the receipt of frame.** In some of the cases the frame does not reach to the destination. It may be lost during passing through the physical medium. In this case destination machine will not send any acknowledgment to the source machine.

Setting Timer

Data link layer uses timer to conquer this problem. When the frame is sent from source to the destination, timer is set for receiving the acknowledgment from destination. Source timer starts counting the time as soon as the frame is delivered.

If the acknowledgment is received by the source before the set time the timer stop.

If the acknowledgment is not received till the stipulated time set on the timer, the source machine retransmits the same frame. Each frame is provided sequence number so that receiving machine can discard the duplicate frames.

There are two sub-layers of data link layer:

1. Logical Link Control (LLC)
2. Media Access Control (MAC)

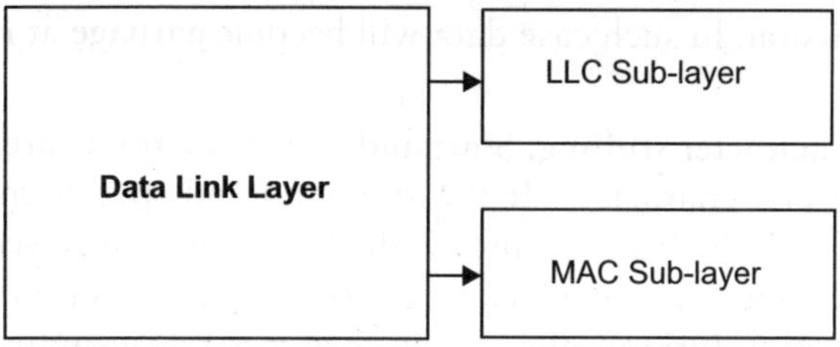

1. Logical Link Control (LLC). The Logical Link Control (LLC) sub-layer controls the data transfer between devices over a single link of a network. LLC supports both connectionless and connection-oriented services used by higher-layer protocols. Number of fields in data link layer frames are defined that enable multiple higher-layer protocols to share a single physical data link.

2. Media Access Control (MAC). Media Access Control (MAC) sub-layer controls protocol access to the physical network medium. MAC addresses are defined by IEEE MAC specification, which enables various machines to uniquely recognize one another at the data link layer level.

Framing

Data link layer receives the data packet from network layer and converts them into frame. The frames are formed in such a manner that after reaching to destination they can be assembled to get the original data. There are following three methods used for formation of frame:

1. Character count,
2. Character stuffing,
3. Bit stuffing.

1. Character count. The first character of frame is the special character that contains the count of characters. When the data are received by the destination computer, data link layer confirms the receipt of complete data by counting the total number of characters in the message. The frame is transferred to the network layer. This simple way of framing works nicely till there is no error in transmission of data. It is possible that character that counts the characters may lost or may changed its value during transmission. In such case data will become garbage at receiving end.

2. Character stuffing. Start and end of the frame are marked with special characters. If the start and end special characters appear with the frame, it means the full frame is received. These two characters are removed to get the original data. In case the frame is lost during transmission then it is retransmitted. It can be recognize by these two characters. Suppose the frame also contains the same character, in such case destination machine is not able to recognize the original special character and the frame may be lost. To avoid this problem bit stuffing is generally used.

3. Bit stuffing. Bit stuffing is similar to character stuffing. In this case bits are used at the starting and the end of the frame. These bits are predefined. The frame dose not contains the similar types of bits so this method is more reliable.

7. Physical Layer

Physical layer transfers physical data in the form of bits from source to the destination. It uses physical medium like telephone wire, coaxial cables or wireless media. Just above the physical layer there is a layer called data link layer. This layer adds header and trailer to the packet and transfer it to physical layer. Now physical layer converts these data into bits and these bits are then transformed into signals and then sent to the destination.

In the following figure it is clear that data link layer adds header and trailer to the data packet. The header contains the address of source and destination. Header also controls the frame. Trailer contains the information for finding errors of data packet.

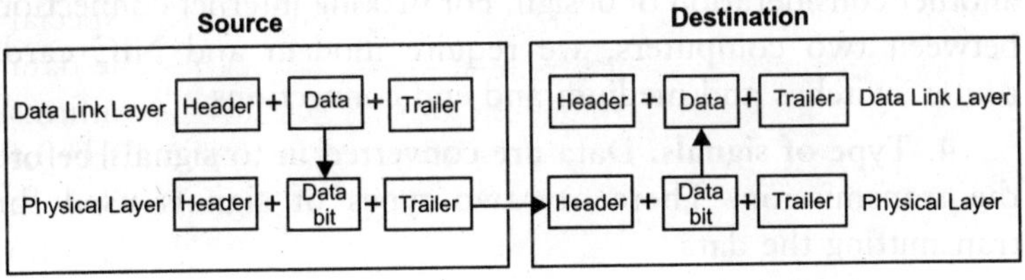

The data packet is now transferred from data link layer to physical layer along with header and trailer. Physical layer transforms these data into bits. These bits are further transformed into signals. These signals are then transferred through the medium to the destination.

Before transferring the data packet to the destination, physical layer has to consider the following points:

1. Two devices which are to be connected physically,
2. The medium of transmission,
3. Architecture,
4. Type of signals,
5. Data Encoding.

1. Two devices which are to be connected physically. Before any transmission of data can takes place, we have to decide the source and destination machines. Then the two machines are physically connected by a guided medium.

2. The medium of transmission. For setting up an internet network, it is necessary to select a transmission medium. There are two types of medium used for data transmission. First type of transmission medium includes twisted pair cable, coaxial cable and optic fiber cable. Second type includes the radio transmission and satellite communication. While selecting the medium of data transmission, we have to consider the cost, speed of data transmission, reliability and security of data.

3. Architecture. Architecture of a network is physical concept (layout) of the network. It is a design in which, we fix the positions of all hardware on the network, along with the physical transmission media like cat-5 wires, coaxial cable or wireless connection. The data access method (OSI Layer 2) is one of the another consideration of design. For making internet connection between two computers, we require modem and NIC card, router switches and medium and end connections.

4. Type of signals. Data are converted in to signals before the transmission. There are two types of signals used for transmitting the data.

1. Analog signal
2. Digital signal

1. **Analog signal.** Analog signals are in the form of continuous sine wave and very with the change of voltage. Information in a continuous mode uses analog signals. For example the weight of a student is analog information.

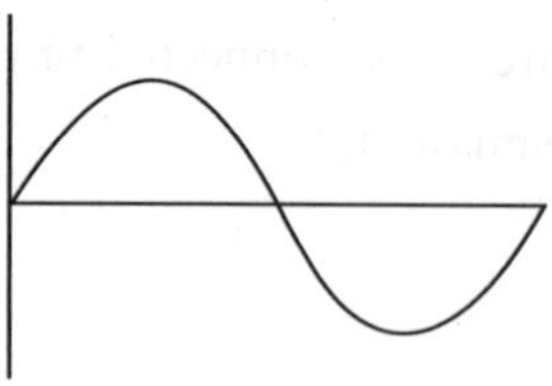

Analog Signals

2. **Digital signal.** Information which can be counted, is transferred in the form of digital signal. Digital signals follow the square wave characteristics, where voltage is kept either maximum or minimum. Number of student in a class is digital information.

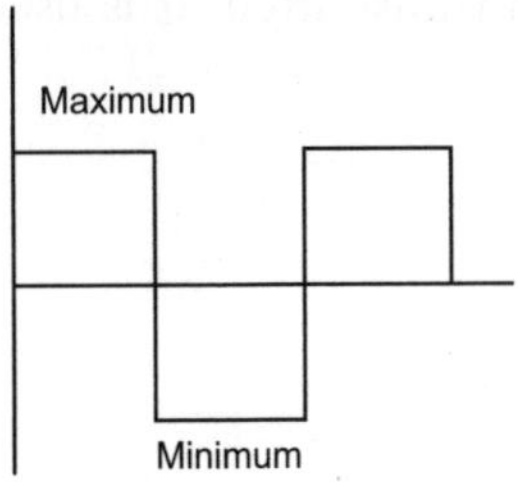

Digital Signals

5. Data encoding. For transmitting the information, signals are created. These signals contain the information in form of bits (0,1). The loading of information in the form of bits is called data encoding. There are four method of data encoding.

1. Digital to analog
2. Digital to digital
3. Analog to digital
4. Analog to analog

Similar method must be used by both the source and the destination machines for encoding and decoding of data.

1. **Digital to analog.** This method is used by telephone lines for transmitting of data, where digital information is converted into analog signals. The source computer generates the information that is coded into analog signals and by the telephone line, it is sent to the destined machine.
2. **Digital to digital.** This method of encoding is used for internal transfer of data. Computer generates the digital signals and transmits them to printer for printing. The digital information is encoded in the form of digital signals.

3. **Analog to digital.** The pictures and video are in the form of analog information. Before transmitting, this analog information is encoded into digital signals at the source level and then transmitted to the destination.
4. **Analog to analog.** Analog information is encoded into analog signal and then transmitted. It is used in radio broadcasting.

Protocols

4

There are four protocols which are commonly used in networking.

They are as follows:

1. NetBEUI
2. IPX/SPX
3. AppleTalk
4. TCP/IP

1. NetBEUI

NetBEUI full form is NetBIOS Extended User Interface. NetBEUI protocol is two layers protocol.

It uses the transport layer and network layer of OSI model. Microsoft and the IBM are the prime users of this protocol. It is a simple and fast network protocol that was designed to be used with the support of NetBIOS.

NetBEUI protocol is programmed to work with the transport and network layers of the OSI model. It is unable to set up communication session between two computers so it takes the help of NetBIOS that is a session layer protocol. NetBIOS sets the session of communication between two nodes of the network for NetBEUI protocol.

Following figure explains the relationship of NetBEUI, NetBIOS and other components for completing the all requirements of data transmission on a small area network.

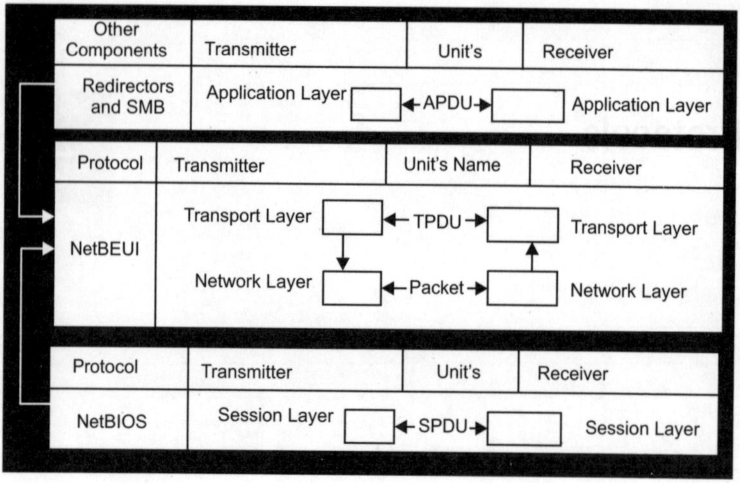

Two other supporting components are the Redirector and the Server Message Block. The Redirector is an application layer component. It provides all the network resources to the client computer like a local server.

Server Message Block (SMB) establishes the peer-to-peer communication between client and server through the redirectors. The Server Message Block is the presentation layer component.

The major drawback of this protocol is that it cannot routes the data through routers on a large networks therefore this protocol is used for small and simple networks only.

IPX/SPX

IPX/SPX full form is Internet-work Packet Exchange/ Sequenced Packet Exchange.

Novell is the designer of network protocol, who has developed it for their own Novell NetWare network operating system. IPX/ SPX uses less overhead support than TCP/IP protocol.

IPX/SPX is a routable protocol therefore it can be used by both small and large area networks.

This is a connectionless transport protocol. It operates at the transport and network layers of OSI model. It controls addressing and routing of the packet on the network.

Protocol	Transmitter	Unit's	Receiver
IPX	Transport Layer	TPDU	Transport Layer
	Network Layer	Packet	Network Layer

SPX full form is Sequenced Packet Exchange. This is a connection-oriented transport protocol.

It operates at the transport layer of OSI model for establishment of internet connections between two computers.

Protocol	Transmitter	Unit's	Receiver
SPX	Transport Layer	TPDU	Transport Layer

IPX/SPX is routing protocol therefore it is suitable for large network. There are two protocols which support the IPX/SPX to establish the network connection and communication between the computers. They are SAP and NCP. They operate at the three layers of OSI model for communication between two nodes.

Protocol	Transmitter	Unit's	Receiver
SAP and NCP	Application Layer	APDU	Application Layer
	Presentation Layer	PPDU	Presentation Layer
	Session Layer	SPDU	Session Layer

1. SAP full form is Service Advertising Protocol. It is used by NetWare File Servers and Print Servers for declaration of the address of the server.
2. NCP full form is NetWare Core Protocol. It is a three layers protocol. The three layers are the Application, Presentation, and Session layers. It transforms the data into packets and provide the connection between client and the server.

AppleTalk Protocol

AppleTalk is a routable protocol, therefore it can be well used with the large area networks.

Appropriate type of NIC is used with this protocol. It can easily be used with Ethernet, Token Ring, and FDDI architectures. Macintosh computers are used most commonly to manipulate the graphics and multimedia services on a network, therefore AppleTalk protocol can be used as an another routable protocol on the wide area network.

AppleTalk protocol is supported by the following group of protocols:

1. Apple Share—This apple protocol works at the application layer and creates an application packet.
2. AFP full form is AppleTalk Filing protocol. This protocol operates at the presentation layer and manages the sharing of files.
3. ATP full form is AppleTalk Transaction Protocol. It operates at the Transport Layer and provides connection between two computers. There are three transaction layers. They are transaction requires (TREQ), transaction response (TRESP) and transaction release (TREL). These three layers are responsible for transfer of the complete data from originating source to the final destination.
4. DDP full form is Datagram Delivery Protocol. It is the network layer protocol. It is a routable protocol and responsible for data packet transportation.

The group of computer in AppleTalk networking is called zone. Zone is like a work groups on a windows network. There are four session layer protocols which control the session:

1. ASP full form is AppleTalk Session Protocol. When two computers are connected on a network, it controls the period of communication from staring to the end point of communication.
2. ADSP full form is AppleTalk data stream protocol. It controls the flow of data between two sockets.

3. ZIP full form is zone information protocol. It maps the zone with the support of RTMP. Routers on the network contains the zone information tables (ZITs). Network addresses and zone names are defined in the zone information tables.
4. PAP full form is Printer Access Protocol. It controls the information between printer and the work station.

TCP/IP

TCP/IP stands for Transmission Control Protocol (TCP) and Internet Protocol (IP). It transports and manages the data across the network. The IP layer requires 4 or 6 bytes address, that is to be assigned to Ethernet card on a computer. IP4 requires 4 bytes address while IP6 requires 6 bytes address of the Ethernet card. This can be done automatically using network software such as dynamic host configuration protocol (DHCP) or by manually entering static addresses into the computer. TCP/IP design for the network is applicable to the current information technology and can accommodate any changes. It can also be used with the TV cable service. Furthermore the gateways can be used for connecting one network with the another one.

Transmission Control Protocol

TCP is a five-layer protocol. The layers used for transmission of data are application layer, transportation layer, network layer, data link layer and physical layer. Following table indicates the functions of five layers:

Five Layers and their Functions

Layer		Function
Application Layer	———	User input message
Transport Layer	———	Set up connection
Network Layer	———	Routes the message from node to node
Data Link Layer	———	Packets are converted into frames
Physical Layer	———	Data conversion into bits and physical transmission

Application layer. It is the layer which gets data from the transmitter and sends them to the destination with the support of other layers. This layer is supported by the protocols like SMTP, FTP, DNS, Telnet, SNMP along with various other protocols.

Transport layer. This layer receives the data from many process by user support layers. The data are then transmitted to the another process at the receiver end. At this level the layer is supported by TCP and UDP protocols. TCP and UDP are supported by various other protocols.

Network layer. This layer transmits the packets from originating transmitter to the final receiver. IP is the protocol that is defined by TCP/IP. IP is supported by other protocols.

Data link layer. Data link layers gets the data from network layer in the form of packets, it converts them into frames and then transmits them from one node to the another. Data travel from one node to the another node and reach the final node. Like physical layer no specific protocol is defined.

Physical layer. This layer is responsible for converting the data into bits, then message is transmitted in the form of bits on the physical medium. No specific protocol is defined for this layer.

The figure on page 51 shows the five layers which are supported by various protocols.

Main Functions of Transmission Control Protocol

1. Multiplexing
2. Error-recovery
3. Windowing
4. Connection establishment and termination

1. Multiplexing. Multiplexing is the process in which the host receives number of applications from the same source and he has to decide, which one should be processed first. For example, Ishita sends three applications, wire application, ad application and web server application to Senjuti. Senjuti has to decide, which application is to be processed first. This process is called multiplexing.

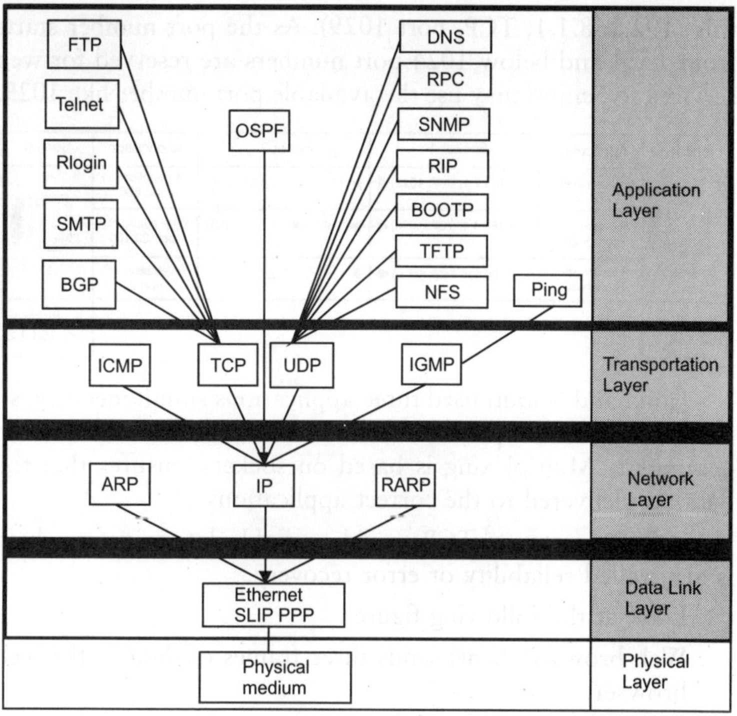

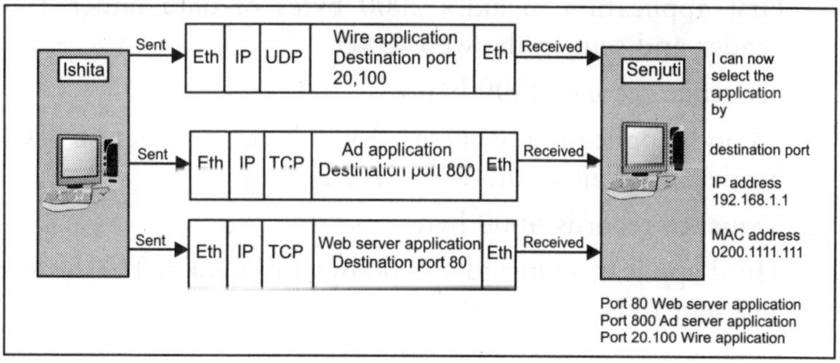

Multiplexing uses a socket. A socket contains, IP address, a transport protocol, and a port number. In the above picture web server application uses, port 80, IP address 192.168.1.1 and protocol TCP, so here the socket would be (192.168.1.1, TCP, port 80).

When Ishita connects her web browser to the web server, Senjuti also uses a socket. The socket used by her may be like this (192.168.1.1, TCP, port 1029). As the port number starts from 1024 and below 1024 port numbers are reserved for web services so Senjuti may use the available port number like 1029.

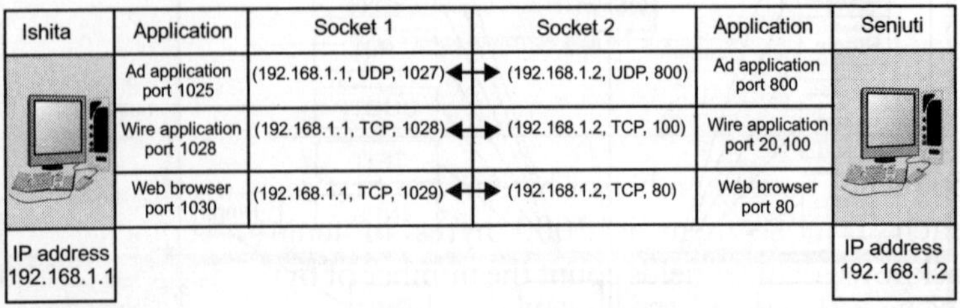

Ishita and Senjuti used three applications simultaneously, so there must be a unique connection in between the sockets of the computers. Multiplexing is based on sockets, ensures that the data are delivered to the correct applications.

2. Error-recovery. TCP provides reliable data transfer, which is also called reliability or error recovery.

Look at the following figure.

Web browser(client) sends three frames of data to the web browser.

First application includes 2000 bytes of data under TCP header and sent to the web server.

Sequence records 2000 bytes.

Second application includes 2000 bytes of data in TCP header and sent to the web server.

Sequence records 4000 bytes.

Third application includes 2000 bytes of data in TCP header and sent to the web server.

Sequence records 6000 bytes.

TCP performs the reliability in both directions. Its sequence number field of one direction from web server to web browser and acknowledgment field from web browser to web server.

The acknowledgment field contains 8000 bytes in the TCP header, sent by the web client because it expects to receive 2000 bytes in the next trip. This is called forward acknowledgment.

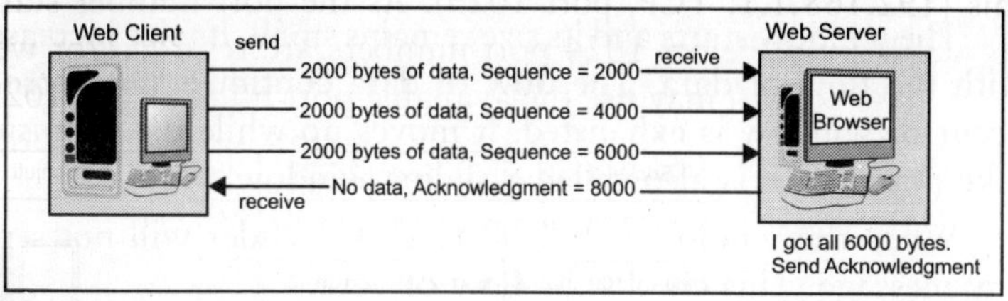

Sequence is the number of byte in the first segment. In this case, each TCP segment is 2000 bytes in length. Sequence and acknowledgment fields count the number of bytes. Suppose second TCP segment was lost or there was an error in it. The web browser acknowledges a field equal to 4000 bytes. The TCP at the web server then recovers the lost data by resending the second TCP segment. After resending the segment TCP waits, for the web client's reply with an acknowledgment that equals to 8000 bytes.

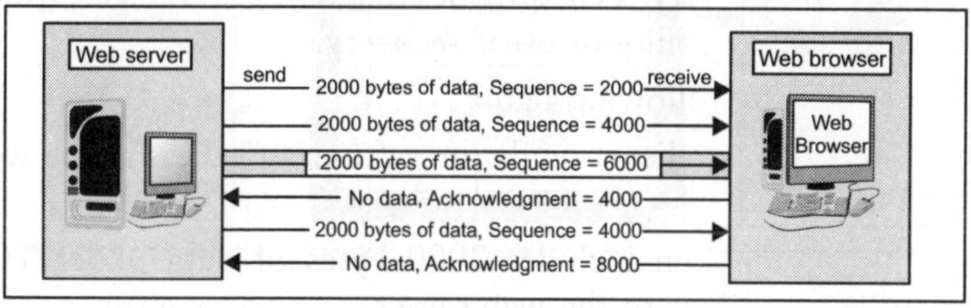

3. Using windowing for error-recovery. TCP implements flow control with the help of sequence and acknowledgment fields in the TCP header. It uses, an another field called the window field. See the following figure.

Bit 0 … Bit 15			Bit 16 … Bit 31
Source Port 16 bits			Destination Port 16 bits
Sequence number 32 bits			
Acknowledge number 32 bits			
Header Length 4 bits	Reserved Field 6 bits	Code Field 6 bits	Window field 16 bits
Checksum 16 bits			Urgent 16 bits
Option field 0 to 32 bits			
Variable data field 32 bits			

The window starts and its size remains small. Its size increases with the flow of data. The flow of data continues until errors occur or window is exhausted. It moves up while data transfer take place, so it is also called a sliding window.

When the window is full of data, the sender will not send any message. This checks the flow of data.

The following figure indicates how windowing is used with sequence.

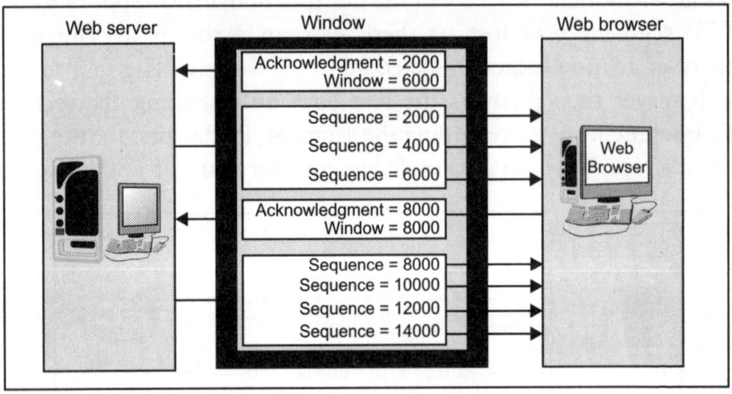

The current window size is of 6000 bytes. Each TCP segment contains 2000 bytes of data. After sending the third segment web server must wait because the window is exhausted. Then web browser sends the acknowledgment to web server. After receiving the acknowledgment, another window can be sent to browser.

If there is no occurrence of errors, the web server provides a larger window to the web browser. Now web browser asks the web server to send 8000 bytes in advance before it receive an acknowledgment.

4. Connection establishment and termination. TCP connection establishment is the first requirement, before any features of TCP is implemented. It is a process which initializes sequence and acknowledgment fields with agreeable port numbers.

Following figure shows the three-way connection establishment. This three-way connections must be established before transfer of any data.

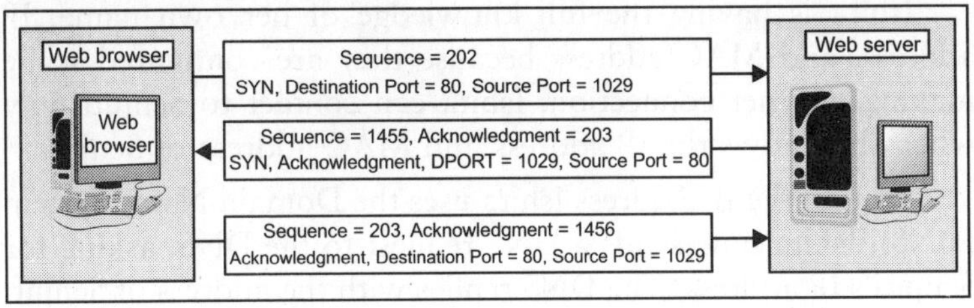

First of all connection between the two sockets must be made, though there is no socket field is mentioned in the TCP header. Socket uses IP address, TCP and port number. In this case TCP is already functioning. TCP is using Protocol field value in IP header, therefore only the port number is required to be included in TCP header to establish the connection between web server and the web browser.

SYN indicates the synchronize the sequence numbers, which is a necessary component in initialization for TCP. The ACK field means "the acknowledgment field is valid in this header". Until the sequence numbers are initialized, the acknowledgment field cannot be used.

You can see in the above figure that the first TCP segment does not contain any acknowledgment number. Actually this number is not valid yet.

Because the ACK field must be present in all the ensuing segments, the ACK bit will continue to be set until the connection is terminated. TCP can initializes the sequence and acknowledgment numbers to some number that is suitable for the four-byte fields.

How TCP/IP Works

TCP/IP means, Transmission Control Protocol and the Internet Protocol. It is a transportation layer protocol. It uses various protocols for different functions of networking.

For getting the concept of TCP/IP, go through the following example. Let us consider two computer named as Ishita and

Senjuti. Ishita wants to send a message in the form of application to Senjuti. Ishita uses her own web browser to access the web server that runs on Senjuti's PC.

Ishita is having the full knowledge of her own name, IP address, and MAC address because they are configured while making internet connection. Ishita can contact to Senjuti only when she knows the IP address and MAC address of Senjuti.

To find the IP Address Ishita uses the Domain Name System (DNS). Ishita now sends a DNS request to the DNS, asking for Senjuti's IP address. The DNS replies with the address of Senjuti as 192.168.1.2.

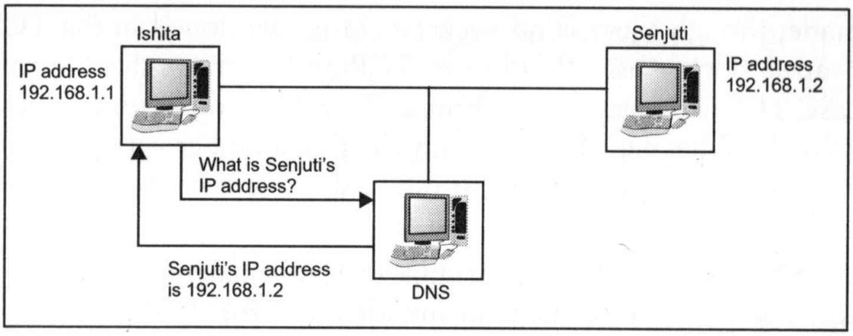

Now Ishita needs to know the Ethernet MAC address used by the IP address 192.168.1.2, therefore she issues an ARP broadcast. An ARP broadcast is sent to broadcast Ethernet MAC address, so every machine on the LAN receives it.

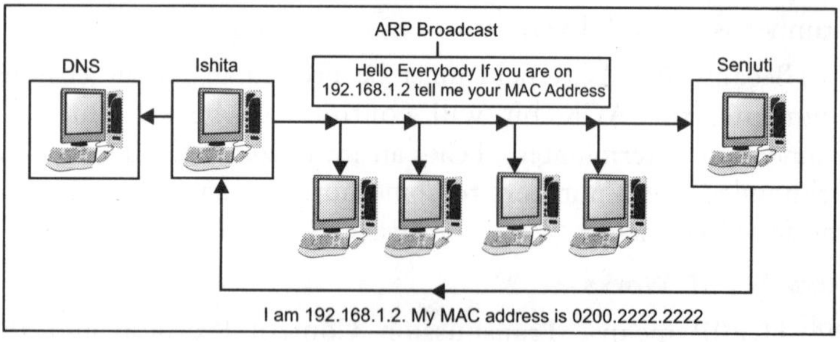

Senjuti is connected to the LAN, so she also receives the ARP broadcast. After receiving the ARP broadcast Senjuti replies with her own MAC address as "I am 192.168.1.2". My MAC address is 0200.2222.2222.

Now Ishita knows the IP address and MAC address of Senjuti so she can send frames to her by using these addresses. But after performing all these activity the applications don't work then you have to test the network connectivity.

For testing the network connectivity you have to use ping (Packet Internet Groper) command. Ping uses (ICMP) Internet Control Message Protocol. It sends a message, which is called an ICMP echo request to another IP address. If you receive ICMP echo reply from the computer with that IP address, you have successfully tested the IP address of the destined computer.

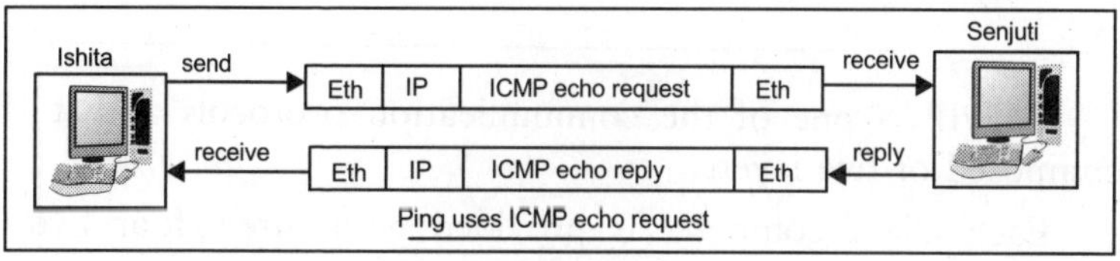

Ping uses ICMP echo request

If still it does work, the problem is more likely related to the application.

ICMP is not used for finding any error of an application, it simply tests basic IP connectivity of the three layers of the OSI model. Following figure shows the three applications model. After the connection between Senjuti's and Ishita's computers Senjuti receives three packets from Ishita.

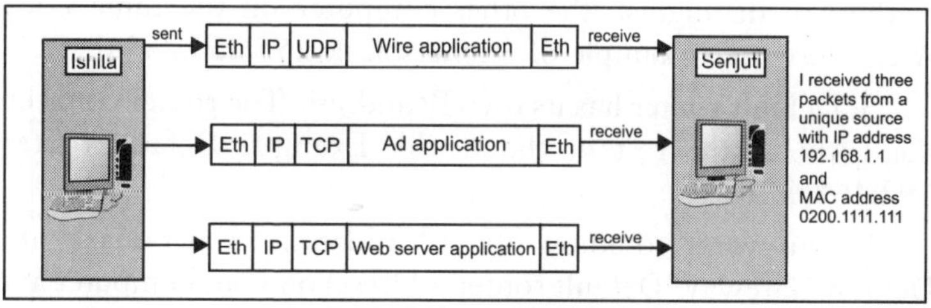

Now Senjuti wants to give data to one of the three applications. But all the application contains the same IP address and MAC address. How to differentiate the three application. As you see from the figure wire application uses UDP protocol and ad application and web server application use TCP protocol. Ishita uses a different port number, for each application, so

Senjuti can choose the application to give the data to because it uses TCP protocol.

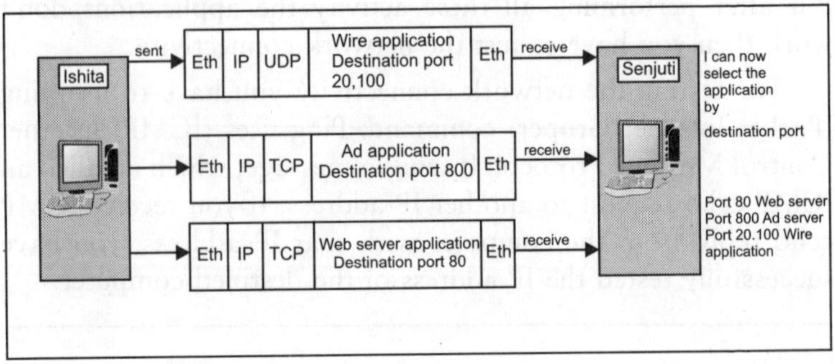

TCP/IP is one of the communication protocols and it is composed of five layers.

Each client computer is provided with three, four bytes information.

1. IP address
2. Subnet mask
3. Default router

1. IP address which is assigned to the computer. Example of IP address: 192.168.1.2.

2. Subnet mask, which is the part of the IP address which enables to distinguish the other computer on the same Local Area Network. Example of Subnet mask 255.255.255.0.

3. Default router has its own IP address. The router connects the LAN to the rest of the world. Example Default router: 192.168.1.1.

If you want to know the IP address, Subnet mask and Default Gateway (Default router address) on your computer and if it is connected with internet then open the MS-DOS command window.

Microsoft(R) Windows 98

(C)Copyright Microsoft Corp 1981-1999.

Type IPConfig in front of C:\WINDOWS> as follows:

C:\WINDOWS> ipconfig <Press Enter>

You will get the following information:

Windows 98 IP Configuration

1 Ethernet adapter:

IP Address . . . . : 192.168.1.2

Subnet Mask . . . . : 255.0.0.0

Default Gateway . . . . : 192.168.1.1

The above information about IP address, Subnet mask and Default gateway is for a particular computer. You may get some other digits for your computer.

For getting all the information related your computer network write the following command in DOS C:\WINDOWS>ipconfig/all and press enter:

Microsoft(R) Windows 98

(C)Copyright Microsoft Corp 1981-1999

C:\WINDOWS>ipconfig/all <Press Enter>

You will get the following information for a particular computer:

Windows 98 IP Configuration:

Host Name . . . . : SANGIA

DNS Servers . . . . : 192.168.1.1

Node Type . . . . : Broadcast

NetBIOS Scope ID . . . . . :

IP Routing Enabled . . . . : No

WINS Proxy Enabled . . . . : No

NetBIOS Resolution Uses DNS : No

0 Ethernet adapter:

Description . . . . : PPP Adapter.

Physical Address . . . . . . : 44-45-53-54-00-00

DHCP Enabled . . . . : Yes

IP Address . . . . : 0.0.0.0

Subnet Mask . . . . : 0.0.0.0

Default Gateway . . . . . . :

DHCP Server	:	255.255.255.255
Primary WINS Server	:	
Secondary WINS Server . . .	:	
Lease Obtained.	:	
Lease Expires	:	
1 Ethernet adapter :		
Description	:	Intel(R) PRO PCI Adapter
Physical Address	:	00-D0-B7-E4-5F-E5
DHCP Enabled	:	Yes
IP Address	:	192.168.1.2
Subnet Mask	:	255.0.0.0
Default Gateway	:	192.168.1.1
DHCP Server	:	192.168.1.1
Primary WINS Server	:	
Secondary WINS Server . . .	:	
Lease Obtained	:	04 15 07 2:02:40 PM
Lease Expires	:	

C:\WINDOWS>

The detail information are for a particular computer machine. This may change with the another computer. You may get some other digits for your machine.

Port

1. The TCP layer requires port number to be assigned to each message.

2. This way it can determine the type of service being provided.

3. This port is totally different from ports that are used for serial and parallel devices, or ports used for computer hardware control.

4. These ports are merely reference numbers used to define a service.

5. For instance, port 23 is used for telnet services, and HTTP uses port 80 for providing web browsing service.

6. Internet Assigned Numbers Authority (IANA) assign the port number for specific services. There are some ports that are kept reserved.

7. There are several unassigned which are used by application programs.

8. Port numbers are unsigned integer which range up to a value of 65535.

Addressing Features

1. Each computer which is connected with the network has an address.
2. This address is used to locate the computer.
3. Data packets are transmitted to the address of the computer.
4. It is similar to the address of the house where the postman delivers the letter or parcel.
5. IPv4 is an internet protocol, which is the improved version of IP protocol.
6. Each IP address is denoted by dotted decimal notation.
7. There are four numbers, which are separated by a dot.
8. The range of number is from 0 to 255.
9. Each number is represented by one byte.
10. Two left-hand side bytes represent the class of network.
11. The third byte indicates the number of the subnet.
12. The fourth number indicates the host number.
13. This numbering system will change according to network.
14. The host number cannot be 0 or 255.

Broadcasting Features

1. Broadcasting is done with all bits set in some bytes.
2. It is a form of communication that all hosts computer on a network can read.
3. It is used for performing various network queries.
4. You cannot assign an address with all 0's.

5. It provides 0.0.0.0 as its address until it receives its assignment.
6. This would occur for machines that are remotely booted or those, that are booted, using the dynamic host configuration protocol (DHCP).
7. The initial part of the IP address defines the network address. It is called network ID.

Before sending the data to the destination TCP converts the data into small frames. These tiny frames are called segment. Each segment is provided with a sequence number. This sequence number is very important for assembling the message at the destination point.

Following figure is the indicator of TCP header of a segment.

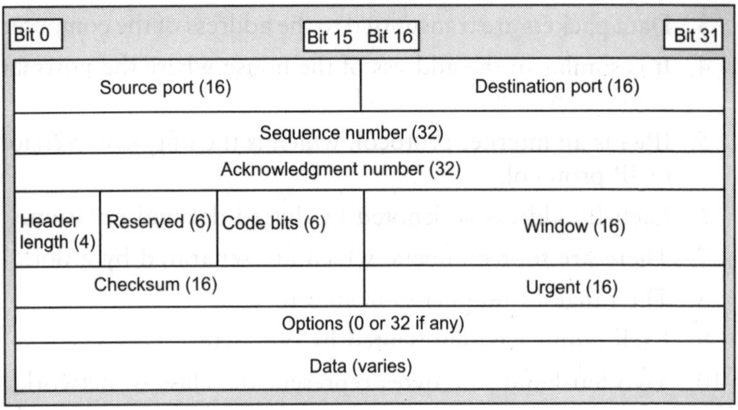

1. Source port. It is 16 bits field that contains the address of source port application.

2. Destination port address. It is also a 16 bits field that indicates the address of the destination port.

3. Sequence number. This is 32 bits field of the TCP header and contains the sequence number of each segment of the message that is going to be transmitted.

4. Acknowledgment number. This is also a 32 bits field of the header and contains the number of acknowledgment sent by the receiver to the transmitter after receipt of the segment. This helps in error detection when due to some reason, segment does processed at the destination computer.

5. Length. Length of the header is a 4 bits field but it can be the multiple of four bits to represent the total length of the header.

6. Reserved. This field is of 6 bits and always reserve for any further use in future.

Code bits: This is a 6 bits field. The six bits are divided into six fields as URG, ACK, PSH, RST, SYN and FIN.

URG: This field specifies that the segment contains urgent data and to be processed immediately.

ACK: This bit confirms the validity of acknowledgment number and works with it.

PSH: If the rate of data processing at the receiver end is more than the rate of data transmission, this bits asks the transmitter to increase the rate of transmission of data.

RST: This bit is used to reset the connection in between source and the destination, if there is problems with the sequence number of the transmitted segments.

SYN: This bit is used to synchronize of the segments.

FIN: This bit is used for terminating the connection in between source and destination machines.

Window: This is the 16 bits field that is used for defining the size of the sliding window.

Checksum: This is also 16 bits field that is used for error detection.

Urgent: It is a 16 bits field that contains a pointer. The urgent pointer confirms the end of urgent data and starting of transmission of normal data.

Options: This 32 bits field is used for alignment of data transfer or any other information related with data transfer in between source and destination.

IP Address Configuration

For connecting your computer with the internet IP configuration is necessary. There are various methods for various version of Windows used by ISP, but the basic configuration technique is described for Windows 98 as follows:

1. Click Start and Click Run in the Start menu of Windows 98.

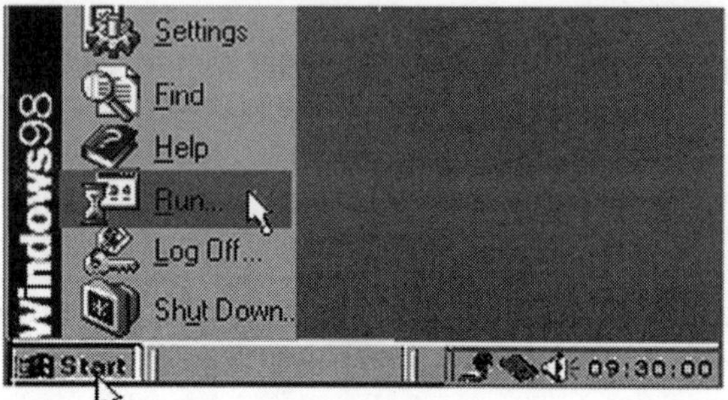

Type winipcfg in the combo box in the following "Run" window and click OK.

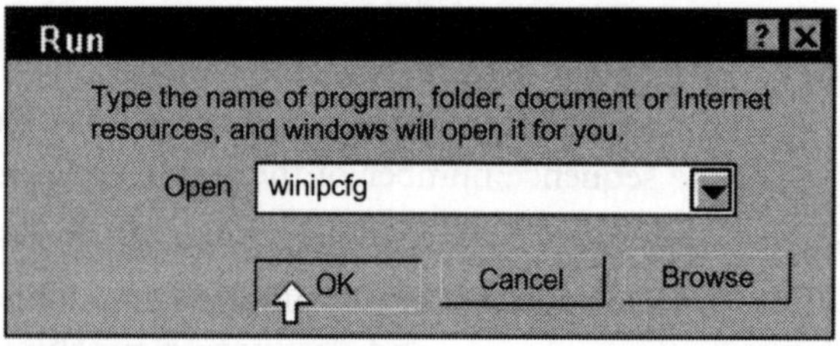

You may open the IP configuration window by command prompt also.

Open the MS-DOS command prompt by clicking on MS-DOS icon on desk top or in program menu.

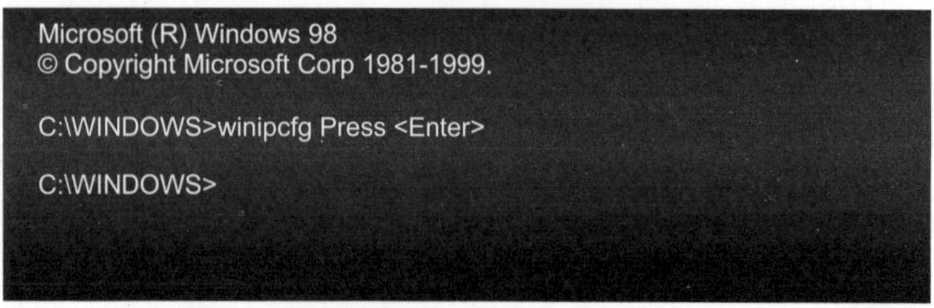

MS-DOS blue screen with command prompt appear on the screen.

Enter winipcfg in front of the command prompt and press enter the following:

IP configuration window will appear on the screen.

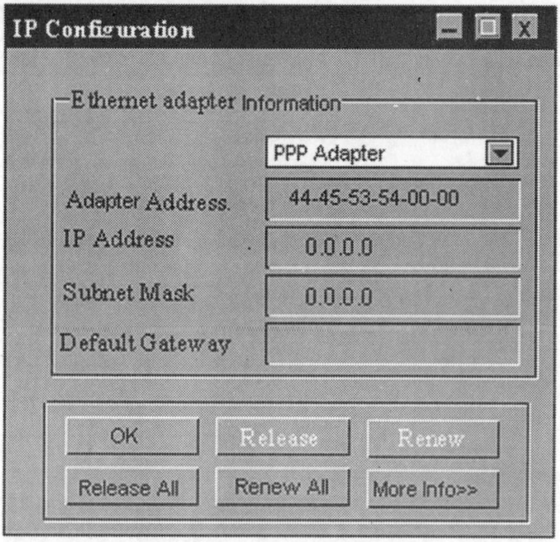

The first IP configuration window will show the configuration of PPP Adapter.

The Adapter Address is indicated as 44-45-53-54-00-00 while IP Address and Subnet Mask are indicated as 0.0.0.0. No default gateway is indicated because no router is used with this LAN.

This Adapter address cannot be changed so Release and Renew button are kept inactive.

For getting more information click on the more info Button in the above IP configuration window.

You will get the following IP configuration window on your screen:

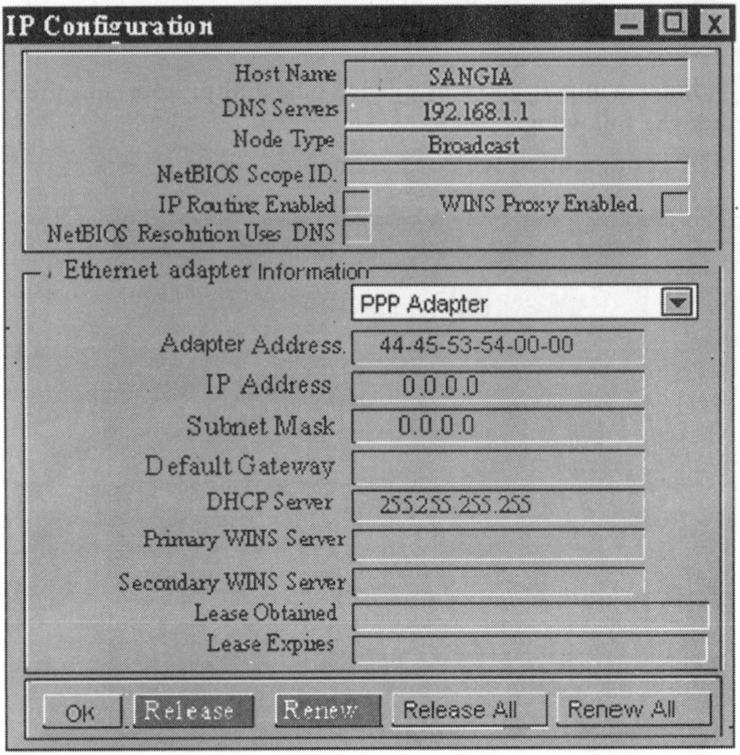

Click the arrow in combo box where you see PPP Adapter.

The second adapter Intel [R] PRO PCI Adapter will appear below the PPP Adapter.

Click the mouse on Intel [R] PRO PCI Adapter.

You will get a different IP configuration window.

This is the active adapter installed on the computer. It has been provided the address to the network adapter as 00-D0-B7-E4-5F-E5. An IP address is provided to the computer automatically as 169.254.74.135. Subnet Mask address is also provided as 255.255.0.0. This is a particular case for this adapter. Data will change with another adapter.

This IP Address Configuration utility enables the users to get the IP address of your hardware and many others information which will help you in configuration of your network. You can change one or more IP addresses. There are two buttons provided in IP Configuration utility window.

They are Release and Renew buttons.

When you click on Release button, a new IP address is popup in the IP configuration window in place of the previous address. Similar is the function of Renew button. Release All or Renew All buttons are utilized for releasing or renewing all the IP addresses.

The new IP addresses are provided by DHCP server. Your computer itself can assign an automatic private IP address. To use a different IP or DNS address for a Dial-Up Networking connection click on the icon My computer on Desk Top.

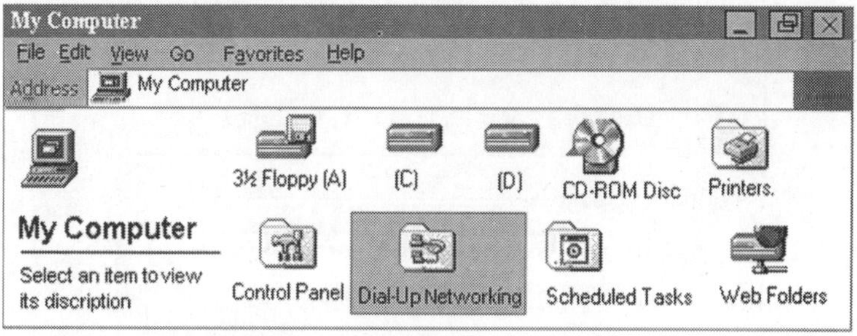

Click on the icon Dial-Up Networking in the above My Computer window.

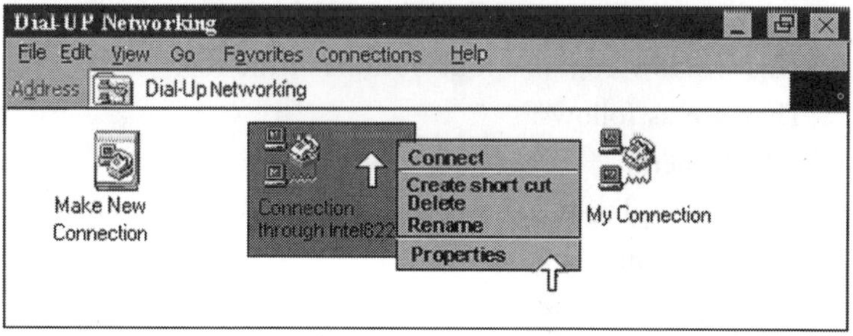

In the Dial-Up Networking window take following two steps:

1. Right click the icon "Connection through Intel 8225".
2. In the connect popup menu click on "Properties. Connection through Intel8255x-based PCI Ethernet Adapter" Window will appear on the screen.

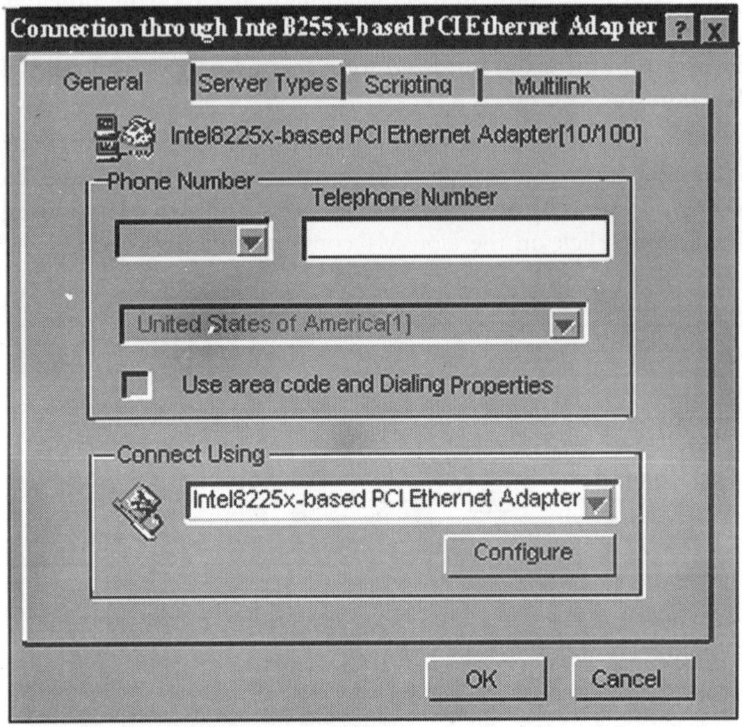

This window contains four buttons at the top.

They are as follows:

1. General
2. Server Types
3. Scripting
4. Multilink

Click the second button "Server Types" in the above window.

When you click on the "Server Types" button the following window will appear on the screen:

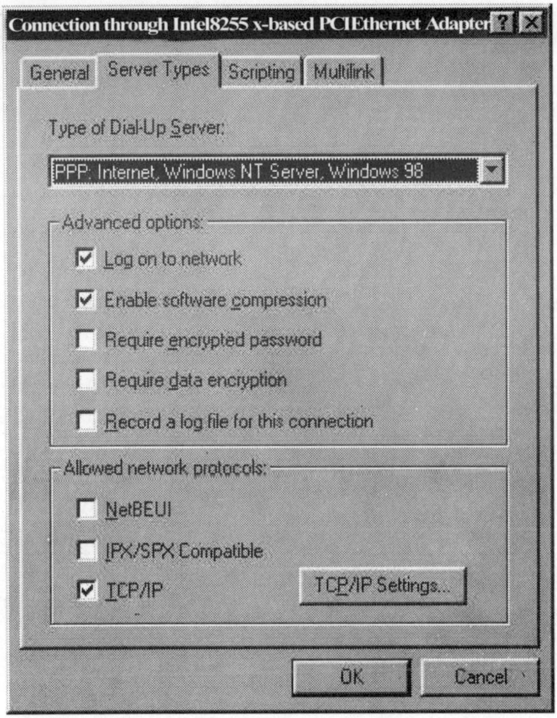

There are two sections of this window:

1. Advance Options
2. Allowed network protocol

1. Advance Options. This section contains the following five items which you can make active by clicking the check boxes:

1. Log on to network.
2. Enable software compression.
3. Require encrypted password.
4. Require data encryption.
5. Record of log file for this connection.

Second section is for Allowed Network Protocols. There are three protocols. NetBUI, IPX/SPX and TCP/IP.

Out of three you have to select TCP/IP protocol. Click on the "TCP/IP Settings..." button.

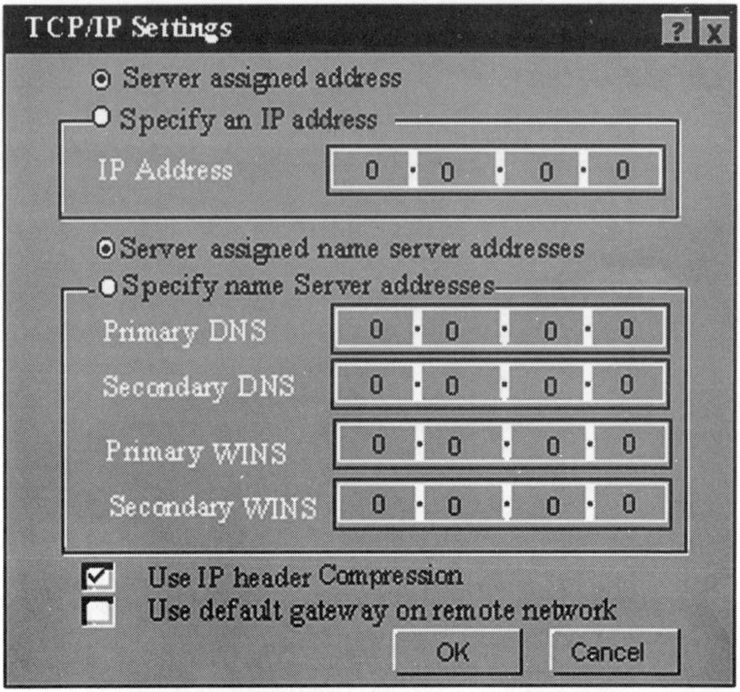

When you click on the "TCP/IP Settings..." button the above window appears on the screen.

There are two default options in each section of TCP/IP Setting window:

1. Server assigned address.
2. Server assign name and server addresses.

When you select the second option, the TCP/IP window looks like this.

First option is to specify an IP address of your computer in the box.

Second section is for specifying the name and server addresses.

Here you can provide three addresses as follows:

1. IP Address
2. Primary DNS
3. Secondary DNS

The following is the example to fill up the above TCP/IP settings for IP address and DNS server:

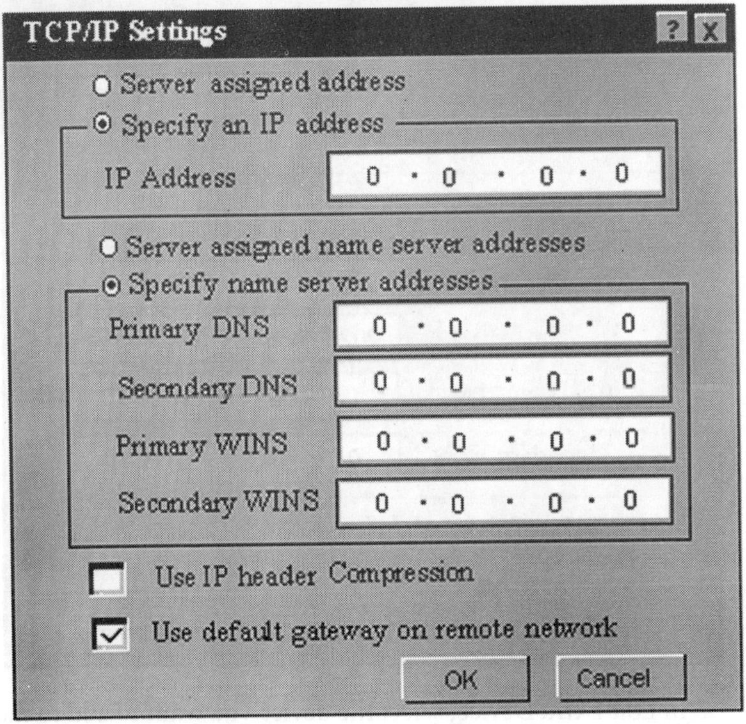

These addresses are provided by a particular network provider to a particular computer on the network.

IP Address......................192.168.1.2

Primary DNS Server 202.56.230.6

Secondary DNS Server.........202.56.224.153

After filling up these addresses click OK. Test the connection now.

To set up a network connection using multiple modems.

Set up a Dial-Up Networking connection using one modem. In the Dial-Up Networking folder, right-click the connection icon and click Properties. On the Multilink tab, click. Use additional devices, and then click Add.

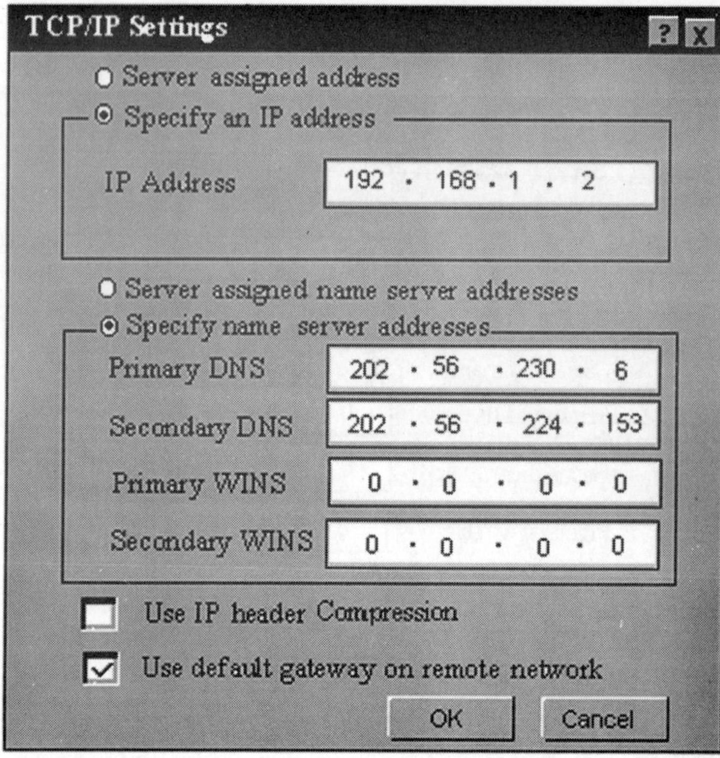

In Edit Extra Device, select the device you want to add to the connection, and then click OK.

Repeat Steps 3 and 4 until you have added all the modems you want.

Short-cut Airtel Connection Method

ISP Airtel uses the different method for connecting your PC with LAN.

It is the direct connection method, where you should know the IP address of your computer.

Take the following steps:

1. Open internet explorer.
2. Switch on your external modem.
3. Type the IP address of your computer like 192.168.1.2 in the address bar of browser and press enter.

4. Type user name and password as “admin” and “password” in the admin window and click OK.
5. A page will open Click on Advance setting.
6. Click on Edit button.
7. A automatic configure window opens, just Click Next.
8. Another window will open, Click Next.
9. Provide your User ID and password and Click Next.
10. This window contains the save button. Click save button.
11. Reboot the router. It takes two to three minutes time and your connection with the internet is set up.
12. See in this case all the four light of your modem will be on.
13. Test by typing the site address http://google.com in address bar and press enter.

Internet Protocol

Internet Protocol (IP) is the network layer protocol. IP main function is to provide a connectionless service. IP deals with the data packets known as datagram. Each datagram is independent. After determination of the routing path, IP transfers the datagram from source to destination. It maintains tables to send a packet according to IP address of host.

Features of Internet Protocol

1. IP transfers the packet from one node to another node.
2. Each node is provided with a four bytes IP address.
3. Every computer that is connected with the network has its IP address.
4. IP address is composed of four bytes, for example IP address: 192.168.1.2.
5. This IP address is provided by the network service provider.
6. Internet service provider provides ranges of IP numbers to sub-company.

7. IP addresses are further distributed to departments to sub-department.
8. IP address of the router is also called gateway.
9. This gateway is responsible for transmitting the data both ways.
10. Internet Protocol (IP) is a network layer of the OSI model.
11. All transport protocol data packets like UDP or TCP are encapsulated in IP data packets and then transmission of data packets is carried out from one host to another.
12. IP is not a reliable protocol because it does not give any guarantee that the data will reach the destination. This is because the datagram may be damaged upon arrival. It may be out of order or it has not reached at all. The upper layer (TCP) above the IP is responsible for delivering the correct data.
13. IP used datagram to send the message from node to node. The format of datagram is shown below that indicates the bits allotted to each field.

<table>
<tr><td>Bit 0</td><td colspan="2">To</td><td>Bit 15</td><td>Bit 16</td><td>To</td><td>Bit 31</td></tr>
<tr><td>Version 4 Bits</td><td>Header Len 4 Bits</td><td colspan="2">Service 8 Bits</td><td colspan="3">Total length 16 Bits</td></tr>
<tr><td colspan="4">Identification 16 Bits</td><td>Flags 3 Bits</td><td colspan="2">Fragment 13 Bits</td></tr>
<tr><td colspan="2">Time to Live 8 Bits</td><td colspan="2">Protocol 8 Bits</td><td colspan="3">Header checksum 16 Bits</td></tr>
<tr><td colspan="7">Source IP address 32 Bits</td></tr>
<tr><td colspan="7">Destination IP address 32 Bits</td></tr>
<tr><td colspan="7">Options 32 Bits</td></tr>
<tr><td colspan="7">Data 32 Bits</td></tr>
</table>

The function of each field of datagram

1. **Version.** It is 4 bits field reserved for IP version. IP version may be IPv4 or IPv6.
2. **Header length.** It specifies the length of the header. It is a multiple of 4 bits field. Length of the header may be in between 20 bytes to 60 bytes.
3. **Service.** This is a 8 bits field. It specifies the level of service to be used by the transmitter. When four bits are on, first two bits represent the maximum throughput of data with high reliability. Other two bits are used for minimizing the delay of data transfer and cost of message transmission.

Table of bits used for service

Service	Bit	Bit
Delay	0 for normal delay	1 for lower delay
Throughput	0 for normal throughput	1 for higher throughput
Reliability	0 for normal reliability	1 for higher reliability
Cost	0 for normal cost	1 for higher cost

4. **Total length.** This is a 16 bits field which indicates the total length of datagram.
5. **Identification.** This is a 16 bits field that contains the information about the each datagram. Each datagram is converted into frame before the data are actually transmitted. To identify the frames, identification field is used. Identification process of the datagram is used to assemble them at the destination end and convert them into a complete message.
6. **Flag.** Flag is the 3 bits field. It is used for identification of frames along with identification field.
7. **Fragmentation.** This is a 13 bits field to point out the offset of data in the original datagram by the process of fragmentation. Bit 0 is used to fragment the packet and bit 1 is used when packed need not to be fragmented.

8. **Time to live.** It is a 8 bits field. Every datagram is provided with the number of router through which it has to pass. This number of routers is called hop. Hop becomes one less, when it passes through a router. When the datagram reaches the final destination, the hop becomes zero and the datagram is deleted. The final router uses ICMP to inform the source router that the datagram is deleted. This hop number indicates the life of the datagram. The hop is generally set from 32 to 64.
9. **Protocol.** There are various protocol which support the Internet protocol. The needed protocol is implemented by using their listed number in protocol field.

Protocols and their associated number as follows:

Protocol	Number Associated
TCP	6
UDP	17
ICMP	1
IGMP	2
OSPF	89

10. **Header Checksum.** It is a 16 bits field. It specifies the IP header.
11. **Source address.** It is a 32 bits field used for indicating the transmitter IP address.
12. **Destination address.** It is also the 32 bits field used for indicating the receiver IP address.
13. **Option.** This is 32 bits field that is used of data management. It provides reliability in data transmission by routing, timing and alignment of data.

It uses the following six options:

1. Restriction and Security
2. Routing Record - IP address is recorded and stored by each router.

3. Stamp Timing	-	Time stamp is provided to each router along with its IP address.
4. Loose routing	-	It is the normal route of datagram and it must go through a set of IP addresses.
5. Strict routing	-	The datagram has to follow the route strictly and must pass through specific IP addresses.
6. Data	-	Hardware data are encapsulated.

Basics of LAN

5

Local Area Network (LAN)

It is a network of computers which works for relatively a small area.

It is generally used for small business and may be located in a small building.

These LANs can be connected with the larger networks, or they can be connected to the Internet. When the LANs use internet protocols, they are known as intranets. These intranets may or may not be the part of bigger internet network.

Local Area Network Components

We need the following hardware or network's components as shown in the following figure:

Components of LAN

1. Two or more than two computers
2. Ethernet card
3. DSL broadband modern
4. Switch or Hub
5. Telephone line connection
6. Power supply Connection at 230 volts
7. Cat 5 wiring

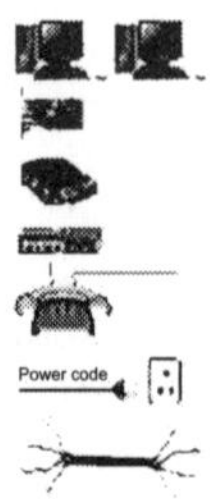

The components of local area network are described below:

1. Computers

For making local area network, we require at least two or more computers.

All the computers must have network interface cards (NIC).

They are three basics: Bus, Star, and Ring topology that are used for connecting the computers in a network.

The network topology is the physical wiring of the network. The computers can share files, folders, printer and scanner, etc.

2. Ethernet card

10/100 Ethernet card is used for making the internet connection. This Ethernet card is installed on the PCI slot of the motherboard of the computer. For making this card workable you have to installed a driver. If the driver is available with the operating system it is automatically installed, when you start the computer, otherwise you have to installed through CD-ROM which contain the appropriate driver. This Ethernet card is provided with an address that is used for internet connection.

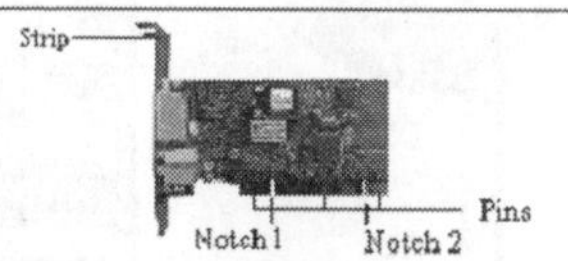

10/100 Ethernet Card

3. Modem

There are five types of modem used in networking:

1. Internal or basic type of modem
2. DSL broadband modem
3. Cable modem
4. Wireless modem
5. Analog or ISDN modem

Modem is the device which is connected with the Ethernet adapter via a switch by cat-5 wiring.

Modem and switch are connected by Ethernet cable and switch is connected with Ethernet adapter by another Ethernet cable. Ethernet adapter is installed on the motherboard of CPU.

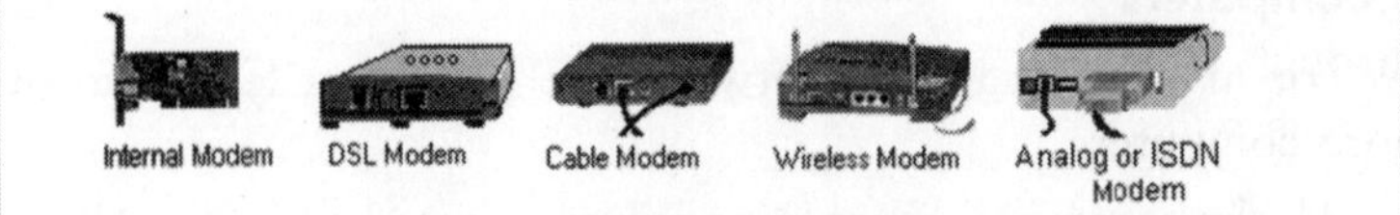

Function of modem is to modulate signals from digital to analog and demodulates analog to digital signals.

1. It modulates digital signals into analog signals, received from digital device of the network and sends them to the other computer through telephone lines.
2. Similarly, it demodulates the incoming analog signals from outside analog device and converts them into digital signals for the digital device.
3. Following figure shows the modem connection with telephone line and the CPU:

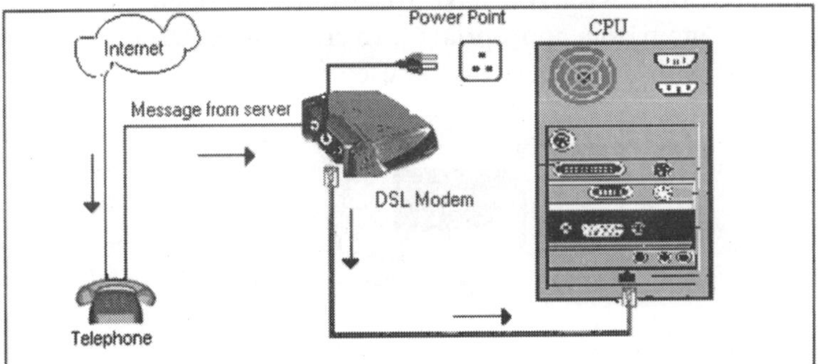

Single PC Internet Connection

4. Switch

Switch connects all the equipments like computers, printer, scanner, etc. in a local area network. It receives the data in the form of packets. It reads the header information from the packet and then after amplification it sends the packets to the destination port of the computer to which the packet belong to. It does not send the packet to all the ports of the network like hub. This reduces the traffic on the network.

Thus the sorting of the packets is performed by the Ethernet switch and the packets are sent to the concerned computer through Ethernet card. The reduction of the network load increases the speed of data transfer.

In the following figure, switch receives the data from modem which is sent through the network to client PC-1. Switch recognizes the IP address of PC-1 and sends the message to PC-1.

If the message packet belongs to PC-2 switch recognizes the address of PC-2 and transmits the message to it.

Following figure shows the switch position in a simple LAN connection of two PCs:

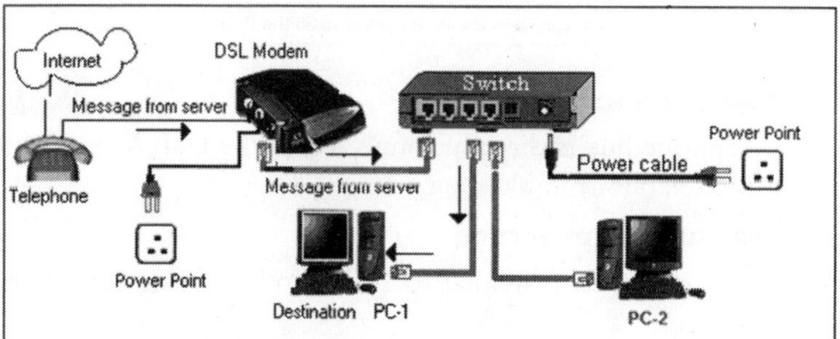

Switch transmits the data to the destined PC

Hub

Hub also connects all the equipments like computers, printer, scanner, etc. in a local area network.

When a hub receives the packet, it passes the message to all the ports of the network.

The packet's destination may be for one port but hub can not recognize the port, therefore the packet is sent to all the machines belong to that network. This causes a heavy traffic on the network and the network response becomes poor.

Hub has to share its bandwidth with each and every one of its ports therefore bandwidth will be divided between all system's machines, which will cause a poor performance.

It is clear from the following figure that message received by DSL modem is transmitted to hub and then hub sends the data to both PC-1 and PC-2, though the message is destined to PC-1 only.

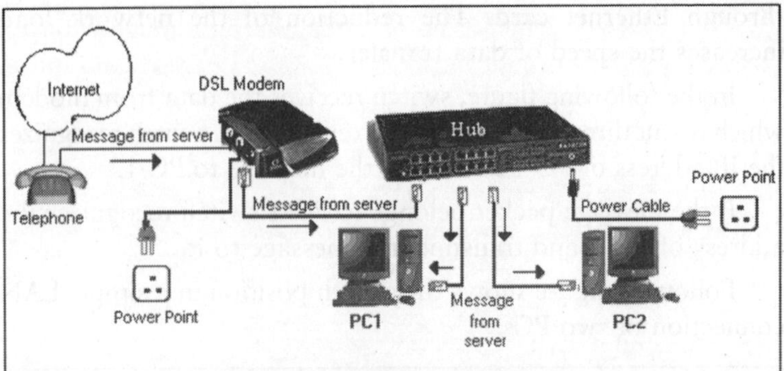

Hub transmits the data packet to all the Ports

5. Telephone line connection

Telephone line is directly connected to the DSL Modem by fixing the telephone cable plug.

6. Power supply connection

Power supply is provided to DSL Modem from 230 Volts supply plug.

7. Cat-5 wiring

Cat-5 wiring means category 5 wiring. It is a special wiring system which is used in Ethernet internet cables. It can transfer the data at the speed of 100 Mbps. Four twisted and insulated sets of copper wires encased inside the insulated sleeve and are connected with the RJ45 connectors at the ends. It can also work with sound frequencies up to 100 MHz. This cat-5 wiring is used to connect modem with switch and switch with computers and other equipments of the network.

Physical LAN Connection Preparation

Before making a physical LAN connection please go through the following check list:

1. Decide which type of cable and how much cable you need for your network.
2. Determine the type of hub or switch you need.
3. It is always better to have a hub or switch with 2-4 more ports.
4. Determine the number of NIC cards, required for your network. Some new computers sometimes come with NIC cards therefore purchase NIC only for those computers which require them.
5. Find out the length of the cable you will require. Measure the length from each computer to the next and from each computer to the hub. It is always better to keep the cables a few feet longer than what you need to allow for moving the location of the computer.
6. If you have not the technical knowledge to cut and crimp your own cables, then it is better to buy your pre-made cables with the predetermined length.
7. Complete all the wiring, card installation, etc. in a day you plan. Do not leave the job for next day.

Installation

Take the steps as given below:

1. Switch off both computers.
2. Connect the modem to the telephone line by the telephone cable number 1.
3. Connect the modem to D-link switch by the cat-5 wire numbered as 2.
4. Connect the two computers PC-1 and PC-2 with the D-link switch by cat-5 wire numbered as 3 and 4 respectively.
5. Fix the power line cable 5 with the modem and power supply point.
6. Fix the power line cable 6 with the D-link switch and power supply point.
7. Switch on both the computers.
8. Switch on the power of modem and the D-link switch.

The following picture shows the connection of your LAN:

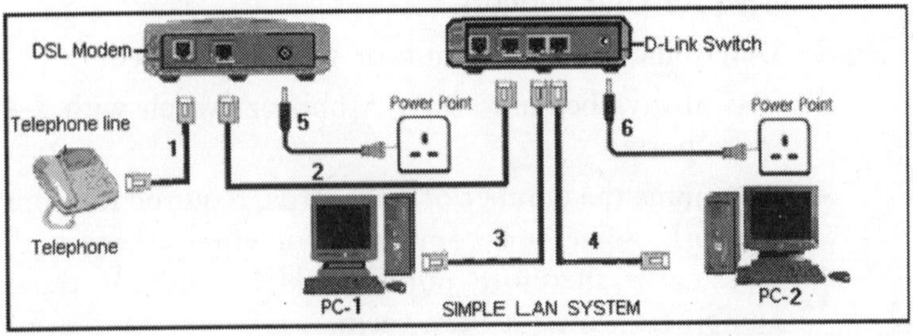

After doing all the connection of LAN you have to carry out the following:

1. Installation of Ethernet card on the motherboard.
2. Verifying IRQ (Interrupted Request).
3. Making LAN Internet connection.

1. Installation of Ethernet card on the motherboard. If your computer does not have an inbuilt Ethernet card, you have to install this hardware on your computer. Take the following steps:

1. Switch off the computer.
2. Remove the CPU cover by opening the screws at the back side of cabinet or remove the side cover so that the motherboard PCI slots are exposed.
3. Pull the cover towards backside because generally the front part of cabinet cover is hoisted inside the front panel of cabinet. Some cabinet provides the side cover with the cabinet to approach the internal part of CPU. You can remove the cover by opening the screw.
4. Locate the PCI slot. In the following motherboard picture three PCI bus extension slots are shown along with the AGP extension slot. Choose any one of the three and fix the Ethernet card.

   Two notches are provided with the Ethernet card. You have to match the notches and the notch-projections of the slot and then press the card gently to fix it. In the left side of the card a metallic strip is provided which sits on the cabinet to fix the card firmly with a screw.

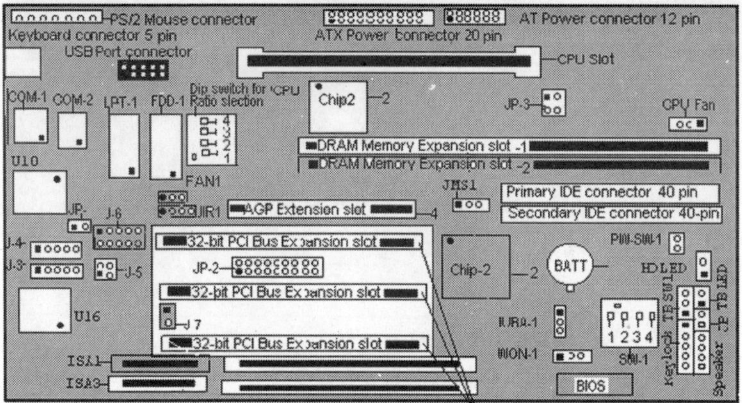

PCI Slots on Mother Board

5. Screw the strip gently. After fixing the Ethernet card on the motherboard place the cover of cabinet in position and screw it.
6. Now switch on the computer. If your system contains the driver for Ethernet card, it will be detected by the operating system and the appropriate drivers will be installed automatically.

   If the system does not contain the appropriate drivers, you will be prompted to insert the CD in CD-ROM that generally provided with the Ethernet card by the seller. Install the Ethernet card driver as directed by the window installer. You have to install the Ethernet card on each computer of your LAN.

2. Verifying IRQ (Interrupted Request). For every hardware of computer, IRQ is allotted by the system. The two hardware devices cannot use the same IRQ, otherwise both the devices will not work properly. After installation of NIC card you have to verify the IRQ allotted to it. NIC card is named as adapter in the device manager list.

If you are using Window XP click on view in Device Manager.

For verification of NIC card IRQ take the following steps:

1. Right click on **My Computer icon** on the Desk Top.

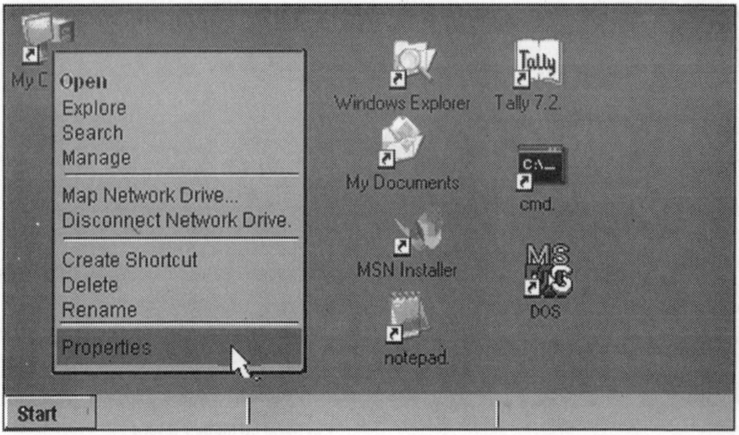

2. Click on **Properties.**
   System Properties window will open with General button.

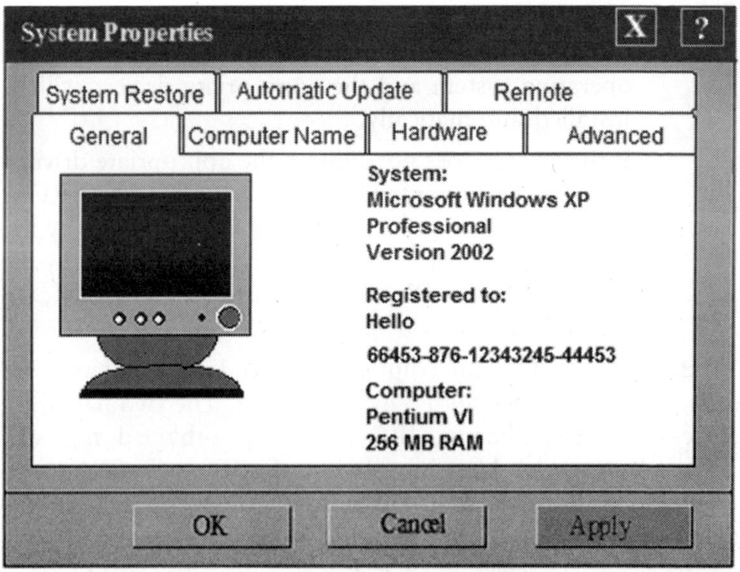

3. Click on **Hardware** button in **System Properties** window.
4. Next click on **Device Manager** button.

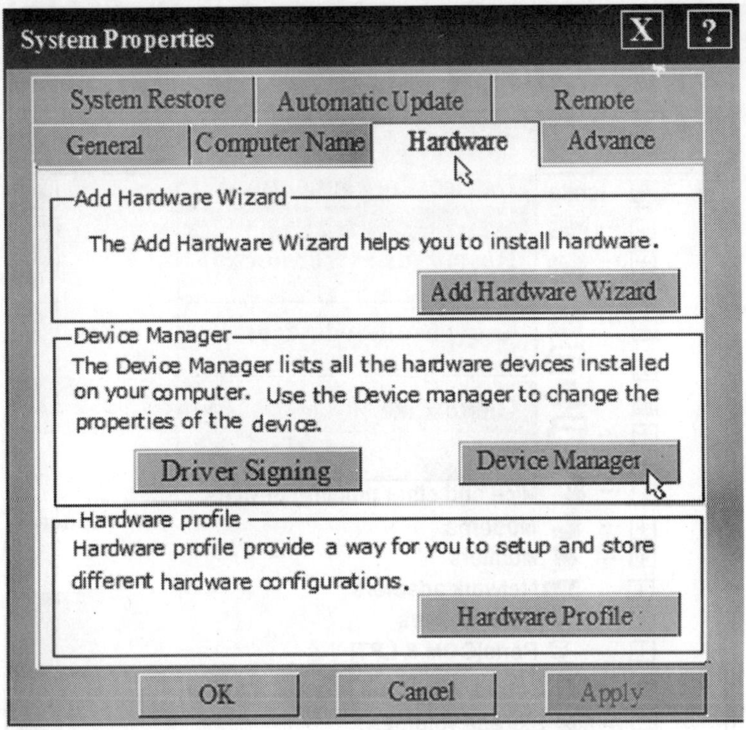

Following **Device Manager** window will open as shown on page 88.

Click on **"View"** and then **"Resources by Type"**

Another Device Manager window will appear on the screen.

Click on the **plus sign** at the **"Interrupt Request"**

This will display the expanded view of IRQ allotted to the each hardware components of the computer.

You can see the IRQ allotted to your NIC card (Adapter) in the list as shown on page 89.

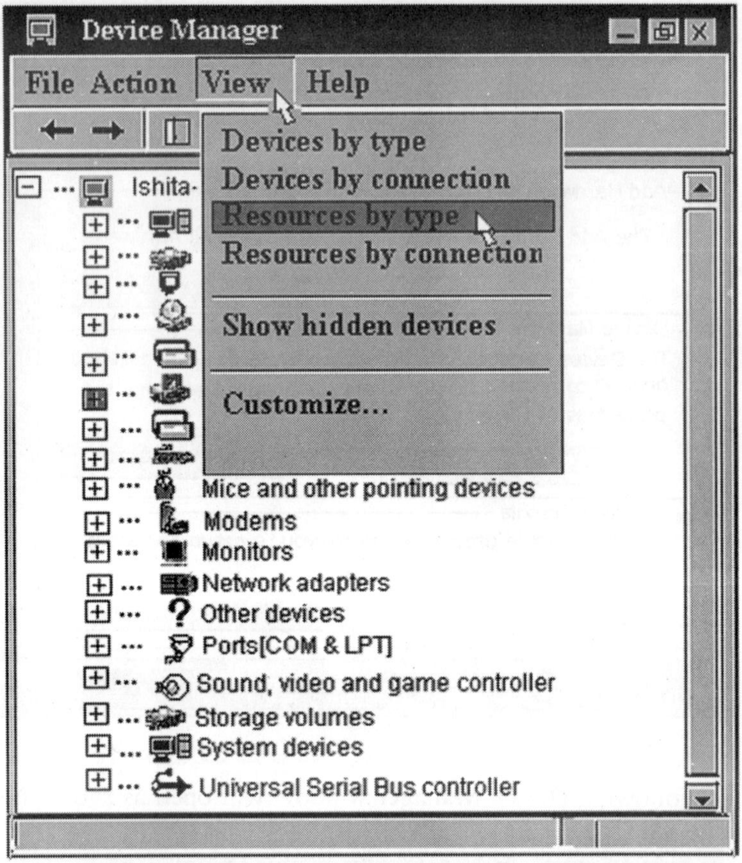
Device Manager
File Action View Help
Devices by type
Devices by connection
Resources by type
Resources by connection
Show hidden devices
Customize...
Ishita-
Mice and other pointing devices
Modems
Monitors
Network adapters
Other devices
Ports[COM & LPT]
Sound, video and game controller
Storage volumes
System devices
Universal Serial Bus controller

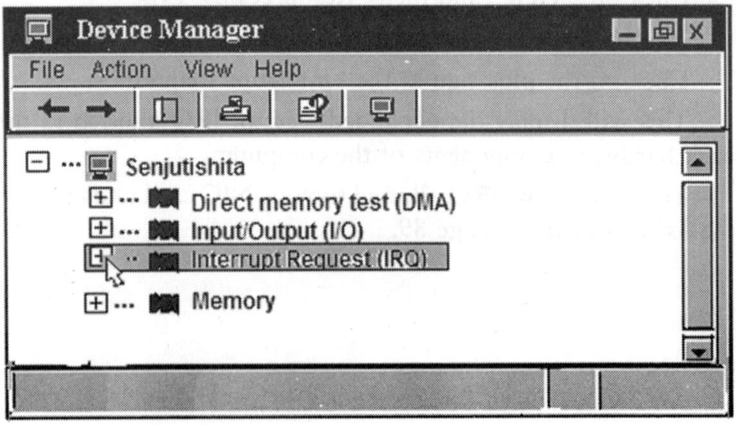
Device Manager
File Action View Help
Senjutishita
Direct memory test (DMA)
Input/Output (I/O)
Interrupt Request (IRQ)
Memory

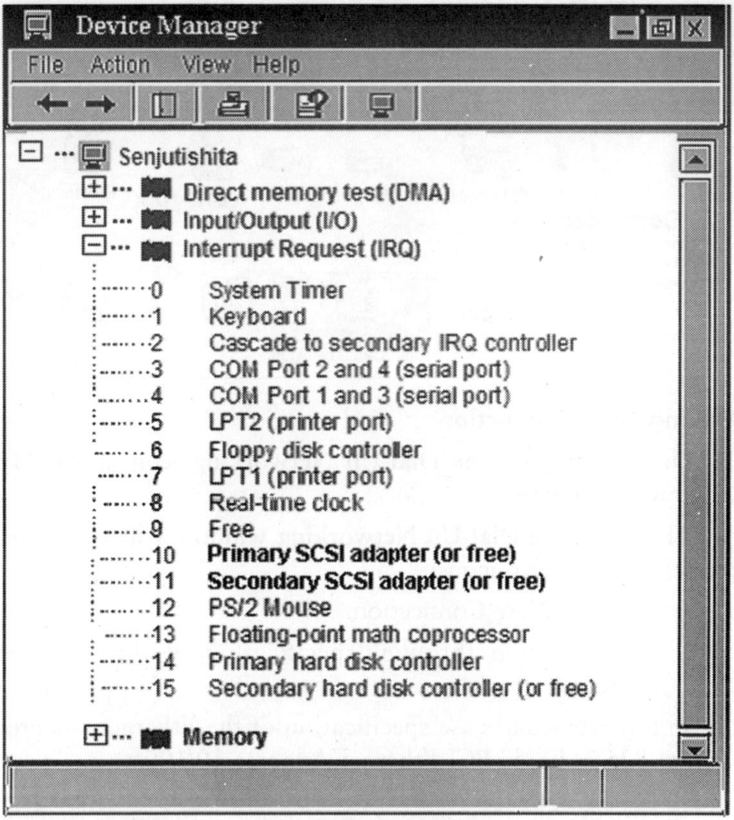

3. Making Internet connection. There are several methods to make internet connection. The procedure of Internet connection varies from one Internet Service providers, to another.

There are following two main methods that are generally in use:

1. Offline Configuration through Internet Explorer.
2. Online Configuration through Internet Explorer.

1. Offline Configuration through Internet Explorer. For making internet connection you may find the **My Computer** icon on the desktop.

The following **My Computer window** will appear on the screen:

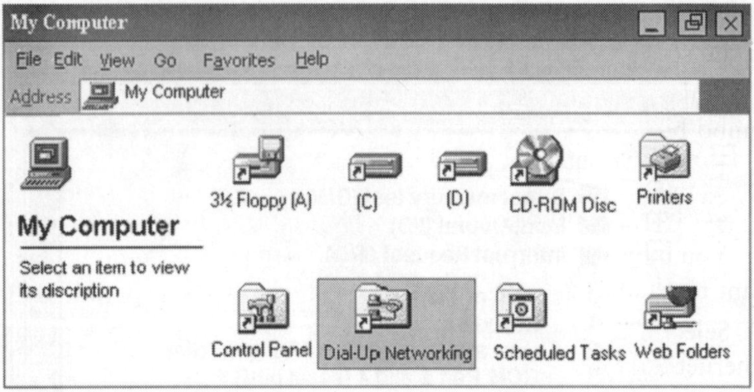

Making New Connection

Double click on the **Dial-Up Networking icon** in the My Computer window.

The following **Dial-Up Networking** window will appear on the screen with two icons:

1. Make New Connection.
2. Connection through (specification of the Ethernet Adapter).

In this particular case specification of the Ethernet Adapter is Intel 8255×-based PCI Ethernet Adapter 10/100.

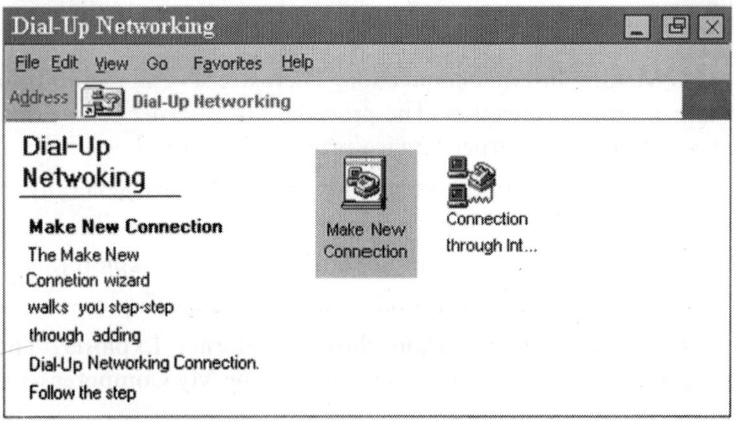

Double Click the **Make New Connection icon** in the Dial-Up Networking Window.

The following "Make New Connection window" will appear on the screen.

Make New Connection window has a text boxes and a combo box.

1. Type a name for the computer you are dialing.
2. Select a device.

You may see the text My Connection in the text box. If you want to change the text. You can type your own text.

Select a device combo box displays the specification of the Ethernet Adapter.

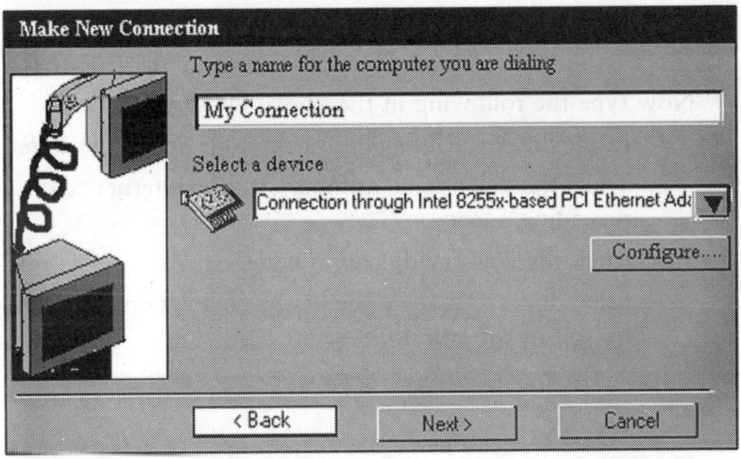

Click the Next button in the above Make Connection Window.

The following window will appear on the screen:

1. Area Code which is the country code.
2. Telephone number of the service providing agency.
3. Name of the country from where you make this internet connection.

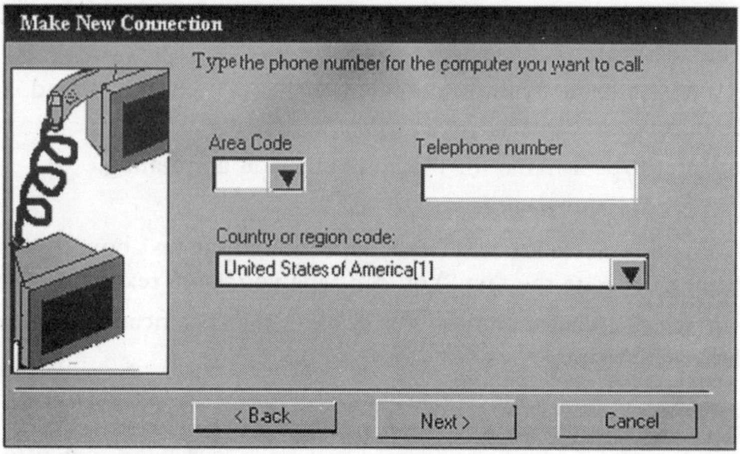

Now type the following in the above window:

1. Inside the Area Code type 91 the code of country India.
2. Type the telephone number of the internet service providing agency.
3. Click the country or region code.
4. Select India (91) from the list by clicking on the arrow button of the combo box.

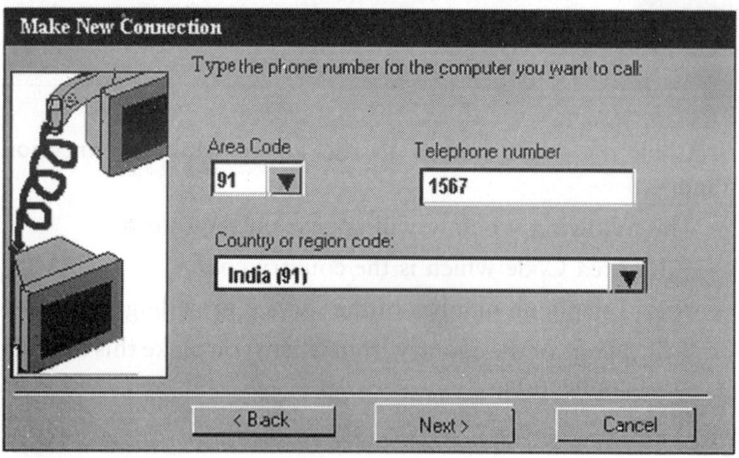

Click the Next button in the above window, you will see the following window:

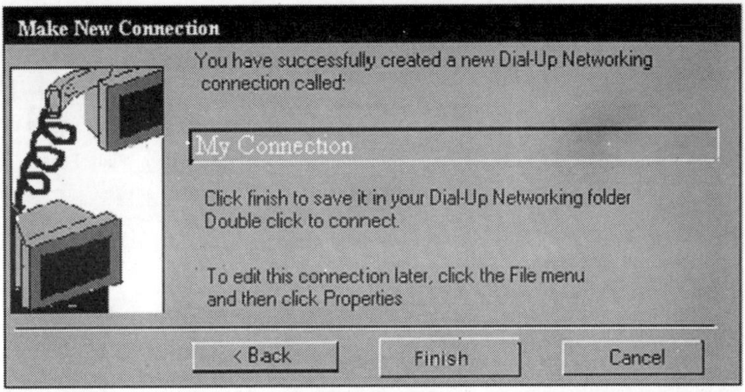

Click the Finish button in the above window. Your internet connection is now made with the server.

If your network is provided with broad band facilities then you have to edit the following:

1. IP address, subnet mask address,
2. Default gateway address,
3. DNS server address.

1. Click Start button at the taskbar then go to settings and then click on control panel as directed in the following figure:

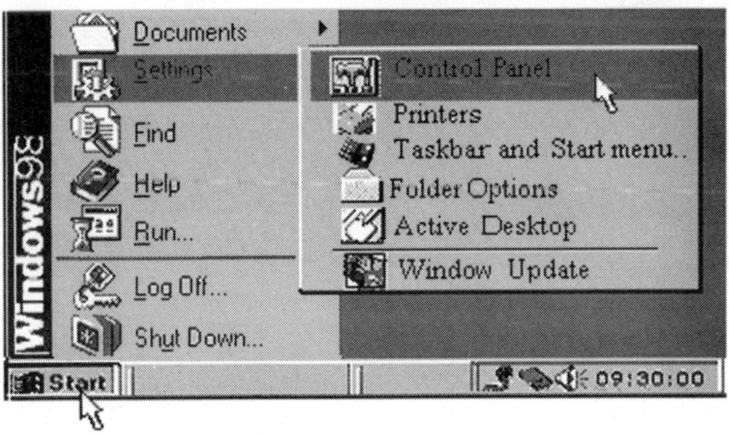

As soon as you click **Control Panel** icon Control panel window will be displayed on screen as follows:

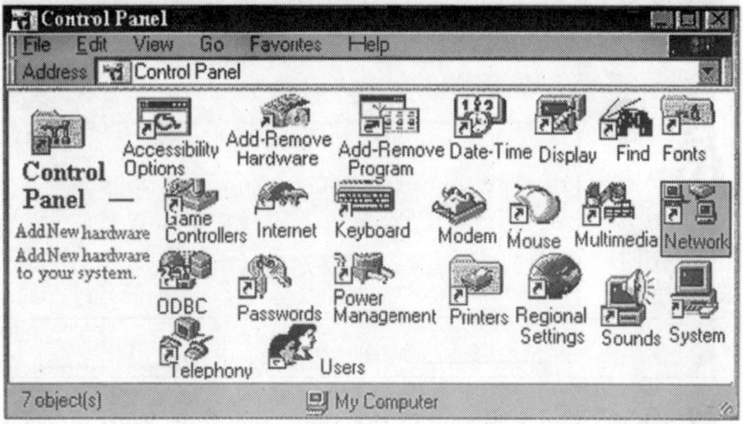

Double click on the **Network icon.** If you are using Windows 98, the following **Network Connections** window appears on the screen.

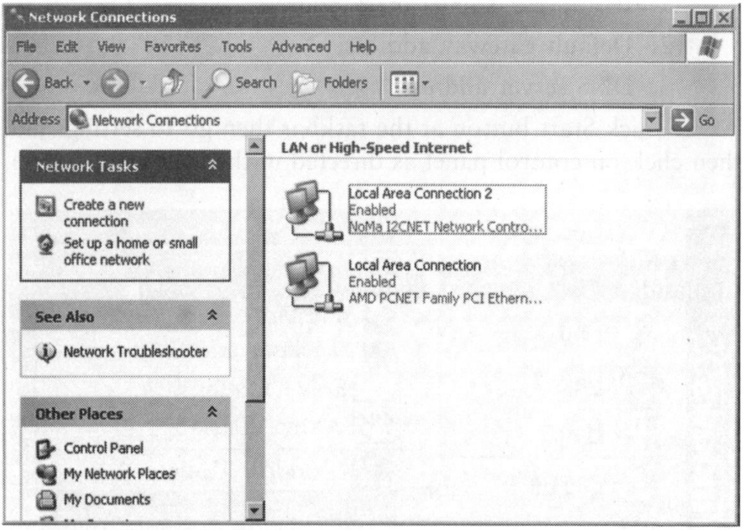

Select **Local Area Connection** and right click and then click on Properties.

Following **Local Area Connection Properties** window will appear on the screen:

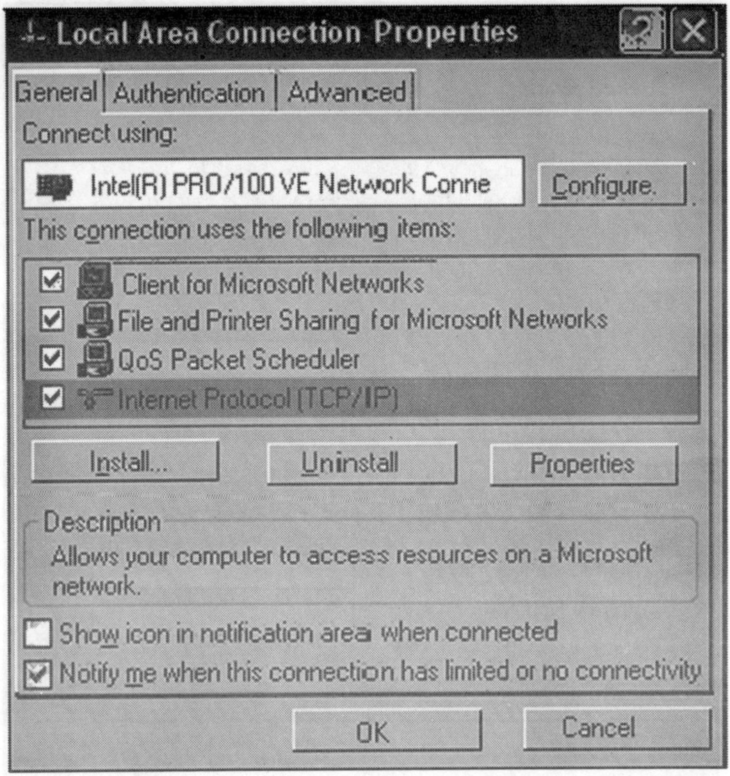

Local Area connection properties window contains the following:

1. Client for Microsoft Network
2. File or Printer Sharing for Microsoft Network
3. QoS Packet Scheduler
4. Internet Protocol [TCP/IP]

Select **Internet Protocol** (**TCP/IP**) and click on **Properties button.**

The following Internet Protocol (TCP/IP) Properties window will appear on the screen:

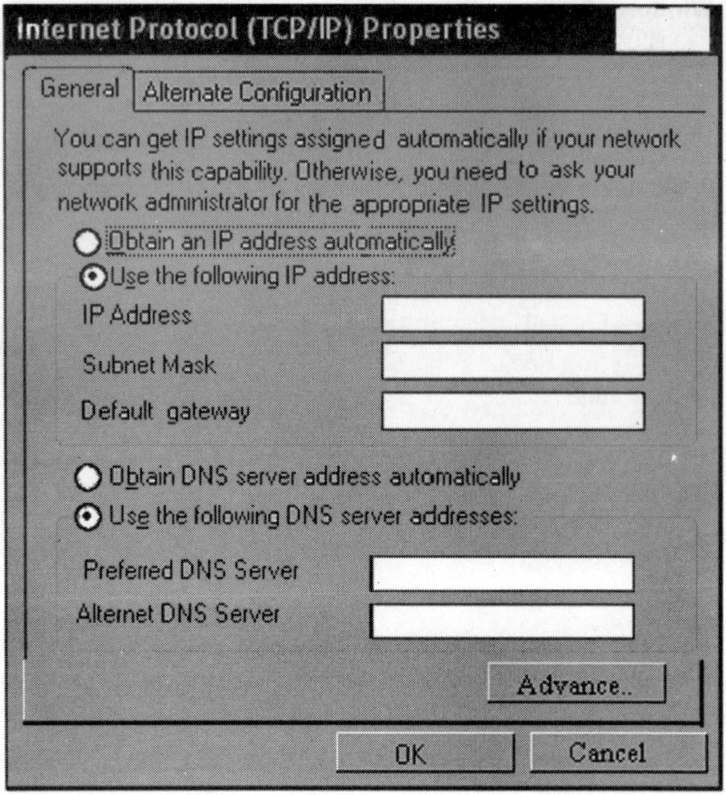

If you have chosen option for setting the **IP address and DNS server address** automatically, then you need not to do any thing with this window.

If you have taken **DSL broadband** connection for unlimited time then select the second option for both IP address and DNS server address in the above window.

For getting IP Address, Subnet mask and Default gateway for your computer network, write the following command in DOS C:\WINDOWS>ipconfig/all and press enter.

Microsoft(R) Windows 98

(C)Copyright Microsoft Corp 1981-1999.

C:\WINDOWS>ipconfig/all <Press Enter>

You will get the following information:

Windows 98 IP configuration

```
Host Name . . . . . . . . . . . . . . : SANGIA
DNS Servers . . . . . . . . . . . . . : 192.168.1.1
Node Type . . . . . . . . . . . . . . : Broadcast
NetBIOS Scope ID . . . . . . . . :
IP Routing Enabled . . . . . . . : No
WINS Proxy Enabled . . . . . . : No
NetBIOS Resolution Uses DNS : No
```

0 Ethernet adapter

```
Description . . . . . . . . . . . . . : PPP Adapter
Physical Address . . . . . . . . . . : 44-45-53-54-00-00
DHCP Enabled . . . . . . . . . . . : Yes
IP Address . . . . . . . . . . . . . . : 0.0.0.0
Subnet Mask . . . . . . . . . . . . : 0.0.0.0
Default Gateway . . . . . . . . . . :
DHCP Server . . . . . . . . . . . . : 255.255.255.255
Primary WINS Server . . . . . . :
Secondary WINS Server . . . . . :
Lease Obtained . . . . . . . . . . . :
Lease Expires . . . . . . . . . . . . :
```

1 Ethernet adapter

```
Description . . . . . . . . . . . . . : Intel(R) PRO PCI Adapter
Physical Address . . . . . . . . . . : 00-D0-B7-E4-5F-E5
DHCP Enabled . . . . . . . . . . . : Yes
IP Address . . . . . . . . . . . . . . : 192.168.1.2
Subnet Mask . . . . . . . . . . . . : 255.0.0.0
Default Gateway . . . . . . . . . . : 192.168.1.1
DHCP Server . . . . . . . . . . . . : 192.168.1.1
Primary WINS Server . . . . . . :
Secondary WINS Server . . . . . :
Lease Obtained . . . . . . . . . . : 04 15 07 2:02:40 PM
Lease Expires . . . . . . . . . . . . :
C:\WINDOWS>
```

The detail information are for a particular computer. This may change with the another computer.

Type the following addresses in the first, second and third box respectively.

IP Address— 192.168.1.1

Subnet mask address— 255.255.255.0

Default gateway— 192.168.1.1

Type the following addresses in the fourth and fifth box respectively.

Preferred DNS Server address— 202.56.230.6

Alternative DNS Server address— 202.56.224.153

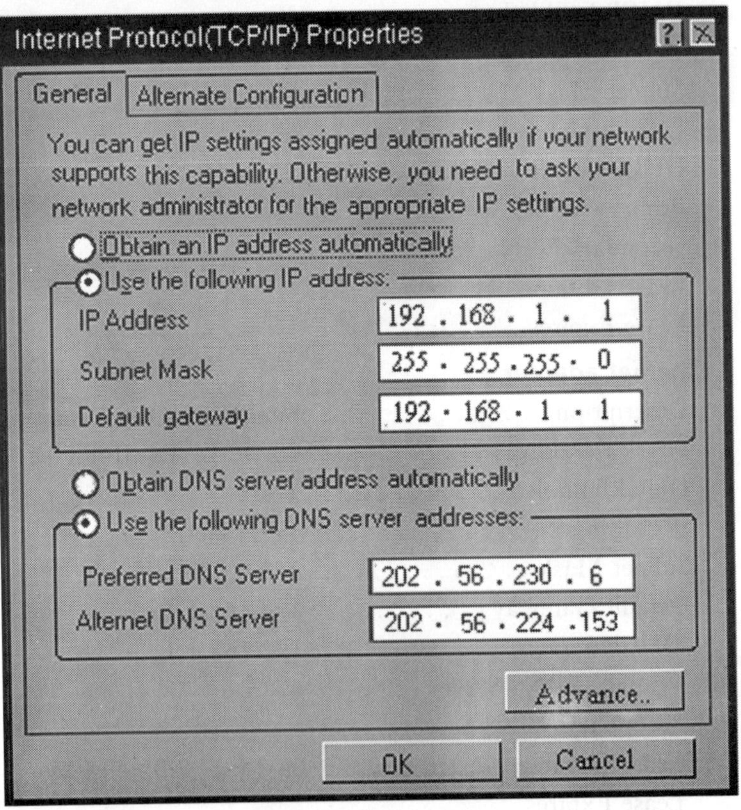

Click OK button. Configuration IP/TCP setting is completed.

The IP address, Subnet mask, and Default gateway addresses you may get from the DOS but the Preferred DNS Server and Alternate DNS Server addresses you have to get from the internet service providing authority.

Your host computer is connected with the internet through dedicated connection. Now you can configure the other computer on your LAN by the following ways.

Configure PC-2

Start the second computer and open the Internet Protocol (TCP/IP) Properties window as you have done with main host computer. Simply go to the IP address and type the address as 192.168.1.2 as shown in the following window:

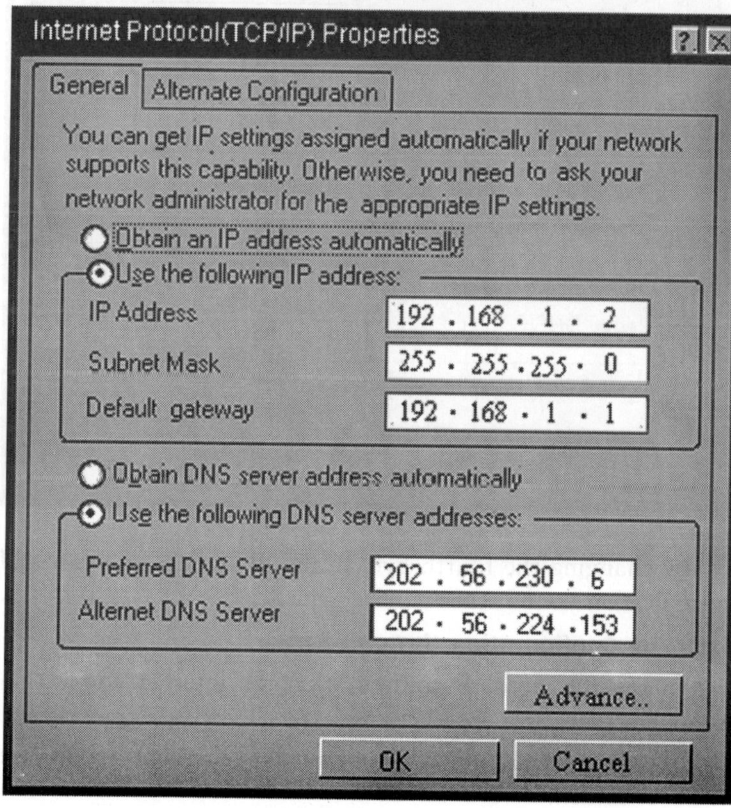

Connecting with More PC on LAN

In a similar manner start the third computer and open the Internet Protocol (TCP/IP) Properties window as you have done with main host computer. Simply go to the IP address and type the address as 192.168.1.3 as shown in the following window:

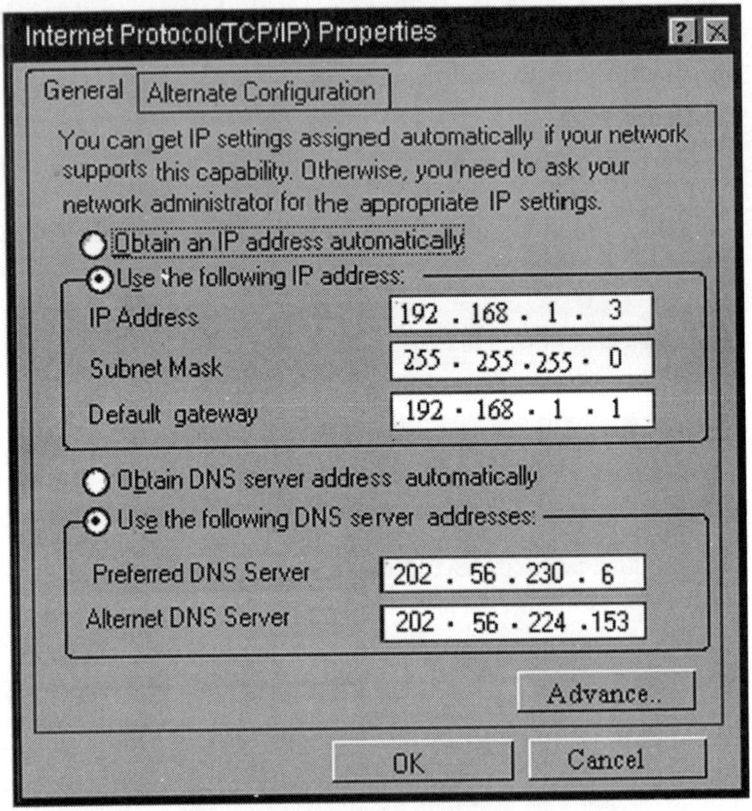

By changing the fourth byte in the IP address you can add more PCs on your LAN.

1. Online Configuration through Server

Follow the steps to configuration the internet connection through server.

1. See all the connections of modem telephone and PC are intact.

2. Power on your modem and start your computer.

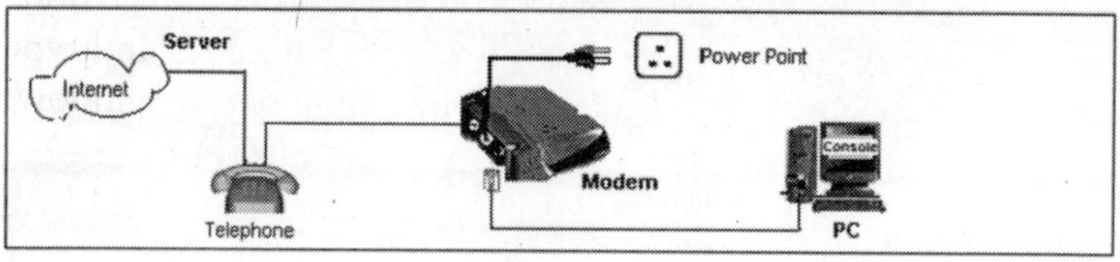

3. Double click on internet explorer icon "e" on the desktop. Internet explorer window appears on the screen as shown in the following figure.
4. Type the IP address of your computer as 192.168.1.1 in the address bar and press enter. Following information appears in your web browser:

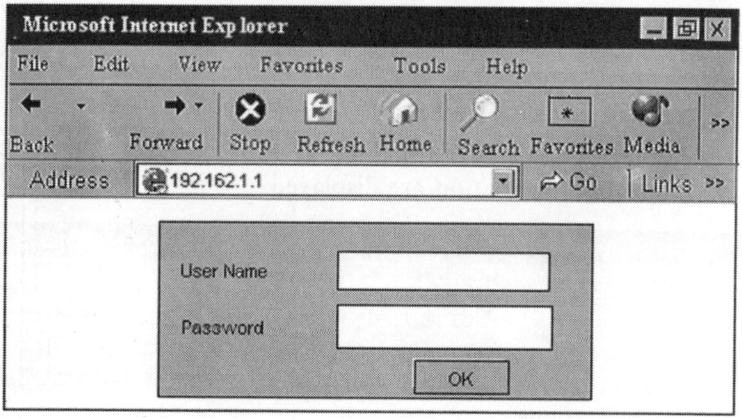

5. Type user name as "admin" and password as "password" and click on OK. Following information will be displayed in the browser:

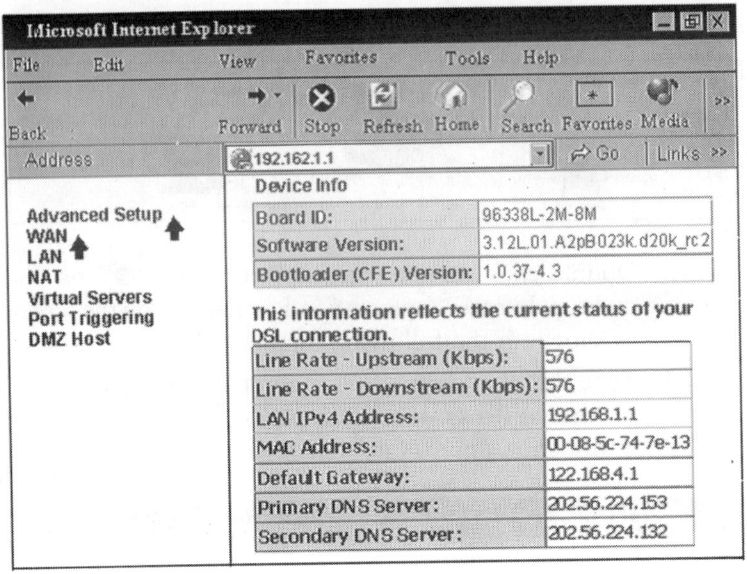

6. Click on Advance Setup.

7. Next click on WAN. Following Wide Area Network (WAN) setup information are displayed:

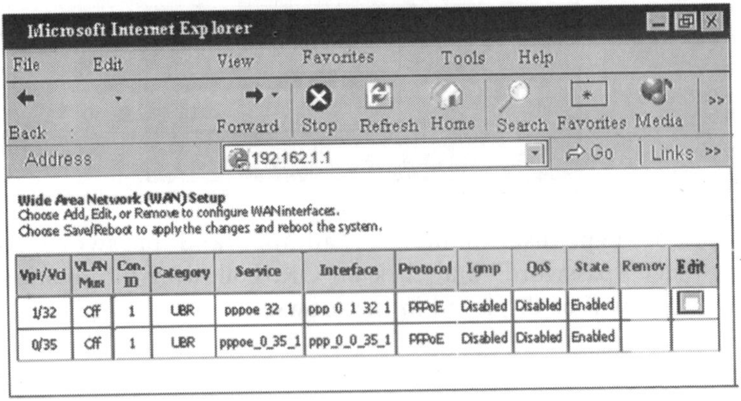

8. Click on the Edit button in the above Wide Area Network (WAN) setup details.

The following information will be displayed in the browser:

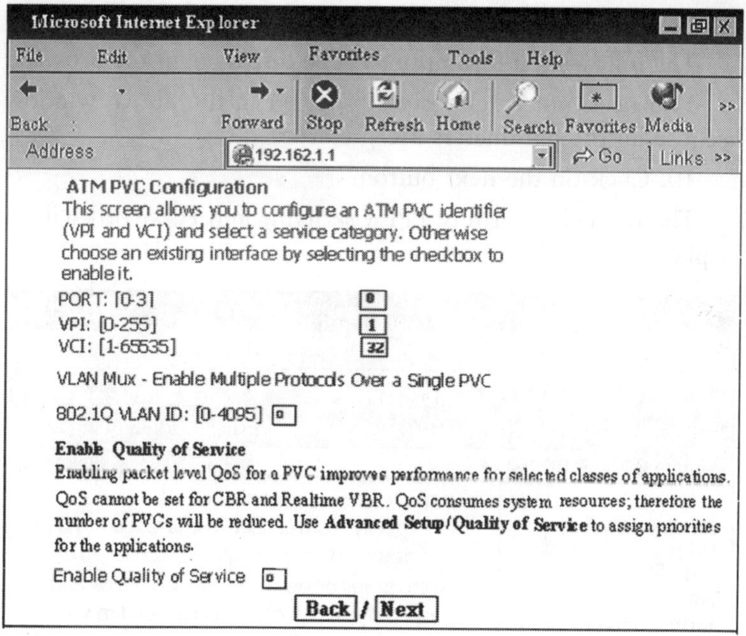

You need not to do any entry in the above window because all the parameters are preinstalled.

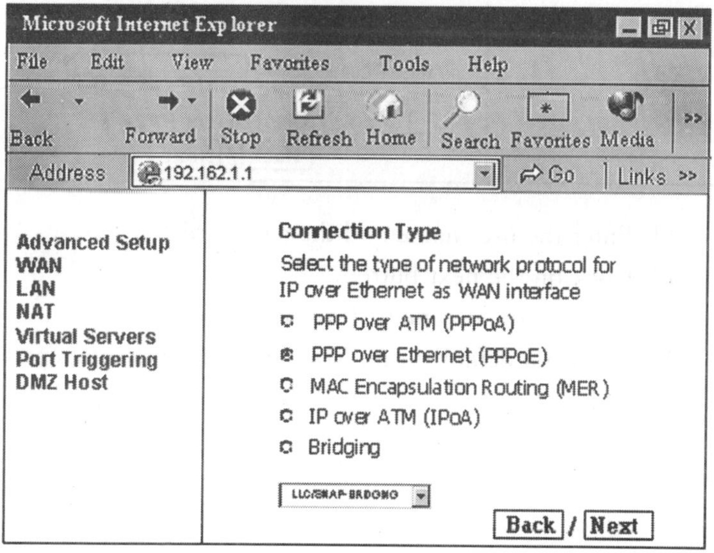

9. Click on the next button.

The following information will be displayed in the browser:

You need not to choose any option in the above window because all the parameters are preinstalled.

10. Click on the next button.

The following form of PPP Username and Password will be displayed in the browser:

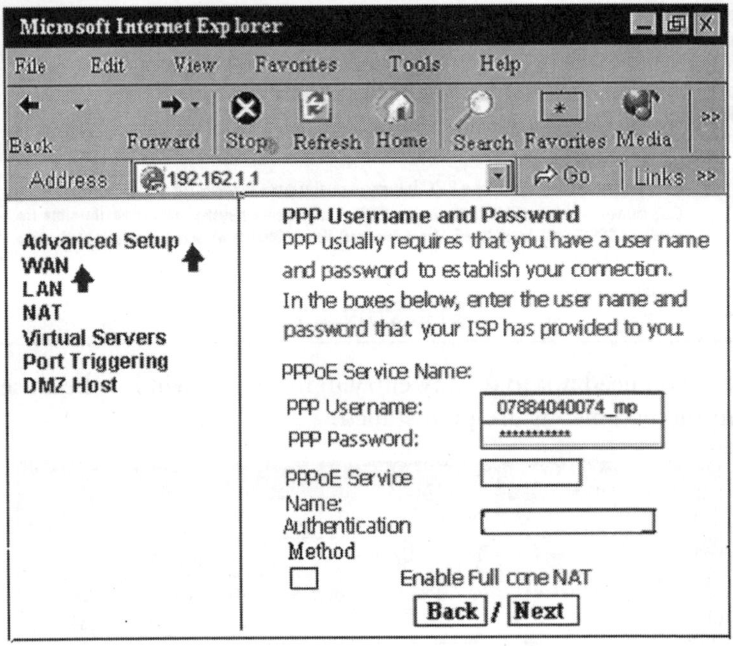

11. Enter the user name and the password.

12. Click on the next button.

Following manual connect form will be displayed:

This is also a default form. You need not to do any entry.

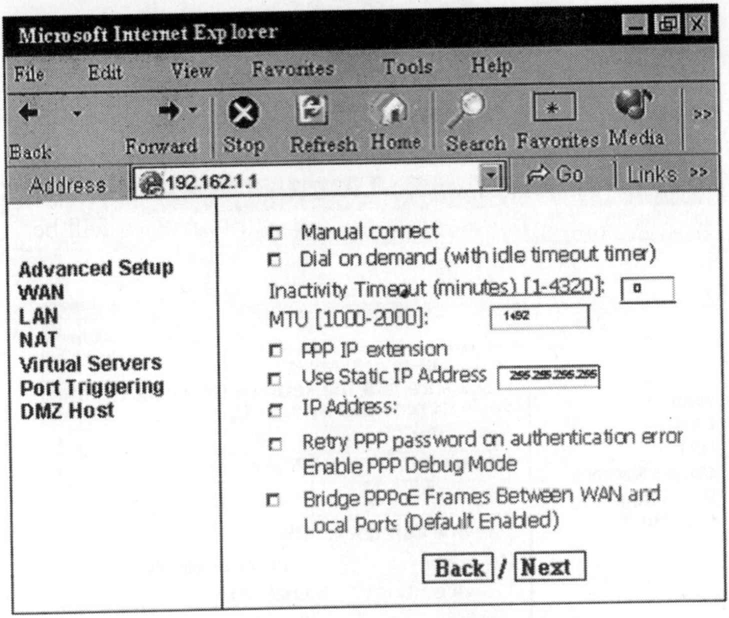

13. Click on the 'Next' button. The following "Network Address Translation setting will be displayed in a window.

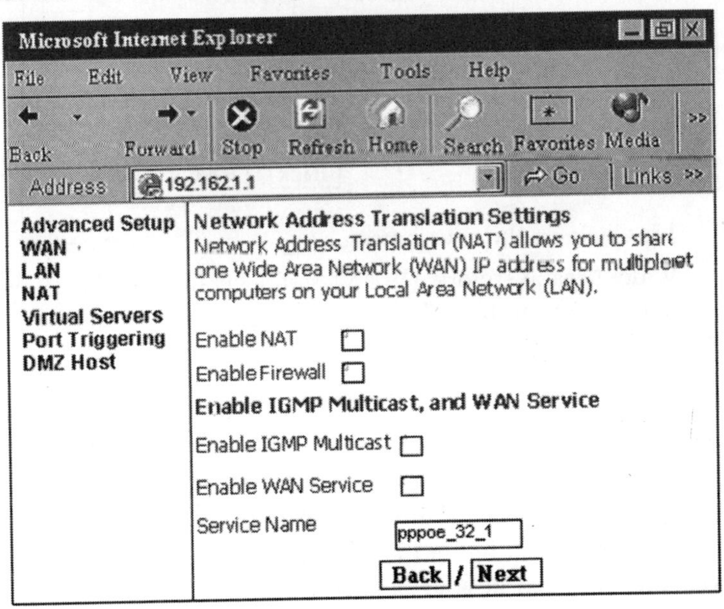

This is also a default form.

14. Click on the next button.

Following WAN Setup Summary will be displayed in the browser:

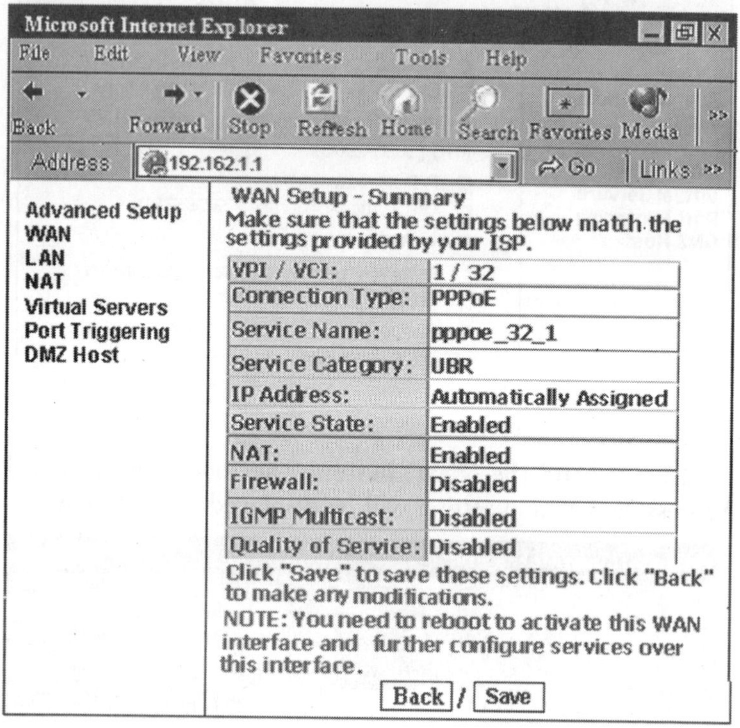

15. Click on the save button.

Wide Area Network (WAN) setup details will be shown again as shown on page 107.

16. Click on Reboot.

The system will save the configuration and reboot the router.

Wait for two to three minutes.

Now try to connect your computer to any known site by typing the site address in the address bar and press enter.

If you have configure the internet connection properly, the web site will open in your browser.

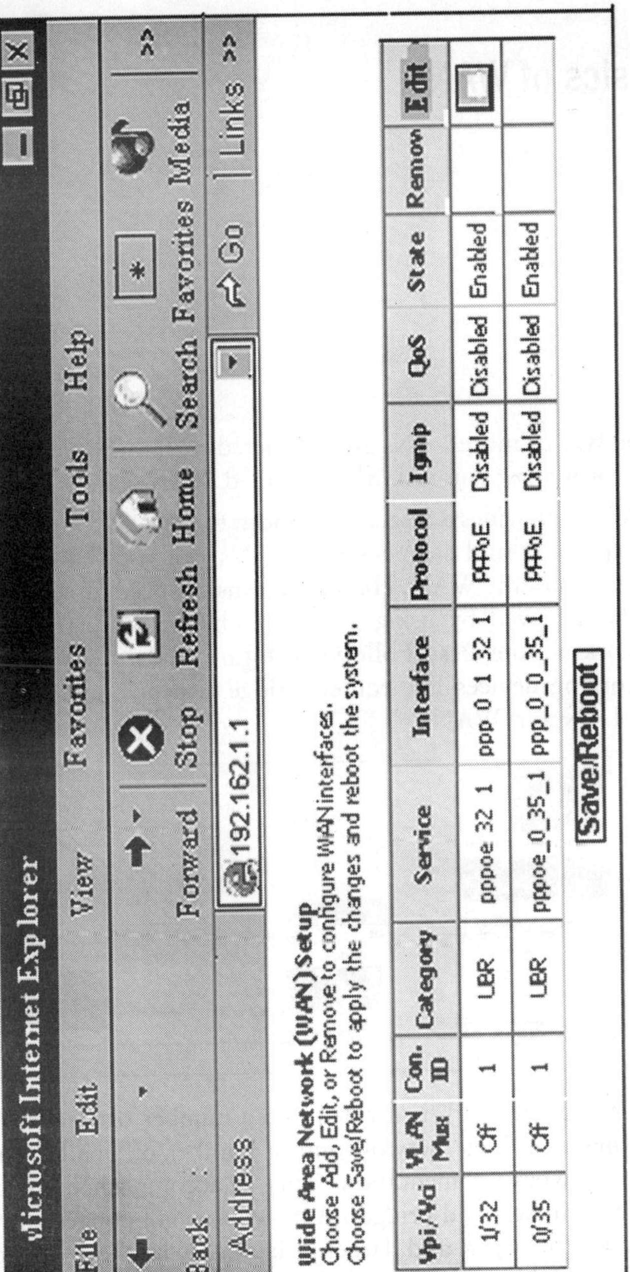
Microsoft Internet Explorer
File Edit View Favorites Tools Help
Back Forward Stop Refresh Home Search Favorites Media
Address 192.162.1.1
Go Links
Wide Area Network (WAN) Setup
Choose Add, Edit, or Remove to configure WAN interfaces.
Choose Save/Reboot to apply the changes and reboot the system.
Vpi/Vci VLAN Mux Con. ID Category Service Interface Protocol Igmp QoS State Remove Edit
1/32 Off 1 UBR pppoe 32 1 ppp 0 1 32 1 PPPoE Disabled Disabled Enabled
0/35 Off 1 UBR pppoe_0_35_1 ppp_0_0_35_1 PPPoE Disabled Disabled Enabled
Save/Reboot

Basics of WAN

6

When two or more LANs are connected with the large network, they form a big network, that is called WAN.

WAN provides a larger bandwidth to LAN to communicate. By expansion and segmentation LANs can use the maximum bandwidth of the WAN. High data transfer speed up to 10 Mbps can be achieved by using 10 baseT channel with the various networking devices. Following figure shows some of the networking devices like router, bridge, repeater and hub used with LAN and WAN:

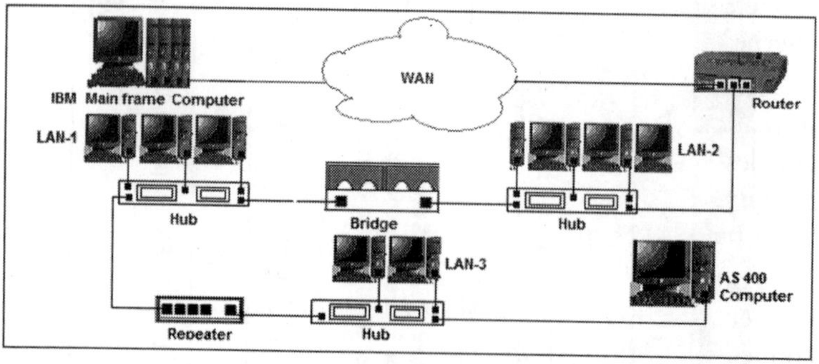

A large network is divided into a number of smaller ones. Breaking up a huge network into a number of smaller ones is called network segmentation. This is accomplished by using routers switches, and bridges. A network is got congested when it grows to larger and larger. The followings are the main reasons of LAN traffic congestion:

1. Too many hosts use a single broadcast domain
2. Broadcast storms
3. Multicasting
4. Low bandwidth
5. Adding hubs for connectivity to the network
6. A large amount of ARP or IPX traffic

For expansion of the network and achieving maximum bandwidth several networking devices are used with the network. Following are the devices that are used on wide area network expansion and segmentation:

1. Routers
2. Switches
3. Hubs
4. Bridges
5. Repeaters
6. Gateways

1. Routers: Routers are Network Layer devices of OSI model. Routers work as a node to connect networks of various types like token rings, FDDI, etc. They are supported by hardware devices and various softwares. Routers divide the network into subnets to control the traffic. They also control the broadcast overhead and prevent the failure of network.

Router is used to route data packets between two networks. It reads the information from the header of the packet and decides its destination. Destinations may by either the receiver machine of the same network to which the router belongs or the node (router) of remote network.

Following figure shows the connection of two LANs with the network. Router-1 is connected with LAN-1 and Router-2 is connected with LAN-2. If any message is transmitted from a LAN-1 computer to LAN-2 computer, it has to pass through Router-1. Router-1 determines the best suitable path and transmits the message to another router. Message may pass through Router-1 to Router-2 directly or through, through Router-1, 3, 4, 2 or Router-1, 3, 2 whichever route is suitable at the time of

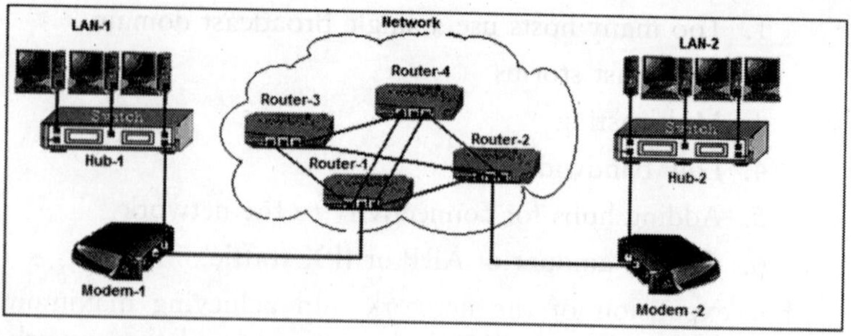

packet transmission. When a packet reaches the Router-2, it finds out the destination NIC address and passes the message to it.

2. Switches: Switches are networking devices of Layer 2 of OSI model. They also transmit the packets to the destination after determining the MAC address. Their functions are similar to bridges. Switches are supported by the hardware therefore they transmit packets faster than a bridge. They transmit the packets to the machine to which the packets belong.

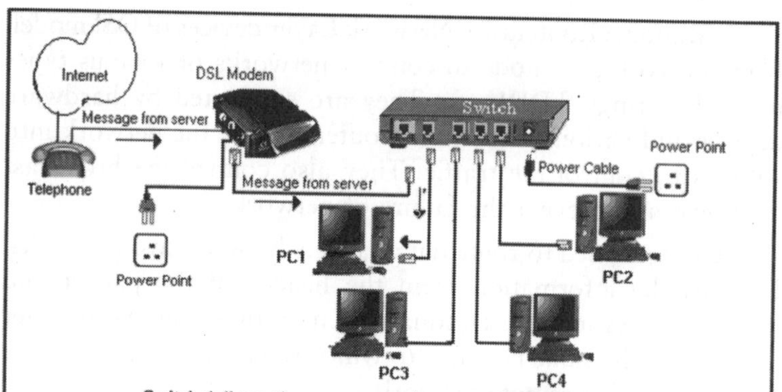

Switch delivers the message to the appropriate PC only

There are two types of switches used in a network:

1. Store-and-forward switches.
2. Cut-through switches.

1. **Store-and-forward switches.** This type of switches first stored the packet temporarily and then transmit to the segment. They read the MAC address of the destination

from the packet and check the error by Cyclical Redundancy Check (CRC). CRC is implemented for determination of the noise level in the serial cable for checking the length of the cable from router to the CSU/DSU. CRC also calculate the remainder by dividing the frame content by prime binary divisor.

This type of switches remove the damaged data packet and then transmitted to the network.

2. **Cut-through switches.** Cut-through switches transmit the frame to the segment as soon as they read the MAC address of the destination from the header of packet. In other words cut through switch checks the destination address (DA) as soon as the header is received and immediately begins forwarding the frame. The delay in cut-through switching remains constant regardless of the size of the frame, because this switching mode starts to forward the frame as soon as the switch reads the DA. Cut-through switches are faster than the store-and-forward switches.

3. **Hubs:** A hub can be called as a multiple-port repeater. Function of a repeater is to receives a digital signal and amplifies or regenerates that signal, and then forwards the digital signal to all active ports without taking any action on data. A hub functions in the same way. Digital signal received from a segment on a hub port is regenerated or amplified and transmitted to all the ports

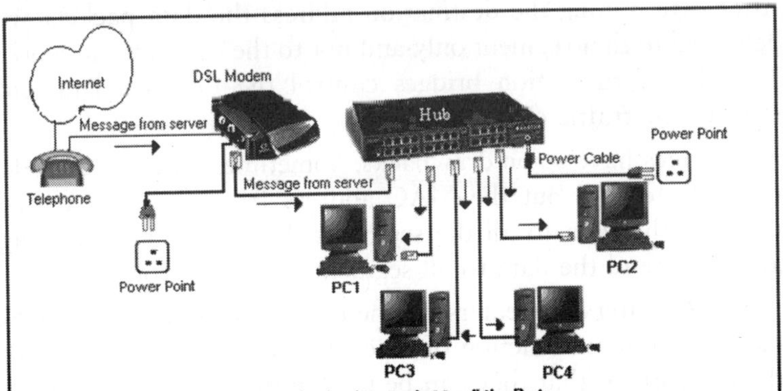

Hub transmits the data packet to all the Ports

on the hub. This makes all the devices plugged into a hub are the member of same collision domain and they have also have the same broadcast domain.

4. Bridges: For using of the maximum bandwidth bridges divide network into group of LANs. This is called the segmentation of the network. Following figure shows the simple segmentation of a network. Each segment contains several LANs.

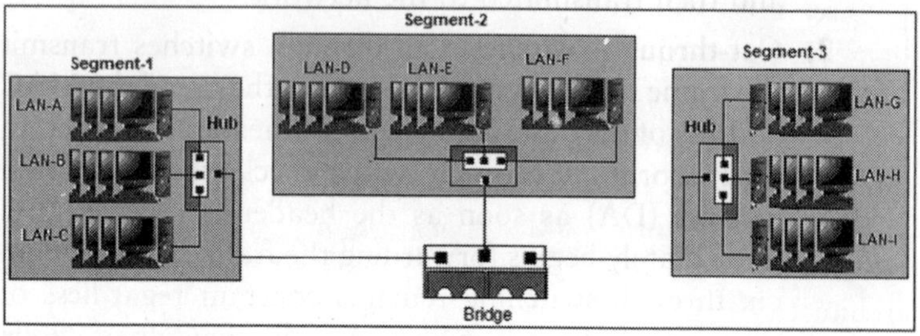

Bridges are the Data Link device of OSI model. When the computer belongs to the X segments sends the packets to another computer which also resides on the X segment, bridges inspect the NIC address (MAC address) from the packet and allow the packet to circulate within the segment. When packets reached the destination they are destroyed.

Secondly when data are transferred from one segment to another segment bridges examine the NIC address from the packet and determine to which segment the packet belongs. After determining the destination address the data packets are delivered to that segment only and not to the complete network. Thus by segmentation bridges control the flow of data and reduces the traffic on the network.

Bridges have some drawbacks. Sometimes when bridges do not able to find out the MAC address from the packet they transmit the data to all the segments. In case of broadcasting also they send the data to all segment of the network.

5. Repeaters: Repeaters are the Physical layer devices of OSI model. The main function of repeater is to boost the signals of the network so that they can be transmitted to larger distance.

Repeaters are simple devices unlike gateways. Following figure illustrates the connection of repeater in between two LANs.

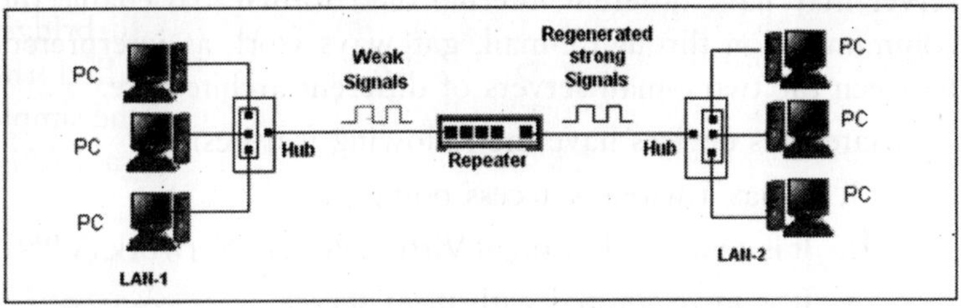

6. Gateways: Gateways are the Upper layer devices of OSI model. Gateways functions are implemented through transport, session, presentation, and application layers. They enable to connect the two LANs which use the computers of different architectures. Gateways are also supported by both hardware and software to perform their functions. Following figure shows the connection and concept of gateway.

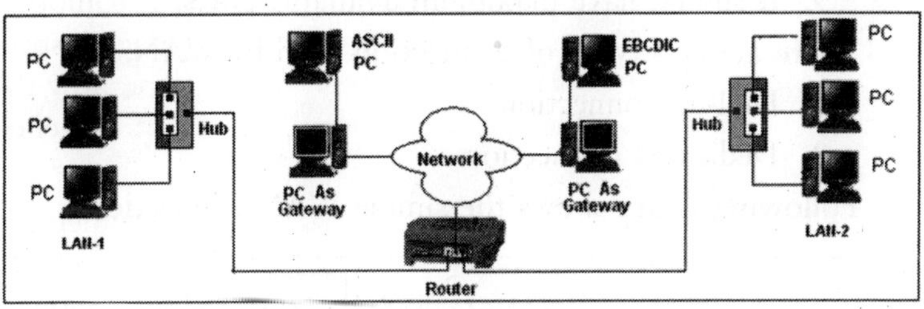

A computer in a network, itself performs the function of a gateway. There are computers of different architectures that use different type of operating system. Some computers use ASCII data format and other use EBCDIC data format.

Gateway translates the data from ASCII to EBCDIC and *vice versa* with the support of presentation layer.

Gateways connects the two machines of different architecture using FDDI networks, along with the LANs via routers. As it is necessary to use gateways for connecting the two machines of different architecture but it result in a slow traffic on the network. Secondly its configuration becomes more difficult than the other devices of the network.

E-mail uses various types of servers like Mail server, Microsoft e-mail server and Lotus notes, etc. The computers used as a server may have different internal data format. To enable the communication through e-mail, gateways work as interpreters between the two e-mail servers of different architecture.

Gateways devices have the following features:

1. It has a wireless access point.
2. It is connected through Virtual Private Network (VPN).
3. It is incorporated with print server.
4. It protect your PC through the firewall.
5. It is provided with multi-port.
6. It has the ability to filter the content.
7. Modern gateways have built in hubs or switches.
8. It should support the dual speed i.e. 10 Mbps and 100 Mbps.
9. It should have maximum available ports.

There are two types of connection used by WAN:

1. Dial-up connection
2. Dedicated connection

Following figure shows the simple WAN connection:

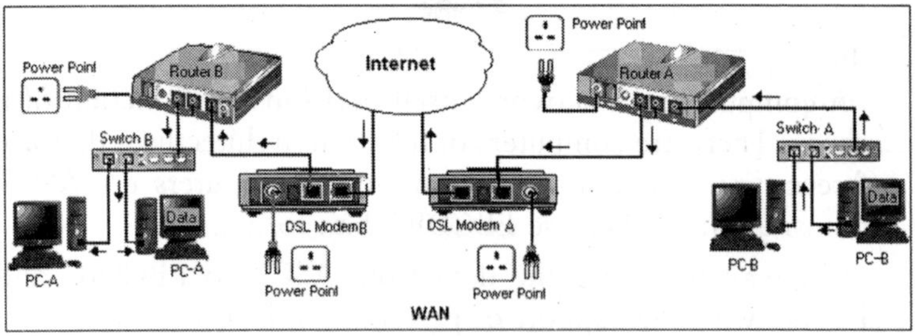

1. Dial-up connection: It is simple and most economic internet connection for small amount of data transfer for a short time. It uses modem to connect the host with the server. This type of connection is most suitable for sending and receiving e-mail and accessing internet for short duration. Dial-up connection used to connect with the server by dialing the telephone number allotted to the server. You have to type the User name and password in the Dial-up connection window and click on connect button.

The server is first connected to the client through telephone line and then verify the User ID and the password. When connection is made, client can send and receive data from remote source. Modem, router, switches, hub, media, other devices and software are used to perform the communication between two computers. Installation of such network connection is easy. It is also flexible and can be converted to dedicated connection by configuring the connection properties. It does not require any maintenance.

Following figure shows the simple Dial-up connection with a single computer.

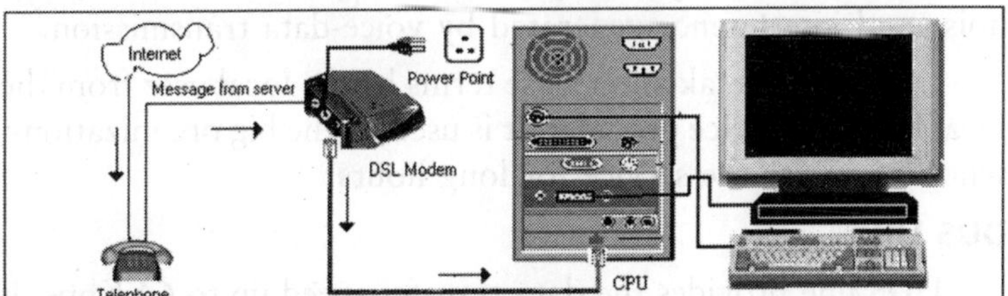

Dial-UP Connection

2. Dedicated connection: Dedicated connection is a 24 hours full time connection. You need not to dial the server for connection through Dial-up connection window. As soon as you start your computer it will be connected to the server automatically. The charges for such connection are fixed on the monthly basis. Access to the internet is unlimited, therefore it is most suitable, for large business organization, cybercafé, etc.

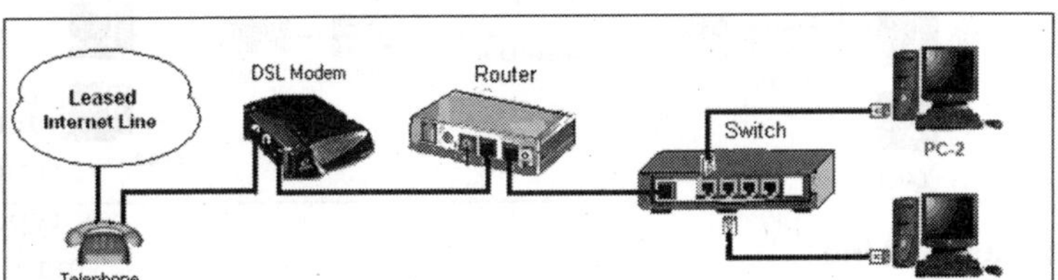

Dedicated Leased Line Connection

This connection is provided with larger bandwidth. It uses digital data service (DDS) and the T-carrier system lines which makes it more efficient. Larger amount of data can be transferred at faster rate as compare to Dial-up connection.

There are three type of lines which provide internet connection:

1. Leased line,
2. Digital Data Service line,
3. T-carrier line.

Leased Line

Leased line uses digital data services. It establishes dedicated connection and provide unlimited access to internet. It joins the two networks through the PSTN. The bandwidth used by leased line is greater than the analog lines. It is capable to withstand the noise and interference generated by voice-data transmission.

Leased line is taken on lease terms by the local user from the local internet service provider. It is used by the big organizations, who like to use the service for long hours.

DDS Line

DDS line provides the data transfer speed up to 64 Kbps. It provides full-duplex connection by which you can send and receive data simultaneously. Two LANs are used to join by Channel Service Unit (CSU) and Data Service Unit (DSU). Leased digital lines of both the LANs is connected to CSU ports while DSU ports are connected to the LAN through bridge. Following figure illustrates the concept of leased line connection to the LANs through the DSU/CSU and bridges.

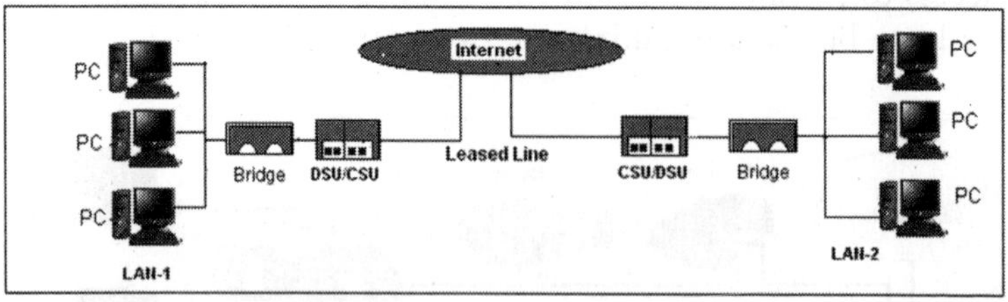

T-Carrier Line

T-carrier line can transfer data to several channels by using multiplexors on a single digital data line.

Multiplexors are used to make digital connections in between two LANs through T-carrier line.

The function of multiplexor is to combine or separate a group of channels. There are four T-lines used by T-carrier system. They are T-1, T-2, T-3 and T-4 lines.

Multiplexor separates the T-1 line into 24 channels with the data transfer speed up to 1.5 Mbps. T-2 line is separated into 96 channels with the data transfer speed up to 6.4 Mbps. T-3 line is separated into 672 channels with the data transfer speed up to 44.8 Mbps. T-4 line is separated into 4032 channels with the data transfer speed up to 274.8 Mbps.

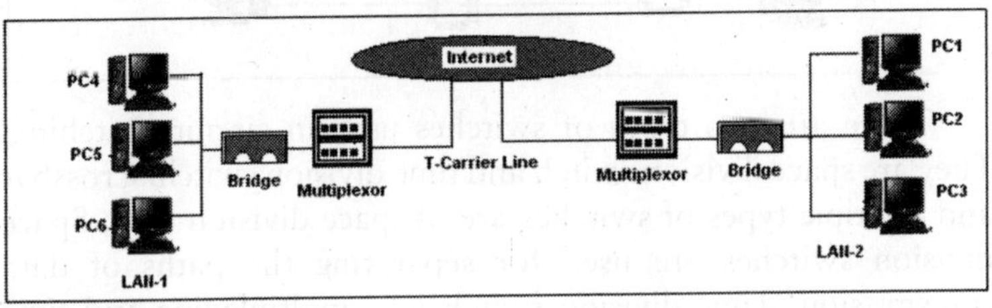

Switched Network

When many clients wanted to use same line or the same bandwidth of the line is called switched network. Switching is the physical method of data transfer through physical media.

There are following three methods of switching to transfer data on a network:

1. Circuit switching,
2. Packet switching,
3. Message switching.

1. Circuit switching: Circuit switching is similar to communicate on telephones. Cost of telephonic communication depend upon the time used by the user. User pays for the time he actually use the telephone. In a similar way the client is charged by the internet service provider for the time he has actually used the internet.

It is a temporary connection between two computers. Source and destination computers are connected by the PDN. Circuit switching uses telephone line to transfer data from source computer to the receiver for a session. When the session or period of communication is over the connection between the source and the destination computer is terminated. Local service provider provides the internet connection to the users and charges the amount for using it. They may charge for the duration for which the user had utilized the internet for data transfer.

Following figure illustrates the simple circuit switching.

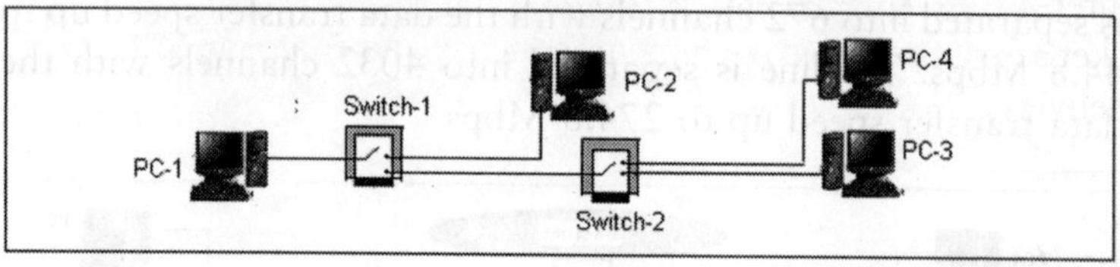

There are two types of switches used in circuit switching. They are space division switch and time division switch. Crossbar and multiple types of switches are of space division type. Space division switches are used for separating the paths of data transmission. Time division switch uses multiplexing and time slot interchanging for data transfer from source to destination.

2. Packet switching: In WAN connections that use Packet switching converts the data into small packets. Data are transferred effectively and at faster rate if they follow the best possible path. Actually the source computer sends the packets after providing the sequence number to each packet. Best possible route always changes according to network condition therefore the data packets reach the destination from different routes. In this case the data packets received by the receiver will not be in the same sequence in which they are transmitted by the source computer. Destination computer reassemble these packets into proper sequence according to there sequence number and convert them into a complete message.

Packet switching is not a continuous process unlike circuit switching. Data packets are sent at different intervals from node to node. These packets are stored first at a node and then forwarded to next node. The forwarding process ends when all the packets reach the final node. Performance can be enhanced if packet switching process uses the virtual circuit, because virtual circuit transfer the data to the destination, through a single route continuously, though this route is shared by other network.

The following figure shows the simple packet switching, from source PC to the destination PC. The data are converted to small packets at the source PC and by Router-1 they are sent to Router-3 directly to destination PC. Router-1 can also send the packet through Router-2 to Router-3, if Router-1 finds the Router-1 to Router-3 route is too busy. At the destination PC the packet are reassembled in original sequence and complete message is delivered to the destination PC.

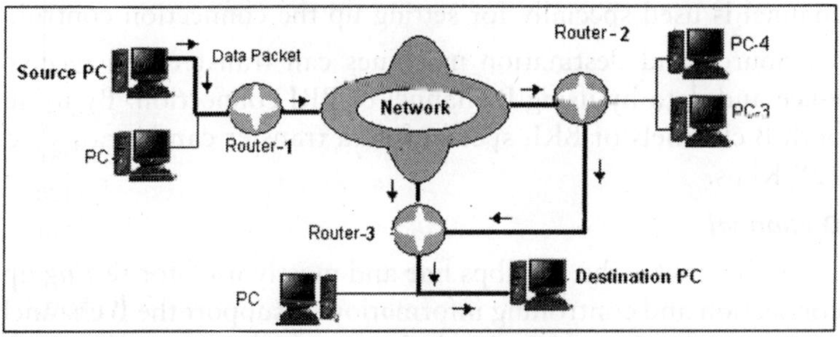

3. Message switching: Message switching is similar to packet switching. In message switching the packets are stored at a node. The router at the node finds the shortest route and then transfers the message to the destination. No restriction to the size of message is applied in case of messages switching, therefore large storage is required at each node.

Node waits for the best possible route then only it start to send the message to the next node. Message switching is not suitable for chatting or any other interactive communication. Message switching is not time bound therefore it engages the network for long duration. Following figure shows the storage with each node for storing high volume of data.

Basic Rate ISDN (BRI)

BRI provides three channels, two B channels and one D channel.

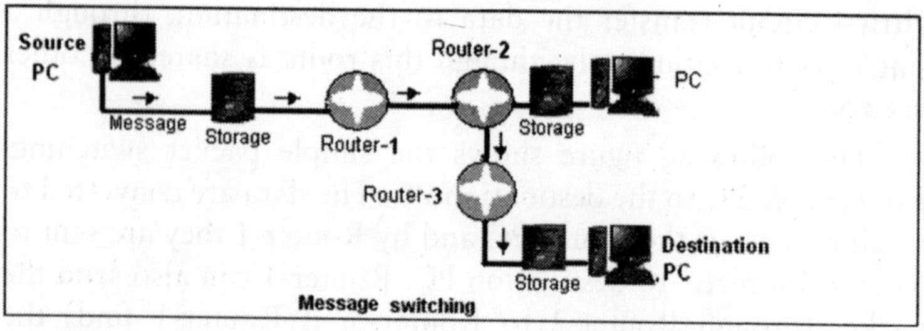

B channel

B channel provides the speed of data transfer at the rate of 64 Kbps while D channel works at the speed of 16 Kbps. D channel is used specially for setting up the connection control.

Source and destination machines can transfer and receive voice and data by using B channel of BRI connection. By using both B channels of BRI, speed of data transfer can be raised to 128 Kbps.

D channel

D channel is the 16 Kbps line and mostly used for setting up connection and controlling information. It support the B channel for setting up the connection before transmitting any data.

Primary Rate ISDN (PRI)

Primary rate ISDN is used with higher bandwidth for big organization. High bandwidth enable the user to transfer large volume of data with greater speed. It uses 23 B channels with T-1 line at the data transfer speed up to 1.5 Mbps. D channel is also used for setting up the connection control.

WAN Connection Technologies

X.25. This is a set of protocols which specifies how to connect computers over a network. These protocols are used to check errors concern with unreliable telephone lines. It uses DTEs and DCEs and set point-to-point communication between two LANs of a WAN. The data transfer speed is about 64 Kbps. It is used on packet switching.

For X.25 network connection we have to lease a line from the LAN to a PDN. X.25 sessions are set to communicate between two DTEs. For example, a LAN-1 is connected with Router-1 and the Router-1 is connected to PDN. Similarly LAN-2 is connected with Router-2 and the Router-2 is also connected to PDN.

Now a computer on LAN-1 can communicate with the computer on LAN-2 via Router-1, PDN and Router-2.

The X.25 protocol is supported by a group of protocols that operates at the three layers of OSI model.

Network, Data Link, and Physical layers are the three layers of the OSI model which enable the X.25 protocol to establish the connection between two DTEs and to transmit the packet from node to node.

Frame Relay

Frame relay operates at the data link layer of the OSI model. Errors are checked at both the ends of the internet connection. Frame relay function is to use frames of different length. Frame relay uses permanent virtual circuits (PVC) for communication sessions between LANs on the WAN.

A permanent virtual circuit (PVC) is established between two points on the network. Frame relay transmits data faster than X.25. Its data transfer speed is from 56 Kbps to 1.544 Mbps. By using digital fiber-optic media frame relay, it provides a high-speed connection up to 1.544 Mbps.

Switched Multi-megabit Data Service (SMDS)

No error is checked by Switched Multi-megabit Data Service. In this case checking of errors is done at both the ends by the computer devices. Its data transfer speed is from 56 Kbps to 1.544 Mbps. It uses fixed length cell switching.

Integrated Services Digital Network (ISDN). The service has two types.

Its function is to first convert analog signals into digital signals and then transmit them on network.

Asynchronous Transfer Mode (ATM) Features

1. ATM is used with both baseband and broadband systems.

2. Data packets of 53 bytes fixed length are used by ATM.
3. Information are placed within five bytes.
4. Hardware devices are responsible for performing the switching of the data.
5. Data can be transmitted with the speed of 622 Mbps.
6. It does not check the error. Error is checked at the receiving end.
7. Connection made by ATM is permanent virtual connection.

Synchronous Optical Network (SONET) Features

1. Fiber optic media is used by a standard layer.
2. It defines data and video delivery procedure.
3. Data are defined in terms of optical carrier levels.
4. It defines data rates in terms of optical carrier (OC) levels. OC-1 level has transmission rate 51.8 Mbps. OC has different levels and each level runs at a multiple of the OC-1.
5. The OC-5 data rate is 5 times of OC-1 and equal to 259 Mbps.
6. SONET also defines synchronous transport signals (STS). Copper media is also used for synchronous transport signals (STS).
7. It has the data transmission speed, equivalent to OC levels.
8. Data transmission speed of STS-3 is same as the speed of OC-3.
9. Mesh or ring topology is used to support SONET.

Network Architectures

7

The architecture supports the quick and efficient flow of the data on the network. It defines the network topology as well as the flow of data from node to node. There are four main types of network architectures used in networking. They are named as follows:

1. Ethernet
2. IBM Token Ring
3. FDDI
4. AppleTalk

1. Ethernet

Ethernet architecture is most commonly used throughout the world. This architecture uses the carrier sense multiple access with collision detection (CSMA/CD) to access the network.

When the source node on the network, wants to transmit the packet to the destined node, it first tries to find out that no transmission of packets is taking place and the line is free. When the source node finds that the line is clear, it immediately gains the control of the line and sends the packets to the destined node. If it senses that the other computers on the network are also sending message, it waits till the transmission of packets by those computers is completed.

If this computer does not wait and transmits the data packet, there is every possibility of collision and data may be lost and may not reach to the destination. Ethernet follows the wait and listen method of data transmission. Ethernet is also called as passive architecture.

Ethernet is the best suited protocol to local area network. It is well defined by IEEE 802.3 standard which is known as CSMA/CD protocol. Ethernet is used all over the world. Ethernet technology is simple to implement and very easy to understand. Standard hardware can be used for interconnection of the network. It is easy to manage and cost of maintenance is low.

The original IEEE 802.3 standard was based on the Ethernet Version 1.0 specification. It has accommodated various improvements like high data rate and various new optional network access controls.

Ethernet Network consists of nodes and interconnecting media. The network nodes fall into two major classes:

Data Terminal Equipment (DTE): Source or the destination machines are called Data Terminal Equipment. PCs, workstations, file servers, or print servers, are known as end stations or (DTE).

Data Communication Equipment (DCE): Repeaters, switches, routers, network interface cards, modems which are used to receive and forward data across the network are called Data Communication Equipment.

Connection may be DTE-to-DTE, DTE-to-DCE, or DCE-to-DCE. The cable which connects the two devices is called link. Length of the cable depends upon the transmission process.

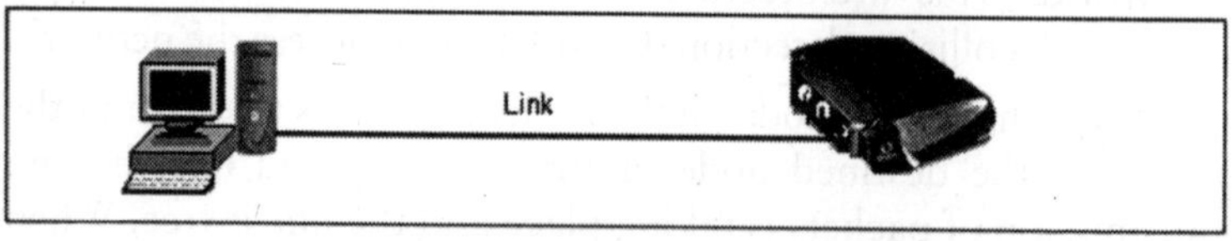

Point-to-Point Interconnection: Coaxial bus structure was initially introduced to form Ethernet network.

The maximum length of the segment was 500 meters. A single segment can accommodate 100 network stations. Repeater can be used to connect these segments with each other.

Point-to-point connection is not suitable in the following cases:

1. If the multiple paths exists in between two stations on the network.
2. The number of DTEs are more than 1024.
3. The total path distance between the most-distant pair of stations is more than the prescribed limit.

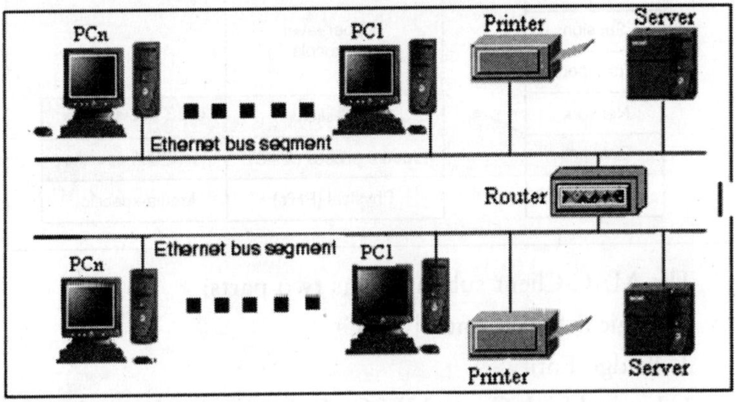

Figure Coaxial Bus Topology

Generally star-connected topology was used for the network configuration during 90's. Multi-port hub or a switch is used in the center of the network. Point-to-point links are formed with either twisted-pair or optical fiber cable.

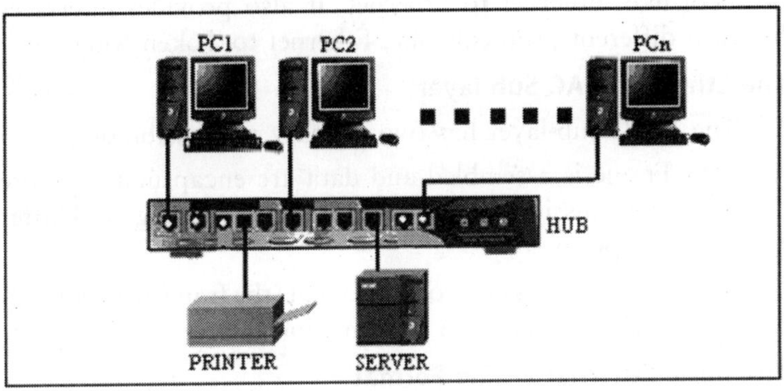

Example Star-Connected Topology

Logical Relationship between IEEE 802.3 and OSI Reference Model in shown in the following figure:

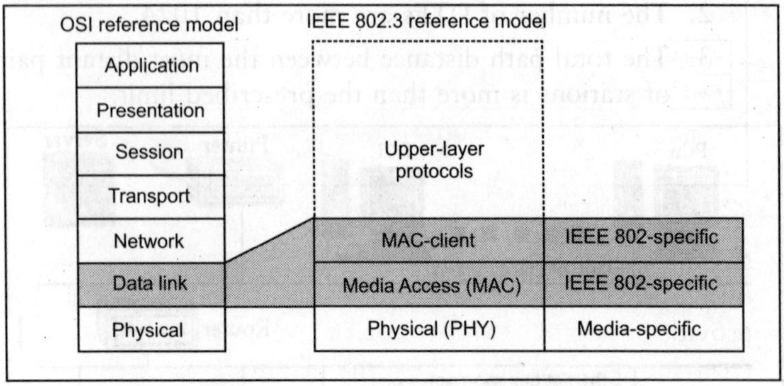

The MAC-Client sub-layer has two parts:

1. Logical Link Control (LLC)
2. Bridge Entity.

1. Logical Link Control (LLC): If the unit is a DTE, then the interface between the Ethernet MAC and the upper layers takes place, in the protocol stack, of the end station. This interface is caused by the sub-layer.

2. Bridge Entity: In this case if the unit is a DCE, it provides LAN-to-LAN interfaces between LANs that use the similar protocol like, Ethernet to Ethernet. It also provides interfaces between different protocols like, Ethernet to Token Ring.

The Ethernet MAC Sub-layer

The MAC sub-layer has two primary responsibilities:

1. Frame is assembled and data are encapsulated before transmission. Errors are detected during and after reception.
2. Media access control implements the frame transmission and recovery from transmission failure.

The Basic Ethernet Frame Format

The basic data frame format contains the seven fields shown in the following figure:

FCS error detection coverage (from DA through Pad)

FCS generation span (from DA through Pad)

Field Name	PRE	SFD	DA	SA	Length/Type	Data	Pad	FCS
Field Length in Bytes	7	1	6	6	4	46-1500		4

Transmission order ⟶ From Left to Right

1. Preamble (PRE): It consists of 7 bytes. The PRE is binary stream of ones and zeros. It informs the receiving stations that a frame is going to be delivered. It tells the receiving station to provide a means to synchronize the frame-reception portions of receiving physical layers with the incoming bit stream.

2. Start-of-frame delimiter (SFD): It consists of 1 byte. The SFD is binary stream of ones and zeros. At the end of stream two consecutive 1 are necessary. These bits are used to determine destination address.

3. Destination address (DA): Consists of 6 bytes. The DA field identifies the address of the destination which is going to receive the frame. The 0 in left-most bit in the DA field indicates an individual address and 1 in left-most bit indicates the group address.

The second bit 0 from the left indicates that the DA is globally administered and the second bit 1 from the left indicates locally administered. The remaining 4 bits are used to identify a single station, a defined group of stations, or all stations on the network by assigning the appropriate value.

4. Source addresses (SA): It consists of 6 bytes. It identifies the sending station. It is always an individual address and the left-most bit in the SA field is always 0.

5. Length/Type: It consists of 2 bytes. This field indicates the number of MAC-client's bytes that are contained in the data field of the frame. If field value is less than or equal to 1500, the number of LLC bytes in the Data field is equal to the Length/Type field value.

Optional type frame contains the Length/Type field value is greater than 1536.

Length/Type field value indicates the particular type of frame being transmitted or received.

6. Data: It is a sequence of n bytes of any value, where n is less than or equal to 1500. In case the length of the Data field is less than 46, it should be increased by adding a filler to form the Data field length to 46 bytes.

7. Frame check sequence (FCS): It consists of 4 bytes. It is the series of 32 bits. Cyclic redundancy check (CRC) carried out. It is created by sending MAC and is recalculated by the receiving MAC to check for damaged frames. This sequence contains a 32 bits value and is generated over the DA, SA, Length/Type, and Data fields.

The Basic IEEE 802.3 MAC Data Frame Format

Whenever an end station MAC receives a transmit-frame request with the accompanying address and data information from the LLC sub-layer, the MAC begins the transmission sequence by transferring the LLC information into the MAC frame buffer.

Half-Duplex Transmission—The CSMA/CD Access Method

The CSMA/CD protocol enables two or more stations could share a common media in a switch-less environment. Central arbitration, access tokens, or assigned time slots methods are not needed by the protocol to specify when a network station will be allowed to transmit. Each Ethernet MAC is independent for sending a frame.

The CSMA/CD access rules are summarized by the protocol's acronym:

1. **Carrier sense:** Each station continuously informed about the traffic on the medium. It will allow the station to find out the gap between frame transmissions.
2. **Multiple access:** Whenever the stations detect the no traffic (There is no traffic) condition on the network, they begin transmitting the frame.
3. **Collision detect:** If two or more stations in the same network begin transmitting the data frame simultaneously, the streams of bits transmitted from

stations will collide with each other. This interference or collision will make the data unreadable. Before sending a frame, each station must be capable of detecting the collision condition in advance. This will enable the station to stop transmitting as soon as it has detected the collision and then it may wait for a length of time.

2. IBM Token Ring

IBM Token Ring is known as a fast and reliable network that uses token. It follows media access strategy. Token Ring networks are wired in a star configuration with a Multistation Access Unit (MAU) providing the central connection for the nodes. There is an actual ring, on which the token is circulated.

The token moves in one direction as characterized by the ring topology. The token ring program controls the passing of token. It accesses the computer that is ready to send the message. As soon as the token is passed to this active computer it takes the possession and starts sending the messages. As soon as the session of this computer is over token is passed to the next computer.

A computer that passes the token to the next computer on the logical ring would be called the nearest active upstream neighbor (NAUN). The computer being passed the token is the nearest active downstream neighbor (NADN).

After a computer takes possession of the token and transmits data, it then passes a new token to its NADN and the token makes its way around the ring until a node on the network takes possession to transmit.

Token Ring is characterized by no collisions and equal access to the network media by all the nodes on the network. It is slower than some implementations of Ethernet but the network degrades more gracefully during times of high traffic.

Token Ring also provides some fault tolerance to the network with its error detection strategy.

When the computers on the network are first brought online, the first computer powered on is designated as the Active Monitor.

The Active Monitor sends out a data packet every seven seconds that travels around the ring to determine, if any of the nodes on the network are done.

For example, if a particular computer doesn't receive the packet from its NAUN, it creates a packet containing its address and the NAUN's address and sends the packet onto the network. This packet provides information that the Token Ring can automatically reconfigure the ring and maintain network traffic.

3. FDDI

The Fiber Distributed Data Interface (FDDI) is an architecture that provides high-speed network backbones. It can be used to connect a number of different network types. FDDI uses fiber-optic cable. It is wired in a ring topology. FDDI uses token passing as its media access method. It can operate at high speeds of 100 Mbps.

Because FDDI uses a token-passing media access strategy, it is reliable and provides equal access to all the nodes on the network. With FDDI you can set priority levels, however, servers on the network could be allowed to send more data frames onto the network than client computers.

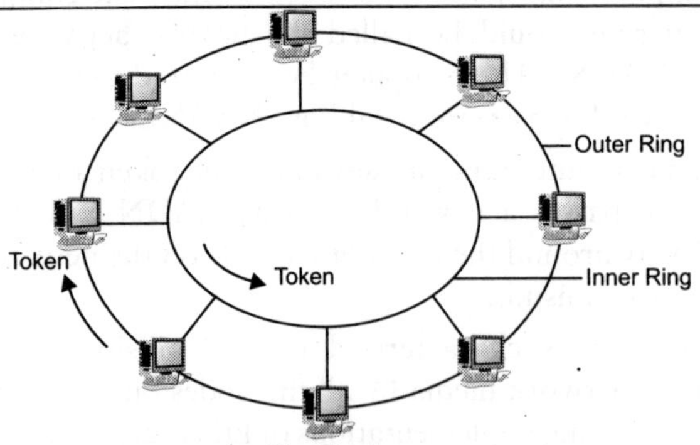

Ring Topology

Because FDDI uses a true ring topology, breaks in the cable system can be a problem. To build fault tolerance into the FDDI network, a secondary ring is used. When a computer cannot communicate with its downstream neighbor, it sends its data to the second ring, which circulates the data in the opposite direction.

4. AppleTalk

AppleTalk is the networking architecture used by Apple Macintosh computers. The networking hardware required is already built into each Macintosh. The cabling system used to connect Macintosh computers is called LocalTalk and uses shielded twisted-pair cables with a special Macintosh adapter.

AppleTalk uses a special dynamic addressing system to determine the address of the nodes on the network. Macintosh computer generates a random address and broadcasts it out onto the network. This random address becomes its network address. AppleTalk is similar to Ethernet and a passive network architecture.

AppleTalk uses Carrier Sense multiple access with collision detection-CSMA/CA. Basically the computers sit on the network and listen to determine whether the line is clear. If the computer finds the clear line on the network, it will send a packet to all the other computers to let them know that it intends to transmit data. The computer then sends out its data.

These announcement packets, however, do have a tendency to slow down the network and Macintosh networks only have a transmission speed of 230.4 Kbps. The fact that the hardware and software needed to network a group of Macintosh computers, comes with each Macintosh makes so it is an easy and inexpensive way, to network several workstations, to share a printer or files.

Network Topologies

There are three types of network topology. They are Bus, Star, and Ring.

The network topology is the physical wiring of the network.

1. Bus network topology: It is the physical wiring of the network which is terminated at both the ends of network with a terminator. It can be further extended with the application of a barrel connector.

It is contention based network. Each computer on the network wait for transmission of packet till the bus becomes free and

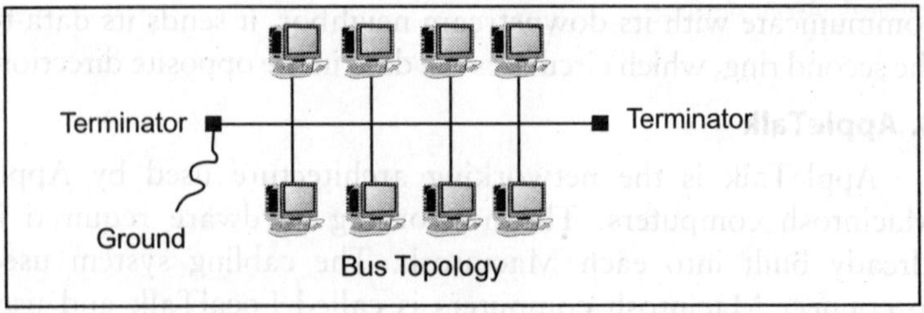

nobody is transmitting any packet. It is generally called passive topology.

Bus networks are easy to assemble and extend. They need a limited amount of cabling. This network uses coaxial cable connected to each computer using a T-connector. It is just a network of cable, connectors, and terminators. No amplification of the signal takes place during physical transfer of data.

Disadvantages

1. Sometimes connectors become loose. In this case complete network stops working.
2. Breakdown of cable is the another problem which is very difficult to detect.

2. Star network topology: There is a hub placed in the center of the network and all the devices are placed around it. This hub controls the network communications, and can communicate with other hubs. About 100 meters distance from the hub is the limit.

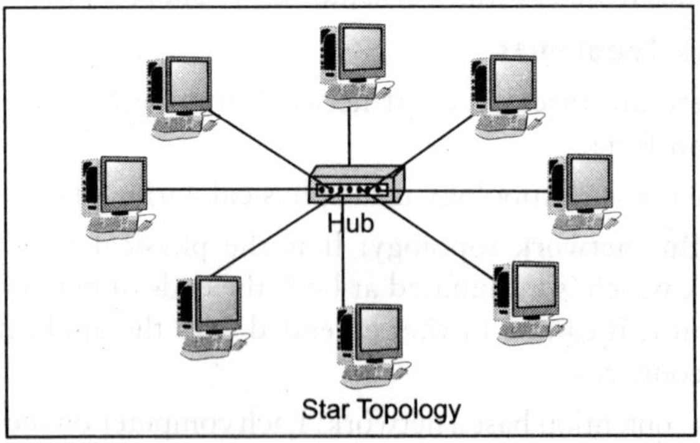

It is also a contention based passive topology like bus topology. In a similar way to bus topology each computer on the network waits for transmission of packet till the bus becomes free and nobody is transmitting any packet.

As each computer is connected to centralized hub so it is easier to add more machines to the network.

The only limitation is the number of ports on the hub, though the number of ports can be increased by connecting the hubs together. It is easy to connect any additional machine on the network by simply connecting it with the hub port.

Disadvantages

1. Each computer is connected with the hub separately so more cable is required than the bus topology.
2. You have to pay the hubs cost for building star topology but it is beneficial in terms of managing the physical aspects of the network.
3. It has also the same problems of cable, connectors and terminators, like bus topology.
4. The biggest disadvantage of star topology is that in case of hub failure complete network comes to stand-still. To avoid this crisis a extra tested hub is kept ready to switch over the network.

3. Ring network topology. All the computers that are called stations are connected to one another in a circle. One of the cards on a computer is the master interface card. This master interface card creates a token.

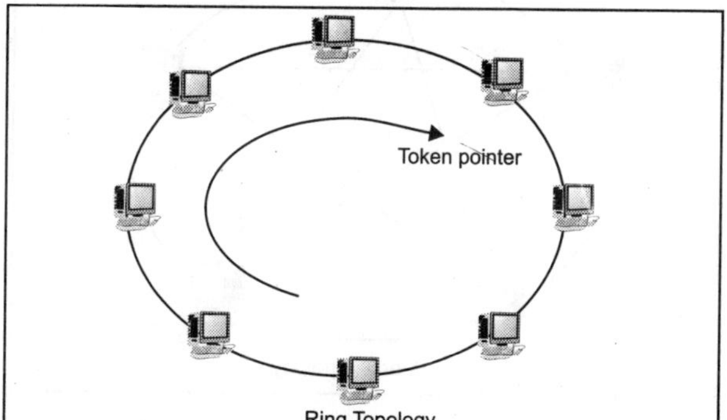

Ring Topology

The token is circulated around the ring to grant permission to a computer around the ring.

Computer waits for the token and when it is allotted, it transmits data to the destined computer. When the source computer receives the acknowledgment from the destined computer that the message is received, the master interface card creates a new token and passes it to the next computer in the ring.

This process allows all the computer on the token ring network an equal access to the network. It is more efficient network topology than other contention based network.

Disadvantages

1. In case of failure of a single computer the whole network stops working because the computers are connected in a ring.
2. If you add or remove any computer from the network, it will disrupt the working of the network.

Mesh Networks

There may be hybrid networks which includes a star-bus hybrid, star-ring network. A mesh networks with connections between various computers on the network may also be used. In a mesh networks each computer is connected with other, this permits each computer to interface directly with each other.

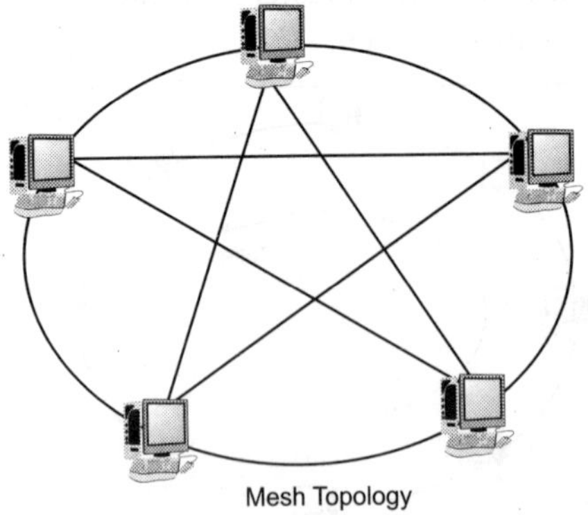

Mesh Topology

In case of the failure of one computer, mesh network continue to work without disruption. You can add or change the computer without affecting the working of the network.

Mesh networks are more costlier than other network. They require a lot of wiring cable for making connections. Installation of mesh network is more difficult than other networks.

Media

8

For transfer of data, from one computer to the another, on a network, some medium is required.

This medium can be a copper or fiber-optic cable. Many types of cables are commonly used with LANs. It is a general practice to use one type of cable for a network. In some case a network may use a varieties of cables. Network topology, protocol, and size is the basis for choosing different type of cable. For designing a successful network we must know the characteristics of each type of cable.

Twisted Pair Cabling

Twisted pair cable is twisted to minimize crosstalk interference.

Twisted pair cabling comes in two varieties:

1. Shielded twisted pair (STP)
2. Unshielded twisted pair (UTP)

Unshielded Twisted Pair (UTP)

Unshielded Twisted Pair (UTP) is the best option for small networks. The following figure is the example of Unshielded Twisted Pair (UTP).

The cable contains four pairs of wires inside the insulated sleeve. Each twisted pair has different number of twist per inch. Different number of twist per inch eliminates interference among adjacent pairs.

Categories of Unshielded Twisted Pair and their uses are given below:

Category 1 - This is used for voice only in telephone wiring.

Category 2 - It is used, where rate of transfer of data is up to 4 Mbps.

Category 3 - This is called Ethernet wiring that can transfer data at the rate of 10 Mbps.

Category 4 - In 16 Mbps Token Ring category 4 UTP cables are used.

Category 5 - For fast Ethernet connections cat-5 cables are used, which can transfer data at the rate of 100 Mbps.

UTP Cable

The tightness of the twisting of the copper pairs is main difference in the UTP category.

Higher the tightness of the pair supports the higher rate of data transfer.

Disadvantage of UTP is that it may be susceptible to radio and electrical frequency interference.

Following figure illustrate the UTP cable, STP cable, Rj-5 and USB connectors.

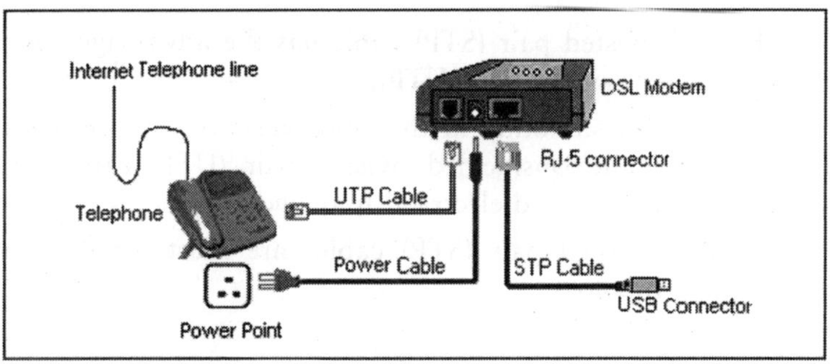

Connectors

Many types of connectors are available to join the Network devices like modem switches, routers, and adapters. RJ-5 USB, T-connector, barrel connector, and terminator are some of the types of connectors that are used for making network connections.

STP: Shielded twisted pair are available with 100 meters in maximum length. They can transfer data at the rate of 16 to 155 Mbps. Shielded twisted pair cables come with an RJ-45 connector. This connector is made up of plastic.

It looks like a large telephone connector. It cannot be fitted wrongly because a slot is provided with it, which permits it to fit with the female slot in only one way.

RJ-45 Connectors

RJ means Registered Jack, which is standard design of connector. It follows a standard which are provided by the telephone industry. The following figure indicates the Shielded Twisted Pair Connector.

Shielded twisted pair (STP) cable has the advantages over the Unshielded twisted pair (UTP).

It can work smoothly in the environments with electrical interference while Unshielded twisted pair (UTP) cables are susceptible to radio and electrical frequencies.

Shielded twisted pair (STP) cables are most suitable for Token Ring topology.

USB Connectors

Shielded twisted pair (STP) cables are also supplied with USB connectors and can easily be installed on the network. Generally the one end of such cable is provided with USB connector and the other end is with the RJ-45 connector. USB connector is always fixed on the USB port of CPU and the RJ-45 connector is fixed with the modem or router.

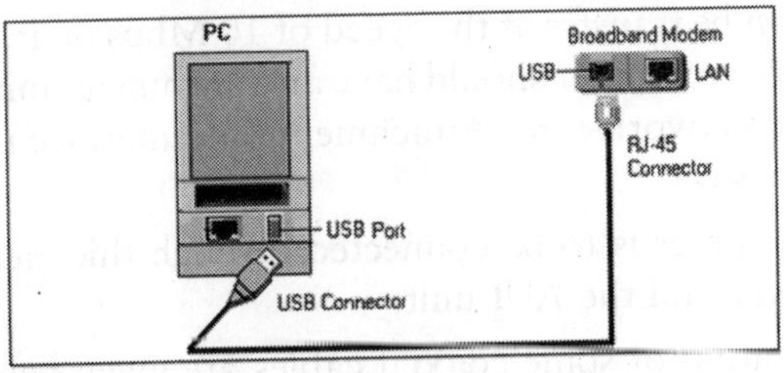

Coaxial Cable

Coaxial cable has a single copper conductor at the center of the cable. It is coated with the plastic layer throughout its length. A braided metal shield is provided on the plastic layer. The plastic layer keeps the copper conductor and the braided metal shield away from each other. All the three parts of the coaxial cable are coated with the thick plastic sleeve.

Coaxial cable is having four parts:

1. Single copper conductor.
2. A plastic layer.
3. Braided metal shield.
4. Outside plastic shield cover.

There are two types of coaxial cables:

1. Thick coaxial.
2. Thin coaxial.

Thinnet: Thin coaxial cable is also known as thinnet. It can carry the Ethernet signals with the segment length of about 185 meters. This type of cables are useful in small local Area Network. The connector which is used at the end of the cable is called British Naval Connector (BNC). Thinnet coaxial cables are the part of the RG-58 family of cable. It can transmits the data with the transmission speed of 10 Mbps. Thinnet cable and its terminator must have the 50 ohm impedance.

Thicknet: Thick coaxial cable is also referred to as thicknet. It can carry the Ethernet signals with the segment length of about 500 meters. Thick coaxial cable is provided with an extra protective plastic cover, which increases its tensile strength and also keeps moisture away from the center core.

Data can be transfer at the speed of 10 Mbps on it. For using thicknet cable computer should have an attachment unit interface (AUI) on its network card. Attachment unit interface is a 15 pin DB-15 connector.

The computer is to be connected through thicknet cable to its transceiver and the AUI unit.

Specification of some coaxial cables are given below:

Specification		Description
RG-58/U	-	It has 50 ohm resistance has a solid copper wire core.
RG-58 A/U*	-	It also has 50 ohm resistance and has a stranded wire core.
RG-58 C/U*	-	This is the Military version of RG-58 A/U.
RG-59	-	It has 75 ohm resistance and good for broadband transmission such as cable TV.
RG-62	-	It has 93 ohm resistance and primarily used for Arc Net.
RG-6	-	It is a high quality cable used for satellite.

Following figure shows the connection of Modem and Router Through coaxial cable:

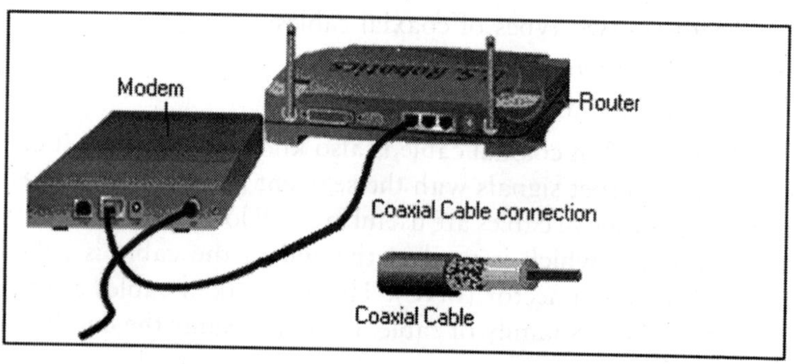

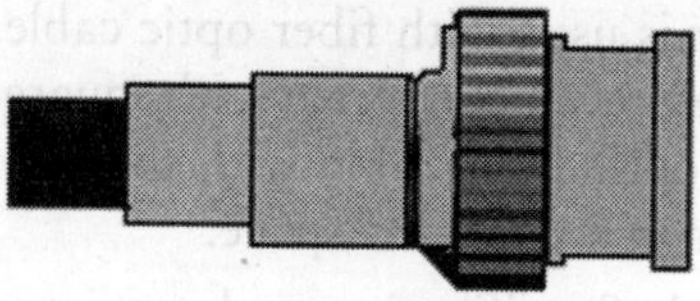

Coaxial Cable Connector

Fiber Optic Cable

Fiber Optic cable is having four parts:

1. Center glass core.
2. Layers of protective materials.
3. Fiber Optic.
4. Outside plastic shield cover.

Fiber optic cabling consists of a center (core), which is made of glass or plastic fibers.

This core is surrounded by protective materials. A plastic coating is used to cushion the fiber center.

The protective layers is surrounded by optic fibers. A thick insulating jacket, made of Teflon or PVC is coated over the optic fibers. Kevlar fiber helps to strengthen the cable and prevent breakage. Optic fiber transmits light instead of electronic signals. This eliminates the electrical or magnetic interference.

Usually there are two fibers, one for each direction. Fiber optic cable can transmit signals over longer distances than coaxial and twisted pair with greater speed. Cable length can be of 2 Kilometers. Speed of transmission of data from 100 Mbps to 2 Gbps is possible.

This is the most expensive and most difficult to install, but is not subject to interference.

There are two types of fiber optic cable:

1. Single mode cables used with lasers.
2. Multimode cables used with Light Emitting Diode (LED) drivers.

Fiber optic cable

ST connector is used with fiber optic cable. It is similar to a BNC connector. A newer connector with squared face is generally used to connect optic fiber cable with the internet devices. It is easier to connect in a confined space.

Ethernet Cable Specification and maximum length.

Specification	Cable type	Maximum length
10BaseT	UTP	100 meters
10Base2	Thin Coaxial	185 meters
10Base5	Thick Coaxial	500 meters
10BaseF	Fiber Optic	2000 meters

Fiber-optic—Data are transmitted using light, rather than electrons.

Installation of Network Cables

Simple rules for laying network cables:

1. Cable length must be kept more than the need with plenty of slack.
2. Each and every part of the network cable must be tested even it may be brand new.
3. While installing network keep the safe distance of all parts about three feet from the sources of electrical interference.
4. All cables which run across the floor must be protected by a proper cover.
5. It is good practice to label all the cables at the both ends.
6. Use the cable fasteners to keep the cable in its proper location.
7. Power cable must be kept away from the network cable.

Ethernet Cabling

Ethernet cabling is physical connections of networking components.

The following are the types of Ethernet cabling:

1. Straight-through cable
2. Crossover cable
3. Rolled cable

Straight-through Cable

The straight-through cable are connection in between:

1. Host computer to switch or hub.
2. Router to switch or hub.

Ethernet devices are connected directly through four wires.

Following figure indicates the straight-through Ethernet cabling.

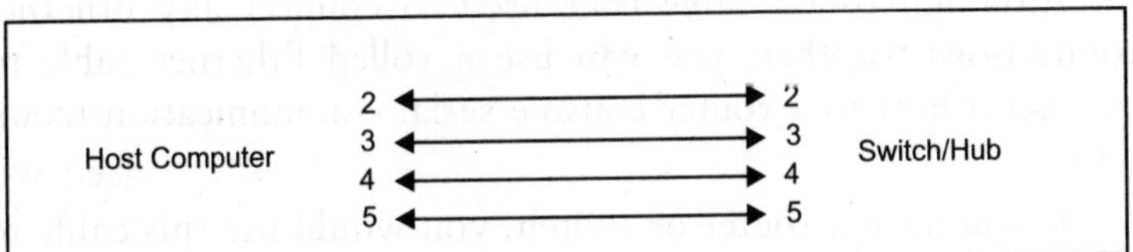

It is clear from the above figure that connection of the pins are made with similar numbers.

We have connected the host computer pin2 with pin2 of switch or hub,

host computer pin3 with pin3 of switch or hub

host computer pin4 with pin4 of switch or hub

host computer pin5 with pin5 of switch or hub

This type of cabling is only applicable for an Ethernet cabling. It does not work with Voice, Token Ring, ISDN, etc.

Crossover Cable

The crossover cable can be used to connect:

1. Switch to switch
2. Hub to hub
3. Host to host
4. Hub to switch
5. Router direct to host

It is similar to the straight-through cabling. We just change the number of pins.

Instead of connecting 1 to 1, etc., we connect pins 2 to 4 and 3 to 5 on each side of the cable.

Crossover Ethernet Cable

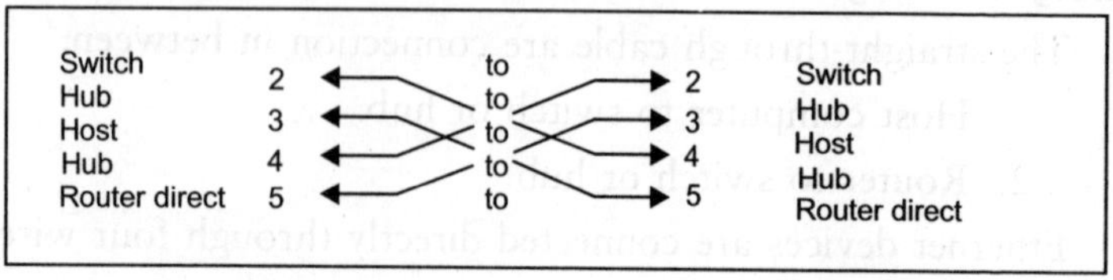

Rolled Ethernet Cable

Although rolled cable isn't used to connect any Ethernet connections together, you can use a rolled Ethernet cable to connect a host to a router console serial communication (com) port.

If you have a router or switch, you would use this cable to connect your PC running from HyperTerminal to the hardware. Eight wires are used in this cable to connect serial devices, although not all eight are used to send information, just as in Ethernet networking.

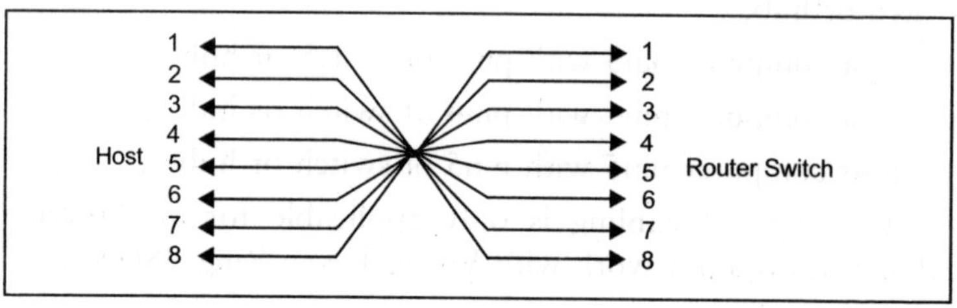

Once you have the correct cable connected from your PC to the router or switch, you can start HyperTerminal to create a console connection and configure the device.

9

Modem

There are four types of modem used with internet network:

1. Internal or basic type of modem
2. DSL broadband modem
3. Cable modem
4. Wireless modem
5. Analog or ISDN modem

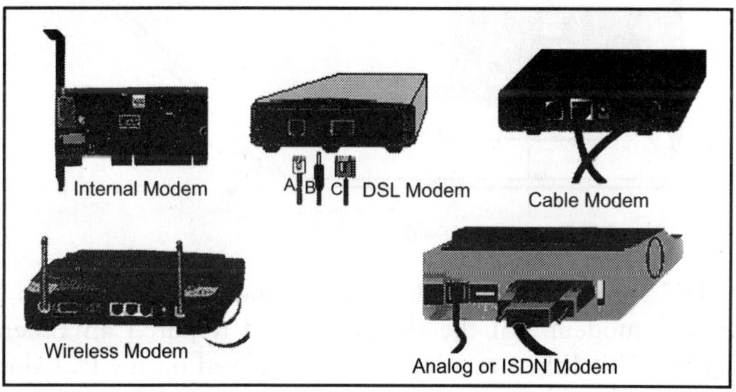

Use of Modem

The modem physically connects the client computer with the remote computer depend upon the type of network. For internal or DSL modems, telephone line is necessary to connect the two computers. For cable modem coaxial wiring is used but for wireless modem no physical connection is required.

If the modem is properly installed and configured, we can use our computer for sending and receiving message. We can also talk or see the person, who is residing in a remote area, by installing audio and video facilities, on our computer.

General Construction Basic Modems

Modem is an electronic printed circuit board comprises of chips and other electronic components.

These components are connected with thin copper strips on a insulated fiber sheet. There are connecting pins at the bottom of modem which are fixed in a PCI slot on the motherboard.

Basic type internal modem are directly connected to the telephone lines. At one side of the fiber sheet there is a metallic strip which is screwed with the body of the cabinet after installing the modem into PCI slot. This strip keeps the modem firmly fixed with the PCI slot.

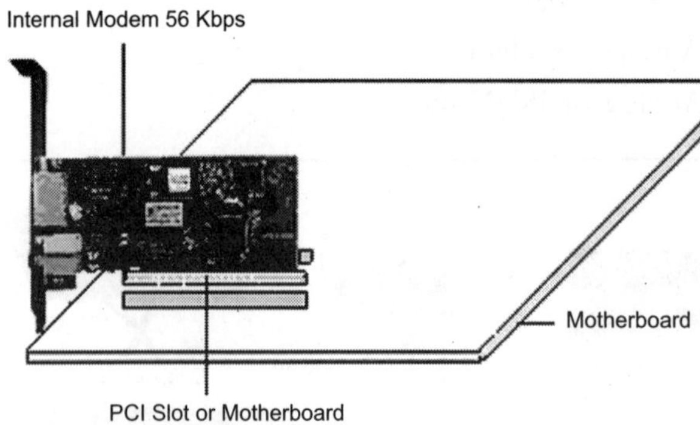

DSL broad band, cable modem and wireless modem are external modem. All the three modems required an Ethernet adapter. This Ethernet adapter is to be fixed on the PCI slot of the motherboard.

This Ethernet adaptor is then connected to the DSL modem with Ethernet cable or USB cable. DSL modem or cable modem are connected with telephone line or coaxial cable. They also have power connection for power supply. In some modern computers adopter and modem are inbuilt. Lap tops have inbuilt adopter and modem.

Function of Modem

Function of modem is to modulate signals from digital to analog and demodulates analog to digital signals.

1. It modulates digital signals into analog signals received from digital device of the computer and sends them to the other computer through telephone lines.
2. Similarly, it demodulates the incoming analog signals from outside analog device and converts them into digital signals for the digital device of the client computer.

Speed of Modem

Initially the speed of modem was designed to 2400 bit per second which was very slow for transfer of data signals. Such modems are now obsolete. Further improvement raised the modem speed of data transfer from 14.4 Kbps to 28.8 Kbps but it was also found insufficient for the present requirement. At present the 56 Kbps modems are used with the new computers.

Further improvement brought through ISDN adapter to increase the speed of data transfer. This adapter is installed on the PCI slot of the motherboard and then connected through USB wire with the DSL modem. DSL modem is connected to telephone lines.

Digital Subscriber Line (DSL) systems has been adopted by most of the internet authorities. This system has the data transfer speed in mega bytes.

Simple Internal Modem Connection

Figure on next page indicates the connections of internal modem with the telephone line.

Installing Internal Modem

For installing internal modem follow the following steps:

1. Close all programs and shut down the computer.
2. Switch off the main supply.
3. Open the side or top cover of CPU.
4. Fix the internal modem on PCI slot on the motherboard.
5. Screw the strip of modem with the cabinet.

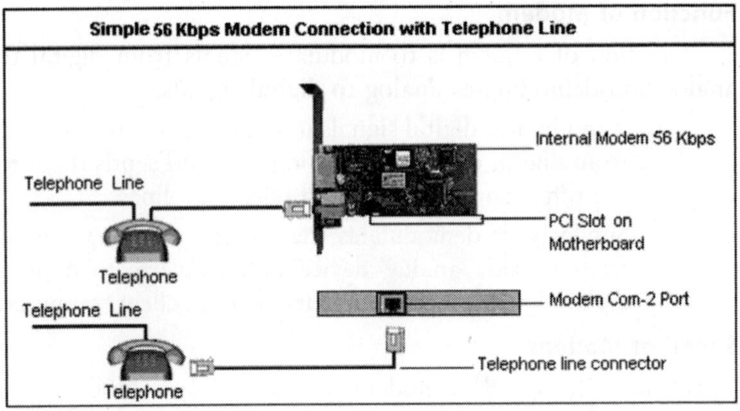

6. Connect the modem with telephone line by fixing the one end of it with COM1/COM2 and other end with the telephone.
7. Fix back the cabinet cover.

You have installed the modem on your computer but to make it work, you have to installed the appropriate driver.

Configuration of Modem: The following example is for a particular type of internal modem. It is conexant Soft 56 Data, Fax Speakerphone PCI modem. You may install any other modem as per your choice, but the installation of driver procedure is the same.

1. Click Start button at the task bar then go to settings and then click on control panel as directed in the following figure:

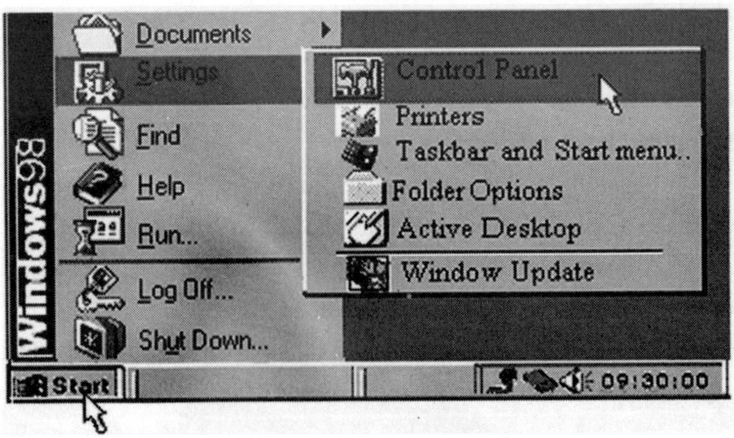

As soon as you click Control Panel icon Control panel window will be displayed on screen as follows:

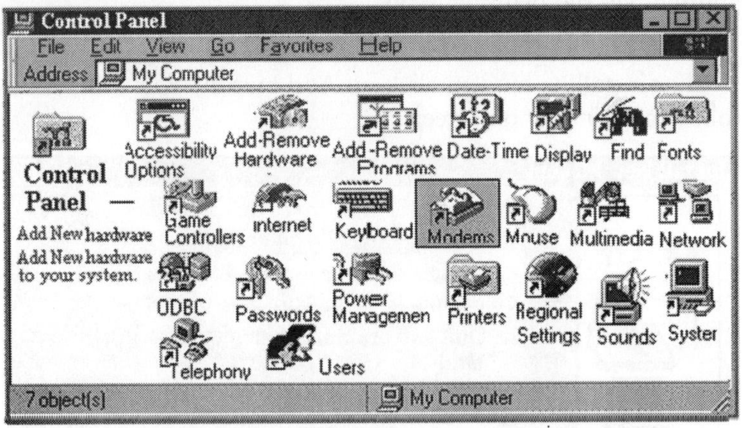

2. In control panel double click on Modems icon. You will see Modem Properties window on the screen as follows:

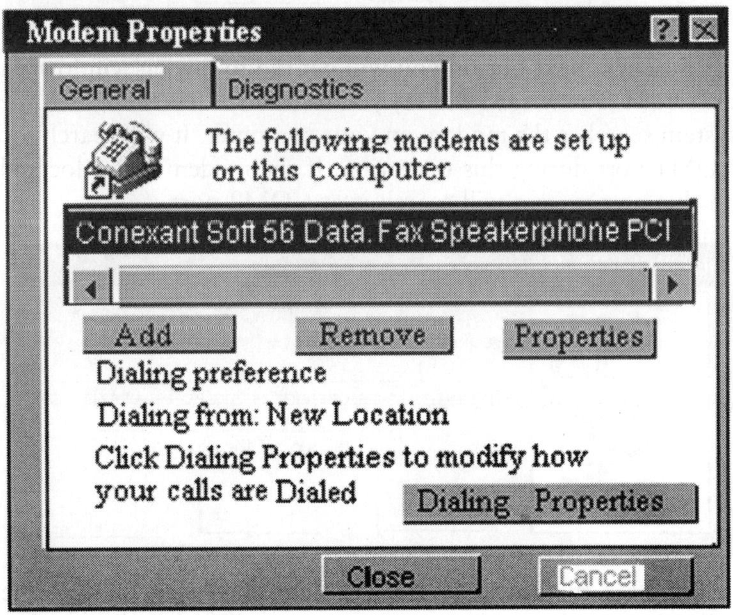

If there is any modem already installed on your computer you will get the name of the modem in the window otherwise you will get the blank window.

3. There are three Add, Remove and Properties buttons.

For installing modem click on Add button. You will see the following window on screen.

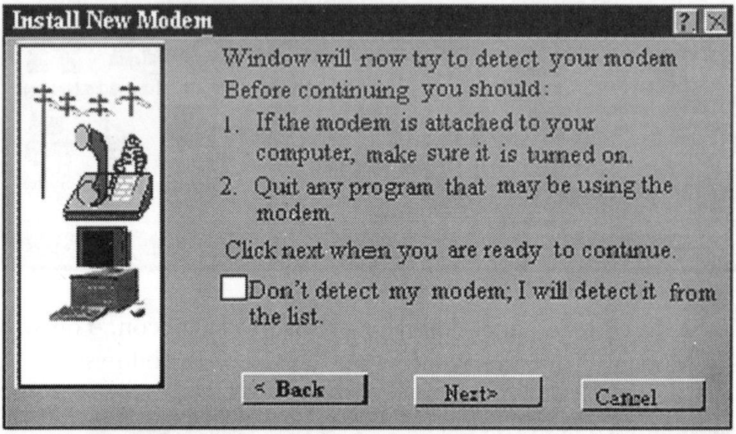

4. Click Next button you will get the following window on the screen. The wizard will say you to wait for few minutes while system searches the modem on your computer. It will search the COM1 port during this operation. If the modem is not located on this port system will search it at COM2 port.

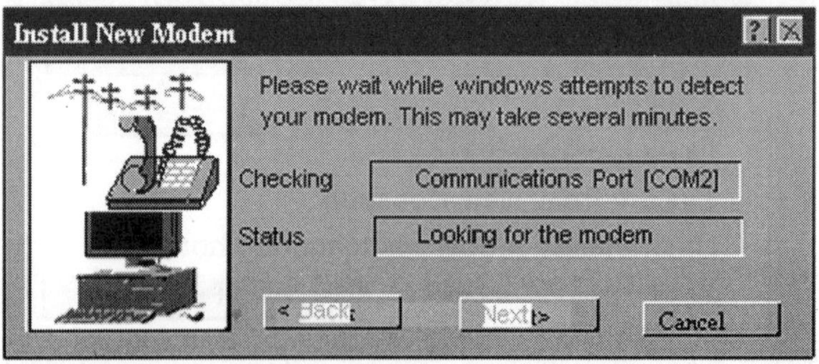

If after the search system did not find any modem the following window will appear on screen. Which indicates that window did not find any modem on your computer. Select the modem from Next window shown after this window.

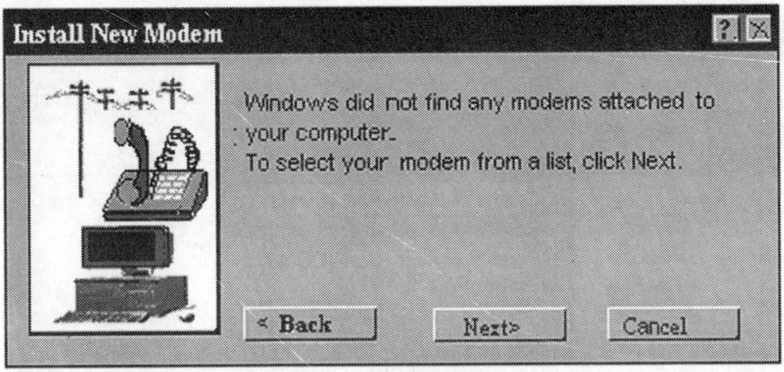

5. Click Next button in the above window. The following window will appear on screen.

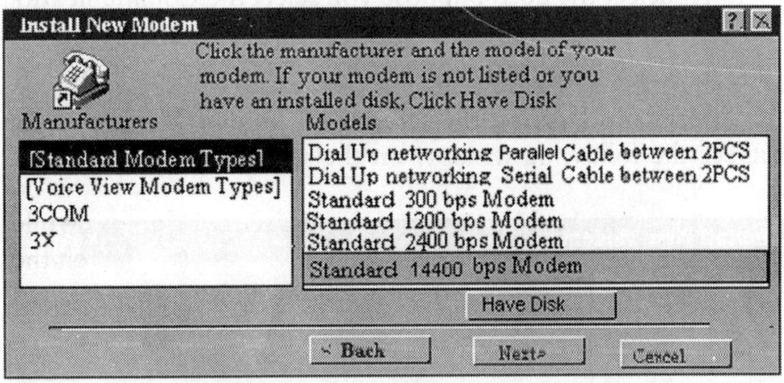

There are the two ways of installing the modem:

1. Installation of modem from the list of manufacturer and model available in your computer.
2. Installation of modem from CD.

1. From the given list of manufacturer and model available on your computer.

If you find the suitable driver for your modem from the given list you may click on the manufacturer and select the model from the model list. Suppose the manufacturer name you select "Standard Modem types" and "Model as Standard 14400 bps Modem" in the above window and then click on the Next Button. Following window will appear on screen.

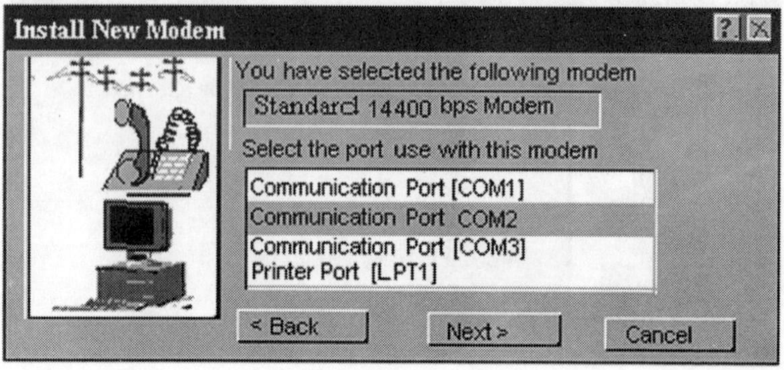

In the above window do the following operations:

1. Select the port. Suppose you select the Communication Port [COM2].
2. Click Next Button.

After a short period the screen will become blank and you will see the following window on the screen:

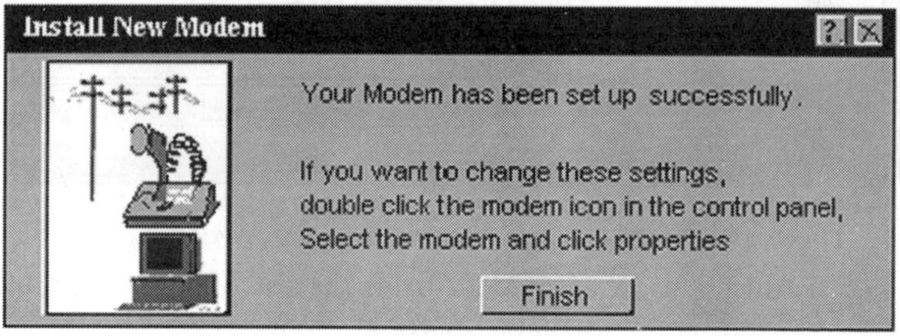

3. Installation of modem from CD.

If we do not find the suitable modem in the above list of manufacturers and models, then click the next button.

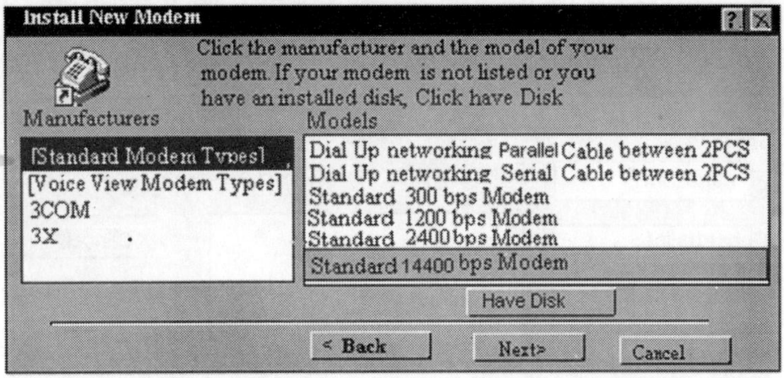

The following window will appear on the screen.

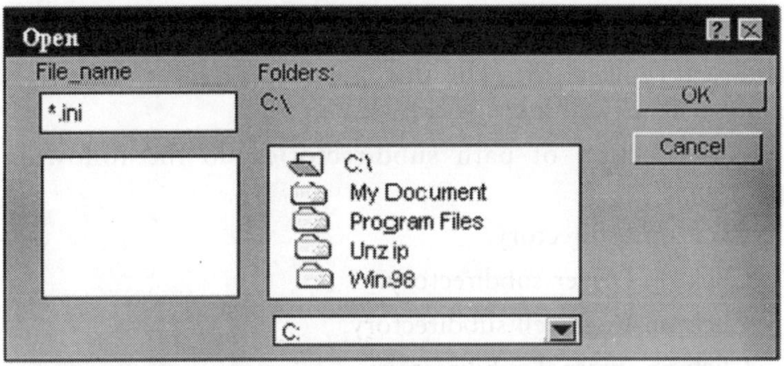

Click on the arrow button.

Select the CD-ROM drive. Here we select (f:) as CD-ROM drive.

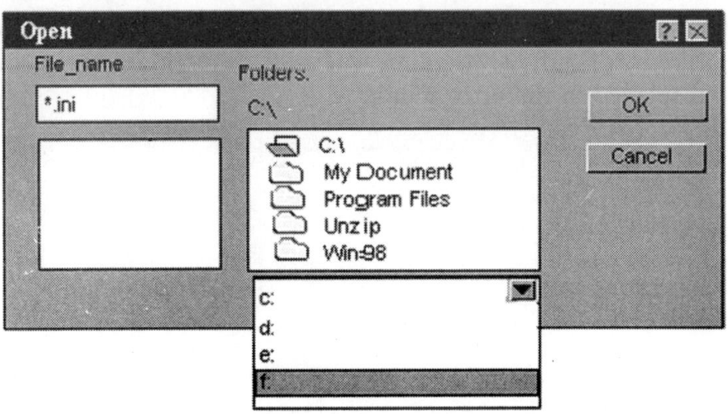

Insert the CD, which contains the modem installation program, into CD-ROM drive.

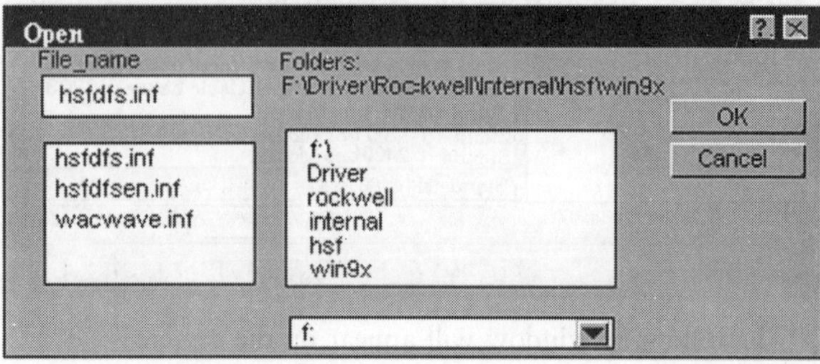

Now you should know the path of the driver, in which subdirectory it resides. In this particular case the path is F:\Driver\Rockwell\Internal\hsf\win9X.

For selection of path subdirectories do the following operations:

Click on f; directory.

Click on Driver subdirectory.

Click on Rockwell subdirectory.

Click on internal subdirectory.

Click on hsf subdirectory.

Click on win9x subdirectory. win9x is the actual modem installation program.

As soon as you click on win9x, you may observe that three files hsfdfs.inf, hsfdfsen.inf, wacwave.inf with .inf extension displayed in the open window.

Now click OK in Open window of previous page 154.

Installation of modem will start.

Click Next button. Following window will appear on screen.

The window contains the communication port number.

You have to select the port number. In this particular case we select the Communication port [COM2].

Click the next button.

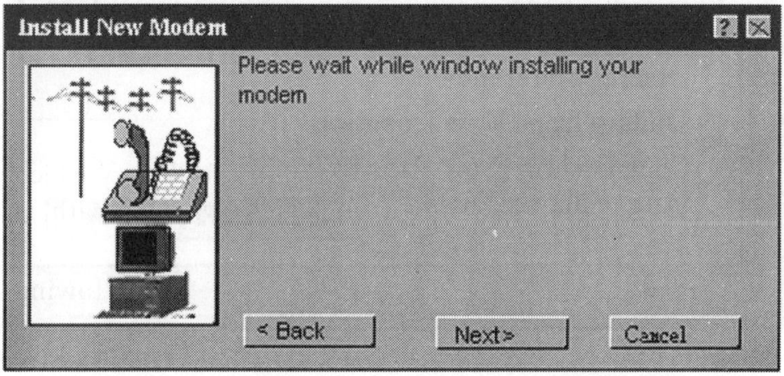

After a short period the screen will become blank and you will see the following window on the screen.

Click finish button in the window shown below. Restart the computer.

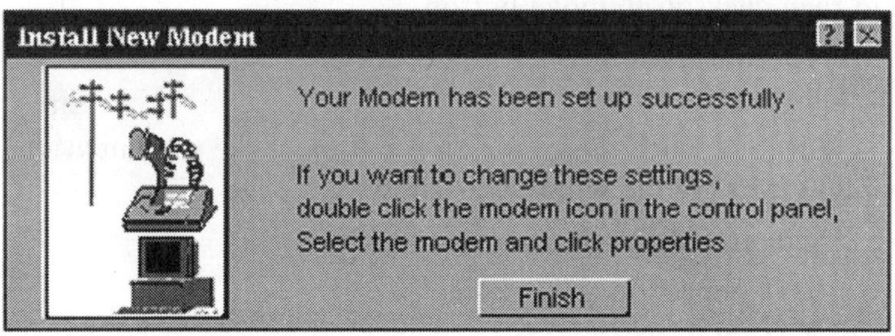

If you again click the modem icon in the control panel you will get the Modem Properties window as follows. In the Modem Properties window you will see the name and specification of the modem which is just installed.

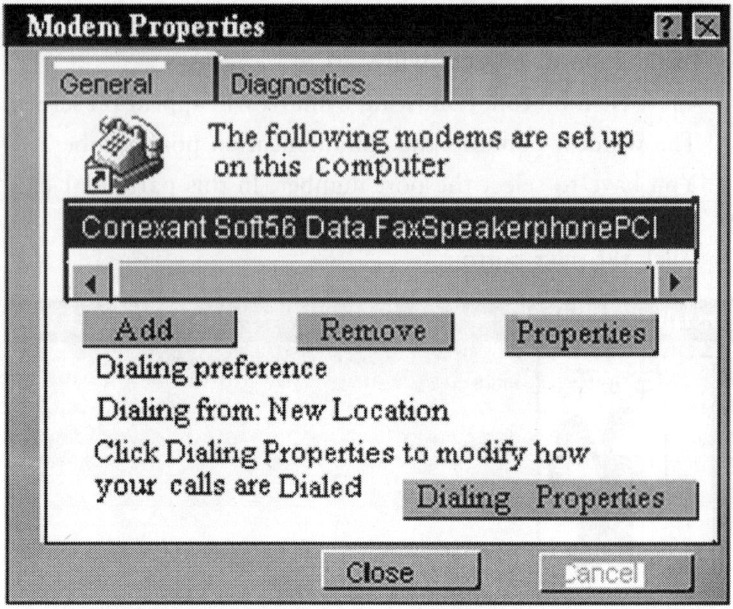

There are three buttons in the above window.

Add button: You have already used this button for installation of modem.

Remove button: It can be used for removal of installed modem. For removal of the installed modem select the modem and then click on Remove button.

Properties button: Click the Properties button you will get the following window.

When you click the connection button at the top line of the window you get the window as shown on page 157.

There are two preference groups:

1. Connection preference.
2. Call preference.

1. Connection preference

This group has data bits.

Parity and stop bits which are set as 8, None and 1 by default. You need not to change the setting.

2. Call preference

There are three check boxes:

(a) Wait for dial tone before dialing.

Click the check box if not checked.

(b) Cancel the call if not connected within 60 seconds. Click the check box and set the duration for 60 seconds.

If you use less duration for connection your call may be terminated before it is connected with the server.

(c) Disconnect the call if idle for more than minutes. You tick the check boxes and set the durations as per your requirement.

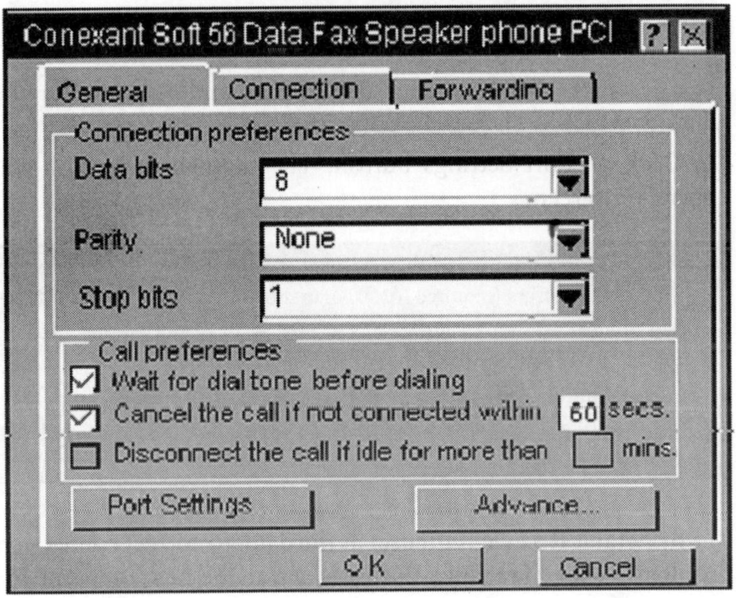

3. Forwarding

Now click the Forwarding button in the above window. The following window will appear on screen.

This window contains a check box which you may use for call forwarding.

Tick the check box and then fill the two boxes with activation code and deactivation code.

By default the box is unchecked.

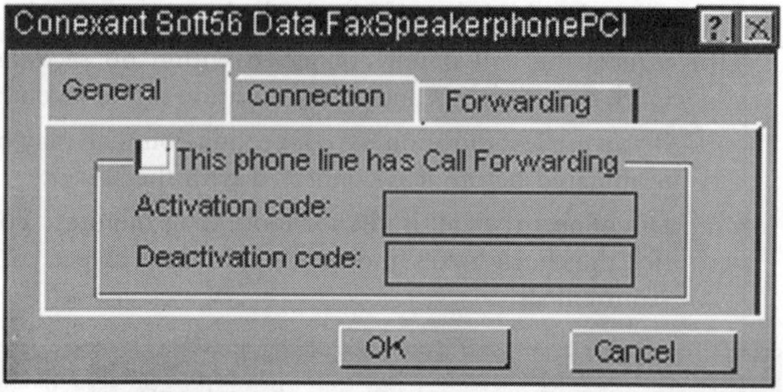

There are two buttons Port Settings and Advance in the window which is shown on page 157.

Click on Port Settings button. The following window will appear on screen:

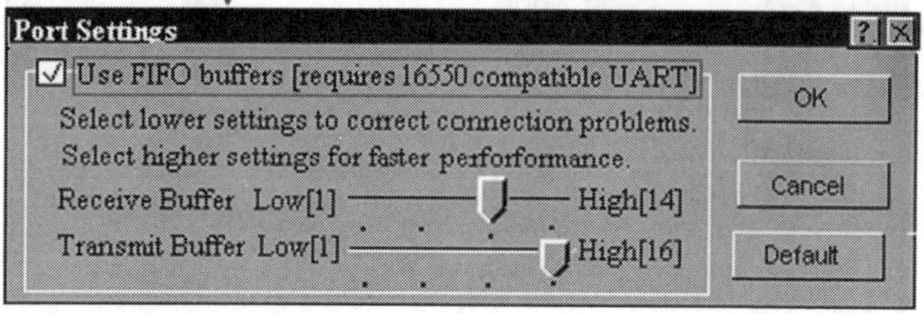

By default Receive Buffer set at third dot to correct connection problems, while Transmit Buffer is set at the highest point for faster performance. You may change the setting according to your requirement.

DSL Broadband Modem. See next page 159.

DSL broadband modem has three connection points:

1. Power supply point which is connected through a power cable.

2. Telephone female connector through which you connect the modem with telephone line.
3. USB port through which you connect the modem with the adapter by USB cable.

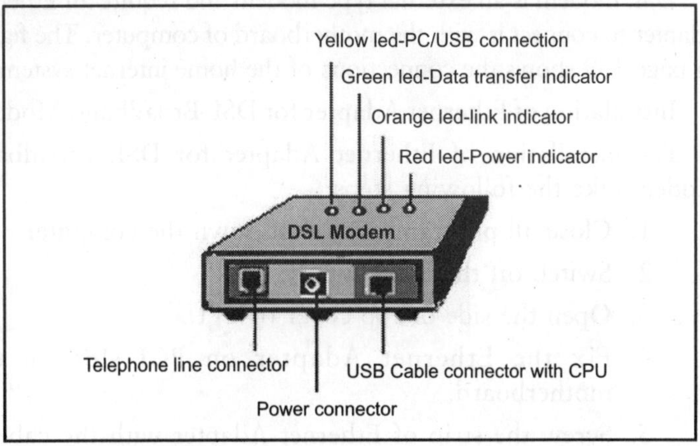

There are four tiny indicators at the top of the modem.

1. Red light indicates that the power supply is on.
2. Orange light indicates the link connection of client computer with the server.

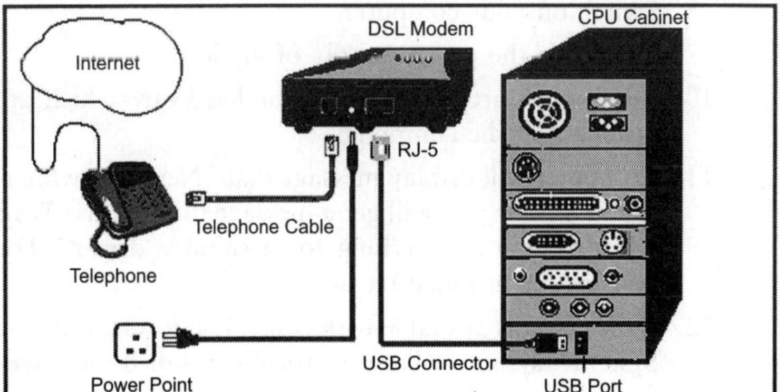

DSL Modem Connections

3. Dark green light indicates that the computer is ready for data transfer.
4. Yellow light indicates the USB connection with PC is OK.

DSL modem is an external type modem and require an Ethernet Adapter to connect it with the motherboard of computer. The figure on page 159 shows the connections of the home internet system.

Installation of Ethernet Adapter for DSL Broadband Modem.

For installation of Ethernet Adapter for DSL Broadband Modem take the following steps:

1. Close all programs and shut down the computer.
2. Switch off the main supply.
3. Open the side or top cover of CPU.
4. Fix the Ethernet Adapter on PCI slot on the motherboard.
5. Screw the strip of Ethernet Adapter with the cabinet and fix the side cover.
6. Connect the Ethernet Adapter with the DSL modem by Ethernet cable.
7. Connect the DSL modem with telephone line as shown in the above figure.
8. Switch on your computer.
9. Switch on the power supply of modem.
10. BIOS will start searching all the hardware which are installed on the computer.
11. Computer will display message that "New hardware is found". Next you will get a message that "Please Wait while System is searching for a suitable driver." For your newly installed hardware.
12. If the driver is available with your "Windows Operating System", system will automatically installed the driver for Ethernet adapter.
13. After installation of the driver, system will display a message window, to restart the computer.
14. Click OK and restart the computer.

After installation of adapter you have to configure the internet connection for accessing the network.

Making Broadband Internet connection.

Some company provide the separate software to connect client computer with the server.

Airtel of India provide the separate software for the DSL broadband modem for making connection with the internet.

Cable Modem

Cable modems are connected by coaxial TV cable. Telephone wire is replaced by coaxial TV cable. The connectors are similar to TV cable connectors. Cable modems are configured in a similar way as we configured other type of modem.

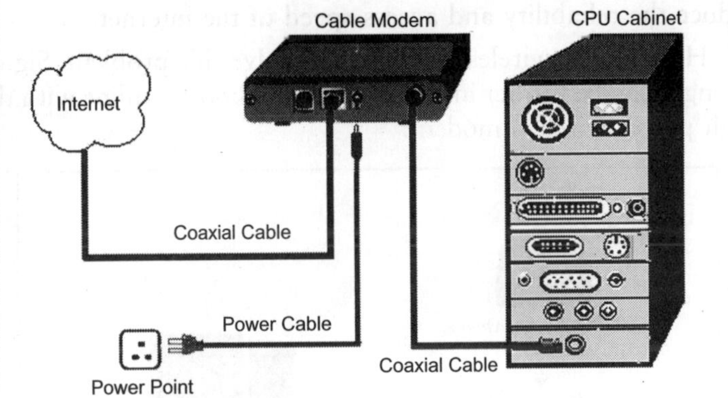

Cable Modem Connections

Wireless Modem

Everybody wants to transfer or receive information with high speed. For making your internet fast you require a high power modem. Modem can be wireless, cable or basic type modem.

Wireless Modem

When we install a wireless modem its configuration is necessary to make our internet system operative.

Initially we have to connect the wireless modem with Ethernet card or network adapter of PC with a UTP or STP cable. Configure the wireless modem as you configure the other modem.

After configuration you may remove the physical connection. For this purpose wireless modem is provided with RJ-5 connector slots. Wireless modem are provided with antenna to catch the signals from internet access device.

We receive the signals of low strength because we are sitting inside the room. The signals, which we are receiving are of low strength, because they are coming to us after passing through many obstructions like trees, buildings and walls. This will reduce the reliability and access speed of the internet.

High power wireless modem can solve this problem. Signal strength can be further increased by using booster inline with the high power wireless modem.

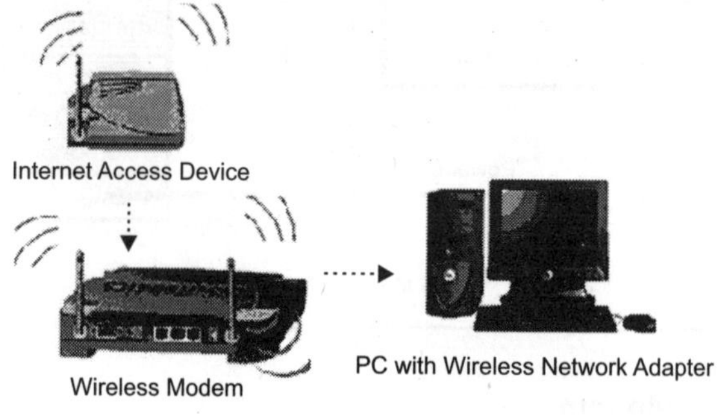

Wireless Internet System

The above figure illustrates the wireless internet system with internet access device, wireless modem and a PC with Ethernet wireless card.

(i) You might have observed when you have tuned your transistor radio inside the room, you may not be able to hear a clear sound but as soon as you go outside the room the performance of your radio becomes better. This is because of the obstacles like wall, door, etc.

In the case of wireless internet, if the outdoor access point is away and the wireless signal are passing through the obstacles like trees and building they become weak before reaching the wireless modem and the PC. A high power wireless modem and a inline booster can solve this problem.

(ii) Outdoor Access Point should be kept at distance of 200 to 500 feet from the PC then high power wireless modem is quite effective. Distance of access point more than 500 feet will reduce the performance of the high power wireless modem.

(iii) If your PC or laptop do not have the wireless network adapter then it is recommend to use a high power wireless modem for getting the best access speed.

(iv) To make a wireless connection each wireless card in the network is to be set to infrastructure mode.

Analog Modem

Analog or ISDN modem are used when you want to use dial up Internet service instead of cable or DSL Internet service. Analog or ISDN modem data transfer speed is better than the basic internal modem. The figure on page 164 illustrates the connections of analog or ISDN modem with the network adapter and with the telephone line.

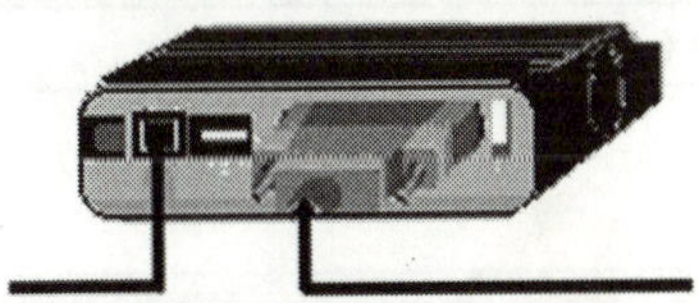

Analog or ISDN Modem

Configuration of modem properties on window Xp.

Open Windows XP and follow the steps. Click Start.

1. Click Control Panel.
2. Click Phone and Modem Options.

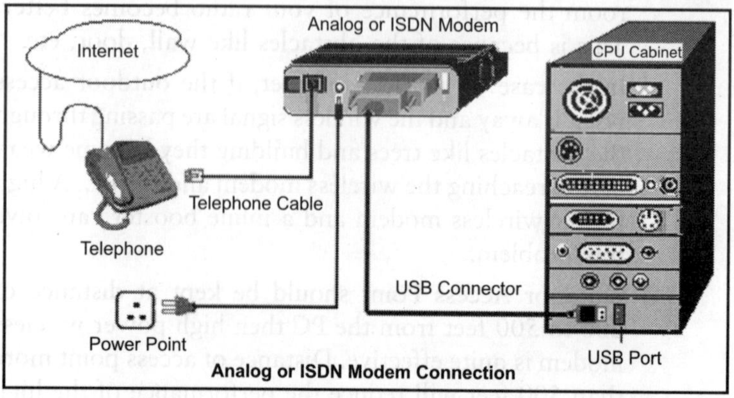

Analog or ISDN Modem Connection

Double click on "Phone and Modem Option" icon in Control Panel "Phone and Modem Option" window will appear with "Dialing Rules", that will display "My Location" with the "Area code".

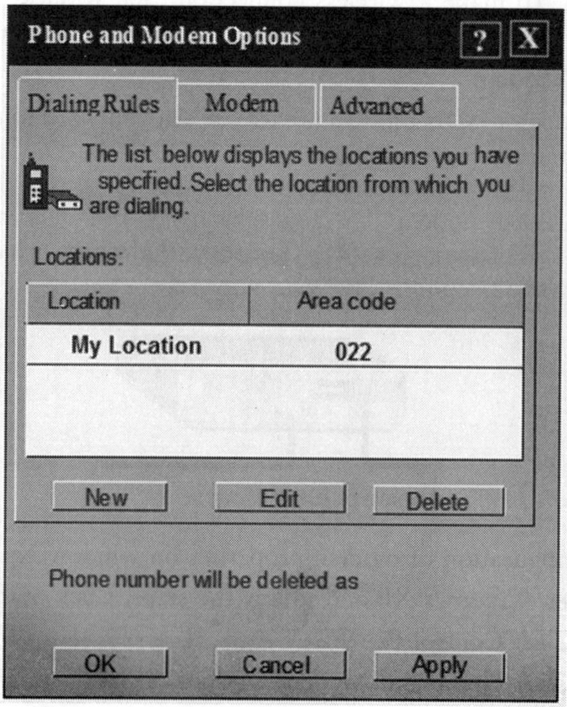

3. Click on "Modem tab" on the "Phone and Modem Option" window. This window will display name and specification of the modem and the COM port.

4. Click on properties button on the "Phone and Modem Option" window. A window with "General" tab will be displayed as shown on page 166.

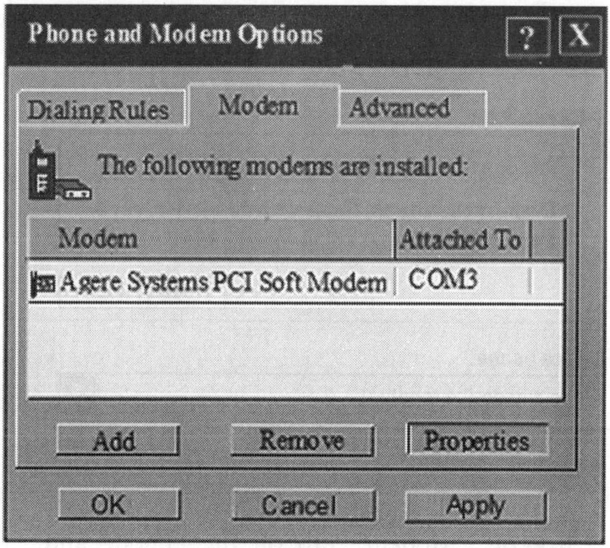

It will show the Name of modem, Device type, Manufacturer name and location of the modem at PCI slot of motherboard. It displays the status of modem. At the bottom you can see the device is selected enabled. If it is selected disabled. You must choose enabled option by using the arrow below the Device Usage.

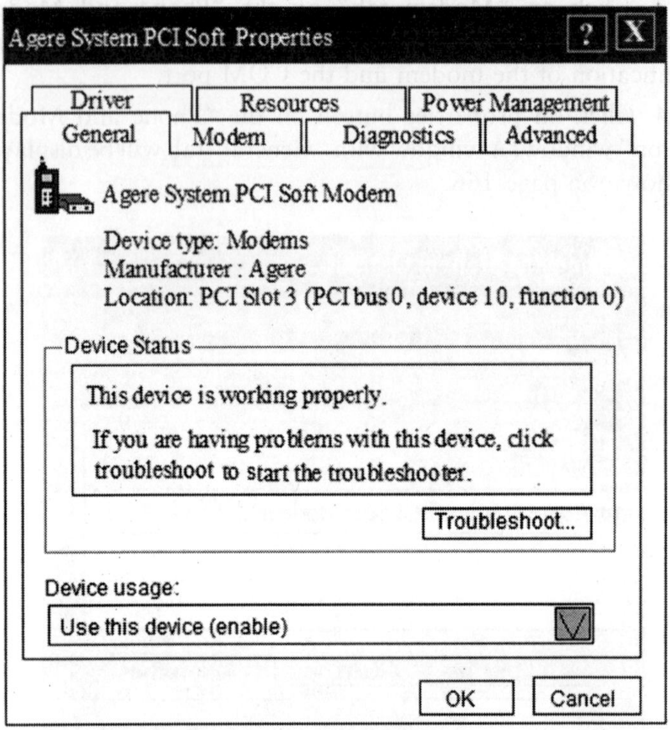

5. Click on "Modem" tab on the "Phone and Modem Properties" window at page 167. This window contains three sections:

1. **Speaker volume:** You can adjust the speaker volume for voice conversation.
2. **Maximum port speed:** Click on the arrow and select the maximum port speed.
3. **Dialing control:** It indicate that you should wait for dial tone before dialing.

6. Click on the "Diagnostics" tab, you will see the following window. It contains the modem information under the "Field" and "Value" columns.

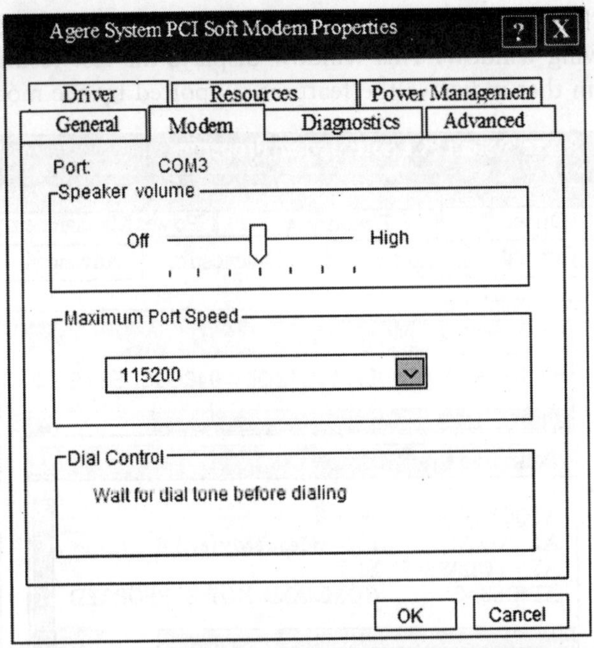
Agere System PCI Soft Modem Properties
Driver
Resources
Power Management
General
Modem
Diagnostics
Advanced
Port: COM3
Speaker volume
Off
High
Maximum Port Speed
115200
Dial Control
Wait for dial tone before dialing
OK
Cancel

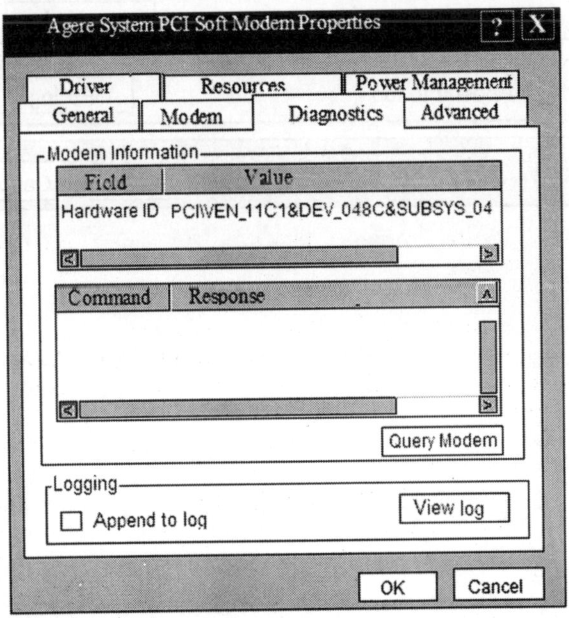
Agere System PCI Soft Modem Properties
Driver
Resources
Power Management
General
Modem
Diagnostics
Advanced
Modem Information
Field
Value
Hardware ID PCI\VEN_11C1&DEV_048C&SUBSYS_04
Command
Response
Query Modem
Logging
Append to log
View log
OK
Cancel

Click on the "Query Modem" button you can see the following window. This window displays the test result of the modem that indicates the features supported by the modem.

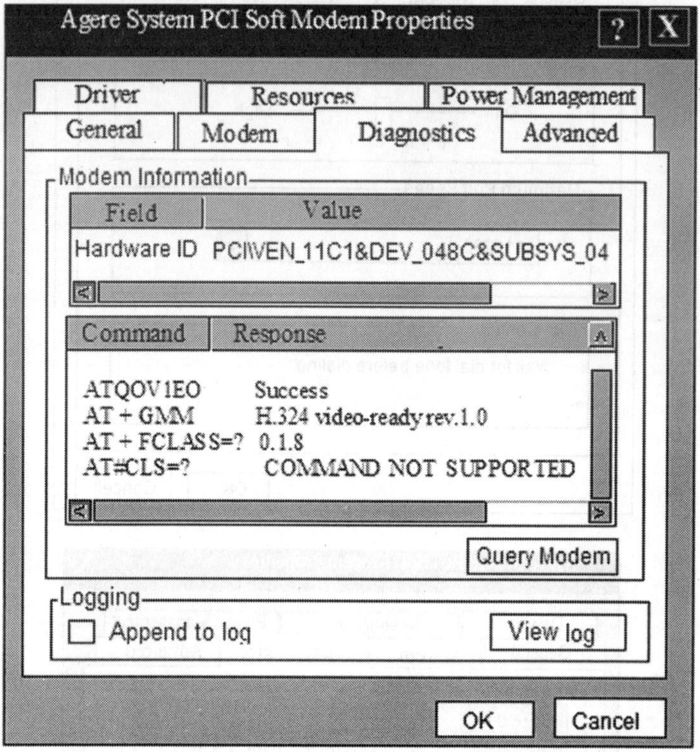

Internet Connection Sharing

10

You can connect your computer with the internet network, using modem, adapter and telephone line.

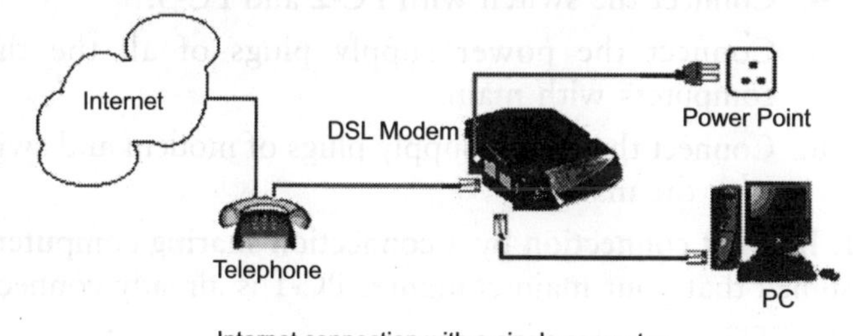

Internet connection with a single computer

The following picture shows the connection of a computer with net.

After installing the physical connection you have to configure the internet connection by using Internet connection wizard as described previously.

You can use more computers machines to access the network in two ways:

1. Internet connection by a connection sharing computer.
2. Internet connection accessed by each computer.

Suppose you add two more computers to your LAN by introduction of a switch. Make the following physical connection as shown in the following picture.

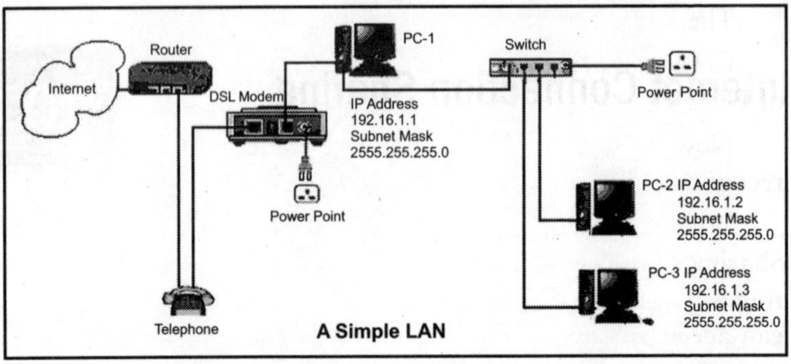

Do the following connections:

1. Connect the telephone line with DSL modem.
2. Connect the modem with the PC-1.
3. Connect PC-1 with the switch.
4. Connect the switch with PC-2 and PC-3.
5. Connect the power supply plugs of all the three computers with main.
6. Connect the power supply plugs of modem and switch with the main.

1. Internet connection by a connection sharing computer. It is assumed that your main computer PC-1 is already connected with internet.

When a singlė computer connected to the home network it is called connection sharing computer.

In the above picture PC-1 is the connection sharing computer. It provides private IP addresses and name resolution services for the other computers PC-2 and PC-3 on the home network.

Thus other computers PC-2 and PC-3 are enabled to access the Internet through the Connection Sharing computer PC-1, using private IP addressing translation.

PC-2 or PC-3 on the network sends a request to the Internet. This request cannot be sent directly to the internet because Internet does not recognize the IP addresses of computers PC-2 and PC-3.

PC-2 or PC-3 therefore sends the request through the connection sharing computer PC-1.

The request of the computer includes its IP address.

Connection Sharing computer PC-1 translates the IP address of PC-2 or PC-3 into its own IP address.

Now the request is sent to the internet with the translated recognizable IP address.

When the response is sent back by the Internet, the Connection Sharing computer PC-1 translates the IP address back again and routes it to the PC-2 or PC-3 on the network. Now PC-2 or PC-3 can access the internet via connection sharing computer PC-1.

2. Internet connection accessed by each computer. Dynamic Host Configuration Protocol (DHCP) dynamically assigns private IP addresses to all computers on the home network. We can change the IP address statically which are assigned by automatic addressing services, to each computer on the network.

Assigning IP Address Statically

Before assigning IP address statically you have to make all the physical connection of your network. Take the following steps:

1. Install physically adapters on all computers.
2. Choose the computer that will be the Connection Sharing computer.
3. Installed DSL modem in your network circuit.
4. Connect the modem with telephone line and adapter.
5. Connect the modem with a power switch.
6. Connect all the computers with power switch.
7. Complete all the connection of your small network.
8. Switch on the power supply of switch, modem and all computers.
9. Run the Internet connection wizard to establish the connection with the Connection Sharing computer. Once your Internet connection is established and found working, then configure the IP addiess and the Subnet mask of all other computers on the network.

Configuration of Other Computers

Start PC-1, PC-2 and PC-3 and do the following on the desk top of PC-2.

1. Click Start button at the task bar then go to settings and then click on control panel as directed in the following figure.

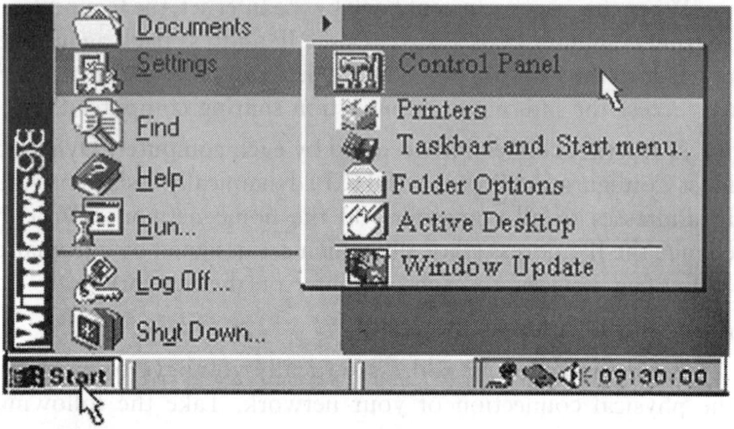

As soon as you click Control Panel icon Control Panel window will be displayed on screen as follows:

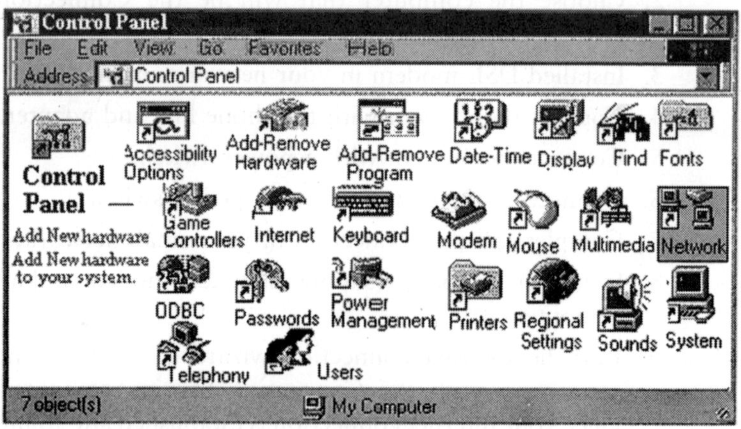

2. Double click on the Network icon in Control Panel. The following Network window will appear on screen.

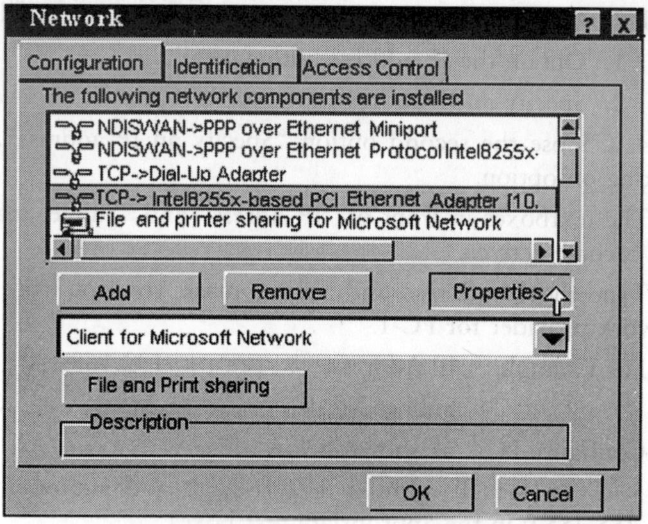

Select TCP→Intel8255-based PCI Ethernet Adapter [10/100] from the Network window components.

3. Click on Properties button.

Following TCP/IP window will appear on the screen.

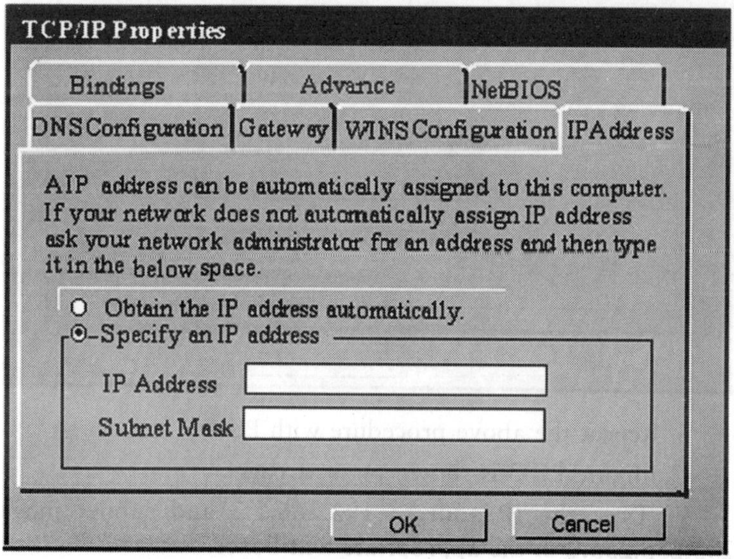

Following are the two options given in the TCP/IP window:

1. Obtain the IP address automatically.
2. Specify an IP address.

4. Choose the second option "Specify an IP address", by clicking on option.

The textboxes in front of "IP Adress" and "Subnet mask" will become active.

Type the IP address and Subnet mask you got from the network provider for PC-1.

For Example IP Address. . . . . : 192.168.1.1
Subnet Mask . . . . : 255.255.255.0

Configure PC-2 as shown below.

5. Type the IP address 192.168.1.2 and subnet mask 255.255.255.0 in the appropriate text boxes.

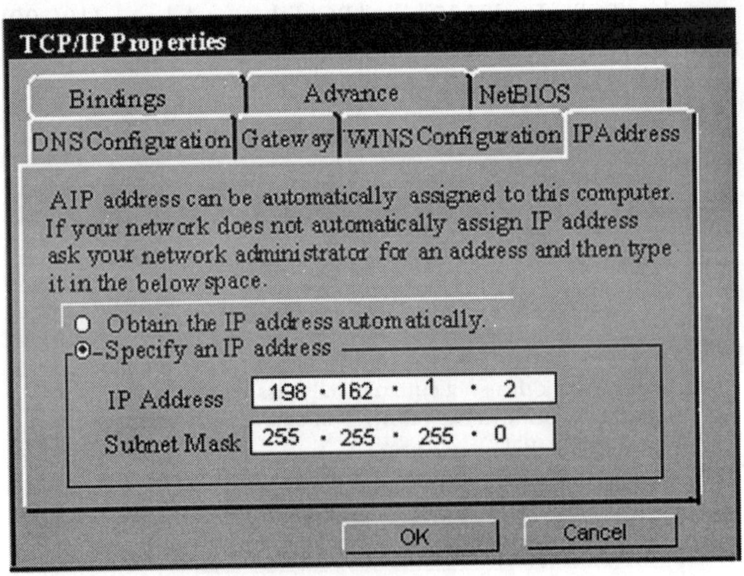

6. Repeat the above procedure with PC-3.

Configure PC-3 is shown on next page.

7. Type the IP address 192.168.1.3 and subnet mask 255.255.255.0 in the appropriate text boxes.

IP Address and Subnet Mask for PC-3

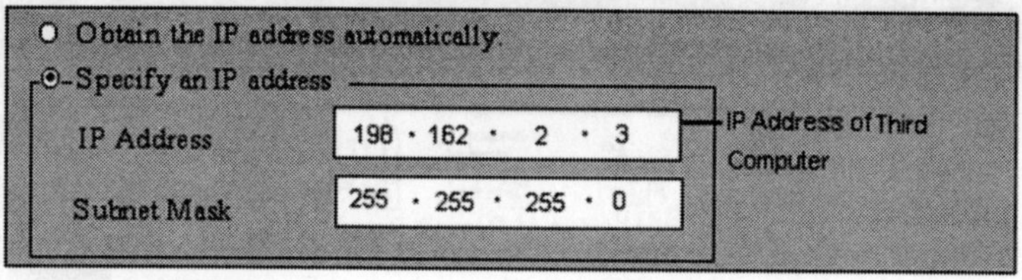

8. Restart the computer.

Now you can access the network by all the three computers.

Installation of Microsoft Service for File and Printer Sharing

1. Click Start
2. Go to Settings
3. Then click on Control Panel.

As soon as you click Control panel icon Control panel window will be displayed on screen as follows:

4. In control panel double click on Network icon.
5. Click on Add button in the Network window shown on page 176.

Following window will appear on the screen.

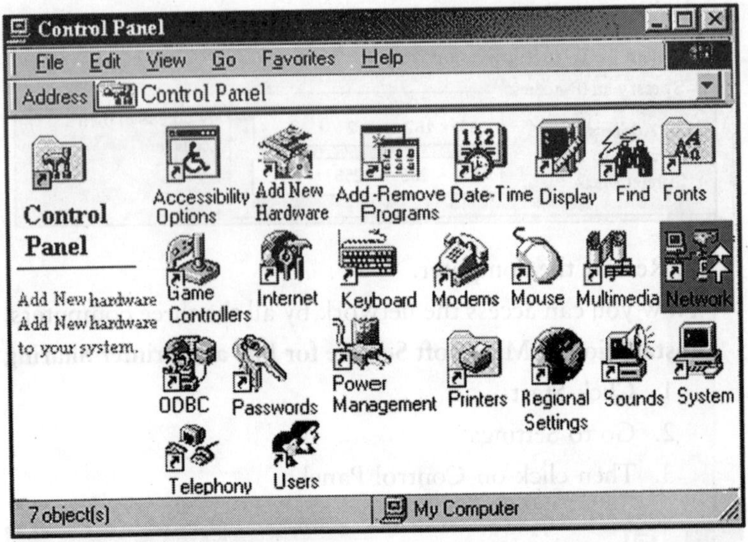
Control Panel
File Edit View Go Favorites Help
Address Control Panel
Control Panel
Add New hardware
Add New hardware to your system.
Accessibility Options
Add New Hardware
Add-Remove Programs
Date-Time
Display
Find
Fonts
Game Controllers
Internet
Keyboard
Modems
Mouse
Multimedia
Network
ODBC
Passwords
Power Management
Printers
Regional Settings
Sounds
System
Telephony
Users
7 object(s)
My Computer

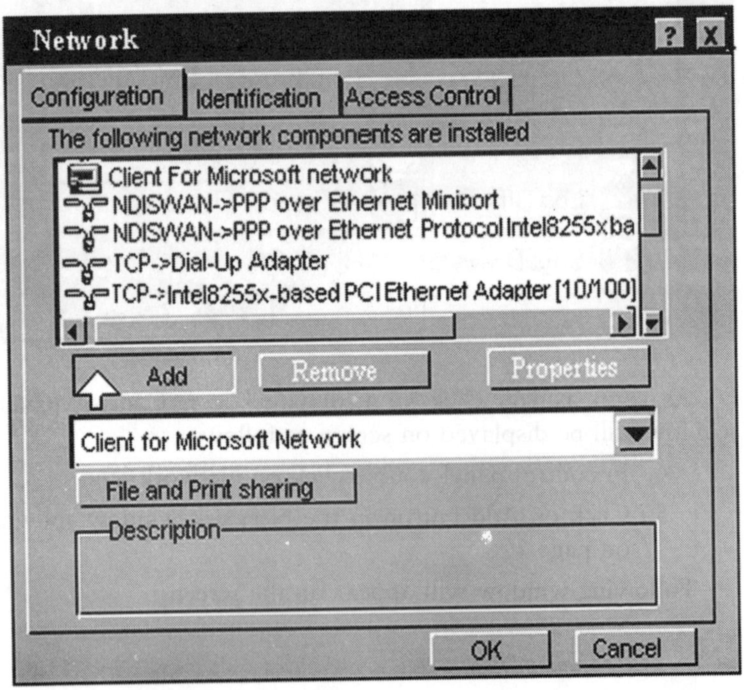
Network
Configuration
Identification
Access Control
The following network components are installed
Client For Microsoft network
NDISWAN->PPP over Ethernet Miniport
NDISWAN->PPP over Ethernet Protocol Intel8255x ba
TCP->Dial-Up Adapter
TCP->Intel8255x-based PCI Ethernet Adapter [10/100]
Add
Remove
Properties
Client for Microsoft Network
File and Print sharing
Description
OK
Cancel

6. Select Service by clicking mouse on it from the network component.

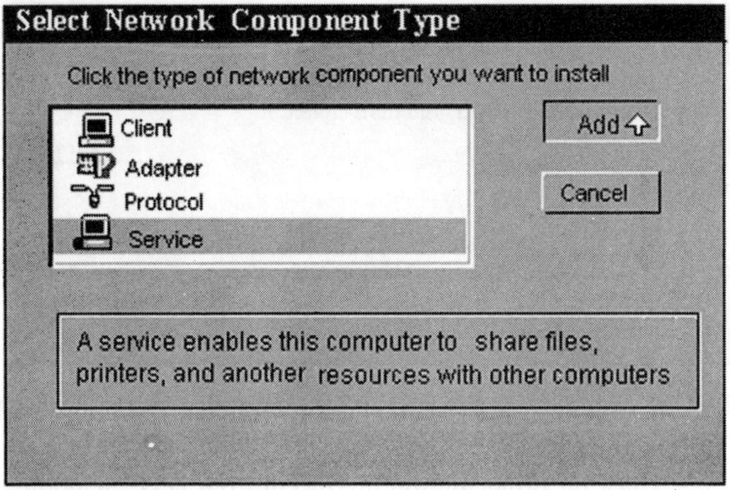

7. Click on the Add button. Following window will appear.

Network Services will be added and you can see it in the list box.

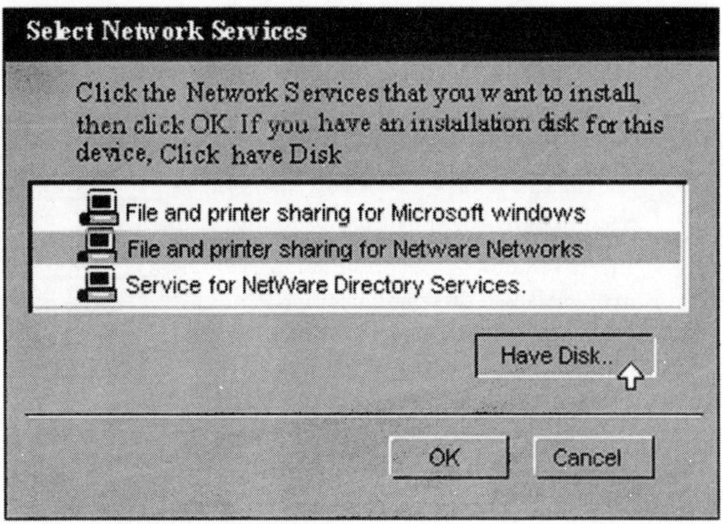

8. Select File and printer sharing for NetWare Networks from the list.

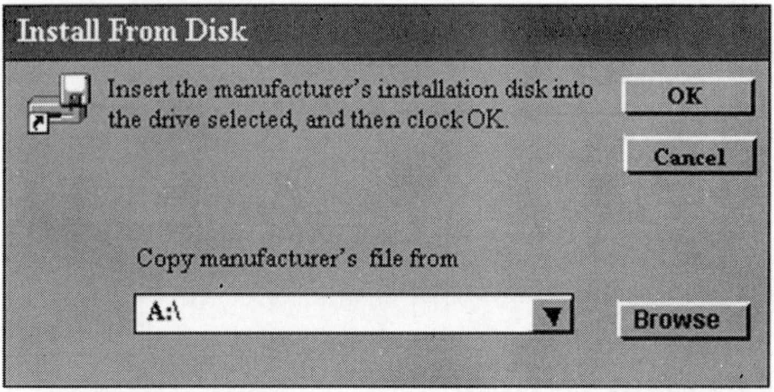

9. Click on Have Disk button. Following window will appear.

9. Click on Brows button in "Install from Disk" window.

The following "Copying Files" window will appear.

The "Copying File Window" will prompt you to insert the (Window98SE) Disk in CD-ROM.

Insert the Disk (Window98SE) into CD-ROM

Click Browse button.

10. Select CD-ROM drive and then click open.

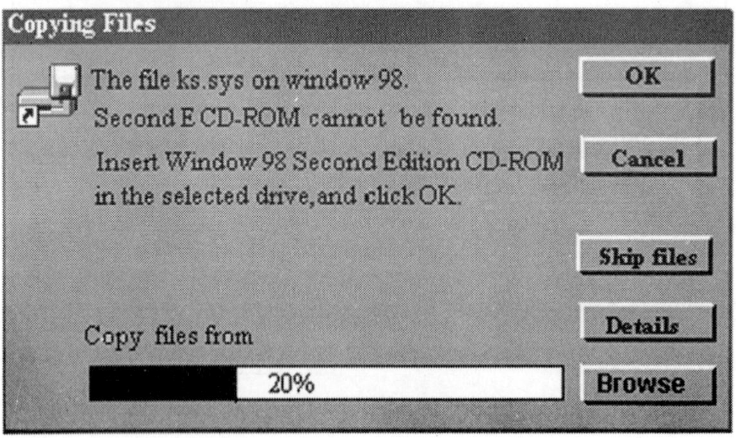

11. After selection of CD-ROM drive click OK in "File Copying Window".

Installation of program will start and you can see the progress in "File Copying Window".

After installation of the shared files and printer you are prompted to restart your computer.

12. Restart the computer.

13. Open the Network window by clicking Network icon in the control panel.

You will get the following window.

You can see the text "File and printer sharing for NetWare network" is added in the Network window.

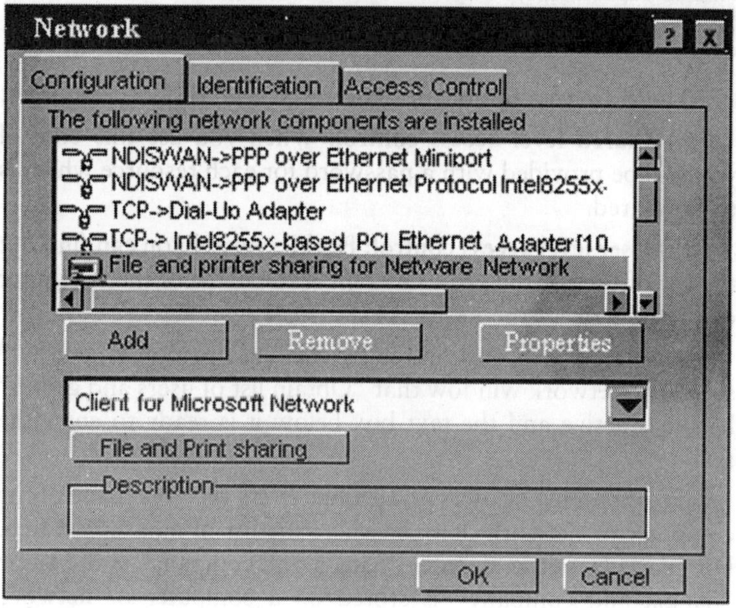

To install file or print sharing for NetWare networks, you must have user-level access control.

To control access by using a list of names:

1. Open the Network window.
2. Click on Access Control.

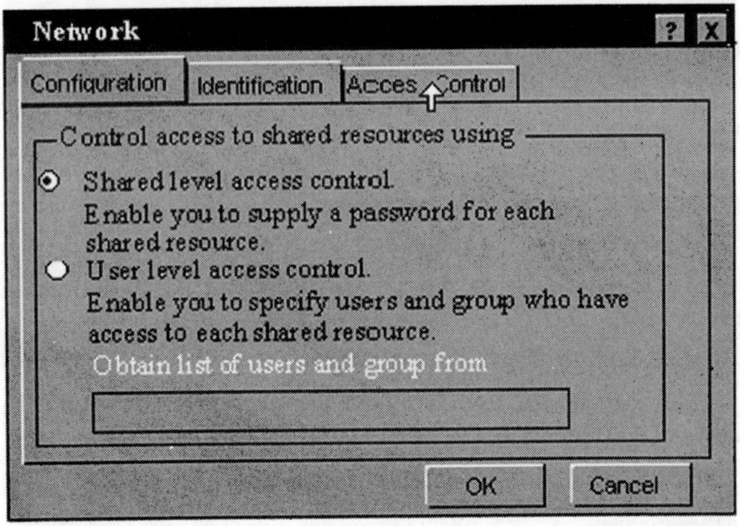

There are two options for control access to share resources.

(i) **Shared level access control:** When you use this control you will be provided with a password for each resource which is to be shared.

(ii) **User level access control:** By this control you can find out the list of user or the group by typing the name of the computer or the domain of the network.

3. Select the second option by clicking the mouse. You will see in the network window that "Obtain list of users and group" becomes active and the text box below it is ready to enter the text.

To obtain list of users and groups from, type the name of the computer or network domain where the list of names is stored. For example, you may enter "Sangia and company" if the name "Sangia and company" is stored on a computer or network domain list. The User-level access control is applicable only when our network is configured for it. In case of any problem you can consult with the network service provider.

Files and printers are shared by others.

1. If you want that your files are printers are shared by others then click in the network window on File and Print sharing button.

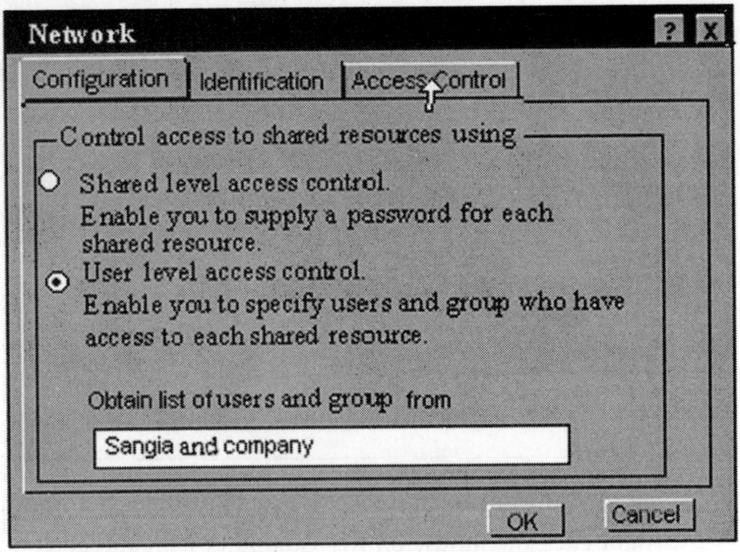

File and Print sharing window will appears.

There are two check boxes you will see in the File and Print sharing window.

2. Check both the boxes.

Now your computer is configured for files and printers shared by others.

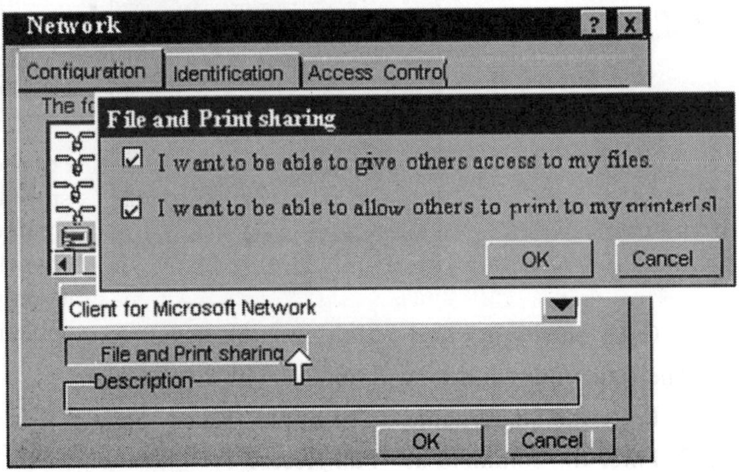

Marking files or folders which are to be shared by others.

3. Click on My Computer icon on the Desk top. The following window will appear.

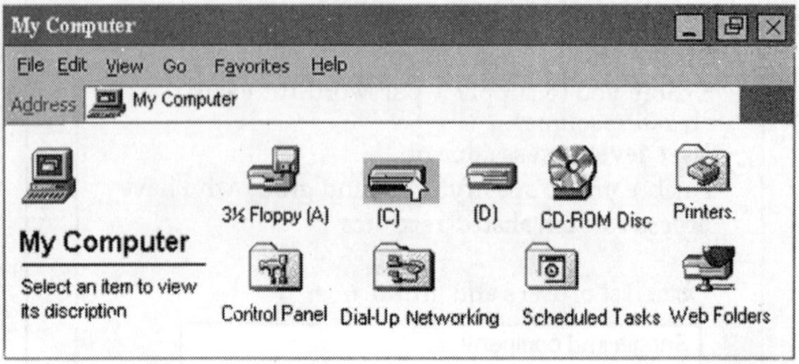

Suppose you want to share My Document folder by others.

4. Right click the mouse on My Computer icon and click on sharing. You will see a pop down menu.

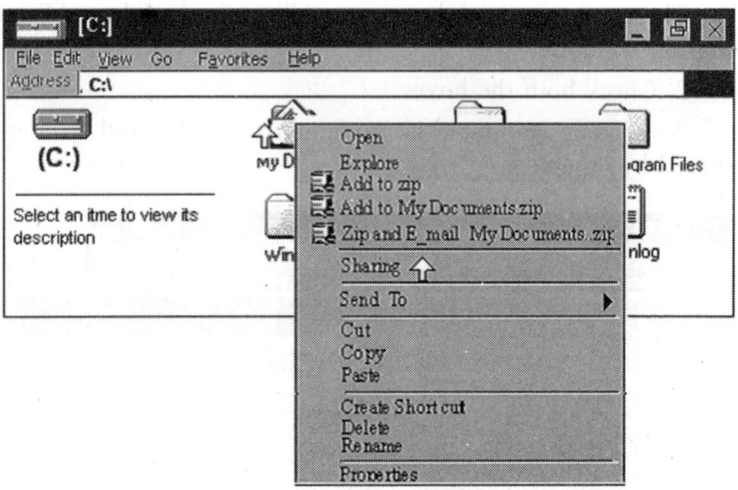

5. Click on sharing in the above.pop up menu.

The following window will appear with two sections:

1. Enter the Share name for example "Rajeev Sangia".

2. Enter the comment as "Full Access".

There are three options for Access type:

(a) Read only

(b) Full

(c) Depend on password

6. Select the option you like.

Suppose you select Full option.

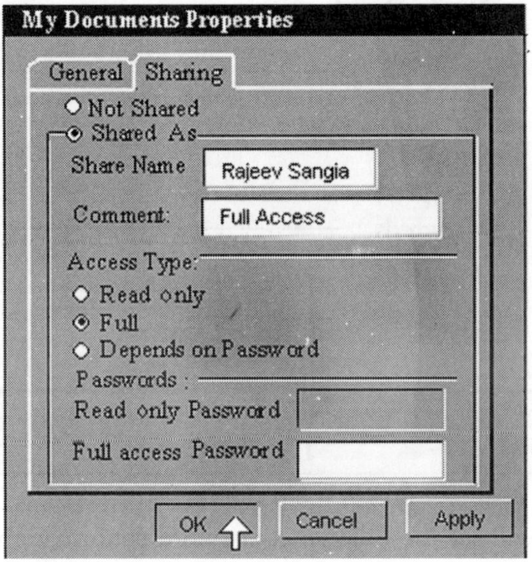

Read only password text boxes will become inactive while full access password will remain active.

7. Enter the password and then click OK.

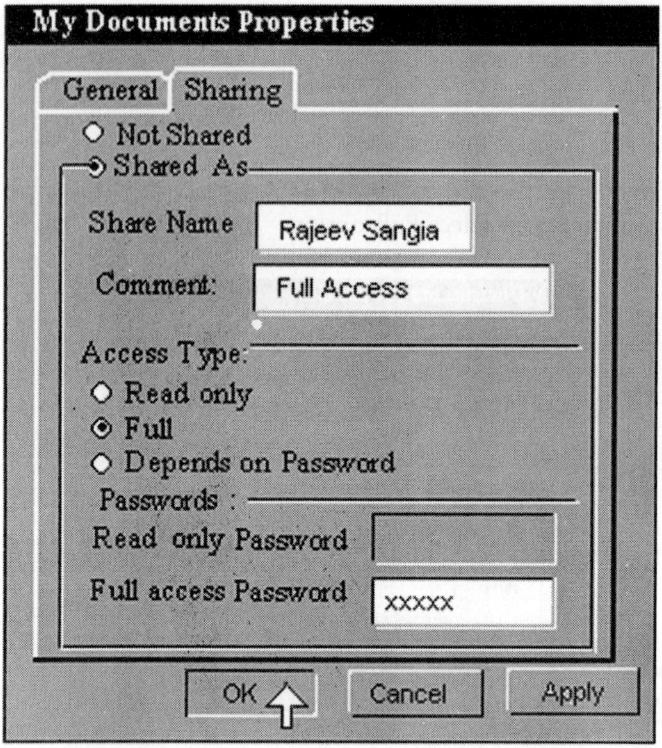

You will see the following password confirmation window on the screen.

8. Retype the same password and click OK.

Now Rajeev Sangia as user and has full access to share My Document folders.

Printer and Fax sharing on window Xp.

1. Click on Start button.
2. Go to Setting.
3. Click on Printers and Faxes from the side menu.
4. Right-click the Printer(1), you want to share, and then click sharing.
5. A Properties window will appear.
6. You will find two options in this window:
   (i) Do not share the printer.
   (ii) Share the printer.
7. Chose Share the printer.
8. Type the name of the printer.
9. Click OK.

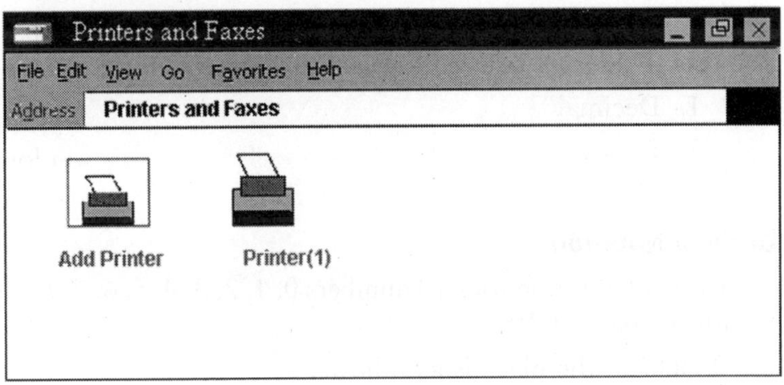

If you are using different version of window then you have to install an additional driver.

10. Click on Additional Driver button.
11. Install the driver through CD-ROM and after installation restart the computer.
12. Now check the file and printer sharing.

Network Addressing System

11

Addressing terms

The following terms are base of network addressing.

Bit: A bit is binary number that uses, 1 or 0.

Byte: Byte is group of eight bits, for example 00010001.

Network addressing uses three types of numbers to form four bytes IP address.

IP address uses 32 bits in four section. Each section consists of eight bits or a byte.

This IP address may be indicated by three notations:

1. Decimal
2. Binary
3. Hexadecimal

Decimal Notation

Decimal notation uses 10 numbers 0, 1, 2, 3, 4, 5, 6, 7, 8 and 9 with the base of 10.

Weight of the place is as follows:

First place $10^0 = 1$

Second place $10^1 = 10$

Third place $10^2 = 100$

Fourth place $10^3 = 1000$

Nth place $10^n = 1$ (with n zeros)

We calculate the value of a digit at its place by multiplying with 10n, where n is the number of place and adds all the individual values and find the total value.

Consider the digit 1234. Start from right to left 4 is at the place of Ones, 3 is at the place of Tens, 2 is at the place of Hundreds, 1 is at the place of Thousands

$1\times10^3 + 2\times10^2 + 3\times10^1 + 4\times10^0$

$1\times1000 + 2\times100 + 3\times10 + 4\times1$

$1000 + 200 + 30 + 4 = 1234$

Binary Number

Binary numbers contains 0 and 1. Their counting can be done on the basis of the decimal digits.

Counting Binary Numbers

Suppose you want to count from 0 to 10000 the number which contains 0 and 1 are:

Range	Binary numbers	Decimal equivalent
From 0 to 10	0, 1 and 10	0, 1 and 2
From 11 to 100	11 and 100	3 and 4
From 101 to 1000	101, 110, 111 and 1000	5, 6, 7 and 8
From 1001 to 10000	1001, 1010, 1011, 1100, 1101, 1110, 1111, 1,0000	9, 10, 11, 12, 13, 14, 15, 16

Normal decimal numbers and Binary number.

We count a decimal number, by considering the position of number from left to right as oncs, tens, hundreds, thousands, ten thousands, hundred thousands and so on.

For decimal notation we use power of 10 like 10^0, 10^1, 10^2, 10^3, 10^4 and so on to denote the position of number. The base digit is 10.

For binary notation we use power of 2 like 2^0, 2^1, 2^2, 2^3, 2^4 and so on to denote the position of number.

In binary notation base digit is 2. The number are called octet.

Octet Number		Decimal Number
2^0	=	1
2^1	=	2
2^2	=	4
2^3	=	8
2^4	=	16
2^5	=	32
2^6	=	64
2^7	=	128
2^8	=	256

Conversion of binary number to decimal number.

Consider the binary number 101010. It contains six digits:

1 0 1 0 1 0

$2^5 \times 1 + 2^4 \times 0 + 2^3 \times 1 + 2^2 \times 0 + 2^1 \times 1 + 2^0 \times 0$

Write the power of 2 starting from 0 to 5 from left to right and multiply by 0 or 1 as per bit position:

$32 \times 1 + 16 \times 0 + 8 \times 1 + 4 \times 0 + 2 \times 1 + 1 \times 0$

$32 + 0 + 8 + 0 + 2 + 0 = 42$ Decimal number

For conversion of binary number into decimal number take the following steps:

1. Write the binary number.
2. Consider the numbers of bits.
3. Write the power of 2 starting from 0 to maximum number of bits with plus sign from left to right as shown above.
4. Calculate the each 2 with its power and multiply with 0 or 1 according to the position in binary number.
5. Add all the numbers, you will get a decimal equivalent of the given binary number.

Conversion of decimal number to binary number.

The best procedure to convert the decimal number into binary number is to divide the decimal number by 2 and then divide the quotient by 2 and continue the process till the quotient becomes zero.

Let us convert the decimal number 187 to binary.

	Quotient	Remainder	
2	187	1	——— Least significant bit
2	93	1	
2	46	0	
2	23	1	
2	11	1	
2	5	1	
2	2	0	
2	1	1	——— Most significant bit

Write the most significant bit first and the least significant bit in the last.

You will get the binary number 10111 011 equivalent to decimal number 187.

Hexadecimal Number

Hexadecimal number are used when we want to denote the higher value decimal number. It is difficult to convert a high value decimal number into binary because it will contain a large numbers of 0s and ones. Hexadecimal number contains the symbols from 0, 1, 2, 3, 4, 5, 6, 7, 8, 9, A, B, C, D, E and F. The base is used in this case is 16. Here A, B, C, D, E and F denote the numbers 10, 11, 12, 13, 14 and 15. Only four bits are used to represent a hexagonal digit.

Table of hexagonal digit

Binary	Hexagonal	Decimal
0000	0	0
0001	1	1
0010	2	2
0011	3	3
0100	4	4
0101	5	5

0110	6	6
0111	7	7
1000	8	8
1001	9	9
1010	A	10
1011	B	11
1100	C	12
1101	D	13
1110	E	14
1111	F	15

Conversion from Hexadecimal to Decimal

$$\begin{aligned}(C6B1)_{16} &= 12 \times 16^3 + 6 \times 16^2 + 11 \times 16^1 + 1 \times 16^0 \\ &= 12 \times 4096 + 6 \times 256 + 11 \times 16 + 1 \times 1 \\ &= 49152 + 1536 + 176 + 1 \\ &= 50865\end{aligned}$$

Network Addressing

Network addressing specify the address of network.

IP address of the computer and the address of the NIC card have unique addresses.

Network address is called network number and associated with the IP address.

Network address is unique therefore it is never duplicated. For example, 192.168.1.2 is the IP address of source or destination which consists of four bytes.

First two bytes 192.168 indicate the network address.

Last two bytes 1.2 indicate the node address.

The node address is also unique.

Several computers with their unique addresses can share a single network address.

Network can be classified into five categories on the basis of network-IP or Host-ID.

Class of network	First Byte	Second Byte	Third Byte	Fourth Byte
Class A	Network-ID	Host-ID	Host-ID	Host-ID
Class B	Network-ID	Network-ID	Host-ID	Host-ID
Class C	Network-ID	Network-ID	Network-ID	Host-ID
Class D			Multicast Addresses	
Class E			Reserved	

Example of A, B and C type of network address

10.0.0.0	First one byte is used for in A type network.
172.32.0.0	First two bytes are used in class B type network.
192,164.2.0	First three bytes are used in class C network.

Class A Network

Class of network	First Byte	Second Byte	Third Byte	Fourth Byte
Class A	Network-ID	Host-ID	Host-ID	Host-ID

Range for Class A Network Address

The first bit of the first byte in a Class A network remains always off and represented by 0.

Now turning off all the remaining seven bits, you will get 00000000 = 0

Turning on all the remaining seven bits, you will get 01111111 = 127

Range of Network Address of Class A type of Network

1st	2nd	3rd	4th	5th	6th	7th	8th		
off	off	off	off	off	off	off	off		
0	0	0	0	0	0	0	0	=	0
off	on	on	on	on	on	on	on		
0	1	1	1	1	1	1	1	=	127

This means a Class A address must be between 0 and 127.

0 is the invalid bit to represent any network address and 127 reserved for loop-back testing.

Network address 127 is used for loop-back testing. This network address is allotted to all local machine that transmits the data to itself. No internet connection is required in this case.

Valid Host Address in Class A Type Network

Here's an example of how to figure out the valid host IDs in a Class A network address: Consider the IP address 10.0.0.0 where 10 represent the network address .0.0.0 represents the zero host on the network while in case of IP address 10.255.255.255, 10 is the network address and 255.255.255 represents the maximum number of host.

Decimal form		Binary form	
N.H.H.H.		Network Host .host .host	
10.0.0.0	=	00001010.00000000.00000000.00000000	(1)
10.255.255.255	=	00001010.11111111.11111111.11111111	(2)

For the valid host IDs: All the bits in host section can't 0 or 1.

For forming the valid host ID we replace the last bit of the fourth byte, 0 by 1 in the equation (1) and 1 by 0 in the equation (2) as follows:

Decimal form		Binary form	
10.0.0.1	=	00001010.00000000.00000000.00000001	(3)
10.255.255.254	=	00001010.11111111.11111111.11111110	(4)

10.0.0.1 indicates a single valid host in the network and 10.255.255.254 indicates the maximum number of host in the network.

Class B Network

Class of network	First Byte	Second Byte	Third Byte	Fourth Byte
Class B	Network-ID	Network-ID	Host-ID	Host-ID

Range for Class B Network Address

The first bit of the first byte in a Class B network remains always on and represented by 1 but the second bit is kept always off and represented by 0.

Keeping first bit on and second bit always off.

1. Turning off all the remaining six bits, you will get 10000000 = 128
2. Turning on all the remaining six bits, you will get 10111111 = 191

Range of Network Address of Class B type of Network

1st	2nd	3rd	4th	5th	6th	7th	8th		
on	off	off	off	off	off	off	off		
1	0	0	0	0	0	0	0	=	128
on	off	on	on	on	on	on	on		
1	0	1	1	1	1	1	1	=	191

Class B address is denoted by decimal number from 128 to 191.

Valid Host Address in Class B Type Network

Decimal form		Binary form	
N.N.H.H.	=	Network . Network . Host . Host	
172.32.0.0	=	10101100.00100000.00000000.00000000	(5)
172.32.255.255	=	10101100.00100000.11111111.11111111	(6)

For the valid host IDs: All the bits in host section can't 0 or 1.

For forming the valid host ID we replace the last bit of the fourth byte 0 by 1 in the equation (5) and 1 by 0 in the equation (6) as follows:

Decimal form		Binary form	
172.32.0.1	=	10101100.00100000.00000000.00000001	(7)
172.32.255.254	=	10101100.00100000.11111111.11111110	(8)

Host address represented from 172.16.0.1 to 172.16.255.254 are valid.

Class C Network

Class of network	First Byte	Second Byte	Third Byte	Fourth Byte
Class C	Network-ID	Network-ID	Network-ID	Host-ID

Range for Class C Network Address

In class C network first 2 bits are kept on and represented by 1 and the third bit is kept always off and denoted by 0.

It means first three bits are fixed and remaining five bits vary.

Keeping first two bits always on and third bit always off.

Now turning off all the remaining five bits, you will get 11000000 = 192.

Turning on all the remaining five bits, you will get 11011111 = 223.

Range of Network Address of Class B type of Network

1st	2nd	3rd	4th	5th	6th	7th	8th		
on	on	off	off	off	off	off	off		
1	1	0	0	0	0	0	0	=	192
on	on	off	on	on	on	on	on		
1	1	0	1	1	1	1	1	=	223

This indicates that the class C network address range is from 192 to 223.

Valid Host Address in Class C Type Network

If you denote the broadcasting address as 192.160.12.0. Fourth byte contains 0, that indicates there is no host connected with the network 192.160. For broadcasting a message there must be maximum number of host connected with that network. If in the broadcasting address 192.160.12.0 we replace the 0 by 255 the broadcasting address becomes 192.160.12.255.

The broadcasting can be carried out to all the host. Decimal number 255 is denoted in binary form as 11111111. For the valid host IDs.

All the bits in host section can't 0 or 1, therefore in the fourth byte we replace first seven bits by 0 and last bit by 1.

The byte becomes as 00000001 = 1.

In other process we turn on first seven bits on and turn off the last bit.

The byte format becomes 11111110 = 254.

The range from 192.160.12.1 to 192.160.12.254 is the valid number for host address.

Class D Network

Class of network	First Byte	Second Byte	Third Byte	Fourth Byte
Class D			Multicast Addresses	

Range for Class D Network Address

Class D network address ranges from 224 to 239. In class C network first 3 bits are kept on and fourth bit is kept always off. It means first four bits are fixed and remaining four bits vary. Keeping first three bits always on and fourth bit always off. Now turning off all the remaining four bits, you will get 1110000 = 224.

Turning on all the remaining four bits, you will get 11101111 = 239.

Range of Network Address of Class D type of Network

1st	2nd	3rd	4th	5th	6th	7th	8th		
on	on	on	off	off	off	off	off		
1	1	1	0	0	0	0	0	=	224
on	on	on	off	on	on	on	on		
1	1	1	0	1	1	1	1	=	239

Class E Network

Class of network	First Byte	Second Byte	Third Byte	Fourth Byte
Class E			Reserved	

Range for Class E Network Address

Class E network address ranges from 240 to 255. In class E network first 4 bits are kept on. It means first four bits are fixed and remaining four bits vary. Keeping first four bits always on.

Now turning off all the remaining four bits, you will get 11110000 = 240.

Turning on all the remaining four bits, you will get 11111111 = 255.

Range of Network Address of Class D type of Network

1st	2nd	3rd	4th	5th	6th	7th	8th	
on	on	on	on	off	off	off	off	
1	1	1	1	0	0	0	0	= 240
on	on	on	on	on	on	on	on	
1	1	1	1	1	1	1	1	= 255

Class E network address is used for research and scientific applications.

IP Addressing

Each host on a TCP/IP network is assigned a unique 32 bits logical address. This IP address is divided into two main parts. Two left hand side parts, each consist of 8 bits indicates the network number and the two right hand side parts which also comprises of 8 bits each, indicates the host number. The network number is provided by the Internet Network Information Center. Internet Service Provider (ISP) can obtain blocks of network addresses from the Internet Network Information Center. The host number is assigned by the local network administrator.

IP Address Format

The 32-bit IP address is arranged in a group eight bits at a time. It is separated by dots, and represented by dotted decimal notation. For example, 192.168.1.1

In a binary notation this is 11000000 10101000 00000001 00000001.

IP Address Classes

IP addressing supports five categories of address classes. They are defined A, B, C, D, and E. A, B, and C are the only IP address classes available for commercial use. These classes are already explained above.

The class of address can be known by the first octet of the address and the class range as given in the following table.

Class of Network	Network Address Range in Decimal	Bits Palced in First Byte
Class A	1 to 126	0
Class B	128 to 191	10
Class C	192 to 223	110
Class D	224 to 239	1110
Class E	240 to 254	1111

In an IP address of 174.30.1.2, for example, the First octet 174 of IP address 174.30.1.2 falls between 128 and 191, so it is a Class B address.

If first octet of the network address falls in between 1 and 126, then it is Class A network.

If first octet of the network address falls in between 192 and 223, then it is Class C network.

If first octet of the network address falls in between 224 and 239, then it is Class D network.

If first octet of the network address falls in between 240 and 254, then it is Class E network.

IP Subnet Addressing

IP Sub network is a small network that is formed by dividing the IP network.

Sub-netting provides the following extra facility to network administrator.

1. More efficient use of network addresses.
2. Control over the broadcast traffic.
3. Broadcast cannot cross a router.

Subnets are used by local administration. It is understood by the main network administration that organization is a single network. The main network does not know about the internal structure of the organization.

For example, consider the following four bytes address 172.16.0.0. The first two bytes are 172.16 represent the network address and next two zeros represent it as complete network address because there is no host.

Network address can be broken up into many sub-networks like 172.16.5.0, 172.16.6.0, 172.16.7.0, and 172.16.8.0 are all subnets within network 170.6.0.0.

IP Subnet Mask

Subnet masks have the four bytes separated by dot similar to IP address. First and second bytes indicate the network, third byte indicates the subnet while fourth byte indicate the host. Example of subnet mask address is 255.255.255.0.

In binary form it is represented by 11111111 11111111 11111111 00000000.

Following table shows the sub-netting for class B network.

Number of Bits	Subnet Mask	Number of Subnets	Number of Hosts
2	255.255.192.0	2	16382
3	255.255.224.0	6	8190
4	255.255.240.0	14	4094
5	255.255.248.0	30	2046
6	255.255.252.0	62	1022
7	255.255.254.0	126	510
8	255.255.255.0	254	254
9	255.255.255.128	510	126
10	255.255.255.192	1022	62
11	255.255.255.224	2046	30
12	255.255.255.240	4094	14
13	255.255.255.248	8190	6
14	255.255.255.252	16382	2

Sub-netting for class C network is shown in the following table.

Number of Bits	Subnet Mask	Number of Subnets	Number of Hosts
2	255.255.255.192	2	62
3	255.255.255.224	6	30
4	255.255.255.240	14	14

5	255.255.255.248	30	6
6	255.255.255.252	62	2

Subnet Masks are used to decide the Network Number

The router is responsible to determine the sub-network address. It finds out the IP address of destination from the packet it received. From this IP address it retrieves the sub-netmask.

For determining the network number router performs a logical and operation.

This action of router removes host part of the destination IP address but the destination network number remains the same.

Now router checks the destination network number for matching it with an outgoing interface. After getting the network number, it forwards the frame to the destination IP address.

12 LAN Maintenance

The WAN is consists of group of LANs.

The following are the main areas of troubleshooting which are concerned with LAN:

1. Modem Trouble.
2. Improper configuration of modem.
3. Communication Port COM-1 or COM-2 Problem.
4. Network Adapters Problem.
5. Internet Explorer Trouble.
6. Internet Connection Sharing Trouble.
7. File and Printer Sharing Trouble.

1. Modem Trouble

If your modem does not work, you may not be able to connect your computer with the net. Modem may not function due to the following reasons:

1. The modem is unsuitable for the system.
2. Improper connections.
3. Improper configuration of network protocol.

1. The modem is unsuitable for the system. There are five types of modem used with internet network:

1. Internal or external basic type of modem.
2. DSL broadband modem.
3. Cable modem.
4. Wireless modem.
5. Analog or ISDN modem.

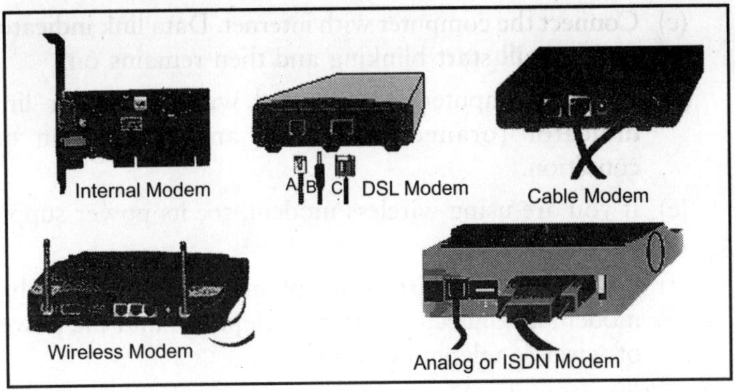

Select the modem according to the type of network connection.

2. Improper connections. In case of improper connections do the following physical check-ups:

1. Check the telephone line connection.
2. See that telephone is kept properly on the cradle.
3. If you are using external modem, see that electric supply of modem is on.
4. If your modem is DSL broad band modem as shown below.

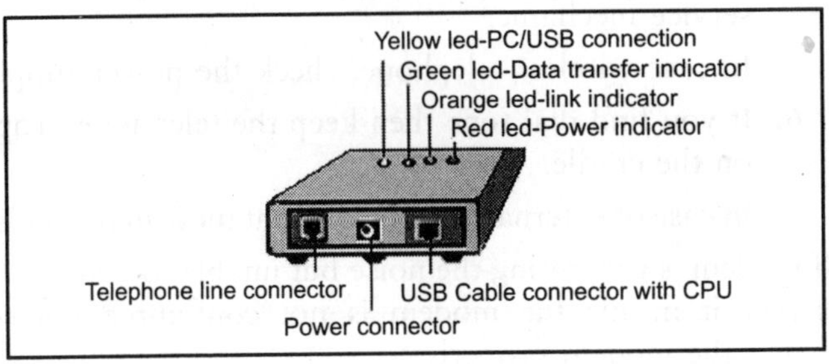

Check that all the four light indicators are on:

(a) Check the electric power connection first. It is shown by red indicator.

(b) Yellow light will blink and becomes stable if modem and PC connection is ok.

(c) Connect the computer with internet. Data link indicator (green) will start blinking and then remains on.

(d) If your computer is connected with the server link indicator (orange) will blink and remains in on condition.

(e) If you are using wireless modem, see its power supply is on.

(f) If you are using wireless telephone connection, see that modem is connected with the telephone and the power of wireless telephone is on.

Modem does not make any sounds

If your modem is configured for dial-up networking, it makes dialing noise and noise stops, when the connection is established with the server. If modem does not make any noise, it indicates that cable connections are not proper.

In this case check the following points:

1. Check the connection of telephone line with the modem.
2. Check the telephone is working by checking the dial tone.
3. If the dial tone is missing, check the telephone line.
4. Still you do not hear the dial tone, call telephone service mechanic.
5. In case wireless telephone, check the power supply.
6. If you find dial tone then keep the telephone properly on the cradle.
7. In case of external modem, see that modem power is on.

If modem is generating the noise but unable to connect with the server it means the modem is not configured correctly. Configure the modem properly.

3. Improper configuration of network protocol. If you have configured the internet protocol incorrectly you may get the following message when you try to connect the computer with the network:

1. The protocol is not configured.
2. A dial-up connection could not be established.

Open internet explorer and click on Tool.

Following Internet Option window appears.

Click on Connection Tab.

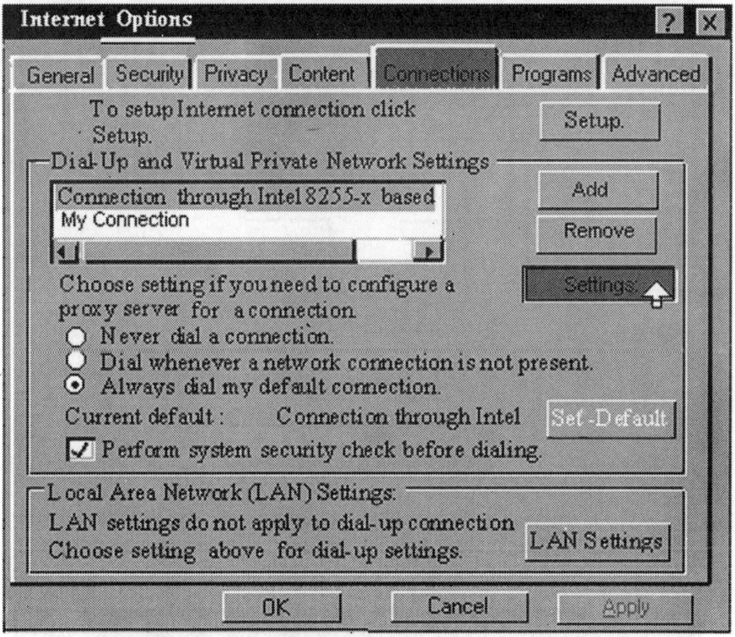

Select the internet connection from the Dial-up and Virtual Private Network Settings box and then click on Settings button. Following window appears which is shown on page 204.

Click on Properties button.

You will see the another window under General button.

Click on Server Type tab of the window which is shown on page 205.

In the "Allowed network protocols" section, click on TCP/IP check box so that check box is checked. If already checked keep it as it is. Remove the check sign from NetBEUI and IPX/SPX Compatible check boxes by clicking on them. Now click on OK. Now you have configured the internet connection for TCP/IP protocol.

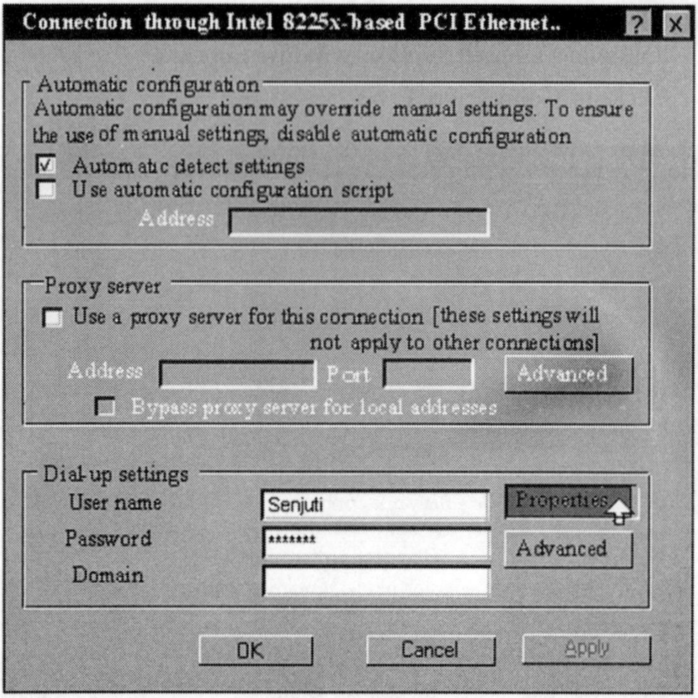
Connection through Intel 8225x-based PCI Ethernet..
Automatic configuration
Automatic configuration may override manual settings. To ensure the use of manual settings, disable automatic configuration
Automatic detect settings
Use automatic configuration script
Address
Proxy server
Use a proxy server for this connection [these settings will not apply to other connections]
Address
Port
Advanced
Bypass proxy server for local addresses
Dial-up settings
User name
Senjuti
Password
Domain
Properties
Advanced
OK
Cancel
Apply

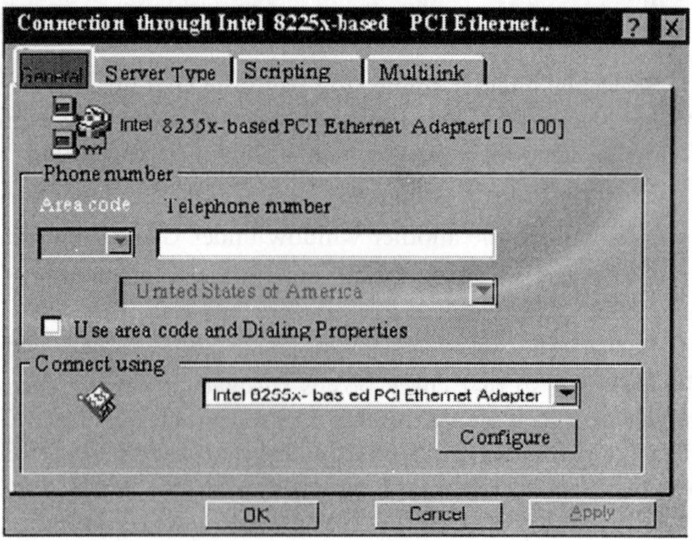
Connection through Intel 8225x-based PCI Ethernet..
General
Server Type
Scripting
Multilink
Intel 8255x-based PCI Ethernet Adapter[10_100]
Phone number
Area code
Telephone number
United States of America
Use area code and Dialing Properties
Connect using
Intel 8255x- bas ed PCI Ethernet Adapter
Configure
OK
Cancel
Apply

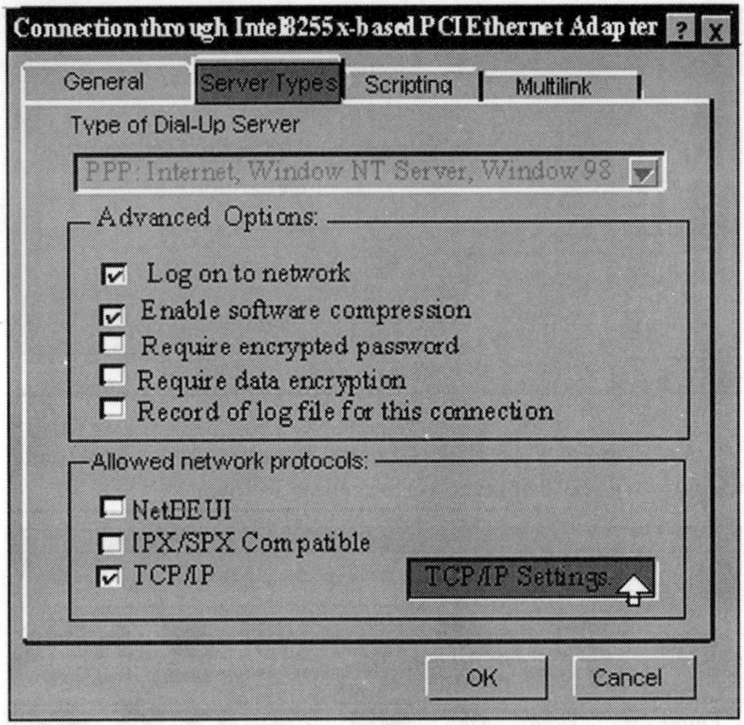

If you are using dedicated internet connection and unable to connect your computer with internet.

Solution: Your network may be provided with dedicated (24 hours Internet service) internet connection facilities then you have to configure the TCP/IP properties by providing the following addresses:

IP address,

Subnet mask address,

Default gateway address,

DNS server address.

During use of internet sometimes the above addresses are vanished. Follow the steps as given below.

Click Start button at the task bar then go to settings and then click on control panel as directed in the following figures.

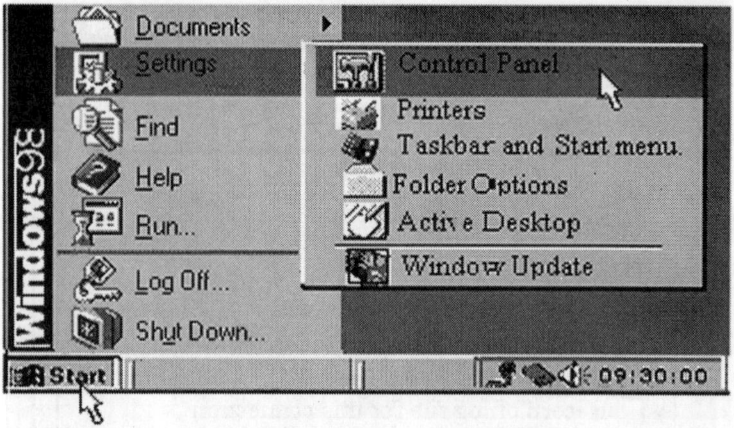

As soon as you click Control Panel icon Control panel window will be displayed on screen as follows:

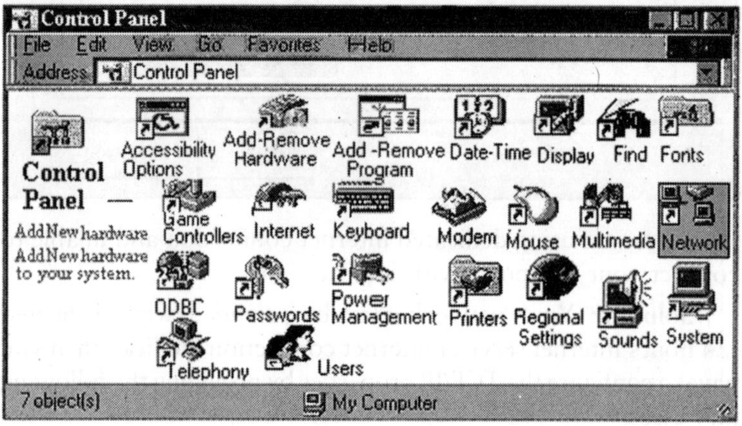

Double click on the Network icon. If you are using Windows XP. The following Network Connections window appears on the screen. If you are using Windows 98 you will get the Local Area Connection Properties window on the screen.

Select Local Area Connection and right click and then click on Properties. Following Local Area Connection Properties window will appear on the screen. There are following line of text along with some other network elements appears in the Local Area connection window.

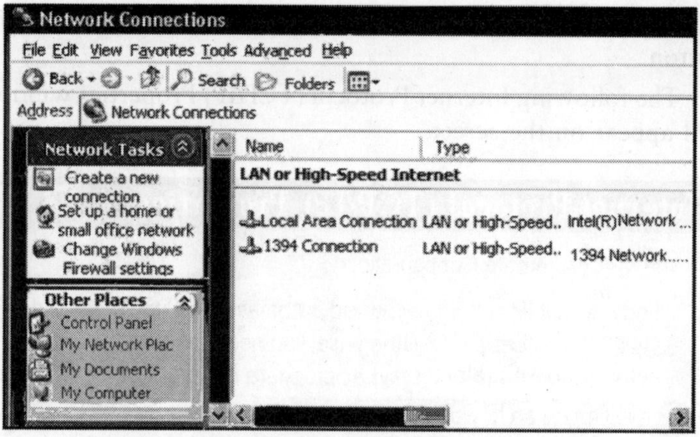

1. Client for Microsoft network.
2. File or printer sharing for Microsoft networks.
3. QoS Packet scheduler.
4. Internet Protocol [TCP/IP].

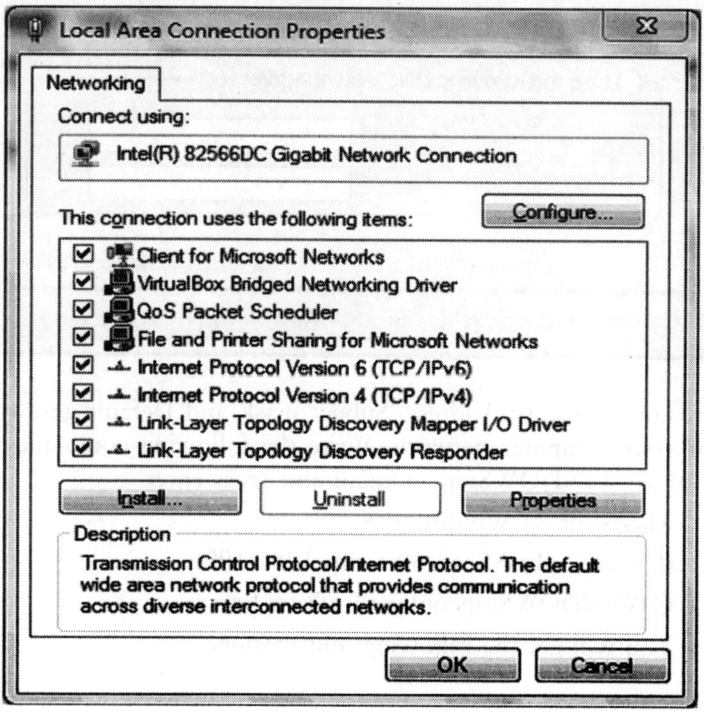

Select Internet Protocol (TCP/IP) and click on Properties button.

The following Internet Protocol (TCP/IP) Properties window will appear on the screen.

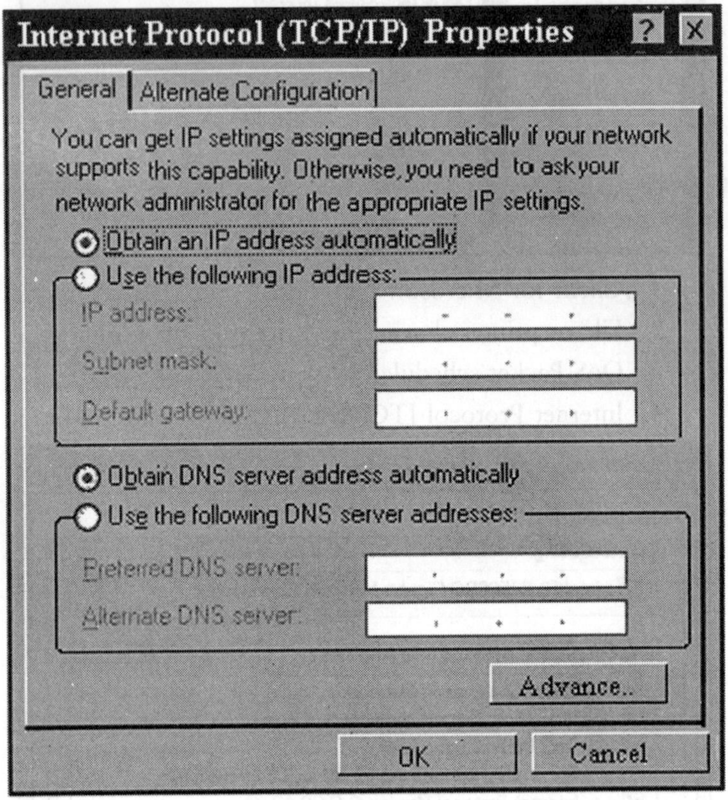

For getting IP Address, Subnet mask and Default gateway for your computer network. Write the following command in DOS C:\WINDOWS>ipconfig/all and press enter.

Microsoft(R) Windows 98

(C)Copyright Microsoft Corp 1981-1999.

C:\WINDOWS>ipconfig/all <Press Enter>

You will get the following information:

Windows 98 IP configuration

Host Name . . . . : SANGIA

DNS Servers . . . . : 192.168.1.1

Node Type . . . . : Broadcast

NetBIOS Scope ID . . . . . . :

IP Routing Enabled . . . . . : No

WINS Proxy Enabled . . . . . : No

NetBIOS Resolution Uses DNS : No

0 Ethernet adapter

Description . . . . : PPP Adapter

Physical Address . . . . . : 44-45-53-54-00-00

DHCP Enabled . . . . : Yes

IP Address . . . . : 0.0.0.0

Subnet Mask . . . . : 0.0.0.0

Default Gateway . . . . . . :

DHCP Server . . . . : 255.255.255.255

Primary WINS Server . . . . :

Secondary WINS Server . . . :

Lease Obtained . . . . . . :

Lease Expires . . . . :

1 Ethernet adapter

Description . . . . : Intel(R) PRO PCI Adapter

Physical Address . . . . . : 00-D0-B7-E4-5F-E5

DHCP Enabled . . . . : Yes

IP Address . . . . : 192.168.1.2

Subnet Mask . . . . : 255.0.0.0

Default Gateway . . . . . . : 192.168.1.1

DHCP Server . . . . : 192.168.1.1

Primary WINS Server . . . . :

Secondary WINS Server . . . :

Lease Obtained . . . . . . : 04 15 07 2:02:40 PM

Lease Expires . . . . :

C:\WINDOWS>

The detail information are for a particular computer. This may change with the another computer.

Type the following addresses in the first, second and third box respectively.

IP Address -- 192.168.1.2

Subnet mask address -- 255.0.0.0

Default gateway -- 192.168.1.1

Type the following addresses in the fourth and fifth box respectively.

Preferred DNS server address -- 202.56.230.6

Alternative server address -- 202.56.224.153

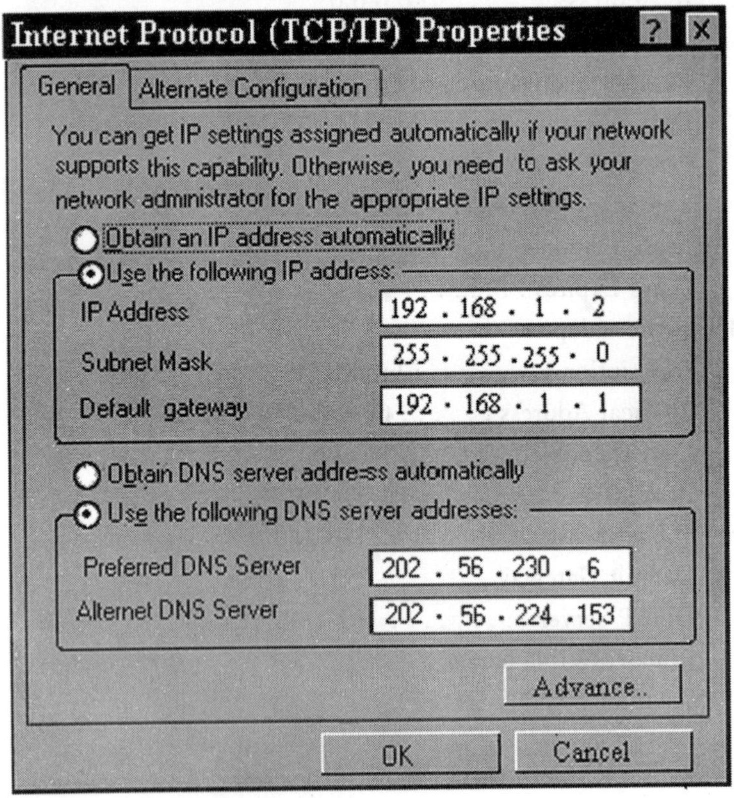

Click OK button. Configuration IP/TCP setting is completed.

The IP address, Subnet mask, and default gateway addresses you may get from the DOS but the Preferred DNS Server and Alternate DNS Server addresses you have to get from the internet service providing authority.

3. Communication Port COM-1 or COM-2 Problem

You will not be able to connect your computer with internet, if the COM port is disabled.

Making COM-port enabled:

1. Right click on My Computer icon on the Desk Top.

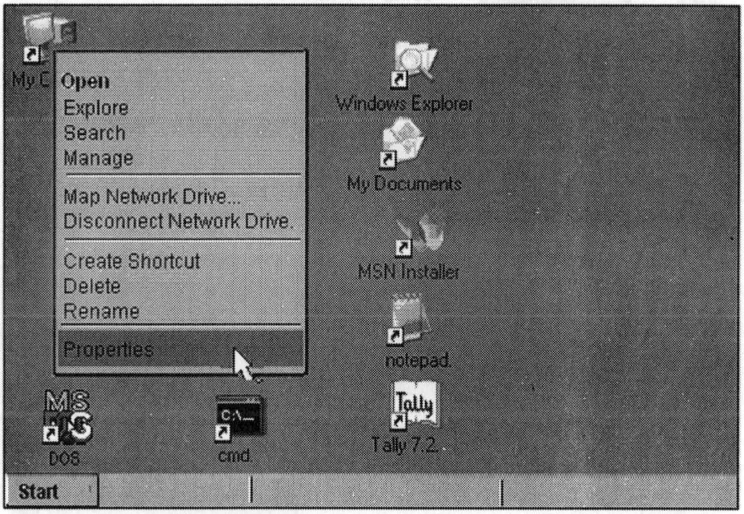

2. Click on Properties.

System Properties window will open with General button.

3. Click on Hardware button on page 212.

Following System Properties window appears as shown on page 212.

4. Click on Device Manager button on page 212.

Following Device Manager window will open as shown on page 213.

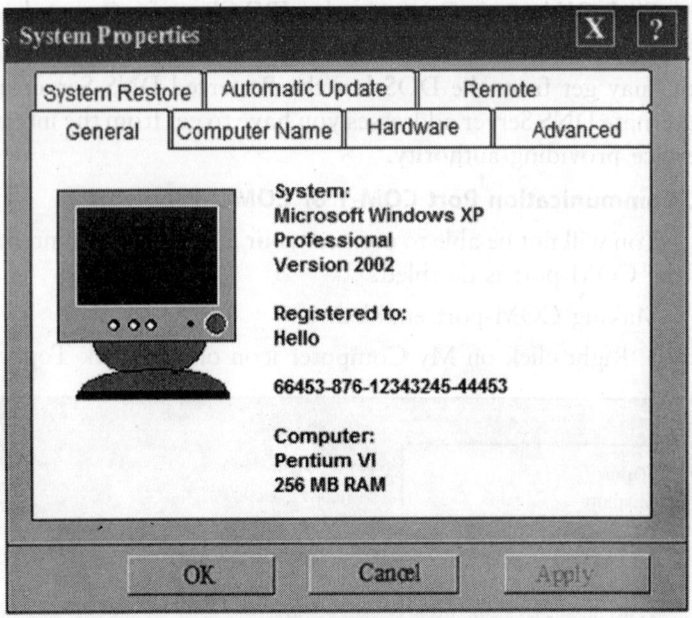
System Properties
System Restore
Automatic Update
Remote
General
Computer Name
Hardware
Advanced
System:
Microsoft Windows XP
Professional
Version 2002
Registered to:
Hello
66453-876-12343245-44453
Computer:
Pentium VI
256 MB RAM
OK
Cancel
Apply

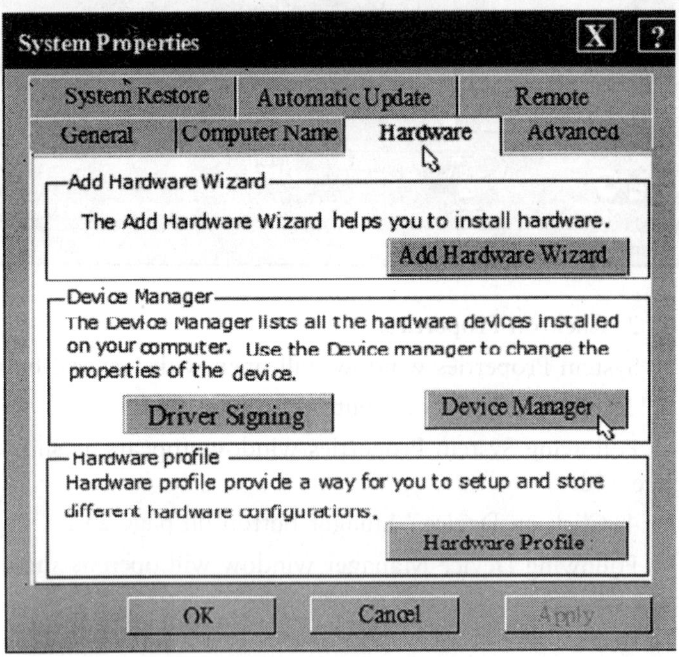
System Properties
System Restore
Automatic Update
Remote
General
Computer Name
Hardware
Advanced
Add Hardware Wizard
The Add Hardware Wizard helps you to install hardware.
Add Hardware Wizard
Device Manager
The Device Manager lists all the hardware devices installed on your computer. Use the Device manager to change the properties of the device.
Driver Signing
Device Manager
Hardware profile
Hardware profile provide a way for you to setup and store different hardware configurations.
Hardware Profile
OK
Cancel
Apply

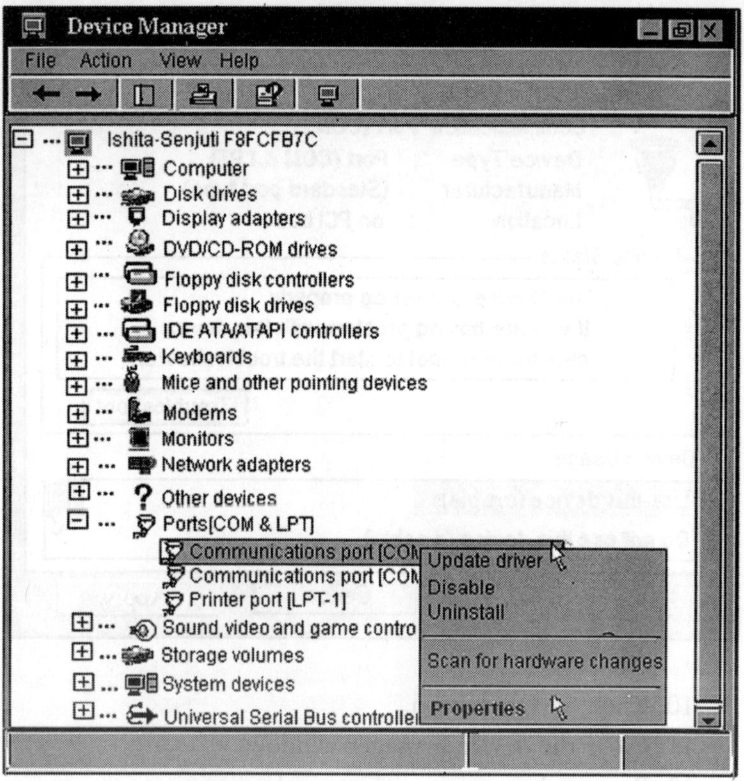

5. Select the item Port [COM & LPT] and click on plus sign. Below Port [COM & LPT] you will see three items.

6. Select Communications port [COM-1]

7. Right click on it.

8. Click on properties.

Communication port [COM-1] properties window will appear as shown on page 214.

At the bottom of window you see a combo box with the text as given below:

1. Use this device (enable).
2. Do not use this device (disable).

9. Click on arrow of combo box and select the text "Use this device (enabled)".

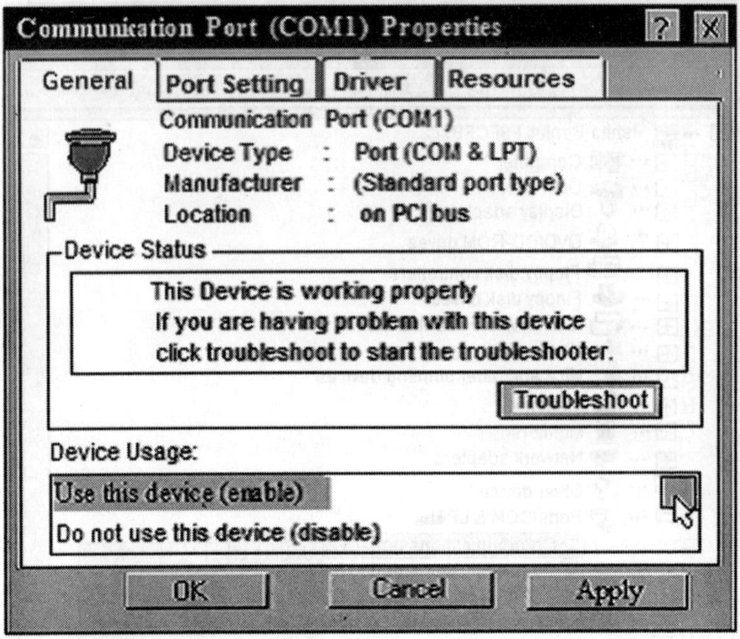

10. Click on OK button.
11. Close the device manager window.
12. Restart the computer to store the setting.

You can connect your computer to internet now.

4. Network Adapters Problem

Basic internal or external modem are directly connected with motherboard through telephone cable connection, while Broadband modem require an Ethernet adapter. For DSL Broadband Modem you have to install an Ethernet adapter. If the network adapter is not functioning you will not be able to connect your computer with internet.

This is due to the following reasons:

1. Network adapter may be disabled.
2. Driver for Network adapter is either improper or not installed at all.

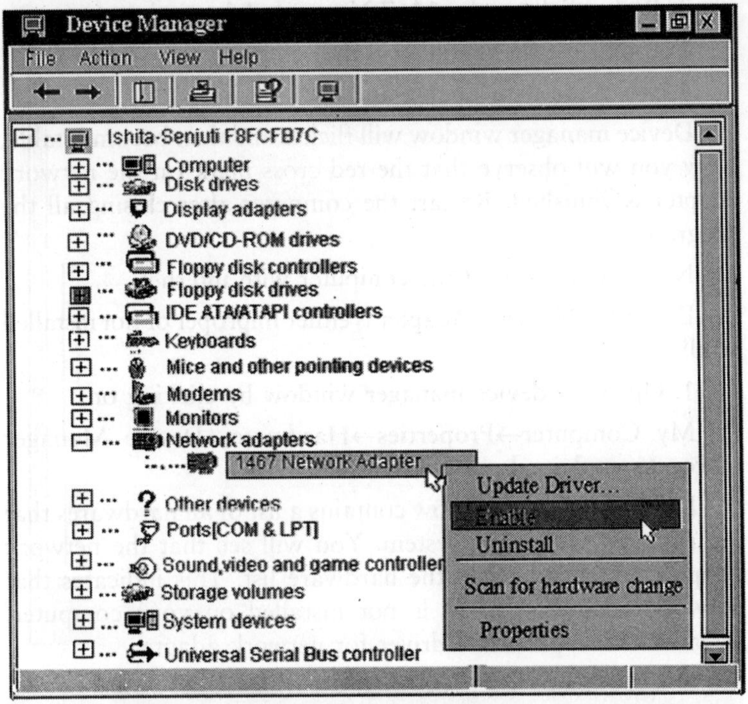

Carryout the following actions:

1. Open the device manager window by clicking on.

My Computer→Properties→Hardware→Device Manager button as explained previously.

2. Click on the plus sign of Network Adapters, as indicated in above window.

Network adapter with specific name will appear below the expanded view.

This is the adapter that is installed on the motherboard of your computer.

Here the name of a particular network adapter is 1467 Network Adapter.

If you see a red cross marks in front of the adapter, this indicates that the adapter is unabled to function.

3. Right click on the 1467 Network Adapter icon:

You will see the menu strip that contains five items.

4. Select the item Enable and click on it:

Device manager window will flicker and then become stable. Now you will observe that the red cross mark on the network adapter is vanished. Restart the computer after closing all the programs.

Now try to connect the computer with internet.

Driver for Network Adapter is either Improper or not installed at all

1. Open the device manager window by clicking on:

My Computer→Properties→Hardware→Device Manager button as explained previously.

Device manager window contains a list of all hardwares that are installed with your system. You will see that the network adapter in not visible in the hardware list. This indicates that network adapter's driver is not installed on your computer. Installed the appropriate driver for network adapter.

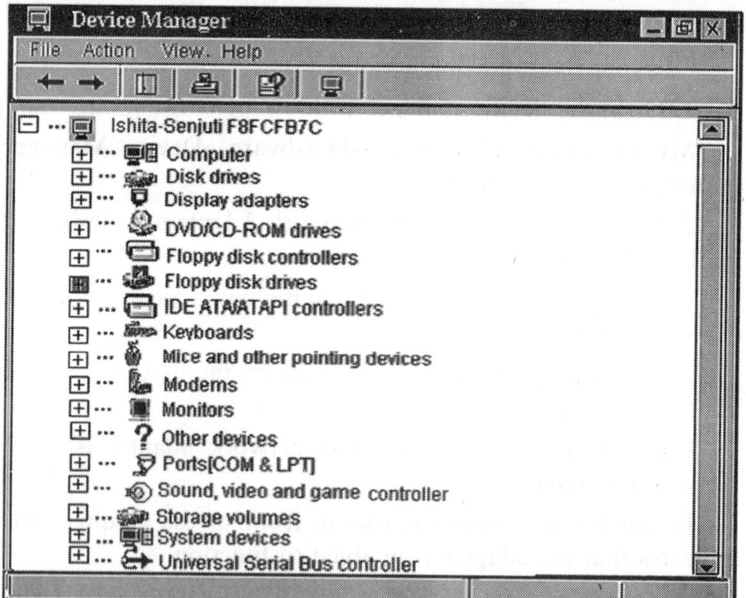

Installation of Network Adapter for DSL Broadband Modem

For installation of Network Adapter for DSL Broadband Modem follow the following steps:

1. Close all programs and shut down the computer.
2. Switch off the main supply.
3. Open the side or top cover of CPU.
4. Fix the Ethernet adapter on PCI slot on the motherboard.
5. Screw the strip of Ethernet adapter with the cabinet.
6. Connect the Ethernet adaptor with the DSL Modem by Ethernet cable.
7. Connect the DSL modem with telephone line.
8. Fix back the cabinet cover.
9. Switch on your computer.
10. BIOS will start searching all the hardware which are installed on the computer.
11. Computer will display message that "New hardware is found". Next you will get a message that "Please Wait

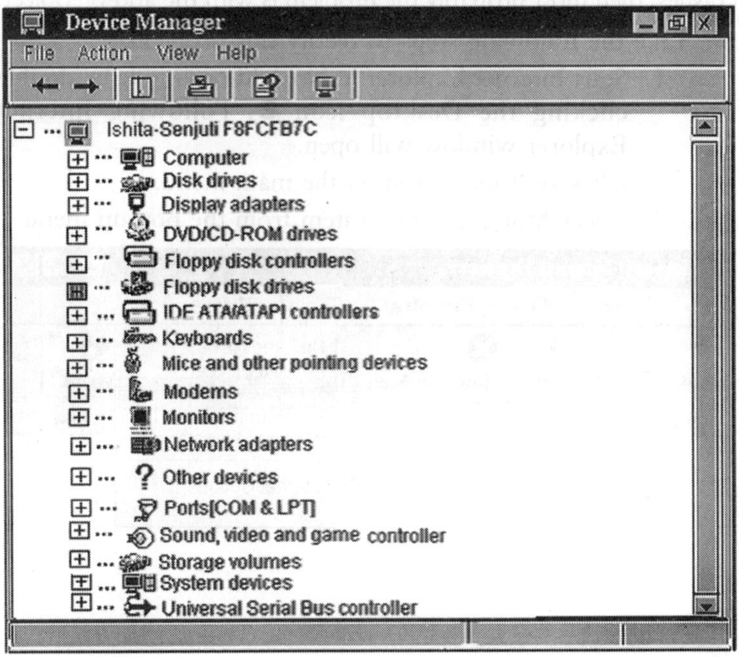

while System" is searching for a suitable driver. For your newly installed hardware.

12. If the driver is available with your "Windows Operating System", system will automatically installed the driver for Ethernet adaptor.
13. After installation of suitable driver system will display a message window to restart the computer.
14. Click OK and restart the computer.
15. Click on My Computer→Properties→Hardware→ Device Manager button as explained previously.
16. Check the adapter is included in device manager list or not.

5. Internet Explorer Trouble

1. Internet Explorer Crashes or hangs.
2. Particular web site is not opening in Internet Explorer.
3. Internet Explorer runs slowly.

1. Internet Explorer Crashes or hangs. If Internet Explorer crashes, then most probably the problem is with the add-on object.

Take the following steps to rectify this problem:

1. Start Internet Explorer in No Add-ons mode by double clicking the Desktop icon. Following Internet Explorer window will open.
2. Click on tool button on the main menu.
3. Select Manage Add-on item from the pop-up menu.

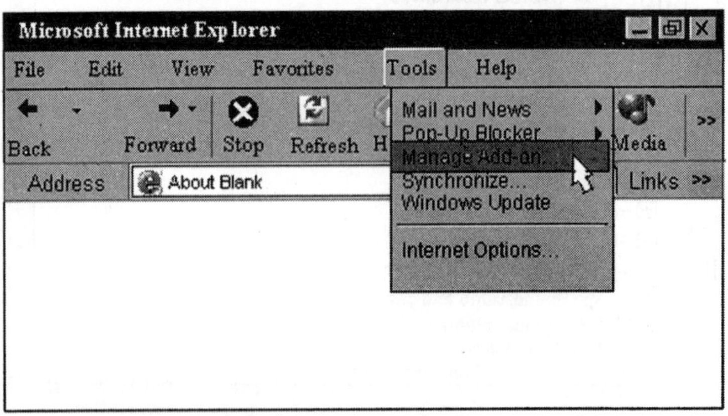

Following Manager Add-on window will open.

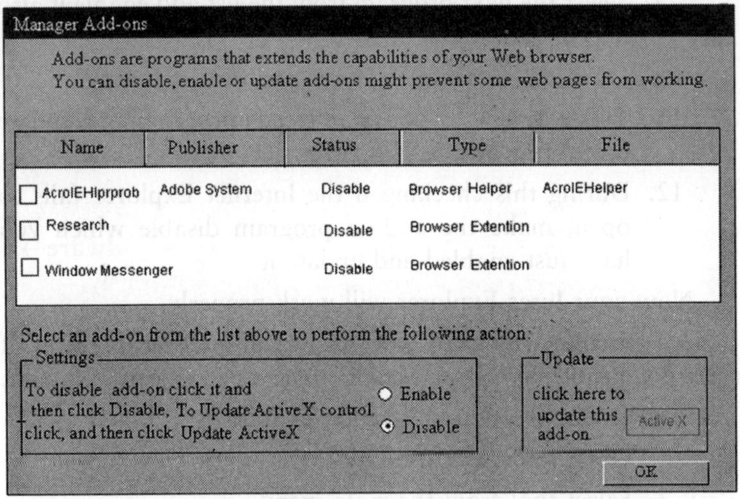

You will see a list of add-on programs. In this list of program, some program prevents some web page from working.

If you select any of the program from the list, the Setting and Update sections become active.

If you deselect the program from the list, the Setting and Update sections become inactive.

In the setting section there are two options:

(i) Enable

(ii) Disable

When you open the Manager Add-on window some program may be enable or disable.

4. Select the program one by one and disable them.
5. After disabling all the listed program start the Internet Explorer.

As you are opening the Internet Explorer without add-on. It will open without any problem.

6. If you want to know which program is creating problem.
7. Select the first program from the list and then enable it and click on Update button.

8. Open the Internet Explorer and test its function.
9. Select the next program from the list and enable it also and update it.
10. Open the Internet Explorer and test its function.
11. This way one by one enable each program and update it and test Internet Explorer.
12. During this checking if the Internet Explorer fails to open, make the add-on program disable which you have just enabled and update it.

Now your Inter Explorer will work properly.

2. Particular web site is not opening in Internet Explorer. If there is a problem with particular site to open in your browser.

You can set the pop-up blocker as follows:

1. Open Internet Explorer.
2. Select tool from the main menu.
3. Click on pop-up blocker item in the drop down menu.

The following pop-up window will be displayed on screen as shown on page 221.

4. Type the web site address in the text box in front of ADD button.

A list of web sites that you have used till now will be displayed automatically.

5. Select the site which is causing problem, from the list or type the full address of the site as www.mywebsite.com
6. Click on add button.

Now the site www.mywebsite.com is added in the list of pop-up blocker setting and allowed to be displayed by your browser.

When the URL are changed from http to https in security mode the execution of java scripts is switched off. The site, whose URL we type, in the address window of internet explorer, does not open.

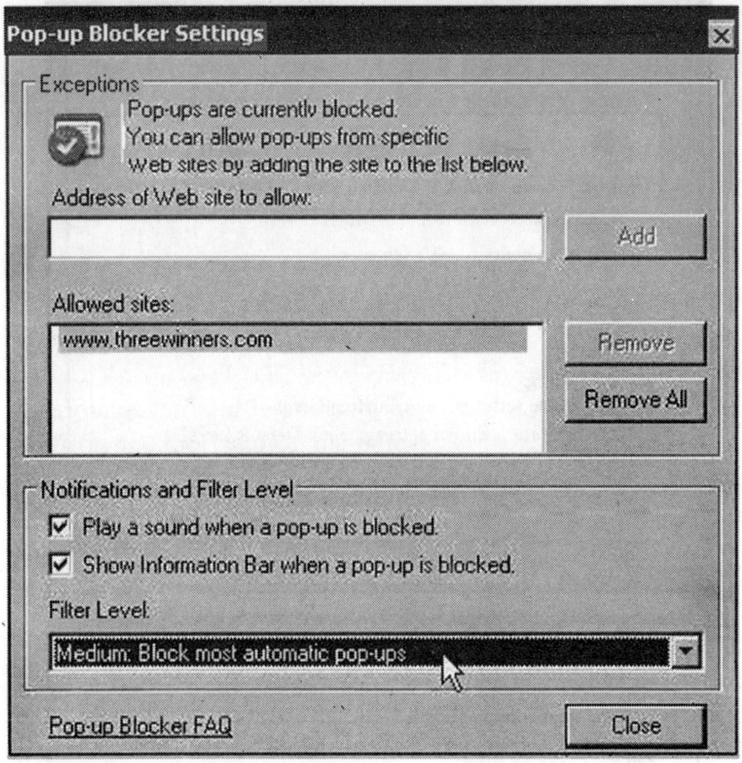

To solve this problem follow these steps:

1. Open Internet Explorer.
2. Select tool from the main menu.
3. Click on internet option from the drop down menu.
4. Following Internet option window will appear as shown on page 222.
5. Click on the Security tab at the top of the Internet option window.
6. Click on the Custom Level button below.

Following Security Setting window will appear on the screen as shown on page 222.

7. Scroll the settings box.
8. Find out Active scripting item.

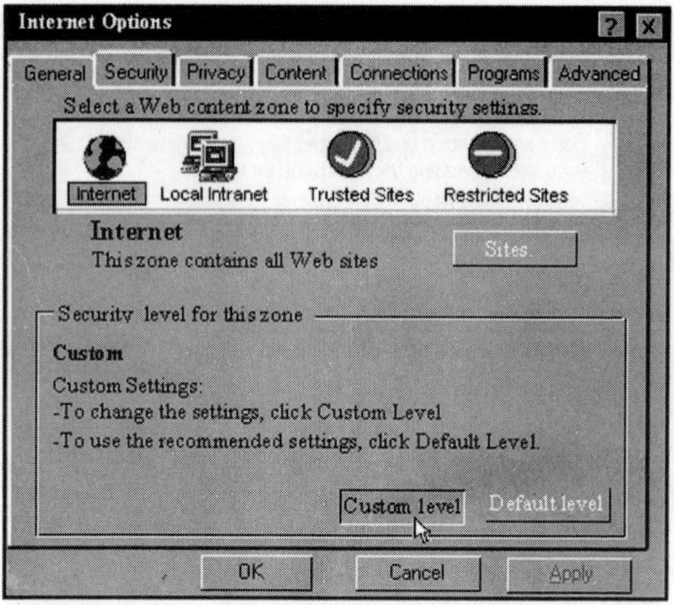
Internet Options
General
Security
Privacy
Content
Connections
Programs
Advanced
Select a Web content zone to specify security settings.
Internet
Local Intranet
Trusted Sites
Restricted Sites
Internet
This zone contains all Web sites
Sites.
Security level for this zone
Custom
Custom Settings:
-To change the settings, click Custom Level
-To use the recommended settings, click Default Level.
Custom level
Default level
OK
Cancel
Apply

Security Settings
Settings:
Scripting
Active scripting
Disable
Enable
Prompt
Allow paste operations via script
Disable
Enable
Prompt
Reset custom settings
Reset to:
Medium
Reset
OK
Cancel

9. Click on the enable option.
10. Finally click OK button.

The script is set to enable so you can see the web site which was not opening in your browser.

3. Internet Explorer runs slowly. Making Internet explorer to run faster:

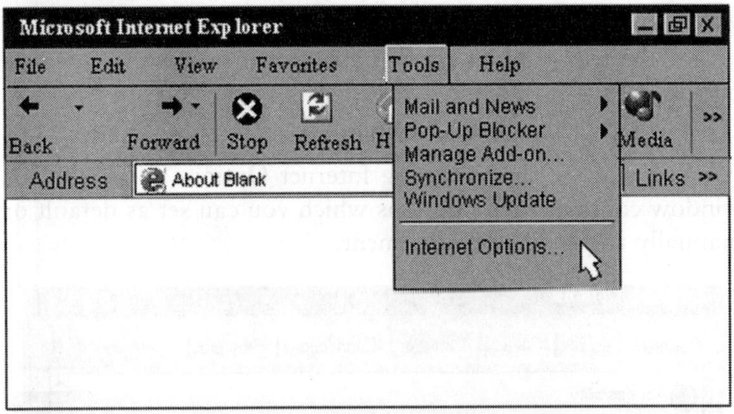

1. Click on Internet Explorer icon at the Task bar or double click it at desk top. The following Microsoft Internet explorer window will appear on the screen.

2. Go to Tools at the standard menu bar and click on it.

A list of sub-menu will appear below the Tools button.

3. Click on Internet Options, a window will appear on the screen.

At the top right of the window you can see the Advance button.

4. Click on the Advanced button.

You will see the following Internet Options window. This window contains many options which you can set as default or manually as per your requirement.

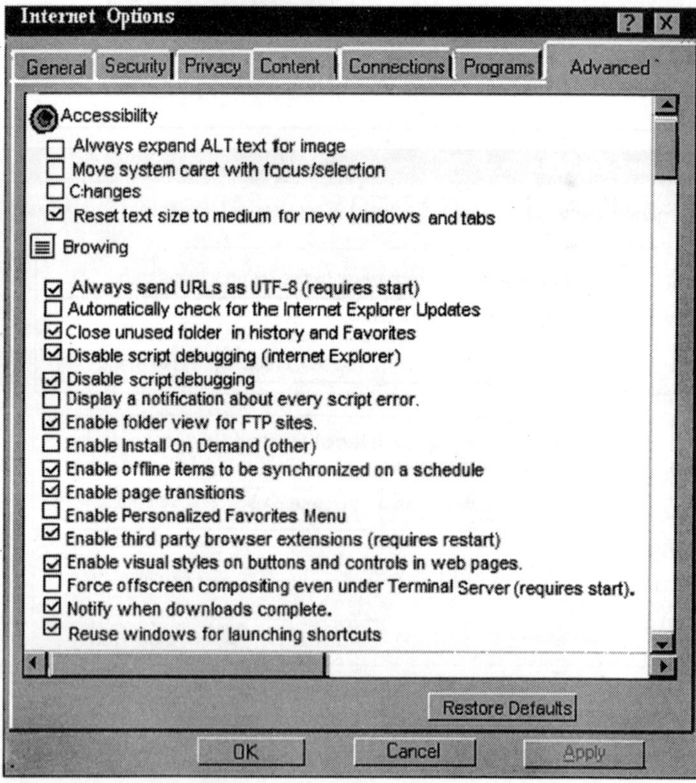

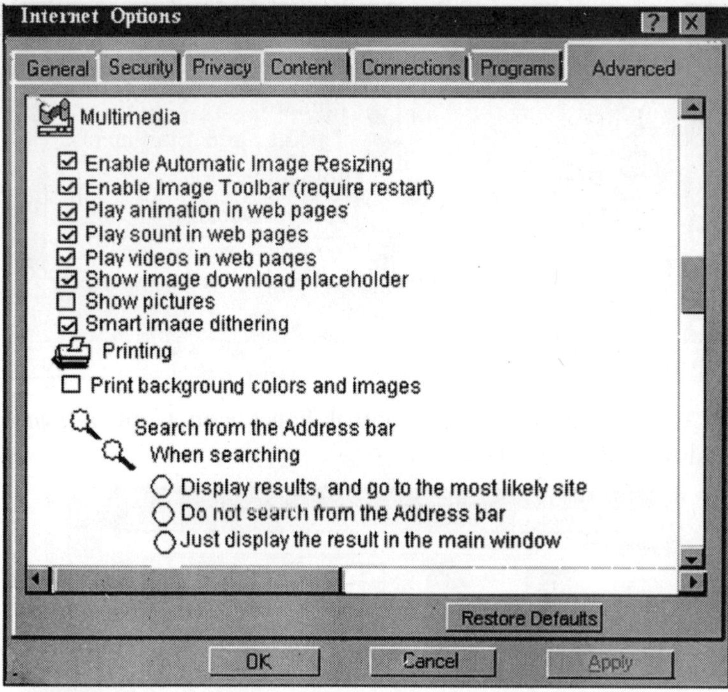

5. Scroll the above window and go to Multimedia.

Click on each check box under multimedia and remove the click sign.

Click on the Apply button. Restart the computer.

Start Internet explorer and connect it with the internet and see the result.

Your Internet explorer will run faster.

6. Internet Connection Sharing Trouble

Problem: Your computer does not share the internet connection with other computer.

If your computer is not sharing the internet connection with the other computer on your LAN.

Take the following steps:

1. Click Start then go to settings and then click on control panel as directed in the figure on next page 226.

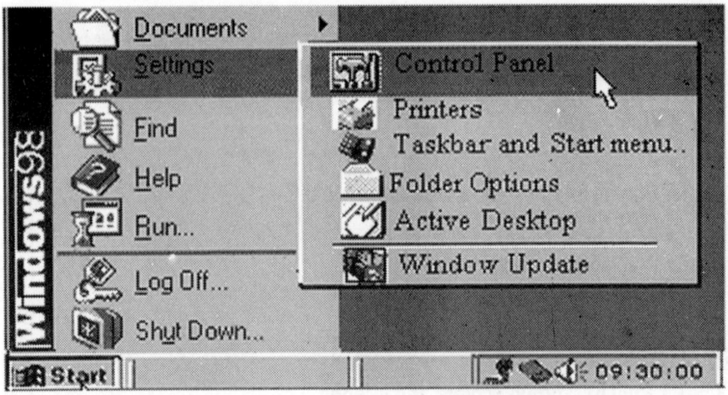

As soon as you click Control Panel icon Control panel window will be displayed.

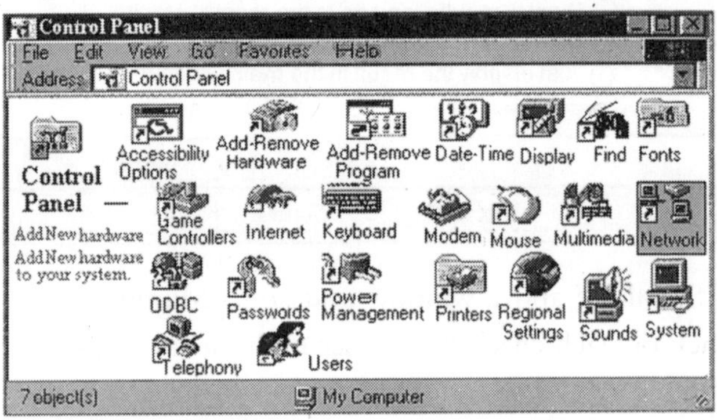

2. Click on Network Connection in the control panel. Following window will be displayed.

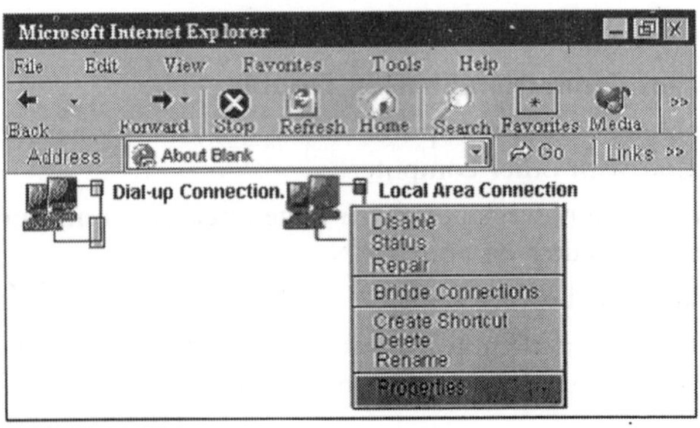

3. Right click the Local Area Connection icon.

4. Click on the Properties from the pop-up menu. You will get the following window.

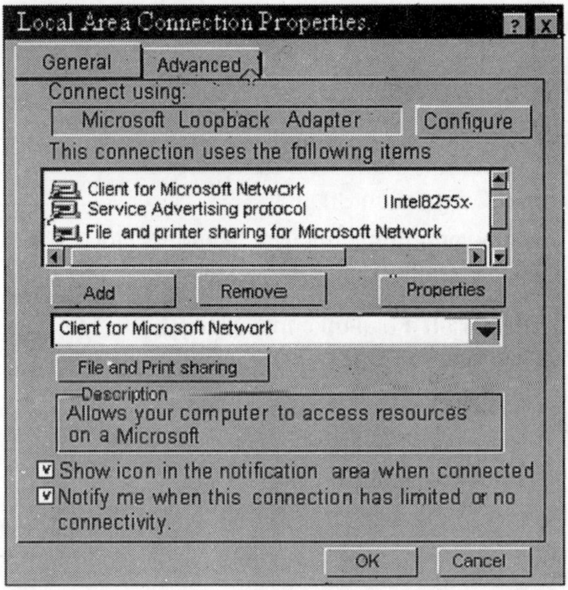

5. Click on Advanced button. You will get the following window Sharing Internet connection with Dial-up connection.

If you are sharing a dial-up Internet connection:

1. Right click on the dial-up icon.

2. Click on the Properties from the pop-up menu.

You will get a "Dial-up connection properties window" opened with General Tab, as shown on page 229.

3. In this "Dial-up connection properties window" click on the "Advanced".

Following "Dial-up connection properties window" with "Advanced" tab will appear on the screen.

Internet connection section contains three check boxes.

Top check box with the following text is active.

Allow other network user to connect through this computer's Internet connection.

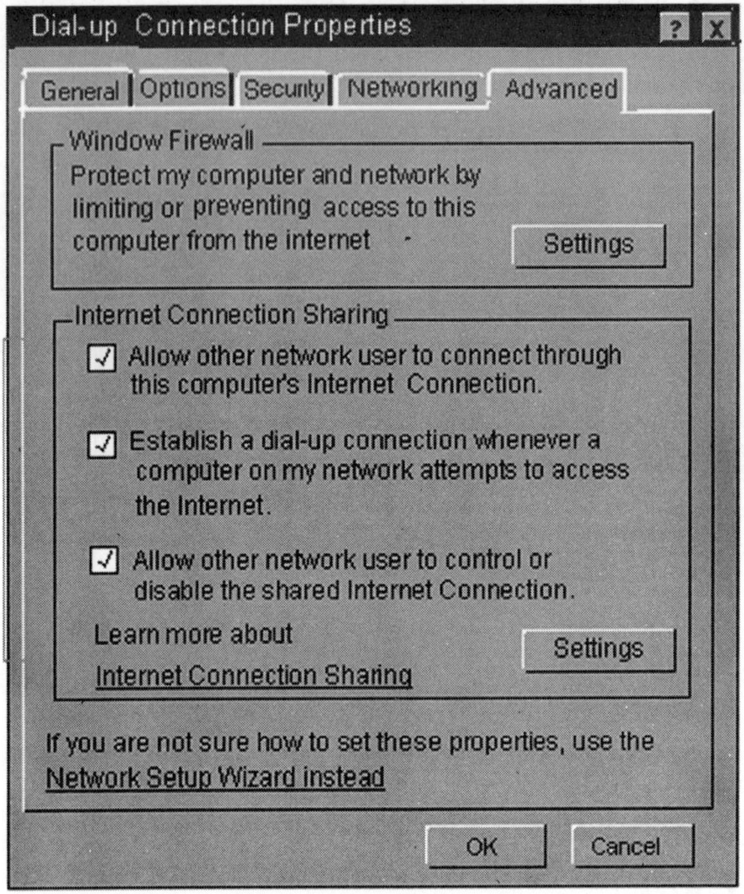

4. Click on this check box.

As soon as you click on this check box other two check boxes will also become active.

5. Now check the other two check boxes by clicking on them.

6. Click OK button.

Your computer is now connected with other computer to share internet connection, through dial-up connection.

7. File and Printer Sharing Trouble

If you want to use a shared folder that is on another computer, but unable to find the folder in My Network Places.

The reason for this may be that your computer name is already exists on the network.

Follow the following steps below to change the computer name:

1. Click Start button at the task bar then go to settings and then click on control panel as directed in the following figure.

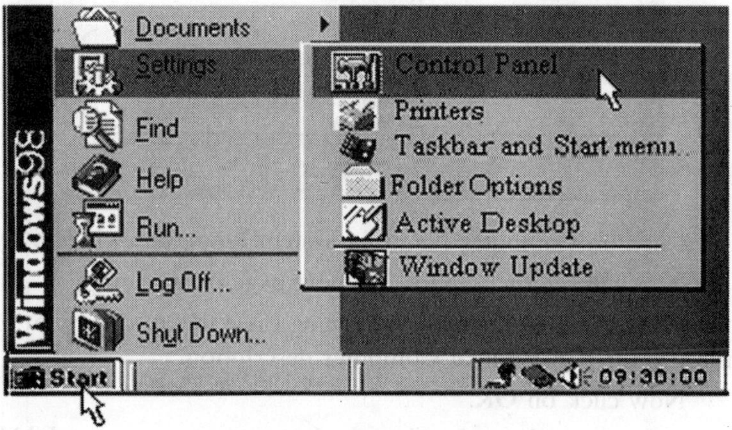

As soon as you click Control Panel icon Control panel window will be displayed on screen as follows:

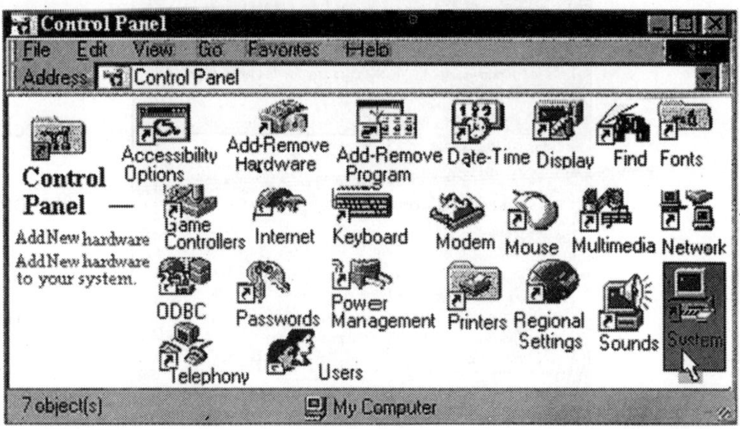

Double click on the System icon in the control panel.

If you are using Windows XP. The following System Properties window appears on the screen.

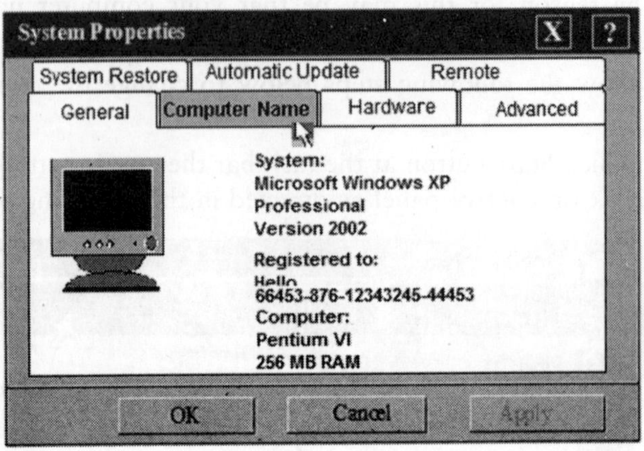

Click on Computer Name in System Properties window.

You will see the window on next page on screen.

Change computer name by typing the name of computer in the text strip in front of Computer description.

Now click on OK.

Now try to share the files of other computer on your LAN.

WAN Maintenance

13

Following are the common tips that can help to isolate and rectify the problems of WAN network:

1. Settings of NICs, of each computer on the network must be correct.
2. All cable connections with the routers, NICs, switches, hubs, repeaters, bridges, and gateways are tightly plugged.
3. If router is not functioning, turn it off for about 30 seconds and then turn it on again.
4. For checking the connection with a remote router ping the IP address of the remote router.
5. Switch on all the network devices such as router, switch, repeater, bridges, etc.
6. Apply local loop testing, signal encoding, and other techniques like framing, clocking and signaling.
7. Check the bandwidth allocation with the WAN troubleshooting tool, to see how much bandwidth is allocated to each remote site. Check network congestion. It may be causing due to the distributed application or may be due to improper bandwidth. Congestion of bandwidth may also occur when somebody is transmitting large chunks of data.
8. Check to see that if there is a malfunctioning in the remote routers/switches or centralized router/switches.

9. See that the firewall software or hardware is configured correctly.

The two levels of network management are listed below:

1. The Fault Level Management.
2. The Configuration Level Management.

1. The Fault Level Management

Network problems that are mostly related with hardware components, at the fault level management.

The faults of the hardware are detected by various troubleshooting devices.

Troubleshooting Hardware Problems

For managing the network at fault level, you must know about the various hardware and software problems.

Network failure may be caused by the following reasons:

1. Hardware problem.
2. Physical problem.

1. Hardware problem. Network's Hardware components like modems, routers, switches, hubs, bridges, repeaters, NIC and server's PCs may be out of order. The problem may lie with hardware or software.

2. Physical problem:

1. Breakage of cable.
2. Loose connections.
3. Wrong type of connection cable or hardware.
4. Hardware device is not receiving proper voltage. Sometimes power supply is off.

For detection and rectification of physical problems of the network there are some troubleshooting tools.

The tools are listed below.

Troubleshooting Tools

1. Digital voltmeter.
2. Time-domain reflect-o-meter.
3. Advanced Cable testers.

4. Protocol analyzers.
5. Network monitors.
6. Terminators.

1. Digital voltmeter. Digital voltmeter is the electronics device that can measure the voltage at various terminals of the network. If the voltage at the particular terminal is found lesser or higher than the specified limit, it is to be rectified immediately. Higher voltage may cause the burning of the component of the network hardware and lower voltage may cause malfunctioning of the hardware.

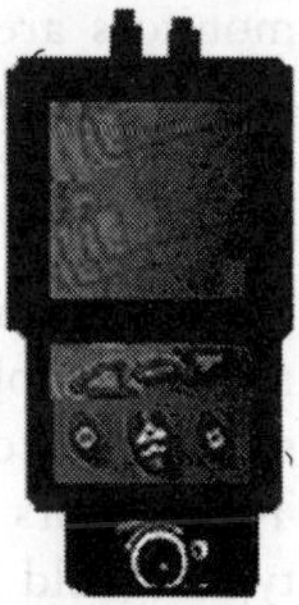

2. Time-domain reflect-o-meter. This is also an electronics device that is used to detect the breakage in the network cable. Time-domain reflect-o-meter generates the sonar like electrical pulses and sends through the network cable. The pulses reach the breakage point of the cable and then return back to the Time-domain reflect-o-meter. This action determines the time of reaching and returning back to the instrument. This total time tells where the breakage of cable lies.

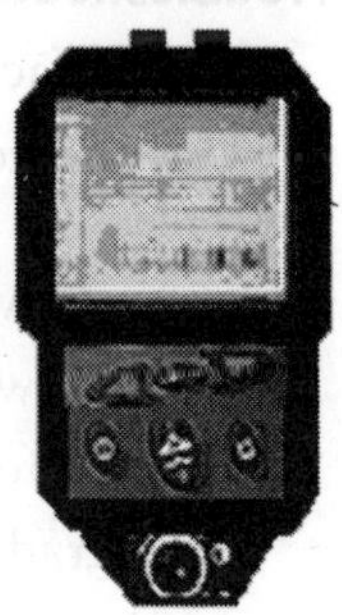

3. Advanced cable testers. Advanced cable testers can measure impedance, resistance, attenuation of the network cables and if the cable is broken or short-circuited the value of impedance, resistance, attenuation will vary from the prescribed limit.

Advanced cable testers is capable of detecting the network collisions, frame counts, and congestion errors. If the network cable is broken its resistance will raised from 50 ohms to infinity.

4. Protocol analyzers. Protocol analyzers are the combination of hardware and software and are also known as network analyzers. They control the network traffic and inspect the packets. They collect the data to determine the performance of the network. They can find the bottleneck of network and the irregular network traffic from a computer. It can detect the faulty NICs or other network components. It can detect the conflicting applications and connection errors of the network.

5. Network monitors. Network monitors control network traffic. They detect the network packets originating source and the destination where they are going. Network monitor are capable of generating the reports and can show the network statistics graphically. The network monitors are functional with all the layers of the OSI model excluding the hardware layer. A software based protocol analyzer is used by Windows NT Server 4.0.

6. Terminators. Terminators are placed at the end of a network cable so that it has proper impedance. The impedance shows the condition of the cable whether it is broken or OK. Terminators are designed to provide optimal performance in typical field installations.

Troubleshooting

1. Interface card or cable problem.

Use the following command to check the status of the interface:

(a) show interfaces serial.

(b) show controllers EXEC.

2. Look for a line down condition and version level.
3. Upgrade the current code if it is older than Version 1.7.
4. Change the faulty cards or cables.

CSU/DSU failure

1. Check the CSU/DSU configuration that serial clock transmit external (SCTE). Enable SCTE terminal timing if it is disabled.

2. See that the CSU/DSU are properly configured, or if intermittent connectivity persists after enabling SCTE/Terminal timing on the CSU/DSU, verify that the correct network entity is generating the system clock. Reconfigure nodes and modems if clocking is not properly configured.

3. If intermittent problems persist, check cable length; if the cable is longer than 25 feet, you might need to invert the clock on the MCI/SCI.

4. Invert the data on the DSU/CSU on both ends of the connection.

5. Lower the line speed to 56 KB or derivative of that speed.

6. Check for possible routing loops, or configurations of routing protocols.

Network generating invalid PRs (X.25)

1. See that the interface default flow control values match the values defined for the switch.

2. Check the switch configuration at command line.

3. Change the switch hardware if necessary.

Router generating invalid PRs (X.25)

1. See that the interface default flow control values and the values defined for the WAN connection should match.

2. Make the debug x.25 events EXEC command enabled and examine the reason and diagnostic codes.

Serial line congestion

1. Make adjustment to hold the queue.

2. Configure buffer sizes to adjust the traffic.

3. Most important message first and the next by applying a priority list.

4. Reduce broadcast traffic by segmentation.

Gateway device is not set properly

Gateway device—Various type of gateway devices are available, that are manufactures by different companies 'like dlink.com, netgear.com and Cisco systems.

Configuration procedures of these devices are different but the basic function of all devices remain the same. The Gateway function is to translate the Network Address. It translates the public IP address into the private IP address on the network, DHCP server and PPP.

Packet Internet Groper Command (Ping)

By the application of ping command you can check the internet connectivity of a host computer with the remote computer on an internet-work. This is the most important DOS command that is used for finding connectivity faults, of node to node, on a network. The same command can also be used in router mode command.

Ping Command

1. Open command prompt.

2. Type ping as C:\Documents and Settings\db2admin>ping <Press Enter>.

Following ping options are displayed

Usage: ping [-t] [-a] [-n count] [-l size] [-f] [-i TTL] [-v TOS]

[-r count] [-s count] [[-j host-list] | [-k host-list]]

[-w timeout] target_name

Options:

-t	Ping the specified host until stopped. To see statistics and continue—type Control-Break; To stop—type Control-C.
-a	Resolve addresses to hostnames.
-n count	Number of echo requests to send.
-l size	Send buffer size.
-f	Set Don't Fragment flag in packet.
-i TTL	Time To Live.
-v TOS	Type Of Service.
-r count	Record route for count hops.
-s count	Timestamp for count hops.

-j host-list Loose source route along host-list.

-k host-list Strict source route along host-list.

-w timeout Time-out in milliseconds to wait for each reply.

C:\Documents and Settings\db2admin>

1. Option -t. This command specified host until stopped. Using "ping -t 192.168.0.1" where "-t" is an option and 192.168.0.1 is the IP address.

1. Type "ping -t 192.168.0.1" in front of command prompt as follows:

C:\Documents and Settings\db2admin>ping -t 192.168.0.1

2. Press Enter. Packet sending process will start and continue. Press "Control +C" to terminate the process.

C:\Documents and Settings\db2admin>ping -t 192.168.0.1

Pinging 192.168.0.1 with 32 bytes of data:

Reply from 192.168.0.1: bytes=32 time=1ms TTL=128

Reply from 192.168.0.1: bytes=32 time<1ms TTL=128

Reply from 192.168.0.1: bytes=32 time<1ms TTL=128

Reply from 192.168.0.1: bytes=32 time<1ms TTL=128

Reply from 192.168.0.1: bytes=32 time<1ms TTL=128

........................nth trip............................

Ping statistics for 192.168.0.1:

Packets: Sent = n, Received = n, Lost = 0 (0% loss).

Approximate round trip times in milli-seconds:

Minimum = 0ms, Maximum = 10ms, Average = 0ms

C:\Documents and Settings\db2admin>

2. Option -a. This option resolve addresses to hostnames.

"Using ping -a 192.168.0.1."

Packets are sent to the destination IP address and reverse name resolution is carried out to find out the name of the computer. On successful application of the ping command the host name correspond to the IP address is displayed.

1. Type "ping -a 192.168.0.1" in front of command prompt as follows:

C:\Documents and Settings\db2admin>ping -a 192.168.0.1

2. Press Enter. Hostname "hi-cvaljbmtkcfx.mshome.net" is displayed with IP address 192.168.0.1

C:\Documents and Settings\db2admin>ping -a 192.168.0.1

Pinging hi-cvaljbmtkcfx.mshome.net [192.168.0.1] with 32 bytes of data:

Reply from 192.168.0.1: bytes=32 time<1ms TTL=128

Reply from 192.168.0.1: bytes=32 time<1ms TTL=128

Reply from 192.168.0.1: bytes=32 time<1ms TTL=128

Reply from 192.168.0.1: bytes=32 time<1ms TTL=128

Ping statistics for 192.168.0.1:

Packets: Sent = 4, Received = 4, Lost = 0 (0% loss).

Approximate round trip times in milli-seconds:

Minimum = 0ms, Maximum = 0ms, Average = 0ms

To ping the destination 192.168.0.1 with "Number of Echo Request messages" = 10.

3. Option -n. This option sends the echo requests n times.

1. Open command prompt.

2. Type ping as C:\Documents and Settings\db2admin> ping -n 10 -l 1000 192.168.0.1.

3. Press Enter. You will see the following result in the command window:

C:\Documents and Settings\db2admin>ping -n 10 -l 1000 192.168.0.1.

Pinging 192.168.0.1 with 1000 bytes of data:

Reply from 192.168.0.1: bytes=1000 time<1ms TTL=128

Reply from 192.168.0.1: bytes=1000 time<1ms TTL=128

Reply from 192.168.0.1: bytes=1000 time<1ms TTL=128

Reply from 192.168.0.1: bytes=1000 time<1ms TTL=128

Reply from 192.168.0.1: bytes=1000 time<1ms TTL=128

Reply from 192.168.0.1: bytes=1000 time<1ms TTL=128

Reply from 192.168.0.1: bytes=1000 time<1ms TTL=128

Reply from 192.168.0.1: bytes=1000 time<1ms TTL=128

Reply from 192.168.0.1: bytes=1000 time<1ms TTL=128

Reply from 192.168.0.1: bytes=1000 time<1ms TTL=128

Ping statistics for 192.168.0.1:

Packets: Sent = 10, Received = 10, Lost = 0 (0% loss).

Approximate round trip times in milli-seconds:

Minimum = 0ms, Maximum = 0ms, Average = 0ms

Ping command "ping -n 10 -l 1000" sends packets to the destination 192.168.0.1 with 10 Echo Request messages, each packet contains a Data field of 1000 bytes.

4. Option -l. This option sends the buffer size.

1. Open command prompt.

2. Type ping command as follows:

C:\Documents and Settings\db2admin>ping-l 56000 192.168.0.1.

3. Press Enter. You will see the following result in the command window:

C:\Documents and Settings\db2admin>ping-l 56000 192.168.0.1.

Pinging 192.168.0.1 with 56000 bytes of data:

Reply from 192.168.0.1: bytes=56000 time<1ms TTL=128

Reply from 192.168.0.1: bytes=56000 time<1ms TTL=128

Reply from 192.168.0.1: bytes=56000 time<1ms TTL=128

Reply from 192.168.0.1: bytes=56000 time<1ms TTL=128

Ping statistics for 192.168.0.1:

Packets: Sent = 4, Received = 4, Lost = 0 (0% loss).

Approximate round trip times in milli-seconds:

Minimum = 0ms, Maximum = 0ms, Average = 0ms

C:\Documents and Settings\db2admin>

In the "ping -l 56000 192.168.0.1" "-l" specifies the length of data field in bytes that is sent to the destination through Echo Request messages. The default is 32. The maximum length of data field is 65,527 bytes and default is 32 bytes.

5. Option -f. This option sets "Don't Fragment flag" in packet.

It specifies that Echo Request messages are sent with the Don't Fragment flag in the IP header set to 1.

The Echo Request message cannot be fragmented by routers in the path to the destination. This parameter is useful for troubleshooting Path Maximum Transmission Unit (PMTU) problems.

C:\Documents and Settings\db2admin>ping -f 192.168.0.1.

Pinging 192.168.0.1 with 32 bytes of data:

Reply from 192.168.0.1: bytes=32 time<1ms TTL=128

Reply from 192.168.0.1: bytes=32 time<1ms TTL=128

Reply from 192.168.0.1: bytes=32 time<1ms TTL=128

Reply from 192.168.0.1: bytes=32 time<1ms TTL=128

Ping statistics for 192.168.0.1:

Packets: Sent = 4, Received = 4, Lost = 0 (0% loss).

Approximate round trip times in milli-seconds:

Minimum = 0ms, Maximum = 0ms, Average = 0ms.

6. Option -i. This option uses time to live (TTL).

It specifies the value of the TTL field in the IP header for Echo Request messages sent. The default is the default TTL value for the host. For Windows XP hosts, this is typically 128. The maximum TTL is 255.

C:\Documents and Settings\db2admin>ping -i 65 192.168.0.1.

Pinging 192.168.0.1 with 32 bytes of data:

Reply from 192.168.0.1: bytes=32 time<1ms TTL=128

Reply from 192.168.0.1: bytes=32 time<1ms TTL=128

Reply from 192.168.0.1: bytes=32 time<1ms TTL=128

Reply from 192.168.0.1: bytes=32 time<1ms TTL=128

Ping statistics for 192.168.0.1:

Packets: Sent = 4, Received = 4, Lost = 0 (0% loss).

Approximate round trip times in milli-seconds:

Minimum = 0ms, Maximum = 0ms, Average = 0ms.

7. **Option -v.** This option indicates the type of service.

It indicates the value of the Type of Service (TOS) field in the IP header for Echo Request messages sent. The default is 0. TOS is specified as a decimal value from 0 to 255.

C:\Documents and Settings\db2admin>ping -v 0 192.168.0.1.

Pinging 192.168.0.1 with 32 bytes of data:

Reply from 192.168.0.1: bytes=32 time<1ms TTL=128

Reply from 192.168.0.1: bytes=32 time<1ms TTL=128

Reply from 192.168.0.1: bytes=32 time<1ms TTL=128

Reply from 192.168.0.1: bytes=32 time<1ms TTL=128

Ping statistics for 192.168.0.1:

Packets: Sent = 4, Received = 4, Lost = 0 (0% loss).

Approximate round trip times in milli-seconds:

Minimum = 0ms, Maximum = 0ms, Average = 0ms.

C:\Documents and Settings\db2admin>ping -s 4 192.168.0.1

8. **Option -r.** This option records route for count hops.

1. Open command prompt.
2. Type ping command as follows:

C:\Documents and Settings\db2admin> ping -r 5 192.168.0.1.

3. Press Enter. You will see the following result in the command window:

C:\Documents and Settings\db2admin>ping -r 5 192.168.0.1.

Pinging 192.168.0.1 with 32 bytes of data:

Reply from 192.168.0.1: bytes=32 time<1ms TTL=128

Route: 192.168.0.1

Reply from 192.168.0.1: bytes=32 time<1ms TTL=128

Route: 192.168.0.1

Reply from 192.168.0.1: bytes=32 time<1ms TTL=128

Route: 192.168.0.1

Reply from 192.168.0.1: bytes=32 time<1ms TTL=128

Route: 192.168.0.1.

Ping statistics for 192.168.0.1:

Packets: Sent = 4, Received = 4, Lost = 0 (0% loss).

Approximate round trip times in milli-seconds:

Minimum = 0ms, Maximum = 0ms, Average = 0ms.

Specifies that the Record Route option in the IP header is used to record the path taken by the Echo Request message and corresponding Echo Reply message. Each hop in the path uses an entry in the Record Route option. If possible, specify a Count that is equal to or greater than the number of hops.

9. Option -s. This option indicates timestamp for count hops.

1. Open command prompt.
2. Type ping command as follows:

C:\Documents and Settings\db2admin>ping -s 4 192.168.0.1.

3. Press Enter. You will see the following result in the command window.

It describes that the Internet Timestamp option in the IP header is used to record the time of arrival for the Echo Request message and corresponding Echo Reply message for each hop. The count must be a minimum of 1 and a maximum of 4.

C:\Documents and Settings\db2admin>ping -s 4 192.168.0.1.

Pinging 192.168.0.1 with 32 bytes of data:

Reply from 192.168.0.1: bytes=32 time<1ms TTL=128

Timestamp: 192.168.0.1: 57047329

Reply from 192.168.0.1: bytes=32 time<1ms TTL=128

Timestamp: 192.168.0.1: 57048329

Reply from 192.168.0.1: bytes=32 time<1ms TTL=128

Timestamp: 192.168.0.1: 57049329

Reply from 192.168.0.1: bytes=32 time<1ms TTL=128

Timestamp: 192.168.0.1: 57050329

Ping statistics for 192.168.0.1:

Packets: Sent = 4, Received = 4, Lost = 0 (0% loss).

Approximate round trip times in milli-seconds:

Minimum = 0ms, Maximum = 0ms, Average = 0ms.

C:\Documents and Settings\db2admin>.

10. Option -j. This option indicates loose source route along host-list.

It specifies that the Echo Request messages use the Loose Source Route option in the IP header with the set of intermediate destinations specified in Host-List. With loose source routing, successive intermediate destinations can be separated by one or multiple routers. The maximum number of addresses or names in the host list is 9. The hostlist is a series of IP addresses (in dotted decimal notation) separated by spaces.

You can send packets to the destination 192.168.0.1 by using ping command and a loose route of 127.0.0.1 10.0.99.221 192.168.0.1 IP addresses can used intermediate destination for test.

Type ping -j 127.0.0.1 10.0.99.221 192.168.0.1 on command line and press Enter.

You will get the following output that indicate the failure of your internet connection.

C:\Documents and Settings\db2admin>ping -j 127.0.0.1 10.0.99.221 192.168.0.1.

Pinging 192.168.0.1 with 32 bytes of data:

Request timed out.

Request timed out.

Request timed out.

Request timed out.

Ping statistics for 192.168.0.1:

Packets: Sent = 4, Received = 0, Lost = 4 (100% loss).

11. Option -k. This option indicates strict source route along hostlist.

It specifies that the Echo Request messages use the Strict Source Route option in the IP header with the set of intermediate destinations specified in HostList. With strict source routing, the next intermediate destination must be directly reachable (it must be a neighbor on an interface of the router). The maximum number of addresses or names in the hostlist is 9. The hostlist is a series of IP addresses (in dotted decimal notation) separated by spaces.

C:\Documents and Settings\db2admin>ping -k 127.0.0.1 192.168.4.1 192.168.3.1 192 .168.5.2.

Pinging 192.168.5.2 with 32 bytes of data:

Request timed out.

Request timed out.

Request timed out.

Request timed out.

Ping statistics for 192.168.5.2:

Packets: Sent = 4, Received = 0, Lost = 4 (100% loss).

12. Option -w. This option indicates time-out in milliseconds to wait for each reply.

It specifies the amount of time, in milliseconds, to wait for the Echo Reply message that corresponds to a given Echo Request message to be received. If the Echo Reply message is not received within the time-out, the "Request timed out" error message is displayed. The default time-out is 4000 (4 seconds).

C:\Documents and Settings\db2admin>ping -w 192.168.0.1.

IP address must be specified.

C:\Documents and Settings\db2admin>ping -w 192.168.0.1 127.0.0.1.

Pinging 127.0.0.1 with 32 bytes of data:

Reply from 127.0.0.1: bytes=32 time<1ms TTL=128

Reply from 127.0.0.1: bytes=32 time<1ms TTL=128

Reply from 127.0.0.1: bytes=32 time<1ms TTL=128

Reply from 127.0.0.1: bytes=32 time<1ms TTL=128.

Ping statistics for 127.0.0.1:

Packets: Sent = 4, Received = 4, Lost = 0 (0% loss).

Approximate round trip times in milliseconds:

Minimum = 0ms, Maximum = 0ms, Average = 0ms.

C:\Documents and Settings\db2admin>.

2. Configuration Level Management

This level of management, includes the monitoring and controlling the operation of the network.

Configuration and addition of hardware like routers switches and bridges are carried out as per network demand.

Configuration of a router.

Examining the routing table

You can use show command to get the information about routing table, specific table of protocols, routing path, connected route's table, static route's table and the summary of all routes.

Router is also just like a PC and has a processor, RAM, ROM, NVRAM, Flash memory, serial port, Ethernet port and a console port connection to connect the monitor and keyboard through a PC. Router has an IOS system that helps to implement all sorts of commands for managing the router. The command are used in the same way as we do on DOS.

For managing a router it is necessary to see its configuration details about it.

We can use the following list of show command to know about the functional details of the router:

1. Show ip route	This command provides information about the routing table.
2. Show ip route protocol	This command displays about the protocol that is used for routing.
3. Show ip route w.x.y.z	This command shows about route used.

4. Show ip route connected — This command displays about the connected route's table.

5. Show ip route static — This command shows static route's table.

6. Show ip route summary — This command shows the summary of all routes.

1. Show ip route command. Type show ip route at R1# prompt and press enter as indicated below:

R1#show ip route<Enter>

You can see the following information about the routing table and short terms used for various protocols.

This is the description of short terms:

Codes: C -connected, S -static, I -IGRP, R -RIP, M -mobile, B -BGP

D -EIGRP, EX -EIGRP external, O -OSPF, IA -OSPF inter area

N1 -OSPF NSSA external type 1, N2 -OSPF NSSA external type 2

E1 -OSPF external type 1, E2 -OSPF external type 2, E -EGP

i -IS-IS, L1 -IS-IS level-1, L2 -IS-IS level-2, ia -IS-IS inter area

*-candidate default, U -per-user static route, o -ODR

P -periodic downloaded static route.

Gateway of last resort is not set.

This description indicate a network whose address is 20.0.0.0/24 and 3 subnets address and interfaces used in sub-netting.

20.0.0.0/24 is subnetted, 3 subnets

C 20.1.2.0 is directly connected, Ethernet0

C 20.1.124.0 is directly connected, Serial1

C 20.1.125.0 is directly connected, Serial0

2. Show ip route protocol. Write the show ip route protocol at the prompt R1# and press enter as shown below:

R1#show ip route protocol <Enter>

In this particular case rip is the protocol whose details are given below:

Routing Protocol is rip

Sending updates every 20 seconds, next due in 10 seconds

Invalid after 190 seconds, hold down 180, flushed after 250

Outgoing update filter list for all interfaces is

Incoming update filter list for all interfaces is

Redistributing: rip

Default version control: send version 1, receive any version

Interface	send	Recv	Triggered	RIP	Key-chain
Ethernet	1	1 2			
Serial 2	1	1 2			

Routing for Networks:

20.0.0.0

172.20.0.0

Routing Information Sources:

Gateway	Distance	Last Update
This router	120	01:10:15
20.1.1.2	120	02:11:03

3. Show ip route x.y.z.w. Type R1#show ip route 10.1.5.8 at the prompt R1# and press enter as shown below:

R1#show ip route 10.1.5.8 <Enter>

The execution of this command will set the route used by the Router 1:

Routing entry for 10.1.4.0/22

Known via "eigrp 9", distance 90, metric 2185984, type internal.

Redistributing via eigrp 9

Last update from 172.16.1.253 on Serial0.2,00:28:36 ago

Routing Descriptor Blocks:

*172.16.1.253, from 172.16.1.253, 00:28:36 ago, via Serial 0.2.

Route metric is 2185984, traffic share count is 1.

Total delay is 20630 microseconds, minimum bandwidth is 1544 Kbit.

4. Show ip route connected. Type show ip route connected at the prompt R1# and press enter as shown below:

R1#show ip route connected <Enter>

The execution of this command will display connected route's table used by the Router 1 as follows:

172.16.0.0/24 is subnetted, 3 subnets

C 172.16.1.0 is directly connected, Serial0.2

C 172.16.2.0 is directly connected, Ethernet0

C 172.16.3.0 is directly connected, Serial0.1

5. Configuration of router for static routing. Static routing is generally used to set the router to route the traffic to a network through a single route.

Manual configuration of the routing table is done and updated route's table are never sent on the link therefore it conserves more bandwidth. You cannot make any change in the existing route's table till the path is active. It must be configured in both directions.

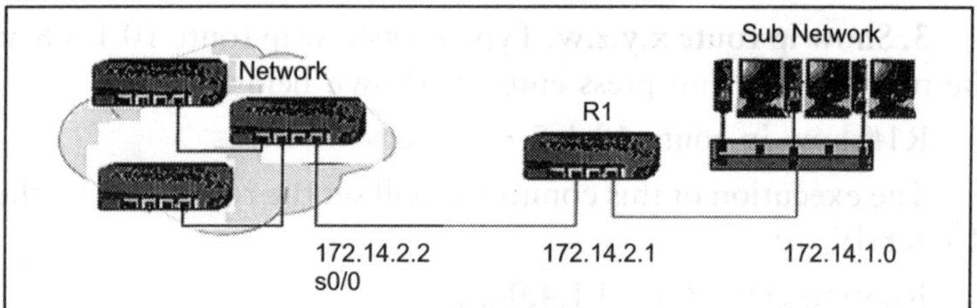

Static Routing

Static Routing

For using ip route command on a router we must know the following:

1. Destination IP address.
2. The destination network address.
3. Subnet mask.

4. Next-hop address.
5. The exit interface.

Execute the following command:

R1(config)#ip route 172.16.20.0 255.255.255.0 s0/0 <Enter>

This command will set the router, to send all packet out interface s0/0 with a subnet mask of 255.255.255.0, for getting the destination network of 172.16.20.0.

In the above command line

172.16.20.2	is destination IP address
172.16.20.0	is destination network address
255.255.255.0	is subnet mask
172.16.10.2	is next-hop address
s0/0	is exit interface

The permanent Keyword (Optional)

Router(config)#ip route 172.16.20.0 255.255.255.0 172.16.10.2 permanent.	Specifies that the route will not be removed, even if the interface shuts down.

Without the permanent keyword in a static route statement, a static route will be removed if an interface goes down. If you don't tighten those serial cables or if you have a bad connector on a UTP cable, a cable can easily become loose, causing an interface to go down. But plugging the cable back in does not add that static route back into the routing table. The only way to get that route back into the table is to reload the router or use the permanent keyword in your ip route command.

Router(config)#ip route 172.14.20.0 255.255.255.0 172.14.10.2 and press Enter.

Formation of above command line:

First	172.14.20.0 is the destination network address we want to get.
Middle	255.255.255.0 is the subnet mask we use.
Third	172.14.20.2 next-hop address where all the packets are to be sent.

R1(config)#ip route 172.16.20.0 255.255.255.0 s0/0 <Enter>

Formation of above command line

First	172.14.20.0	To get destination network address.
Middle	255.255.255.0	is the subnet mask used.
Third	s0/0	From interface s0/0 all packets out.

For viewing the static route's table you can use the following command:

R1#show ip route press Enter.

This will display the current static route's table:

Codes: C -connected, S -static, I -IGRP, R -RIP, M -mobile, B -BGP.

D -EIGRP, EX -EIGRP external, O -OSPF, IA -OSPF inter area.

N1 -OSPF NSSA external type 1, N2 -OSPF NSSA external type 2.

E1 -OSPF external type 1, E2 -OSPF external type 2, E -EGP.

i -IS-IS, L1 -IS-IS level-1, L2 -IS-IS level-2, ia -IS-IS inter area

*-candidate default, U -per-user static route, o -ODR

P -periodic downloaded static route

Gateway of last resort is 0.0.0.0 to network 0.0.0.0

This description indicates a default routing network whose address is 20.0.0.0/24 and 3 subnets address and interfaces used in sub-netting.

20.0.0.0/24 is subnetted, 3 subnets

C 20.1.1.0 is directly connected, Serial0

S* 0.0.0.0/0 is directly connected, Serial0

For configuring the router, to send all packets out interface s0/0 send all packets to 172.16.10.2 IP address with a subnet mask of 255.255.255.0, type ip route 172.16.20.2 255.255.255.0 s0/0 at the R1(config)# prompt and press Enter as follows:

R1(config)#ip route 172.16.20.0 255.255.255.0 s0/0 <Enter>

The drawback of static routing is that in case of failure of the network due to loose connection or interface goes down the static route set on the router is rubbed off. When you activate the network, you have to reconfigure the router for static route static again.

This problem can be overcome by using a keyword "permanent" as follows:

Router(config)#ip route 172.16.20.0 255.255.255.0 172.16.10.2 permanent <Enter>

This command will configure the router's static route permanently and even after the network failure the router retains this configuration.

LAN Connections

Depending on the type of router you have, LAN connections are typically made to an Ethernet or Token Ring interface port on the router and then to a hub or MAU (Multistation Access Unit) that supplies the connections for the various computers on the network.

Let's assume that we are connecting an Ethernet LAN to our router. A hub can be connected to the Ethernet port by Cat 5 twisted pair. RJ-45 female port is generally used in Ethernet Interface. Each computer on the network will then be connected to the hub.

If we want to connect more computers to the network, then connect one of the hub ports on the router, to a port on an additional hub.

Serial Connections

Serial connections on the router can be configured for several different WAN protocols.

The actual physical serial connection on routers is a 60 pin female port.

Connecting the Router on LAN and WAN

After configuration of router keep it in a proper accessible place and firmly fit it with the socket. After placing it, make all the physical connections. Particular type of router is shown in the following figure.

It has two serial port two Ethernet ports a console female connection and a auxiliary connection.

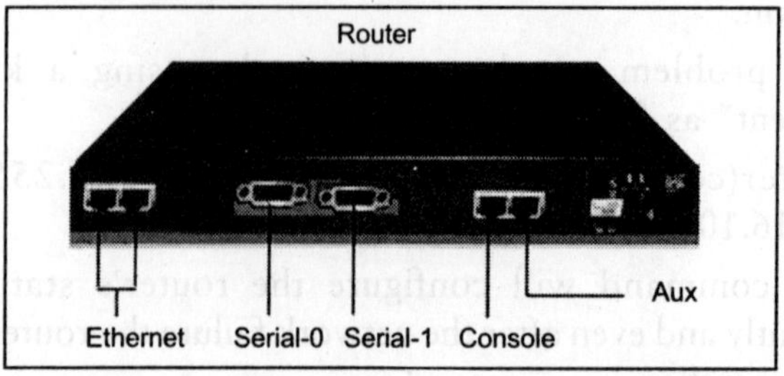

Three signaling standards V.35, X.21bis and EIA-530 RS232 are used for serial communications:

1. One end of V.35 cable with 60 pin male connector is used to connect serial port of router while the other end is used to connect the other device of WAN. V.35 supports packet switching and provide synchronous communications in between various LANs and WANs.
2. X.21bis signaling standard is used to communicate between DTEs and DCEs.
3. EIA-530 RS232 signaling standard used when serial communications is not functioning properly.

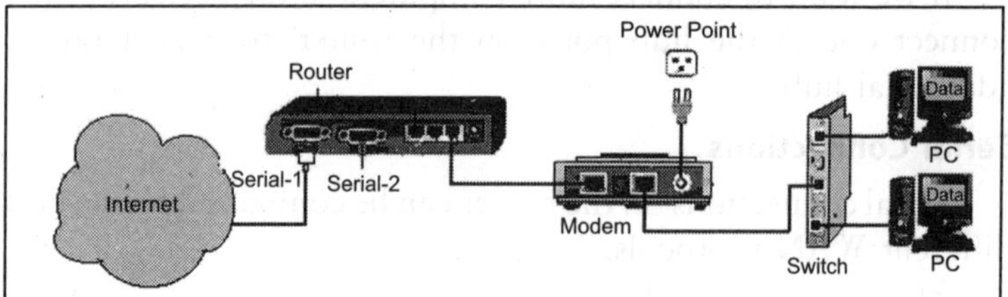

Simple LAN with Router

Router Configuration Modes

1. User mode
2. Privileged mode
3. Global configuration mode

4. Line mode
5. Interface mode and sub-interface mode
6. RXboot mode
7. Router configuration mode

1. User Mode (Router Name>). This mode provides limited access to the router. You are provided with a set of nondestructive commands that allow examination of certain router configuration parameters. You cannot, however, make any changes to the router configuration.

User mode is an informative mode that provide limited information about the configuration of the router.

You cannot make any change in the router's configuration when you work with the user mode. You can only see the configuration information by using a limited command set.

User prompt for the router's configuration on the system dialog window is displayed as follows:

Router Name>

You can give "show interfaces" command to get the details of interfaces set on your router.

User mode is like a read only file where you can read but cannot write.

2. Privileged Mode (Router Name#). Privileged mode also known as the Enabled mode. This mode is equipped with a large set of command that includes the user mode commands. This mode uses a stronger set of commands to examine the router than the user mode.

You can reset the secret/enable password by using this mode.

Privileged mode has a facility to access the configuration commands of the configuration mode therefore you are able to edit the configuration for the router.

You can see the current running status of the router by using show running-config command.

3. Global Configuration Mode [Router(config)#]. Configuration mode is also called the Global configuration mode. This mode is <Enter>ed from the Privileged mode and supplies the complete command set for configuring the router. Subsets of the configuration mode exist for protocols, interfaces, and other aspects of the router operation. The configuration mode allows you to set all the parameters related to the hardware and software running on the router. You can configure interfaces, routed protocols, and routing protocols.

You can also set router passwords and configure the WAN protocols used by the router's serial interfaces.

Some of the configurable options related to the router can be set on a new router using the System Configuration dialog. The configuration mode gives you access to absolutely all the commands that you would use to configure or fine tune the configuration of the router.

4. Line Console Mode. You can enter line console mode from configure mode and can set a password to line console mode to secure your router configuration.

5. Interface Mode. You can enter Interface mode from configure mode and can configure the router's interfaces.

6. RXboot Mode. It is router's maintenance mode. This is also called ROM monitor mode. It is used to recover the lost password of the router.

It is also used to restore the IOS file in flash memory, if it is erased or found corrupt.

You can enter into this mode directly by pressing the Break key after starting the router within 60 seconds.

Following figure (on next page) shows to move in between commands.

1. Entering from User Mode to Privilege Mode. For entering into Privileged mode type "enable" at the User mode prompt as follows:

Router Name>enable Press <Enter>

Router Name#

Your prompt will change to privileged prompt as Router **Name#** and you are now in Privilege mode.

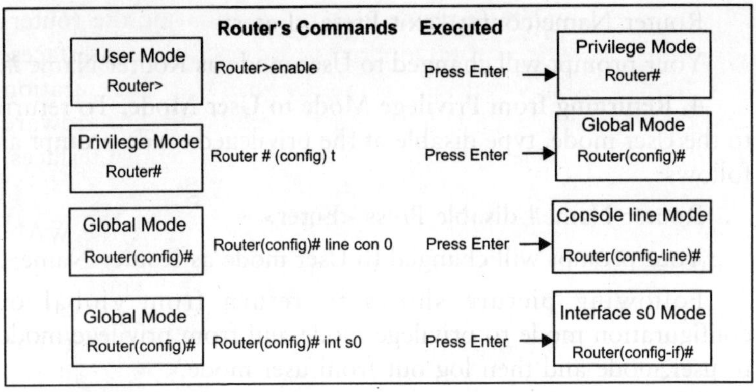

2. Entering from Privilege Mode to Configuration Mode. Type (config) t at the privilege prompt Router# and press <Enter> as follows:

Router Name#(config) t Press <Enter>

Following prompt appear which is the Global mode prompt Router Name(config)#

Router Name(config)# this prompt indicates that you are in configuration or global mode.

Following picture shows to enter from user mode to privilege mode and from privilege mode to global or configuration mode.

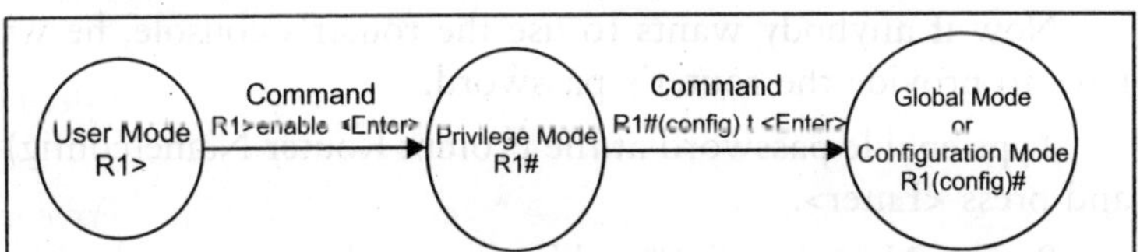

Command used to enter from User Mode to Privilege Mode to Configuration Mode in steps

For security of your router's configuration. It is always better to come back to user mode after completion the work in configuration mode. If you do not exit from the configuration mode somebody can access your router configuration and may change or damage the configuration data file.

3. Returning from Configuration Mode to Privilege Mode. To return from configuration mode to privileged mode, type exit at Router Name(config)# prompt as follows:

Router Name(config)#exit Press <Enter>

Your prompt will changed to User mode as Router Name #.

4. Returning from Privilege Mode to User Mode. To return to the User mode, type disable at the privileged mode prompt as follows:

Router Name# disable Press <Enter>

Your prompt will changed to User mode as Router Name>.

Following picture shows to return from global or configuration mode to privilege mode and from privilege mode to user mode and then log out from user mode.

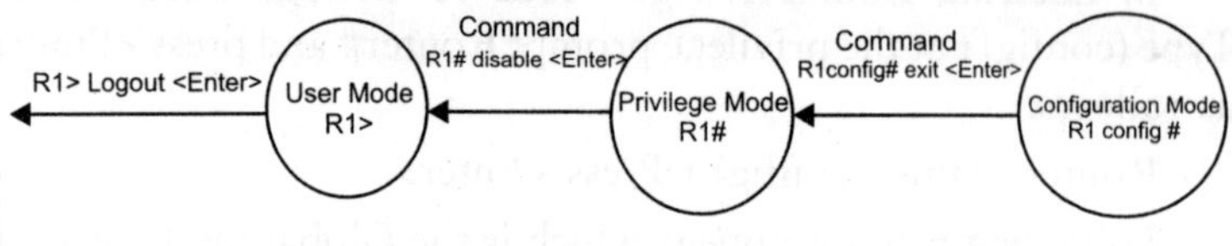

Returning back from Configuration Mode to User Mode and Logout User Mode

5. Log Off from User Mode. If you want to come out of user mode and want to log off the router type logout at the user prompt as follows:

Router Name> logout Press <Enter>

Now if anybody wants to use the router's console, he will have to provide the router's password.

Type enable password at the prompt Router Name(config)# and press <Enter>.

Router Name(config)#enable password

Press <Enter>

You will be prompted to type encrypted password. Type the password and press <Enter>.

Router Name# ******** Press <Enter>.

Router Name# show running-config Press <Enter>.

You can see the current configuration of your router by using show running-config command.

Using the Configuration Mode

1. At the Privileged prompt type config, and then press Enter.

Router# config Press<Enter>

Prompt changes to Router(config)#

2. You will be asked if you want to configure from the terminal, memory, or the network.

The default is the console terminal, so press Enter.

3. Changing the name of the router.

Type host-name [name] at the prompt Router (config)# and Press Enter as follows:

Router(config)# host-name Ishita2002 press Enter.

Ishita2002(config)# Now Ishita2002 is the new name to your router.

4. To set the enable password, type enable secret password at the config prompt, where [password] is the word that you will use as your secret password to get into the Privileged mode. Then press <Enter>.

5. Now you can set a password for the router. This means that anyone logging in to the router will have to provide this password to even access the User mode. To set the password you must get into the Line Console mode.

Type line console 0, and then press Enter.

6. You are now in the line console Configuration mode; type login, and then press <Enter>.

Ishita2002(config-line)# login press <Enter>.

7. To specify the login password, type password [password], where the [password] is the word you have set to log in to the router. For example, Senjutishita2002.

8. When you have completed your configuration changes, press Ctrl+Z. This will save your changes to the router's running configuration and return you to the Privileged prompt.

Using the Different Router Modes

After you have made changes to the running-config, you may want to save them to your startup-configuration in NVRAM. This is the file that is loaded when the router is rebooted or restarted.

At the Privileged prompt, type "copy running-config startup" and then press <Enter>. The new startup-configuration will be displayed on the console screen.

Getting Around Lost Passwords

Sometimes you just forget those passwords, which you need to enter into the Privileged mode and want to change a router's configuration.

Replacing a Lost Password

Take following steps:

1. Switch off router power supply.
2. After a few seconds switch on your router and for rebooting, press Ctrl+Break.
3. This will bring you in ROM Monitor mode. At the prompt ROM Monitor prompt Type "e/s2000002", and press <Enter>. Write down the virtual configuration number that appears.
4. At the ROM Monitor prompt type "o/r0x2142" and press <Enter>. This action will ignore the configuration file in NVRAM by the router.
5. Type i at the ROM Monitor prompt, and press <Enter>. Configuration dialog box will appear after rebooting of router. Click the mouse on "No" and press <Enter>.
6. At the router prompt type "enable" to <Enter> the Privileged mode. Type "copy startup-config running-config", and then press <Enter> to get your original configuration into the router's RAM.
7. At the enabled prompt type "config" and press <Enter>. You are now in the configuration mode. Type new password, and press <Enter>. This new password becomes your new enabled secret password.

8. Now register contents is to be set back to the original contents. At the configuration prompt, type "config-register 0x virtual configuration number" press <Enter>.
9. At the prompt configuration prompt type "end" and press <Enter>. Now you have come out of configuration mode.

Switch off router power supply. After a few seconds switch on your router.

You have replaced the lost password by a new secret password, and the router is configured to its normal state.

Console Line Mode

1. Type "line con 0" at the prompt Router(config)# and press <Enter> as follows:

Router(config)#line con 0 Press <Enter>

Line mode is indicated below:

Router(config-line)#

2. Setting Password to console using console line mode.

Type "password console" at the prompt Router(config-line)# and press <Enter> as follows:

Router(config-line)#password console Press <Enter>.

3. You are prompted to type a password at the auxiliary line mode prompt. Type the password and press enter.

Router(config-line)# ******** Press <Enter>.

4. Now if you want to test the password that you have supplied to the Vty line mode to enter into it, type "login" at the prompt Router(config-line)# as follows and press <Enter>.

Router(config-line)# Login Press <Enter>.

5. You are prompted to type a password at the auxiliary line mode prompt. Type the password and press enter.

Router(config-line)# ******** Press <Enter>.

6. Now if you see the prompt Router(config-line) without any instruction, you can do the router configuration in Vty line mode and can use the telnet facilities. Remember the password.

7. To exit from the auxiliary configuration mode, press Ctrl+Z.

Following figure shows the steps to set password for console line mode.

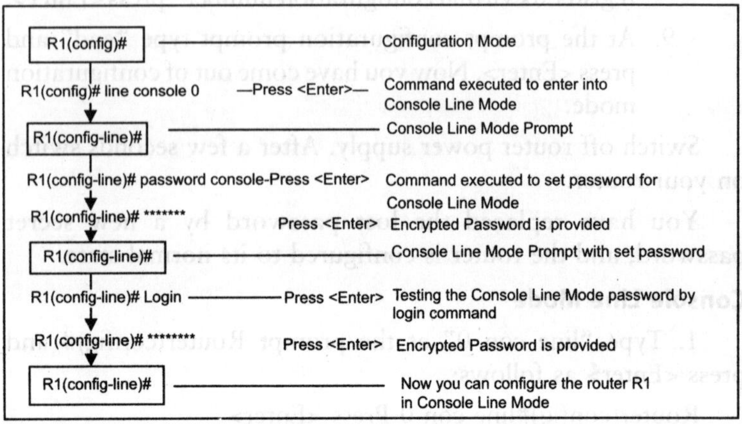

Virtual Terminal Password

If anybody wants to use telnet facilities, he has to provide the telnet password that is called a virtual terminal password.

1. Type line vty 0 4 at the prompt Router Name# as follows and Press <Enter>

Router Name# line vty 0 4 Press <Enter>.

This action will bring you in the Virtual terminal Configuration mode with following prompt:

Router(config-line)#.

2. Type "password telnet" at the Router(config-line)# prompt and press enter as follows:

Router(config-line)# password telnet Press <Enter>.

3. You are prompted to type a password at the Vty line prompt. Type the password and press enter.

Router(config-line)# ******** Press <Enter>.

4. Now if you want to test the password that you have supplied to the Vty line mode to enter into it, type "login" at the prompt Router(config-line)# as follows and press <Enter>

Router(config-line)# Login Press <Enter>.

5. You are prompted to type a password at the Vty line prompt. Type the password and press enter.

Router(config-line)# ******** Press <Enter>.

6. Now if you see the prompt Router(config-line) without any instruction, you can do the router configuration in Vty line mode and can use the telnet facilities.

Remember the password. Come out of the configuration mode press Ctrl+Z.

Following figure shows the step to set the Vty line mode password:

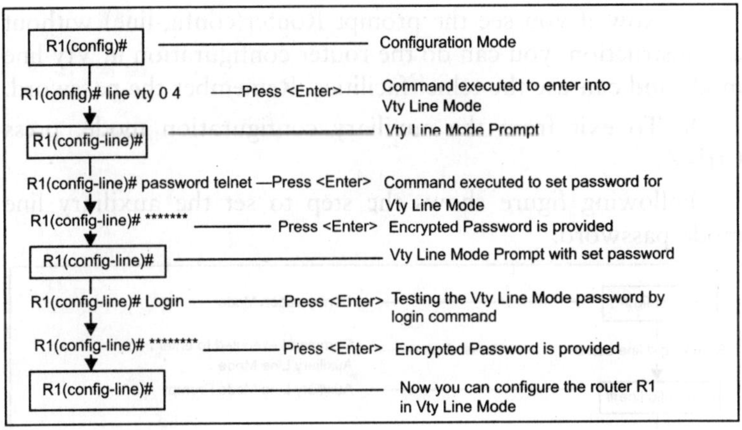

Auxiliary Line Mode

1. Type line aux 0 at the prompt Router(config)# and press <Enter> as follows:

Router(config)# line aux 0 Press <Enter>.

2. You will enter into auxiliary line mode and the prompt changes as indicated below:

Router(config-line)#.

3. Setting auxiliary line mode password to backdoor.

Type "password backdoor" at the prompt Router(config-line)# and press <Enter> as follows:

Router(config-line)# password backdoor Press <Enter>.

4. You are prompted to type a password at the auxiliary line mode prompt. Type the password and press enter.

Router(config-line)# ******** Press <Enter>.

5. Now if you want to test the password that you have supplied to the Vty line mode to enter into it, type "login" at the prompt Router(config-line)# as follows and press <Enter>.

Router(config-line)# Login Press <Enter>.

6. You are prompted to type a password at the auxiliary line mode prompt. Type the password and press enter.

Router(config-line)# ******** Press <Enter>.

7. Now if you see the prompt Router(config-line) without any instruction, you can do the router configuration in Vty line mode and can use the telnet facilities. Remember the password.

8. To exit from the auxiliary configuration mode, press Ctrl+Z.

Following figure shows the step to set the auxiliary line mode password.

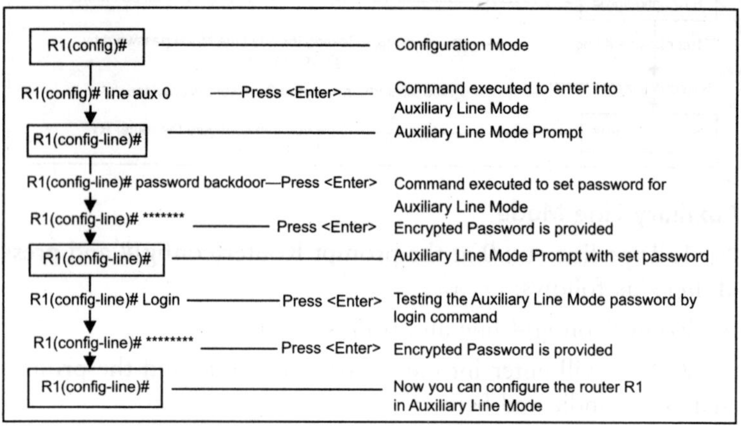

Setting Encrypted Password

You can set an encrypted password by using the

Type "service password-encryption" at the prompt Router (config)# and press <Enter> as follows.

Router(config)# service password-encryption Press <Enter>

This command will set a weak password

Setting enable password to the router

Type "enable password" at the prompt Router(config)# and press <Enter> as follows:

Router(config)# enable password Press <Enter>.

This command will set enable password.

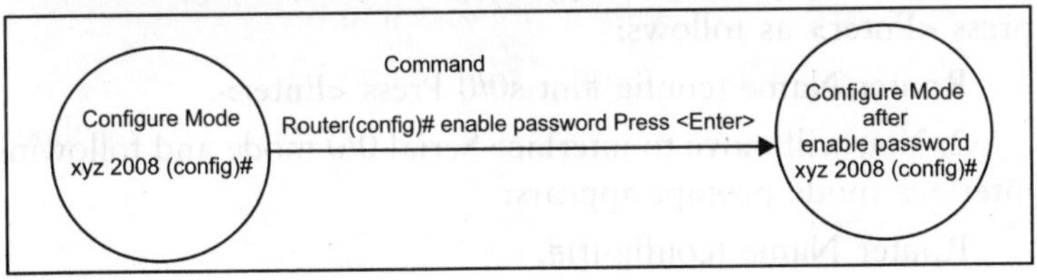

You can turns off password encryption by using following command:

Router(config)# no service password-encryption Press <Enter>.

After this action password cannot be encrypted.

Assigning Hostname to Router

For configuring a router you have to provide a hostname name to it. Hostname may be any string.

Type hostname xyz2008 at the prompt Router(config)# and press <Enter> as follows:

Router(config)#hostname xyz2008 Press <Enter>.

The following prompt will appear:

xyz2000(config)#

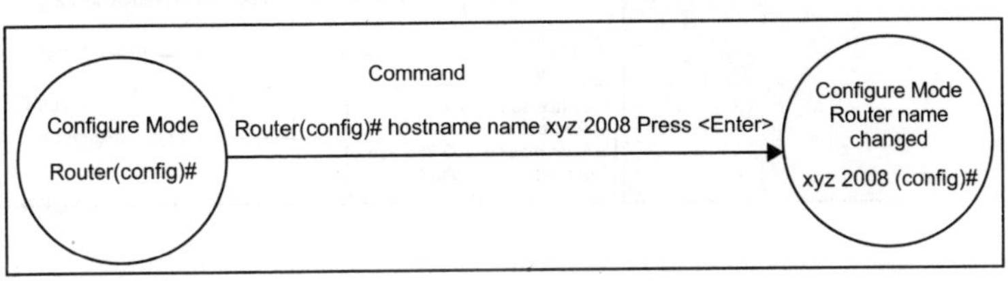

You are in configuration mode to configure a router whose name is "xyz2008".

Serial Interface Configuration

1. Go to global mode prompt Router(config)#.

Type "int s0/0" at the prompt Router(config)# and then press <Enter> as follows:

Router Name (config)#int s0/0 Press <Enter>.

2. You will move to interface Serial 0/0 mode and following interface mode prompt appears:

Router Name (config-if)#.

3. Type "ip address 192.164.20.1 255.255.255.0" at the prompt Router(config-if)# and press <Enter> as follows:

Router Name(config-if)#ip address 192.168.10.1 255.255.255.0 press <Enter>.

This action will provide IP address and subnet mask to the interface.

4. To set the clock rate for the interface s0/0 type clock rate 56000 at the prompt Router(config-if)# and press <Enter> as follows:

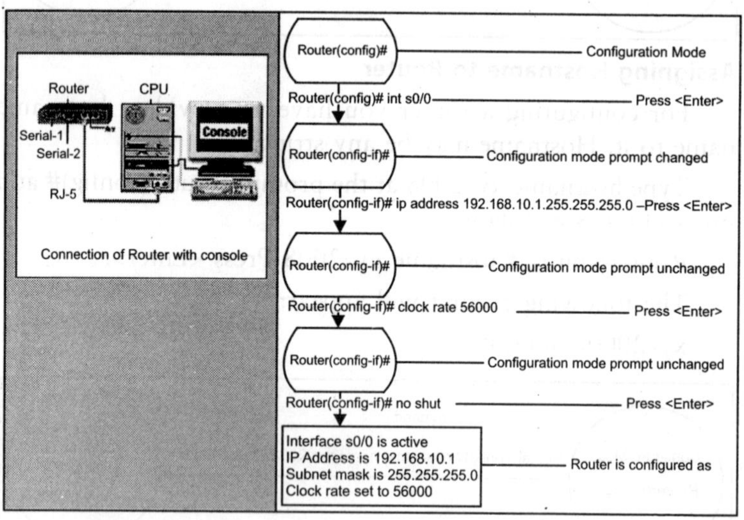

Router Name(config-if)#clock rate 56000 Press <Enter>.

This action will set the interface s0/0 clock rate to 56000.

5. To make interface active, use the following command with the interface Serial 0/0 mode prompt.

Type "no shut" in front of Router(config-if)# and press <Enter> as follows:

Router Name(config-if)# no shut press <Enter>.

Fast Ethernet Mode Configuration

1. Go to global mode prompt Router Name(config)#.

2. Type "int fa0/0" at the prompt Router(config)# and then press <Enter> as follows:

Router Name(config)# int fa0/0 Press <Enter>.

You will move to Fast Ethernet mode and following interface mode appears:

Router Name(config-if)#.

3. Type Router Name(config-if)# description Accounting LAN press <Enter>.

This will sets an optional descriptor of the link that is locally significant.

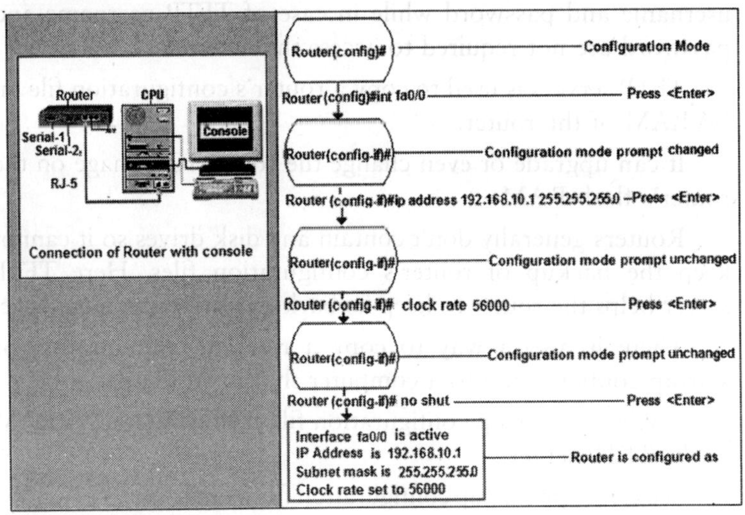

4. Type "ip address 192.164.20.1 255.255.255.0" at the Router(config-if)# prompt and press <Enter> as follows:

Router Name(config-if)#ip address 192.168.10.1 255.255.255.0 press <Enter>

This action will provide IP address and subnet mask to the interface.

5. To make interface active, use the following command with the interface Serial 0/0 mode prompt.

Type "no shut" in front of Router(config-if)# and press <Enter> as follows:

Router Name(config-if)# no shut press <Enter>.

TFTP Server

A PC on which TFTP server software is loaded and connected with the network is known as TFTP server. A transport layer protocol known as TFTP is used by TFTP server.

TFTP (Trivial File Transfer Protocol) is a protocol that is used to transfer file. It is transport layer protocol that is supported by TCP/IP and used by TFTP server. It works in the same manner as FTP.

The difference between TFTP and FTP is that FTP needs username and password while in case of TFTP username and password are not required to access the network.

- TFTP servers is used to copy a router's configuration file on NVRAM of the router.

It can upgrade or even change the router IOS image on the router's flash RAM.

Routers generally don't contain any disk drives so it cannot keep the backup of router's configuration files. Here TFTP server helps the router to keep its backup file intact on its drive.

There is also a way to copy a running configuration or startup configuration to a computer that is on the network.

Coping of startup configuration file from router's NVRAM to the TFTP server.

We can copy startup configuration file from router's NVRAM to the TFTP server whose IP address is known to us.

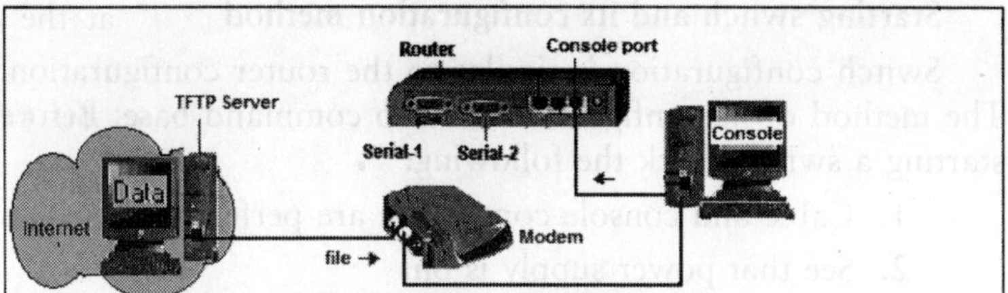

TFTP server copies router's configuration file on NVRAM

For copying the startup configuration file from router to TFTP server go through the following steps:

1. Start the TFTP server software on the server workstation.

2. Open the router console by switch on the router and the console PC.

Type "enable" at user mode prompt R2002> as follows:

R2002>enable Press <Enter>.

You will enter into privileged mode and prompt will be changed to R2002#.

3. Type "copy tftp startup-config" at the prompt R2002# as follows:

R2002# copy tftp startup-config Press <Enter>.

4. You are prompted to type the IP address of the TFTP server. Let the TFTP server IP address is 10.24.0.2.

Type the IP address of the TFTP server at the Router Name# prompt as follows:

R2002#ip 10.24.0.2 Press <Enter>.

5. You are prompted to give name to the configuration file on the TFTP server you want to copy.

Type the <File Name> at the prompt the R2000# press <Enter> as follows:

R2000#<File Name> Press <Enter>.

6. Next step you are prompted to confirm the file name.

7. Press Enter to confirm the file name.

Starting switch and its configuration method

Switch configuration is similar to the router configuration. The method of its configuration is also command base. Before starting a switch check the following:

1. Cable and console connection are perfect.
2. See that power supply is on.
3. Check the Boot sequence.

Points are to be observed

1. All the indicators of the switch are green, at the start.
2. When test is completed, you can notice that all the indicators are off.
3. All the indicator's color will change to amber, if the test fails.
4. System indicator color changes to amber, on failure of any of the test.
5. POST is completed, if all the test are successfully carried out.
6. When the POST is completed successfully, all the indicators start blinking and then turn off.

LAN Switch Configuration

There are three methods to configure switch:

Using console port.

Using Web-based Visual Switch Manager (VSM).

Command-Line Interface (CLI).

Switch Configuration

Once the switch is connected with the console port, system configuration menu is displayed as given below. It contains PCA Number, System serial number along with other numbers.

User can use the following:

Interface Menu

M - Menus

K - Command Line

I - IP Configuration

P - Console Password

You can select any of the above capital letter to activate the menu.

Let us select: K

We are using the command line interface (CLI).

User mode command prompt will be displayed on screen.

>

Type enable in front of User mode command prompt

>enable press<Enter>

Enable mode command prompt change in to pound sign (#), like we have seen in router configuration.

#

Switch is configured with the configure terminal command.

For entering into configure terminal command type config t in front of enable mode command prompt as follows and press enter:

#config t <Enter>

Enter configuration commands, one per line. End with CNTL/Z

(config)#

Allot host name to the switch for its identification.

Type the hostname in front of global configuration mode and press enter.

(config)#hostname Ishita <Enter>.

Prompt will turned as follows:

Ishita(config)#.

If you ever want to get back to the menu-based configuration system from the command line, enter the menu command.

Ishita(config)# menu

Main Menu

[C] Console Settings

[S] System

[N] Network Management

[P] Port Configuration

[A] Port Addressing

[D] Port Statistics Detail

[M] Monitoring

[V] Virtual LAN

[R] Multicast Registration

[F] Firmware

[I] RS-232 Interface

[U] Usage Summaries

[H] Help

[K] Command Line

[X] Exit Management Console

Enter Selection:

From the above menu you can select any of the capital letter for particular purpose.

For example, you can choose 'P' for port setting for the switch.

You can select port addressing for the switch by selecting 'A' and so on.

Similar commands as in case of a router, are used for configuration of switch in most of the cases.

Router Management

14

Router is a network device that is used to route data packets between networks. It reads the information from the header of the packet and decides its destination. If packet is destined for a network to which the router has to access then immediately, it will open the outer packet, readdresses the packet to the proper Ethernet address, and transmits it on that network.

If message is destined for another network and it is to be sent to another router, it will re-package the outer packet and sends it to the next router. The routing theory which depends upon the routing tables to determine packet destinations.

Routing takes place at the network layer of the OSI model. Routing enables to connect the networks of different architectures like Token Ring and Ethernet. At the data link level routers are able to transform information, but they cannot transform the information from one data format such as TCP/IP to IPX/SPX.

Routers are not able to transmit broadcast packets or corrupted packets to any other networks.

When the router receives the broadcast, it discards the broadcast without forwarding it on to other networks.

Packets are discarded when their proper address are not found in the routing table.

There are various type of routers shown below which are used according to the media.

Routers not only able to break up broadcast domains by default, but they can break up collision domains as well.

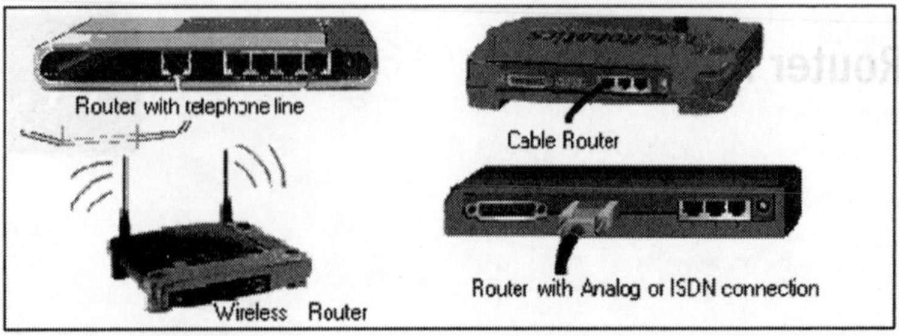

The advantages of using routers in your network are as follows:

About Router

Routers has to execute commands. It has to prepare routing tables and save and store them.

Routers must have processing power along with some storage capacity to carry out all these activities.

An operating system is to be installed on console PC that is used to configure router.

Along with the processing power, routers needs to store configured information in a storage memory chip to boot the router internal operating system (IOS). The other storage devices are used to deal with the dynamic information on the router during packets movement on the network.

Router has following components, which support the router to carry out its network duties:

1. RAM
2. ROM
3. NVRAM
4. Flash
5. Interface
6. CPU

RAM

RAM is just like the dynamic memory of PC.

RAM is a storage device that stores the information temporarily on the router. When packets are received by the router, they are stored on RAM. Router examines the addressing information. It also stores the current router configuration and the current routing table. It runs IOS, routing table, ARP and router configuration.

ROM

ROM is read only memory just like personal computer.

It performs the Power-on Self-Test (POST) and has the bootstrap program for the router.

It stores the subset or the entire router IOS. In case of the failure of Flash RAM, back up of IOS is available on the ROM which help to cope up with any major disaster on network that take place. The ROM chips is a replaceable component and can be upgraded at any time. It has a ROM monitor which is used to manufacture the router in a shop. The complete assembly of the router is tested in a lab and defects are rectified. It is also used for online troubleshooting.

NVRAM (Non-volatile RAM)

Startup configuration file is loaded on the NVRAM. NVRAM is erasable, and writable component. You can write or copy the present configuration on the router to NVRAM.

It retains the stored information even after the power of router goes off like BIOS chip on PC. This feature of NVRAM enable you to keep the router configuration intact and you need not to configure it every time when power of router goes off.

Flash

Flash RAM is non-volatile. It functions like a file system like PC. It is costlier than NVRAM. Flash RAM is a kind of ROM that is erasable and programmable. Flash is used to store the IOS that runs on the router.

There are special kind of Flash RAM that comes with enhanced version of IOS that enables you to upgrade the router easily. Flash RAM are practically SIMMs (Single-Inline Memory Modules). For enhancing the capacity of Flash memory you can install an additional Flash RAM on your router.

Mini-IOS

It is a program file. It is called Boot-loader, and used to bring up an interface and load a IOS into flash memory. It also carries out some maintenance activities.

CPU

Routers has also a CPU like PC. CPU contains a microprocessor.

There are different kind of microprocessor available. Cisco 2505, Motorola 68EC030 and Motorola MC68040 are some of the microprocessor used in router.

Interfaces

Router provides three interfaces. One interface is used for LAN and two serial interfaces are used for connecting subnets like ISDN, T1 leased lines.

Connecting Router with Console

Before installing the router on the network for its actual functions it is necessary to configure the router.

For configuration the router, the console marked terminal is to be connected with PC.

Before connecting the router with the PC, take care of the following points:

1. Power supply switch of router should be in off position.
2. See that power supply of main switch is also off.
3. Now connect the power cord of the router with the main switch.

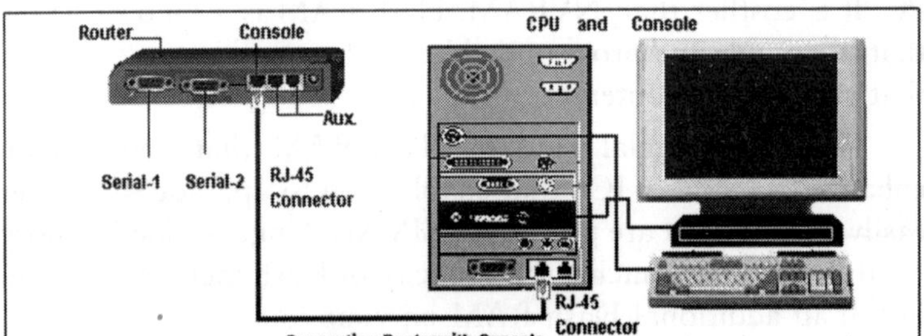

Connecting Router with Console

4. Connect the router terminal marked as console with the CPU through RJ-45 connector as shown below.
5. Switch on the main switch of power supply and then switch on the router switch.
6. Switch on PC also.

It is assumed that terminal emulation software is already installed on your PC. If not, then install this software on your PC. Emulation software enable you to communicates and configure the router. ProComm Plus is a software that supports communication facilities. Tera Term Pro is an another software that can be used to configure terminal emulator.

If you are not having any terminal emulation software then use Hyper Terminal program. Hyper terminal is supported by Windows Operating System.

Setting communication parameters with Hyper Terminal for the serial port take the following steps Select Start→Programs →Accessories→Communications→Hyper Terminal.

Click on Hyper Terminal.

Following Connection Description window will appear.

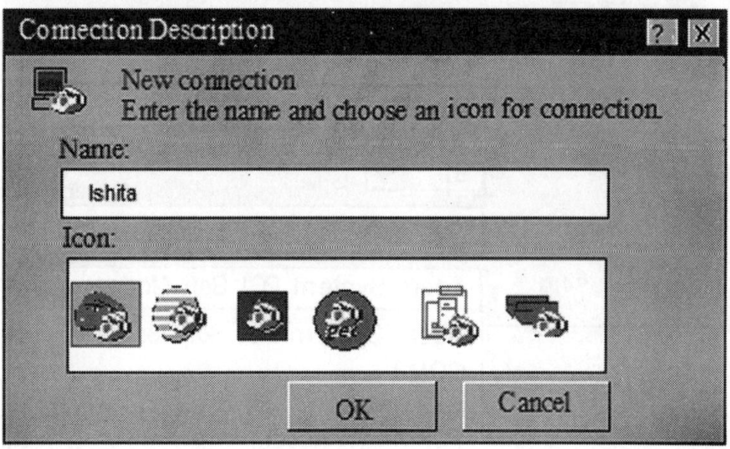

Choose the first icon and click OK.

The following "Connect To" window will appear.

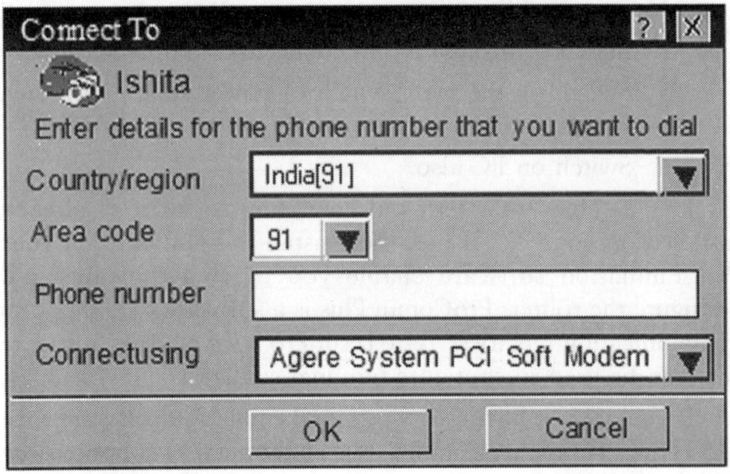

Step 3 Don't attempt to configure a phone number.

Click the arrow "Connect using" combo box.

You will get the following window.

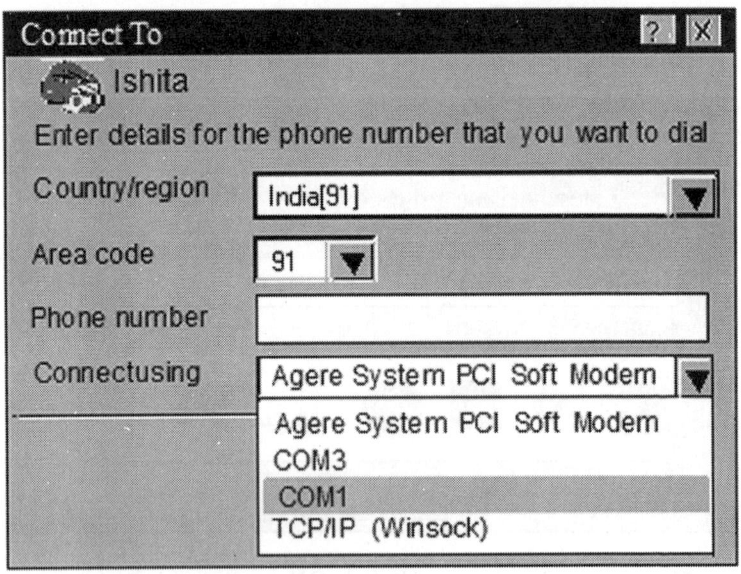

Select COM1 and then click OK.

Following "COM1 Properties" window will appear.

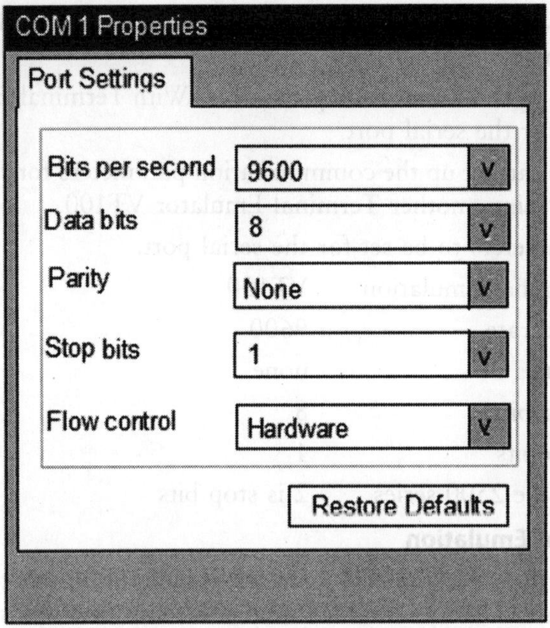

1. Change bits per second from 2400 to 9600 bps.
2. Data bit remain the same.
3. Parity will remain to none.
4. Stop bit also remains unchanged.
5. It is what the router requires the console terminal to operate with.

Your new connection is setup and saved in Hyper Terminal folder.

You can start the hyper terminal program as follows.

Go to Hyper Terminal as follows:

Select Start→Programs→Accessories→Communications→ Hyper Terminal.

You will see two icons one is Hyper Terminal folder without arrow and another is Hyper Terminal program folder with arrow. This contains the executive file "Ishita".

Click on it. Your Hyper Terminal editor will open.

Now you can configure the router using Hyper Terminal program.

Setting communication parameters With Terminal Emulator VT100 for the serial port.

You can set up the communication parameters for the serial port by using another Terminal Emulator VT100.

Parameters to be set for the serial port.

Terminal Emulation	VT100
Baud rate	9600
Parity	none
Data bits	8
Stop bits	1
For the 2500 series	2 is stop bits

Terminal Emulation

VT100 is the standard main-frame and mini-frame terminal. It acts as a dummy terminal and just receives and sends packets through serial port.

Baud Rate

Baud rate is set to 9600. It means that you have set the speed of data transmission to 9600 elements per second. If the element are bits then the speed of data transmission will be 9600 bps.

Parity

Parity is the setting for serial communication for error-detection.

Parity may be even or odd. Odd parity indicates that each data word contains an odd number of bits.

Even parity indicates that each data word contains an even number of bits. This parity setting controls the data transmission and if any data word does not follow the parity rule, it is retransmitted.

Data Bits

Data bits indicates the total number of bits sent and received.

Stop Bits

Stop bits indicates that all the bits of a particular data packets are received and stops the flow of data stream.

Selecting IOS Version

After selecting a router for a specific internet working task, you have to choose appropriate version of IOS that supports the type of routing on your network.

If your network uses IP routing then choose the IOS version that supports IP routing.

Similarly for other protocol like IPX and AppleTalk you must use the appropriate version of IOS.

Establishing communications between the router and the console:

1. Start the terminal emulator and set the communication parameters of appropriate serial port.
2. Switch on the power supply of router. The following booting sequence activities take place on the router.

Booting Sequence

(a) When the router is switched on, the ROM chip performs POST. It checks the presence of all the internal components of the router such as processor, interfaces, and all memories components. It checks the necessary functions of the router's hardware. It locates the presence of all interfaces.

(b) After POST bootstrap code are loaded that boots the router just like PC. ROM runs the bootstrap program and searches for the IOS. Then ROM itself can load the IOS.

A complete or a partial IOS resides on the ROM itself. The IOS program is stored in the Flash RAM.

IOS can be loaded from TFTP server if router is connected with it.

(c) After IOS is loaded on the router the router searches for the configuration file. The configuration file resides in router's NVRAM. By giving copy command running configuration can be copied on NVRAM.

This configuration file can also be loaded on NVRAM through TFTP server. Configuration file contains the information that enables the interfaces for setting parameters related and routing protocols.

3. After booting process of router, a window will appear that will display the specifications of serial port. You can check and confirm the console and serial port connection. If you have selected the correct serial port, you can communicate with the router through the terminal emulator program.

Working with the System Configuration Dialog Box

When you boot up a new router the System Configuration dialog is loaded.

Now system configuration dialog box ask you several questions one after another. If you answer to these questions correctly, the basic configuration for the router takes place.

For answering these questions you must know certain configuration parameters:

1. You must know which network protocols you will route IP, IPX or AppleTalk.
2. You must be acquainted with the parameters related to the different type of interfaces.
3. If you want to use IP as routing protocol, you must know the IP addresses of the router interfaces for its configuration.

Configuring a Router from Scratch

Take the following steps:

1. Erase the configuration file for a router and then start over, building a new basic configuration using the configuration dialog. At the enable prompt type "erase startup-config" and press <Enter> as follows:

   Router# erase startup-config Press <Enter>.

   This action will erase the configuration file from NVRAM.

2. To restart the router at the enable prompt type "reload" and press <Enter> as follows:

   Router# reload Press <Enter>.

   The router will reboot and the System Configuration dialog will appear on the console screen.

   You can confirm from the dialog box that the old configuration file is no more there.

Configuring Passwords using Setup Dialog

The setup dialog can ask you quite a few questions related to setting various passwords for the routers and configuring the interfaces on the router. The first part of the setup configuration relates to setting up enable and virtual terminal passwords for the router.

1. You will be prompted

   "Would you like to <Enter> the initial configuration dialog."

   Press <Enter>.

2. Next you will be prompted

   "Do you want to see the current interface summary."

   Press <Enter>.

   Summary of the interfaces will be displayed.

   The summary indicates that the Ethernet 0 interface is enabled and the serial interfaces on this router are disabled and interfaces are without IP numbers.

3. You are now prompted to write the name of the router which you are configuring.

   Type* hostname "xyz" at the prompt Router(config)# and press <Enter> as follows:

   Router(config)#hostname xyz Press <Enter>.

   The prompt will change to xyz(config)#. You can write even any name.

4. Next you are prompted to provide an enable secret password.

This encrypted password enable you to access to the router's Enable mode.

Type "enable password" at the prompt xyz(config)# and press <Enter>.

xyz(config)#enable password Press <Enter>.

You will be prompted to type encrypted password. Type the password and press <Enter> as follows:

Router Name# ******** Press <Enter>.

5. Next you will be prompted to give an "enable" password.

   This is second password used by earlier versions. It does not provide any encrypted password for the Enable mode. It is just to fill the password blank to proceed further.

   Press <Enter>.

6. Next you have to provide a virtual terminal password for the router.

   Type "line vty 0 4" at the prompt xyz(config)# as follows and press <Enter>.

   xyz(config)# line vty 0 4 Press <Enter>.

   This action will bring you in the Virtual terminal Configuration mode with following prompt: xyz(config-line)#.

   Type Password at the prompt xyz(config-line)# and press enter as follows:

   xyz(config-line)# ******** Press <Enter>.

   This action will set virtual terminal password.

7. Next you will be asked "if you want to enable SNMP".

   Type "No" and press <Enter>.

   Your basic configuration of router is completed.

Configuring Routed Protocols

Following are the steps that you have to take for configuration of the routed and routing protocols on your router:

1. Routed protocol are supported the IOS version. Choose the routing protocol that is to be used on your router.

   You are asked to enable the DEC net protocol.

   By default dialog box displays a negative response as "No".

   Press <Enter>.
2. Next you are asked to enable and configure AppleTalk protocol on your router.

   By default dialog box displays a negative response as "No".

   Press <Enter>.
3. Next you are asked to enable and configure IPX protocol on your router.

   By default dialog box displays a negative response as "No".

   Press <Enter>.
4. Next you are asked to enable and configure IP protocol on your router.

   By default dialog box displays a positive response as "Yes".

   Press <Enter>.
5. You will be prompted to configure IGRP on the router.

   Type "No" and press <Enter>.
6. You will be prompted to configure RIP on the router.

   Type "No" and press <Enter>.
7. You will be prompted to enable bridging.

   Type "No" and press <Enter>.
8. You are able to configure IP protocol now.

Configuring Router Interfaces

Now you have to configure the router's interfaces. You have to choose the router interfaces which appears in the dialog box like Ethernet and serial interfaces. You have to provide the appropriate IP addresses for the interfaces over the router.

Configuring Interfaces with the Setup Dialog

1. You are asked to use Ethernet 0 interface on your router.

   For enabling E0 interface, press <Enter>.

2. Next you are asked to configure IP on this interface.

   Press <Enter>.

3. Next you are asked to provide the IP address of the interface.

   Type the IP address for the E0 interface. For example, type 10.40.2.1.

   Press <Enter>.

4. Next you are asked for the number of bits you want to use for the subnet field. The number of bits indicates the number of subnets you are going to create. Type 4 for creation of four subnets.

   Press <Enter>.

5. Next you will be asked to enable all the ports of the hub.

   Press <Enter>.

6. Next you are asked to configure the next interface.

   The next interface on your router may be serial 0.

   Press <Enter>.

7. Next you are prompted to configure IP on the S0 interface.

   Press <Enter>.

8. You are given the option of configuring the S0 interface as IP unnumbered.

   Press <Enter>.

9. You are now prompted to provide an IP address against the S0 interface.

   Type the IP address. For example, 10.40.3.1.

   Press <Enter>.

10. You will then be asked to provide the subnet field bits. This is defaulted to 4, which was <Enter>ed in step 4.

    Press <Enter> to use the same bit count.

11. Next you are prompted to configure the Serial 1 interface.

    Press <Enter>.

12. Next you are prompted for, disable IP numbered.

    Press <Enter>.

13. Next type the IP address as 10.40.4.1 at the prompt.

    Press <Enter>.

14. Next you are asked to supply the bit for the subnet mask again.

    Type 4 and press <Enter>.

    As soon as you press <Enter>, the screen will scroll and display the link tests for the interfaces configuration.

15. Next you will be asked to confirm the use of current configuration. Type Yes and press <Enter>.

    This will save the configuration file on NVRAM that you have just created by dialog box.

16. Press <Enter> again.

    You will be in the router's user mode prompt.

    Router's user mode will enable you to see configuration parameters.

    Router's user mode will also enable you to use various Router Modes.

    You can use various modes like "User mode, Privileged mode" to edit the router's configuration.

17. Now you can test the availability of different router's mode after the router's basic configuration.

Copying the Startup Configuration to Router

1. Start the TFTP server software on the server workstation.

2 Open the router console by switch on the router and the console PC.

   Type "enable" at user mode prompt R20002> as follows:

   R2002> enable press <Enter>.

   You will enter into privileged mode and prompt will be changed to R2002#.

3. Type copy tftp startup-config at the prompt R2002# as follows:

   R2002# copy tftp startup-config press <Enter>.

4. You are prompted to type the IP address of the TFTP server. Let the TFTP server IP address is 10.24.0.2.

   Type the IP address of the TFTP server at the Router Name# prompt as follows:

   R2002#ip 10.24.0.2 Press <Enter>.

5. You are prompted to give name to the configuration file on the TFTP server you want to copy.

   Type the name at the prompt the Router Name#<File Name> Press <Enter>.

6. Next step you are prompted to confirm.

Show Commands

Show command is widely used for getting information about the router.

R2002#show?

This command will display a complete list of commands.

R2002#show interfaces

This will show all configured interfaces.

R2002#show interface serial 0

This command will describe serial 0 interface statistics.

R2002#show interface serial 0

This command will show of all interfaces, along with the IP address assigned to interfaces.

R2002#show controllers serial 0.

This command will show interface hardware configuration. It also shows the clock rate DCE, DTE cable connection.

R2002#show clock

This command will display clock time set on the router.

R2002#show hosts

This command shows a list of names and addresses of hosts.

R2002#show users

This command shows a list of users.

R2002#show flash

This command will describe Flash memory.

R2002#show version

This command will show software version on the router.

R2002#show arp

This command will show ARP table.

R2002#show protocols

This command will show about Layer3 protocols.

R2002#show startup-config

This command will show the configuration file details that is saved on NVRAM.

R2002#show running-config

This command will show about the current configuration. That is running on RAM.

Setting the Clock Time Zone

Type clock timezone EST 5 at the prompt Router(config)# prompt and press <Enter> as follows:

Router(config)#clock timezone EST 5 press <Enter>

This action will set the time zone that is Eastern Standard Time which is 5 hours behind UTC.

Local Hostname can be used for IP Address

Just like on mobile telephone you can be recognize by your mobile phone number or by your name. In a similar manner IP address of the host can be recognize by host name you configure on your router.

Type "ip host Ishita 192.168.1.2" at the prompt Router(config)# as follows and press <Enter>:

Router(config)# ip host Ishita 192.168.1.2 press <Enter>.

Now you can use Ishita in place of IP address 192.168.1.2.

If you want to test the IP address assigned to your computer by ping command.

You can type ping 192.168.1.2 or ping Ishita at the prompt Router# and press <Enter> as follows:

Router# ping 192.168.1.2 Or Router# ping Ishita and press <Enter>.

Both commands will perform a similar function. Twenty-three is the default port number in the ip host command.

Saving Configuration

When you edit a router's configuration file by using terminal emulator software that is to be saved for further application. It is saved in local NVRAM or on TFTP server.

Command for saving configuration on local NVRAM.

Type "copy run start" at the prompt Router Name# and press <Enter> as follows:

Router#copy run start press <Enter>.

This action will save the current configuration on NVRAM.

Command for saving configuration on remote TFTP server.

Type "copy run tftp" at the prompt Router Name# and press <Enter> as follows:

Router#copy run tftp press <Enter>.

This action will save the current configuration on TFTP server.

Removing Startup-Configurations file from NVRAM.

Type "erase start" at the prompt Router Name# and press <Enter> as follows:

Router Name# erase start press <Enter>.

This action will delete the startup-configuration file from NVRAM.

These are the set of commands that are commonly used to configure a router.

Configuration Example: Basic Router Configuration

Privileged mode

Router>en-<Enter>

Sets local time on router

Router#clock set 18:30:00 15 Nov 2004

Global config mode

Router#config t -<Enter>

Sets router name to Senjutishita

Router(config)#hostname Senjutishita -<Entcr>.

Turns off name resolution on unrecognized commands (spelling mistakes).

Senjutishita(config)#no ip domain-lookup Senjutishita (config)# banner motd #-Creates an MOTD banner.

Sets time zone to Eastern Standard Time (5 from UTC)

Senjutishita(config)#clock timezone EST 5-

Enables secret password set to sisco

Senjutishita(config)#enable secret sisco -<Enter>

Encryption-Passwords will be given weak cncryption

Senjutishita(config)#service password -<Enter>

Line console mode

Senjutishita(config)#line con 0 -<Enter>

Commands will not be interrupted by unsolicited messages

Senjutishita(config-line)#logging sync -<Enter>

Sets password to class

Senjutishita(config-line)#password class -<Enter>

Enables password checking at login

Senjutishita(config-line)#login -<Enter>

Moves to virtual Telnet lines 0 through 4

Senjutishita(config-line)#line vty 0 4 -<Enter>

Sets password to class

Senjutishita(config-line)#password class -<Enter>

Enables password checking at login

Senjutishita(config-line)#login -<Enter>

Moves to line auxiliary mode

Senjutishita(config-line)#line aux 0 -<Enter>

Sets password to class

Senjutishita(config-line)#password class -<Enter>

Enables password checking at login

Senjutishita(config-line)#login -<Enter>

Moves back to global config mode

Senjutishita(config-line)#exit -<Enter>

Encryption-Turns off password encryption

Senjutishita(config)#no service password -<Enter>

Moves to Fast Ethernet 0/0 mode

Senjutishita(config)#int fa 0/0 -<Enter>

Sets locally significant description of the interface

Senjutishita(config-if)#desc Engineering LAN -<Enter>

Assigns IP address and subnet mask to the interface

Senjutishita(config-if)#ip address 172.16.10.1 255.255.255.0 -<Enter>

Turns on the interface

Senjutishita(config-if)#no shut -<Enter>

Moves directly to Serial 0/0 mode

Senjutishita(config-if)#int s0/0 -<Enter>

Sets locally significant description of the interface

Senjutishita(config-if)#desc Link to Bullow Router -<Enter>

Assigns IP address and subnet mask to the interface

Senjutishita(config-if)#ip address 172.16.20.1 255.255.255.0 -<Enter>

Sets a clock rate for serial transmission. DCE cable must be plugged into this interface

Senjutishita(config-if)#clock rate 56000

Turns on the interface

Senjutishita(config-if)#no shut -<Enter>

Moves back to global config mode

Senjutishita(config-if)#exit -<Enter>

Sets a local host name resolution to IP address 172.16.20.2

Senjutishita(config)#ip host buffalo 172.16.20.2 -<Enter>

Moves back to privileged mode

Senjutishita(config)#exit -<Enter>

Saves running-config to NVRAM

Senjutishita#copy run start -<Enter>.

15 Internet Explorer

Internet Explorer-6 is a Web browser. It is a Microsoft product and used by the host computer for internet connection and browsing. When you install windows operating system on your computer, it is automatically loaded.

About Internet Explorer

When you click on Internet explorer icon "e" on the desk top or select it from start program, Internet explorer window appears on the screen as shown in the following figure:

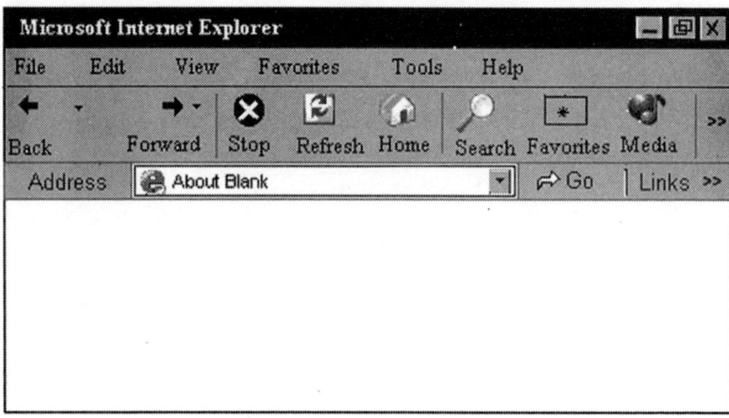

It generally contains three lines of menu items:

1. Top line is the main menu that contains items like, File, Edit, View, Favorites, Tools and Help.
2. Middle line contains a set of icons.
3. Bottom line contains Address bar, go and links items.

Main menu items are actually the set of buttons which is explained as follows:

File Button has the following items:

New, Open, Edit, Save, Save As, Page Setup, Print, Print Previous, Send, Import Export, Properties Work Offline and Close.

File

Click on File and then click on New, a drop down list of items appears on the screen, as shown in the following figure:

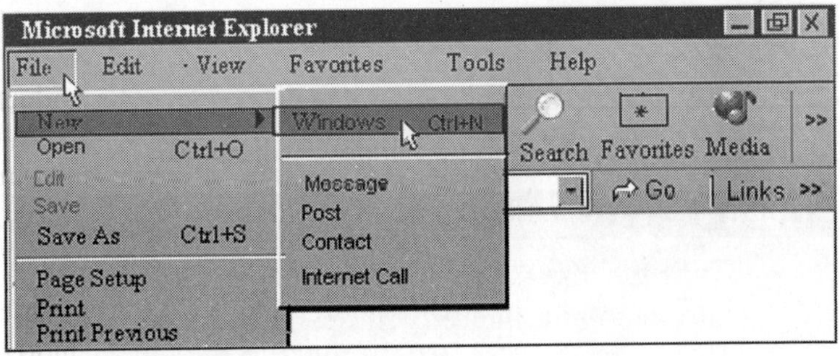

Windows, Message, Post, Contact, Internet Call.

1. Click on Windows, another Internet Explorer window will open.
2. Click on Message, Outlook Express will open to write new message to send e-mail.
3. Click on Post, Internet connection wizard will open to configure the outlook express connection.
4. Click on Contact, Address book of Main Identity will open.
5. Click on Internet Call, a Net meeting window will appear, where you can enter the, Name Address and e-mail address of a person, to whom you may like to contact regularly.

Opening the site through main menu

Click on File and then click on Open As shown in the following figure:

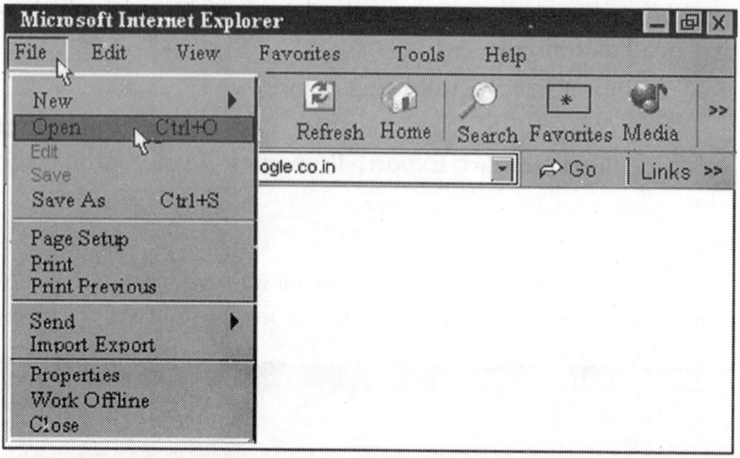

Following "Open" pop-up window will appear.

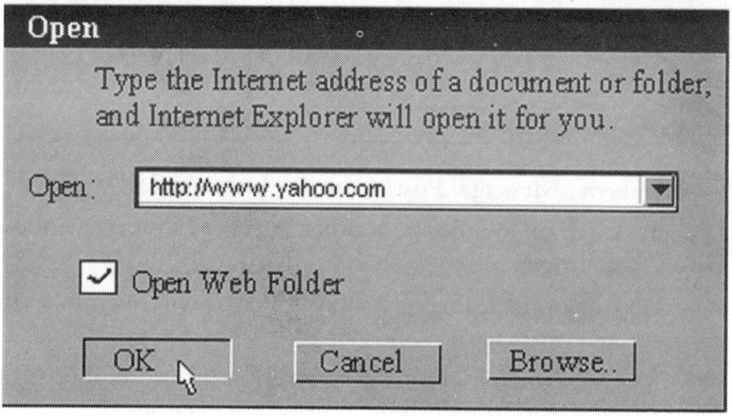

Write the name of URL, File or Folder and then click OK button of the above window.

Internet Explorer will open the file or folder for you. If you write the name of any URL you will be prompted to connect your computer with the server for opening the site.

1. Suppose you type http://www.yahoo.com inside the combo box strip in front of Open and then click OK. If you are online with the server the yahoo.com site will appear on the screen. If you are offline, you will be prompted to connect with the server.

You can also open any folder by using "Browse" button. When your are working offline Edit and Save Buttons are inactive.

Other items of drop down list:

1. Save As is used for saving the web page as HTML documents in your My Documents folder.
2. Items Page set up, Print and Print Previous are used for printing the web page.
3. Send item contains an arrow button and has the three item as follows:
   (i) Page By E-mail
   (ii) Link By E-mail
   (iii) Shortcut to Desktop

The following picture shows the Send items along with its associated items.

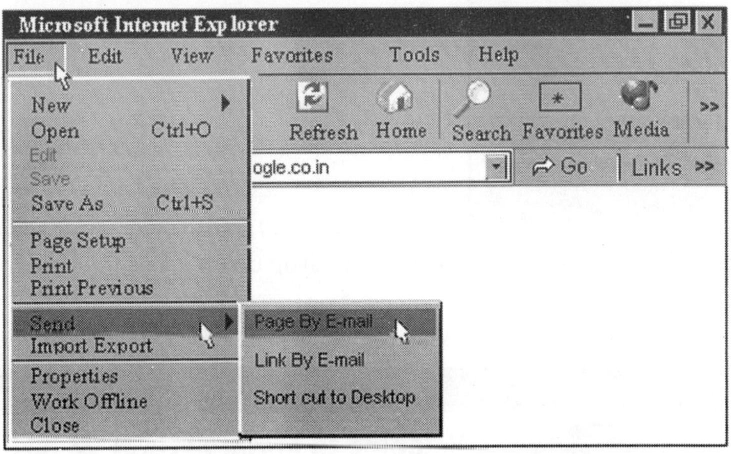

(i) If you click on Page By E-mail, a New Message window will appear on the screen, that will contain the web page which you want to send to your friend. Enter the E-mail address, subject and click on the Send button your message will be sent to the destination.

(ii) If you click on Link By E-mail, a message window will appear in which you can see, that the web page is included as attachment. Subject is also entered as the name of the web page automatically. In the textbox below you can also see the URL address of the web page. Enter the E-mail address click on the Send button. Your web page will be sent to the destination.

(iii) If you click on the Shortcut To Desktop, the web page short cut icon will appear on the Desktop.

Import Export item is used for import cookies and favorites from other resources and export them to other destined folder like Favorites, Link and Media.

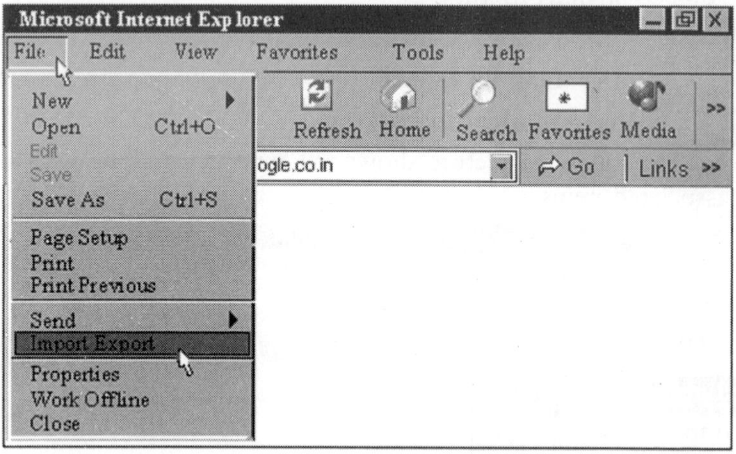

Click on Import Export on the drop down list as indicated in the above figure.

Following Import/Export Wizard will appear on the screen.

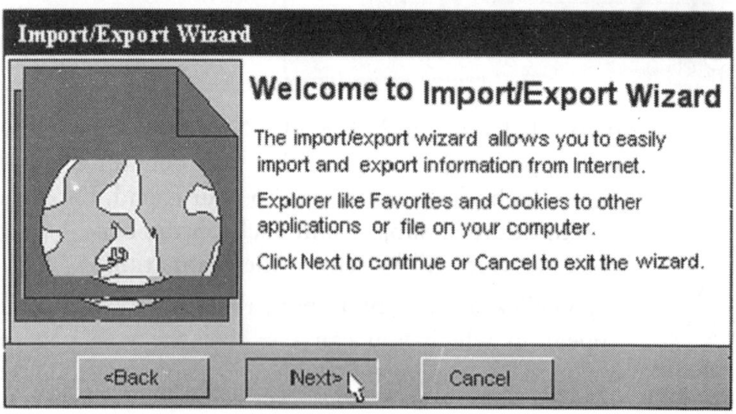

Click Next in the above Import/Export wizard to import or exports the information from Internet.

Following Import/Export wizard will appear.

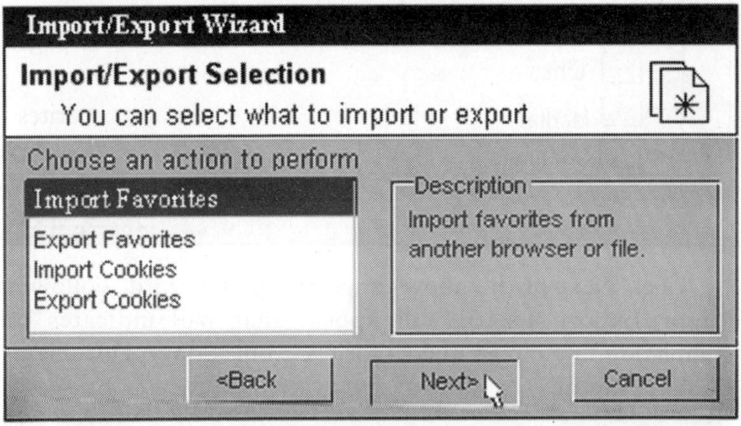

Click Next in the above Import/Export wizard to import favorites from another browser or file.

Following Import/Export wizard will appear.

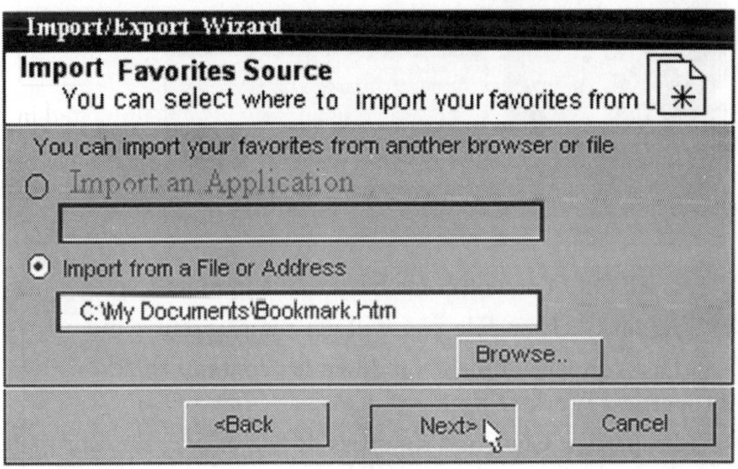

After entering the text "C:\My Documents\Bookmark.htm" click Next in the above Import/Export wizard.

Following Import/Export wizard will appear:

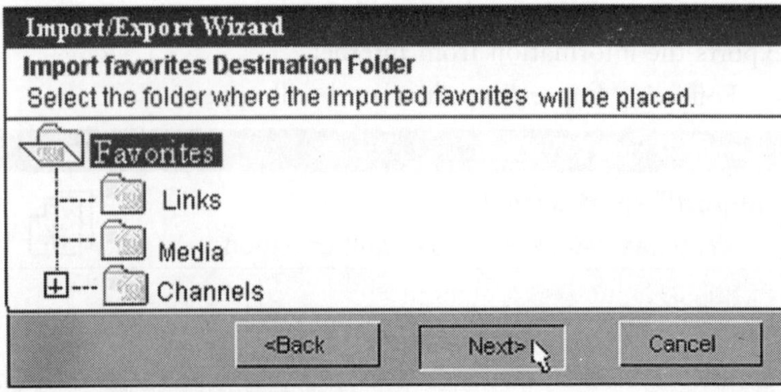

Click Next in the above Import/Export wizard. Following Import/Export wizard will appear that will indicates the completion of import the favorites from C:\My Documents\Bookmark.htm.

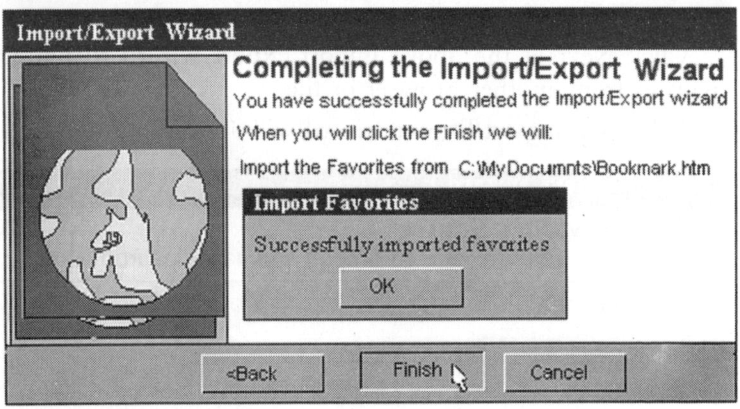

Click OK. You will come back to the Internet Explorer page.

Again Click on File you will get the previous window.

Last segment of the drop down list contains the three items, Properties, Work Offline and Close.

Properties: Click on Properties. It will display the a property window which contains the URL address of the web page.

Work Offline: Click on this item. It will allow you to see the downloaded web pages offline.

Close: Click on this item. It will close the Internet Explorer.

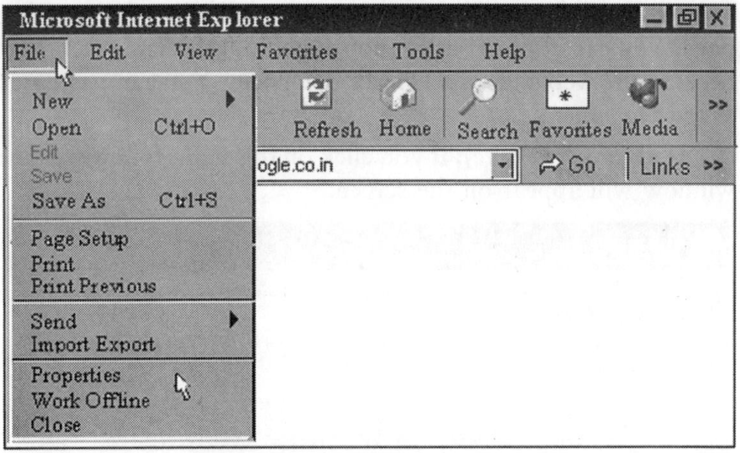

Edit

Edit is the second item of main menu. Click on Edit, the following drop down list under Edit will appear.

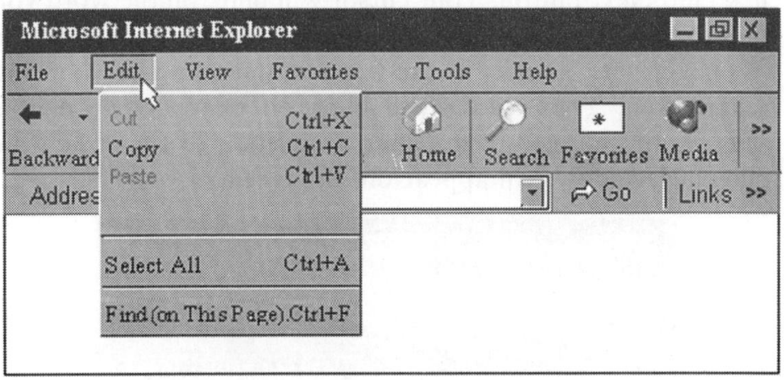

If the web page is open in the browser, item copy will be active, while items cut and paste will be inactive.

You cannot cut and paste the text or picture in the web pages because web pages are written in html language.

You can copy the content of the web page and can paste in word's document. You can even copy the complete web page and paste as document in Microsoft word, but some of the items like picture may not be copied.

Select All: If you click on this item it will select the complete page. You can copy it but cannot paste it on the same web page because the web page is a HTML document. You can paste it in Word Document.

Find (on This Page): If you click on this item, following Find window will appear on the screen.

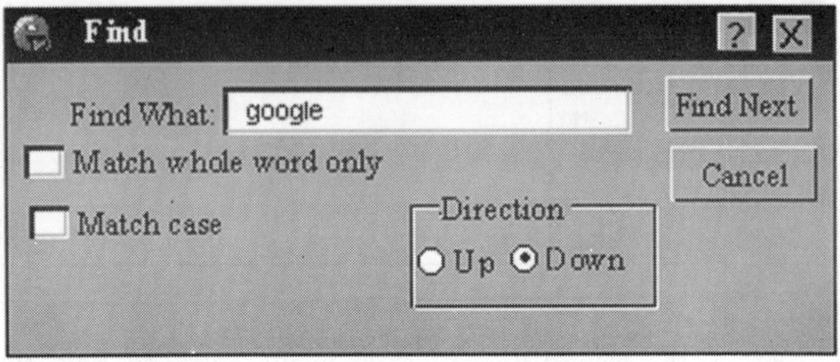

Write the word you want to find, in the textbox and then click Find Next Button. Your cursor will blink on the word you want to find. Suppose you want to find the word 'google' on the web page, type 'google' in the textbox and then click on Find Next button. Your cursor will blink on word google if it is available on the web page. After completion of the search the following window will appear on the screen.

View

View is the third item of main menu as shown below.

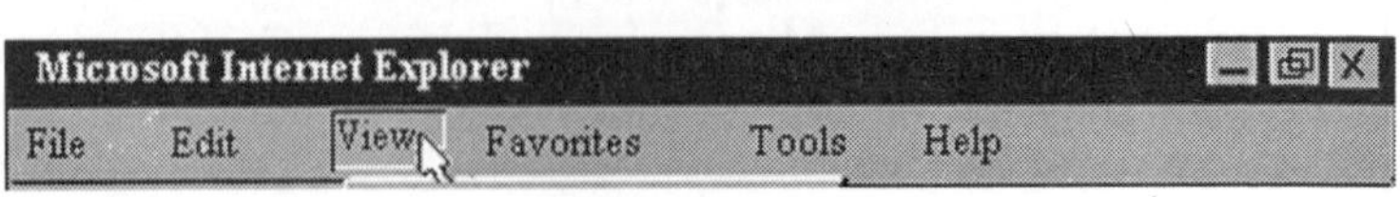

When you click on the View you will get the following drop down list as shown in the following figure.

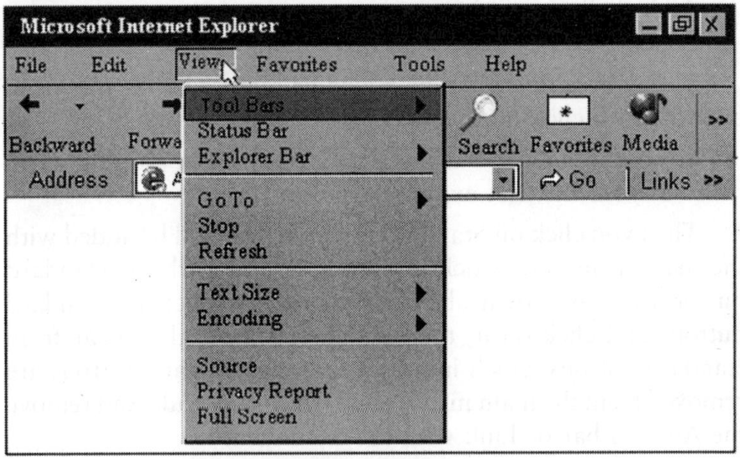

The View item contains four segments as follows:

A: Tool Bars, Status Bar, Explorer Bar

B: Go To, Stop, Refresh

C: Text Size, Encoding

D: Source, Privacy Report, Full Screen

Tool Bars is the first item of drop down list under view item. Toolbars contains five items in two segments.

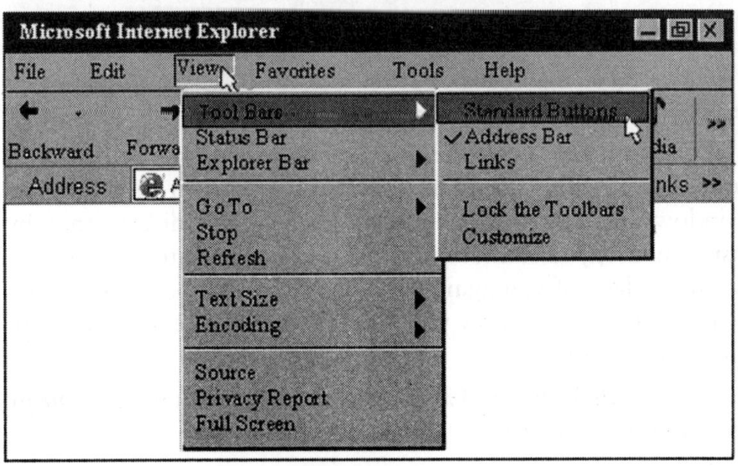

First Segment contains the following items:

✓ Standard Buttons
Address Bar
Links

These three items can be added or removed with the menu bar when we click on them.

Suppose Standard buttons item is not present with the main menu in your Internet explorer window.

Then you click on Standard buttons, they will be added with the main menu and a tick mark will appear with the standard button's bar as shown above. If you again select the standard buttons and click on it, the tick mark '✓' will disappear from standard buttons which indicates that the standard buttons are removed from the main menu. Similarly you can add and remove the Address bar or Link with the main menu.

Second segment contains the following two items:

1. Lock the Toolbars
2. Customize.

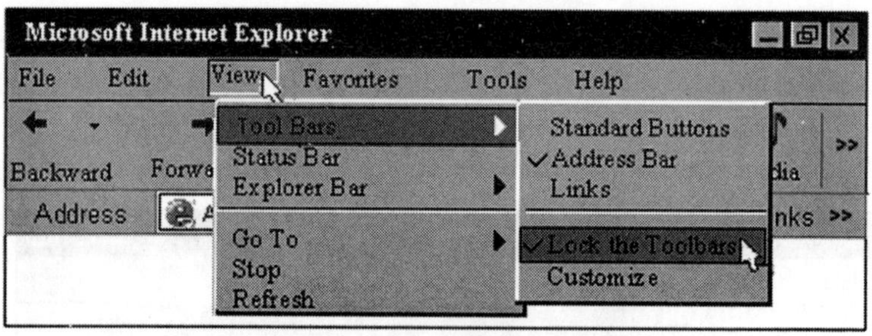

Click on the 'Lock the tool bar' item, a tick mark '✓' will appear with the "Lock the tool bar" as shown in the above window and the toolbars will be locked. It indicates that by using mouse, you cannot move the tool bars of Internet explorer from its place. If you again click on it, the lock on the tool bars will be removed and now you are free to move the tool bars with the help of mouse.

If you click on the Customize item, the following window will appear on screen:

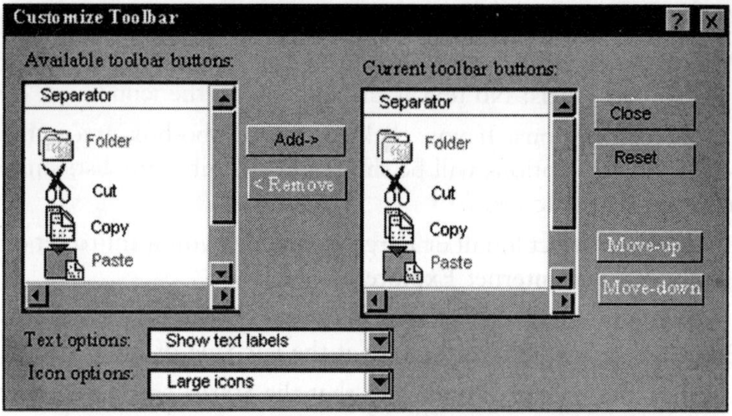

Customize window is used for adding the buttons to the toolbar. There are two section of the Customizes Window:

1. Available toolbar buttons
2. Current toolbar buttons

Select the button from Available toolbar buttons and then click on the Add button. The icon will be added on the Current tool bar. If you want to remove the icon from the current toolbar then select the icon from the current toolbar and then click on the Remove button, the icon from the current toolbar of Internet Explorer will be remove.

At the bottom of the Customize toolbar there are two options with combo-boxes:

1. Text options
2. Icon options

1. Text option: If you click on the combo-box arrow the following three options will be shown on a combo-box list:

Show text labels

Selective text on right

No text labels

Click the mouse on the above items one by one and see the effect on the Internet Explorer's standard tool bar.

Show text labels: At the bottom of the icon on the toolbar, icon name is displayed.

Selective text on right: At the right side of the icon on the toolbar, icon name is displayed.

No text labels: No text is displayed with the icon.

2. Icon options: If you click on the combo-box arrow the following two options will be shown on a combo-box list: small icons and large icons.

You can select Small or Large icon which you want to set on the toolbars of Internet Explorer.

Second item of the View is Status bar. If you click on Status Bar a tick mark '✓' will appear at the left Side of it.

This tick mark '✓' indicates that the Status bar is added at the bottom of the Internet Explorer.

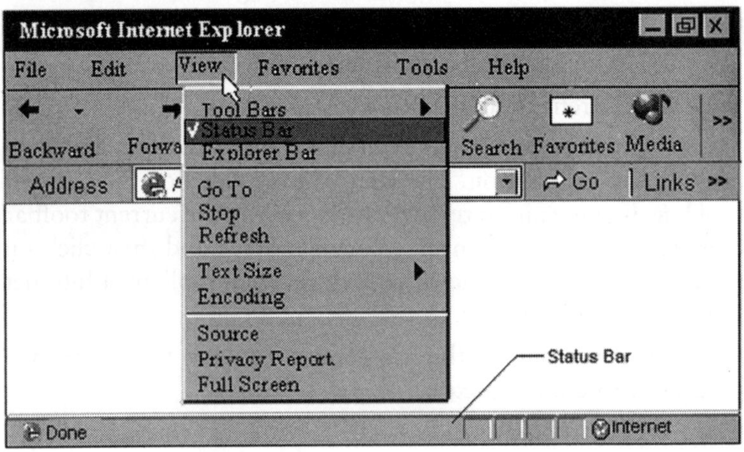

Third item of in the list under View is Explorer bar shown in the expanded form in the figure on next page.

There are two groups of items.

First Group: This group contains the following three items:

Search

Favorites

History

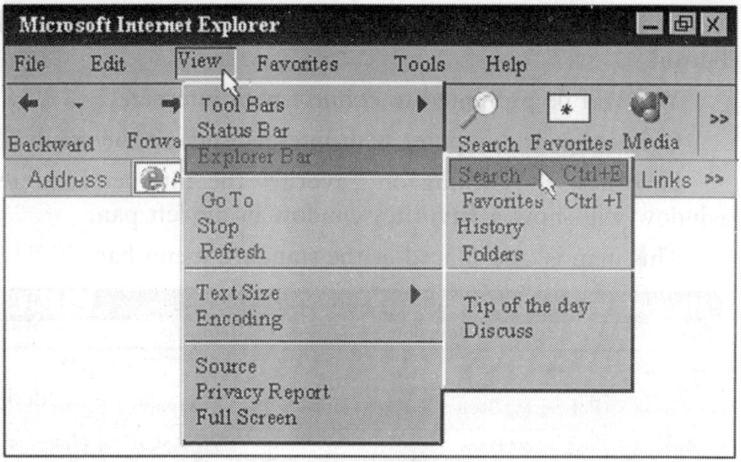

Folders: These items are available on the Standard Buttons Bar (Middle line).

Second Group: It contains two items:

Tip of the day.

Discuss.

Search: By clicking on Search, the Internet Explorer window will show a search window in the left pan.

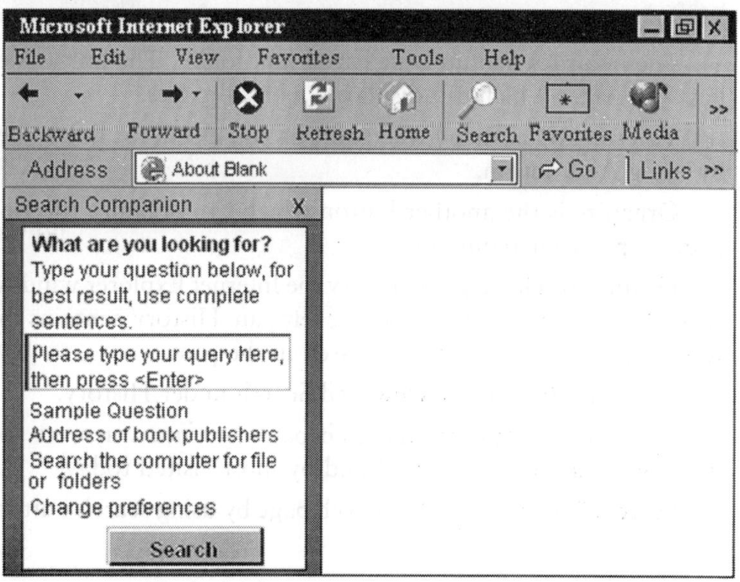

Write the query in the textbox and then click on search button.

You will be prompted to connect with internet.

Connect your computer with internet and get the result.

Favorites: By clicking on Favorites the Internet Explorer window will show a Favorites window in the left pan.

This item is also placed at the standard menu bar.

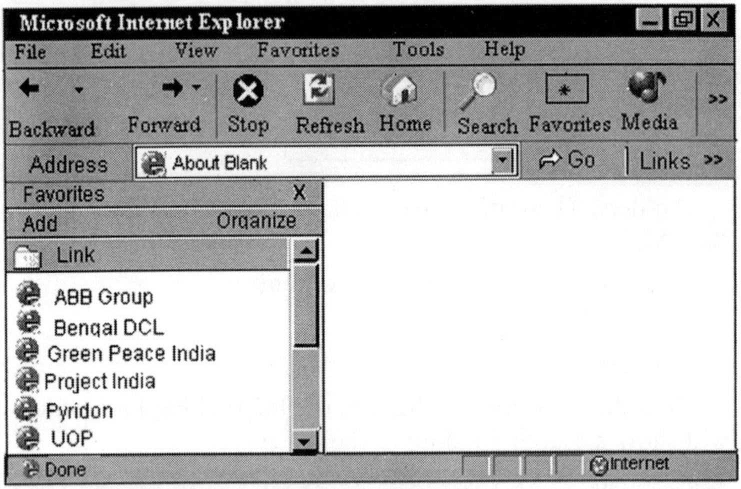

The favorites contains the list of link folder. The link folder has web pages which are displayed as html pages.

You can add as many web pages as you like in the link folder by using Add button.

Organize is the another button which can organize the web page as per your requirement.

History: By clicking on History the Internet Explorer window will show a History window in the left pan. History contains the web pages which you have accessed in the past.

There are two items View and Search under History.

View: View arranges the web pages in four ways, i.e. by date, by sites, by most visited and by most visited today.

Search: You can search the web page by using search button.

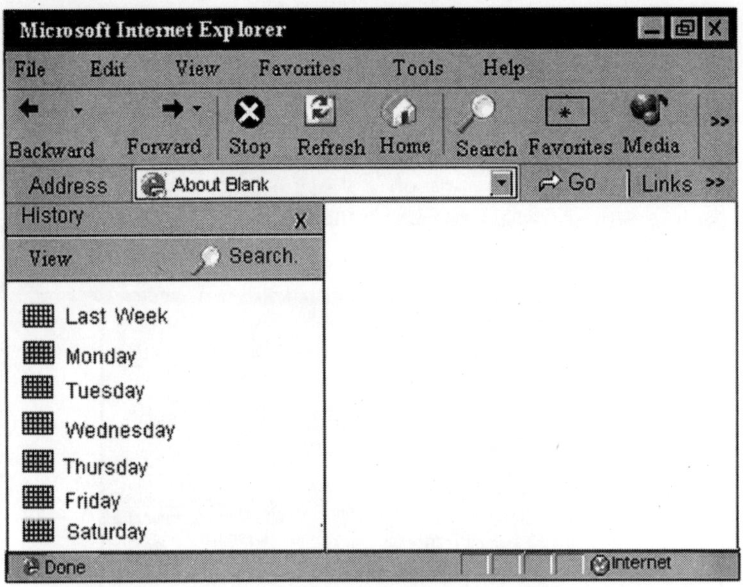

Folder: If you click on this item, you can open window explorer and can access any file or folder that is loaded on your system. Following figure shows the details. Folder section contains the all whatever is there in your computer system. It acts like window explorer.

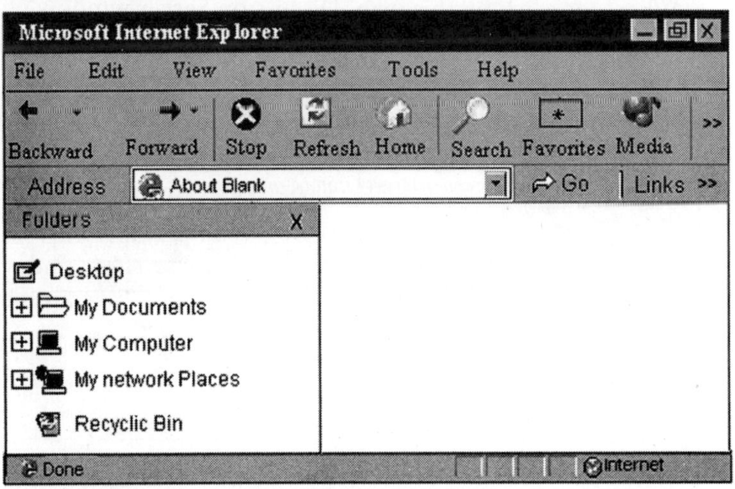

Second Group: This group has two items, Tip of the day and Discuss.

Tip of the day: If you click on this item. Internet Explorer will provide some information, which can be seen at the bottom portion of the Internet Explorer window. For example, you can see the tip of the day in the following picture.

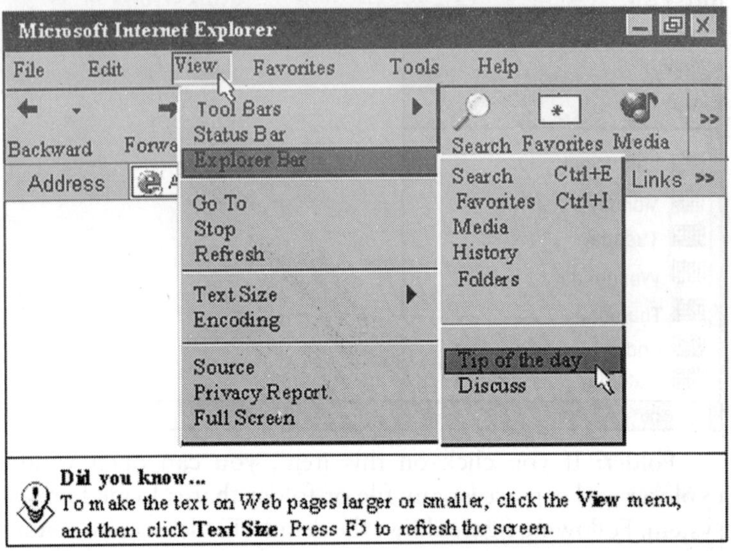

Second item of the group is Discuss.

When you click on this item, Discussion Server window will appear on the screen.

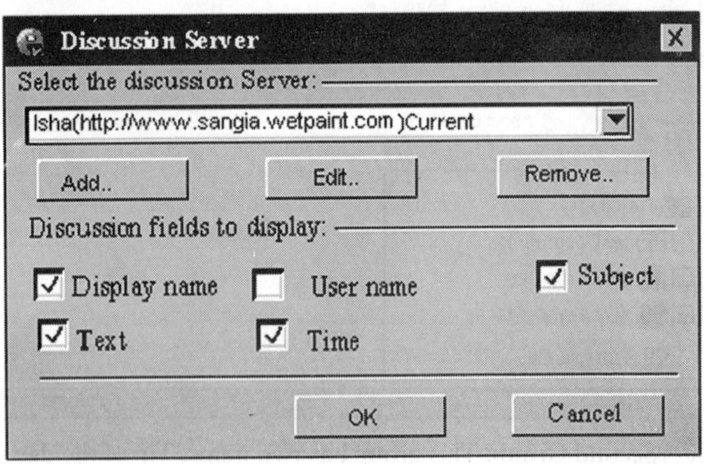

There are three buttons Add, Edit and Remove in the Discussion Server window, which you can use for adding, editing or removal of the discussion server.

There are five fields Display name, User name, Subject, Text and Time which you can use by clicking on them.

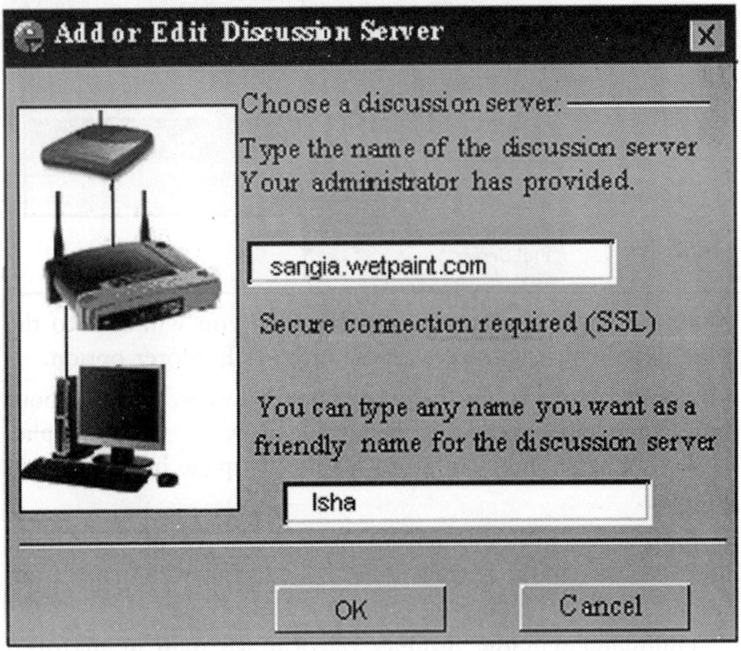

Go to is the fourth item of drop down list. Click on this item the window on next page will be displayed on screen.

Go to item has four sub items, Back, Forward, Home Page and About blank.

Back and forward items remains inactive if there is no web page opened in the browser.

They will be active if there are at least two web pages opened in browser. You can go from second web page to first web page by clicking on Back item and can go from first web page to second web page by clicking on Forward item.

If there are many web pages are opened by you while surfing the net, you can go to back or forward to see the web pages one by one.

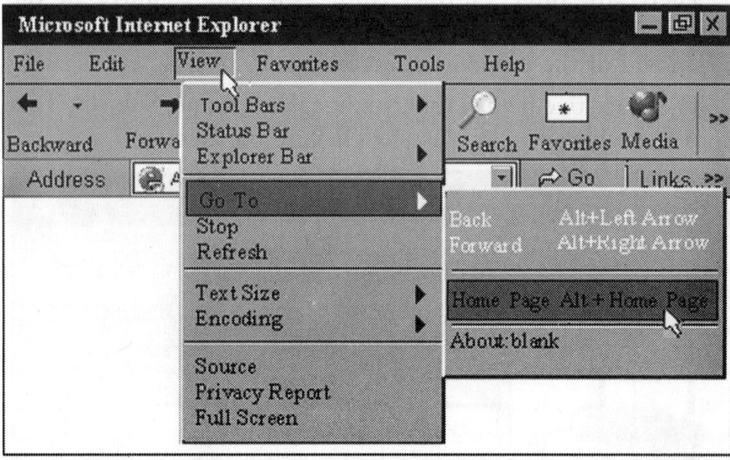

Home Page: If you click on this item you will sent to the home page which you have set by Internet Explorer option.

About blank: If you have set your browser, to use About blank, then whenever you open your browser, it will display blank web page. You can go to blank web page by clicking on this item.

Stop is the fifth sub-item of drop down list of View item. Click on this item, it will stop the current web page from loading.

Following window displays the Refresh item in the drop down list of View.

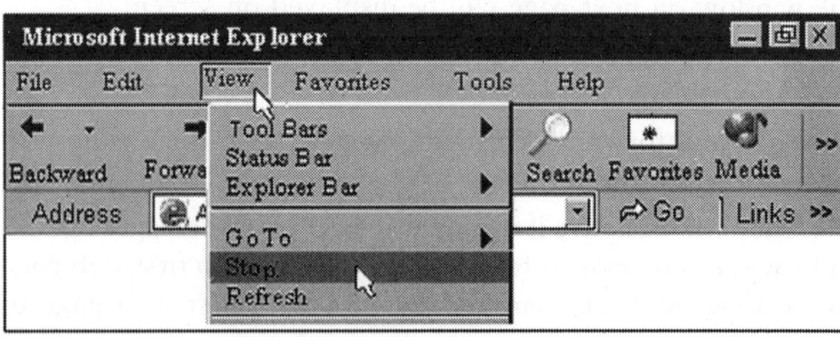

Refresh is the sixth sub-item of drop down list of View.

When the web page is not displayed properly, you can use this by clicking on it, to get the clear web page.

Following window displays the Refresh item in the drop down list of View item.

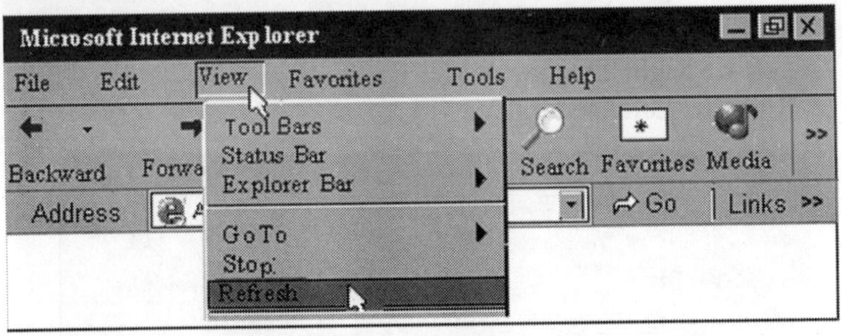

Text Size is the seventh sub-item of the View. When you click on this sub-item, a side list which contains text size as largest, larger, medium, smaller, smallest appears as shown in the following figure.

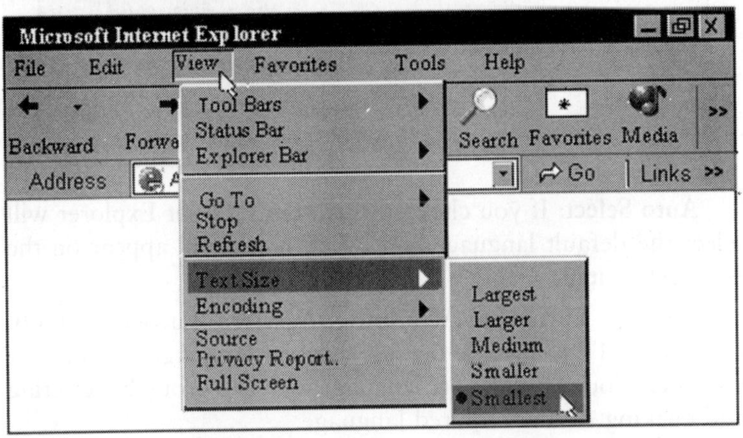

When you click on the item, it is selected and marked by a big dot. The text size of the web page will change to the marked text size. Suppose you click on the item Smallest, then Internet Explorer will change the text size of the web page to smallest.

Encoding is the eighth sub-item of the View item.

It contains following seven items:

Auto Select
Western European (Windows)

Western European (ISO)
Unicode (UTF-8)
More
Left-to-Right Document
Right-to-Left Document

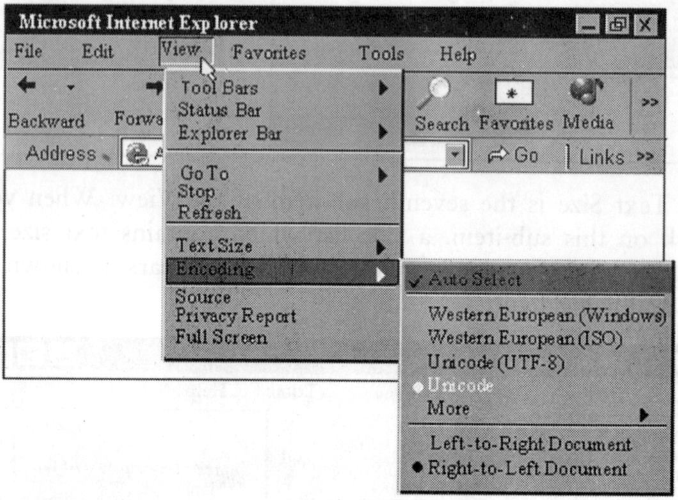

Auto Select: If you click on this item Internet Explorer will select the default language and a tick mark will appear on the Auto select item.

Western European (Windows), Western European (ISO), Unicode (UTF-8) are the default selected language for Internet Explorer. You can add more language with this group by selecting and clicking on the required language.

More: If you select the item More, a list of several languages will appear on the screen. From the list suppose you select Japanese, and click on it, the following window will appear on the screen:

Start the internet connection and download the desired language for your web browser.

If you download Japanese successfully, you can use the browser in Japanese language.

Left-to-Right Document: If you click on it. It will change the scroll bar of the web page from Left-to-Right.

Right-to-Left Document: If you click on it. It will change the scroll bar of the web page from Right-to-Left.

Source is the 9th sub-item of the list under item View. If you click on this item, it will display HTML page in plain text, in Note Pad. This HTML document is the source code for the current web page.

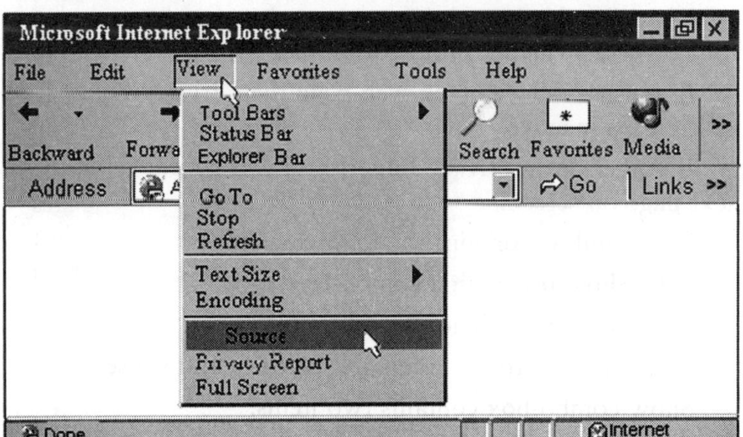

Suppose your current page is the Yahoo.com which is displayed in the web browser.

Now you click on Source item. Following part of HTML text is displayed in note Pad.

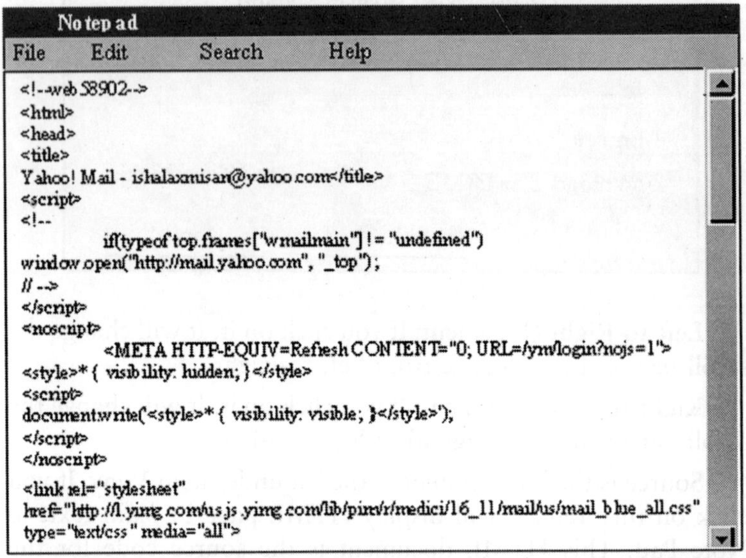

Next item is Privacy Report.

For using this item, it is necessary that a web page exist in your browser whether offline or online.

If you use About blank web page then Privacy Policy item will remain inactive.

If you click on Privacy Report you will get the window on next page on screen.

This window contains the following:

1. Show text with a combo-box.
2. Sites and cookies description.
3. Three buttons, Summary, Settings and Close.

Show combo-box contains two items:

1. All Websites.
2. Restricted Websites.

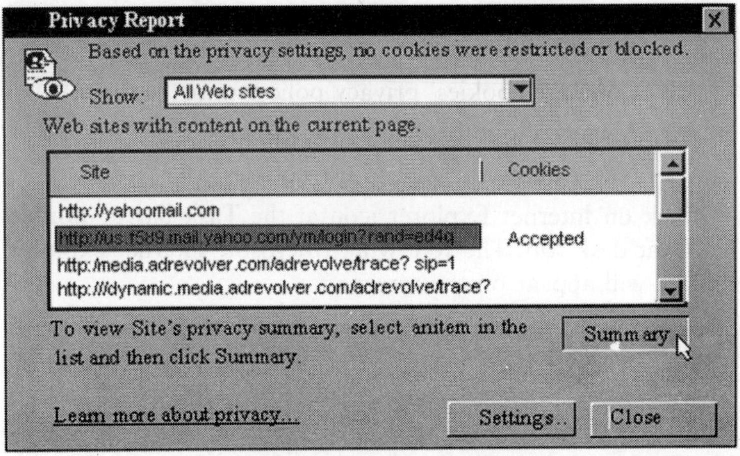

Sites addresses of the all the websites are displayed inside the "Website with content on the current page". Select any website or the content of the current page from the above window and click on Summary button, you will get the following privacy Policy window.

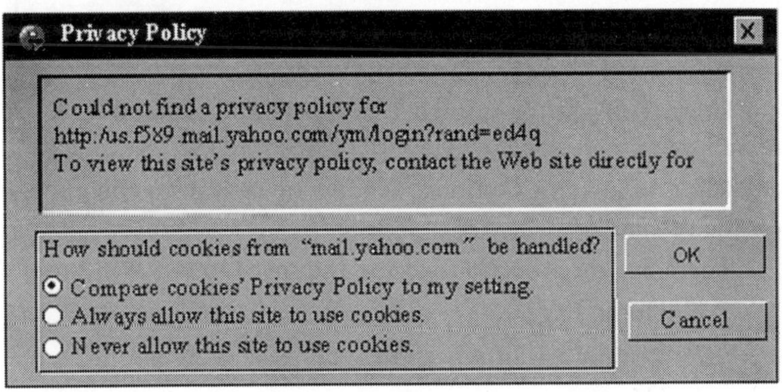

Top line text in the Privacy Policy window indicates that the privacy policy for the selected site could not be found.

To view this site's privacy policy you have to see the privacy policy directly from the site.

There are three options where you can choose any one of them:

1. Compare cookies' privacy policy to my settings.
2. Always allow this site to use cookies.
3. Never allow this site to use cookies.

Click on Internet Explorer icon at the Task bar or double click it at desk top. The following Microsoft Internet explorer window will appear on the screen.

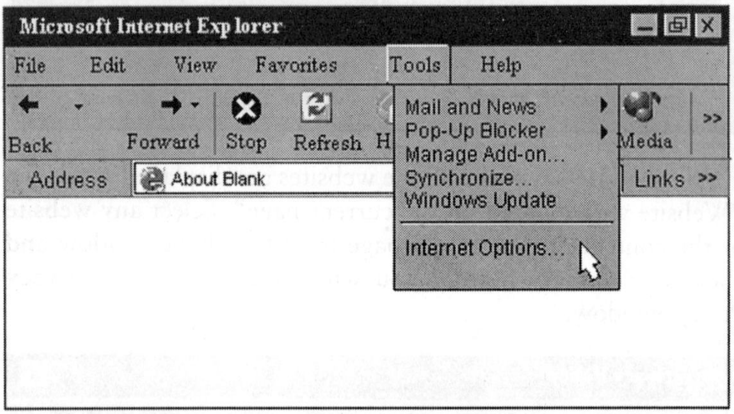

Go to Tools at the standard menu bar and click on it. A list of sub-menu will appear below the Tools button.

Click on Internet Options, window on next page will appear on the screen.

There are three sections of the Internet Option Windows:

1. Home Page
2. Temporary Internet Files
3. History

1. Home Page. This section contains three buttons and a textbox as shown in the following figure.

Text Box: The text in the textbox indicates the current home page. Home page is the web page which appears first, when you start Internet Explorer.

This home page can be set by you, by using any one of the three buttons:

1. **Use Current:** If you click on this button, the web page which is appeared currently will become the home page for your browser. The web page address will appear in the Internet Options textbox.
2. **Use Default:** If you click on this button, the web page which is provided by Microsoft with the Internet Explorer will become the home page for your browser. The web page address will be http://www.microsoft.com with some more text. It will appear in the Internet Options textbox.

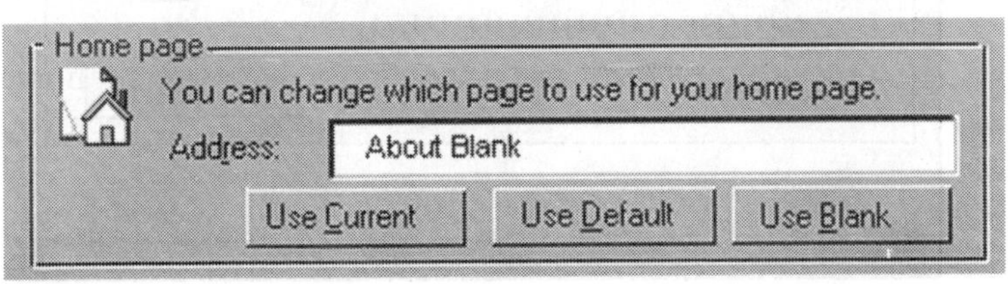

3. **Use Blank:** If you click on this button, a blank web page will become your home page. A text "About blank" will appear in the Internet Option textbox.

2. Temporary Internet Files. This section contains three buttons as shown in the following figure.

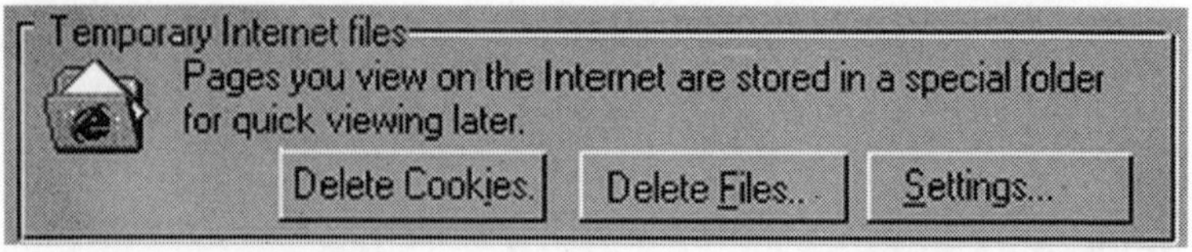

1. **Delete Cookies:** If you click on this buttons, it will delete all cookies which are stored in your temporary folder of window folder.
2. **Delete Files:** If you click on this button, it will delete all temporary files which are stored during surfing the Internet and unnecessarily occupy the hard disc space.
3. **Setting:** If you click on this button, the following Setting windows will appear.

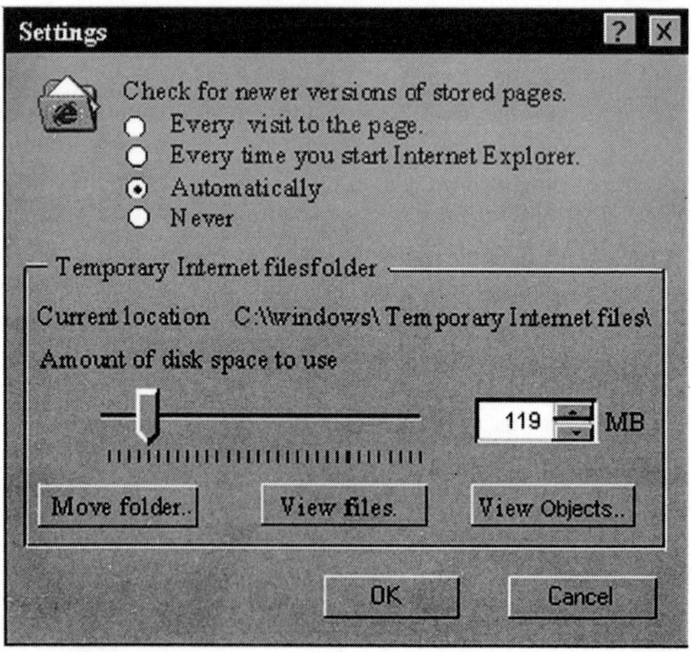

Settings window contains four options, for checking the newer version of web pages which is carried out as per the option you select:

1. Every visit to the page.
2. Every time you start the Internet Explorer.
3. Automatically.
4. Never.

By default setting is Automatically.

Temporary Internet Files Folder

This section contains a combo-box which indicates the space set for the Temporary Internet files folder in MBs.

There is a pointer and scale in front of it. You can change the space on the hard disk by moving the pointer on the scale or directly or by typing the digits in the combo-box. You can also use the two arrows for setting folder capacity in MB.

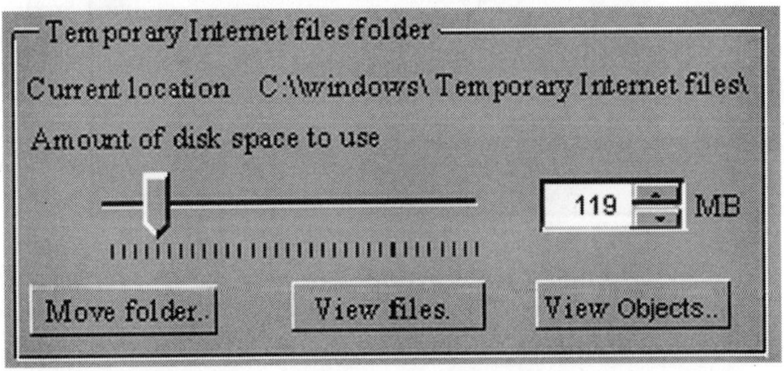

Current location of the Temporary Internet files folder is given as C:\\windows\Temporary Internet files.

This indicates that Temporary Internet files reside in the folder Window of root directory C:/

There are three buttons in the "Temporary Internet files folder" section. They are given below:

1. Move Folder
2. View Files
3. View Objects

1. Move Folder: If you click on this button, "Browse for Folder" window appears on the screen as follows. You can move your Temporary Internet files' folder in C, D drive, My document or any other folder you like.

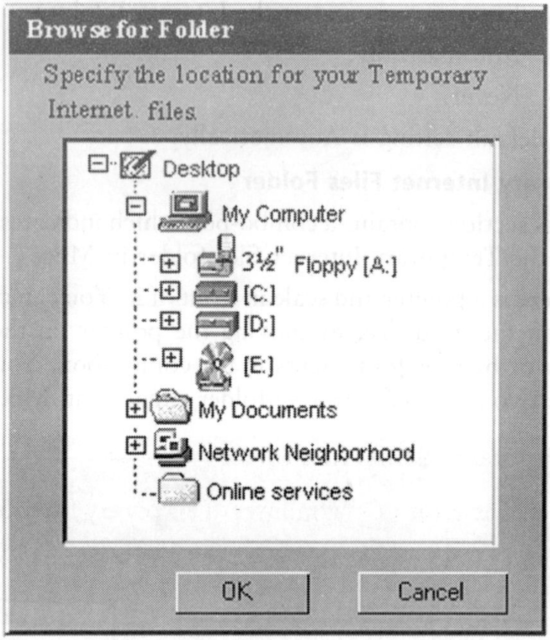

2. View Files: It is the second button of Temporary Internet files folder window. If you click on this button the following window will appear.

This window shows the details about Temporary Internet files folder.

It displays the Internet address, type size and expires details of temporary Internet files. This folder contains all the web pages which you have opened. They are actually copied to this folder automatically. If you open these web pages, they will be displayed very fast.

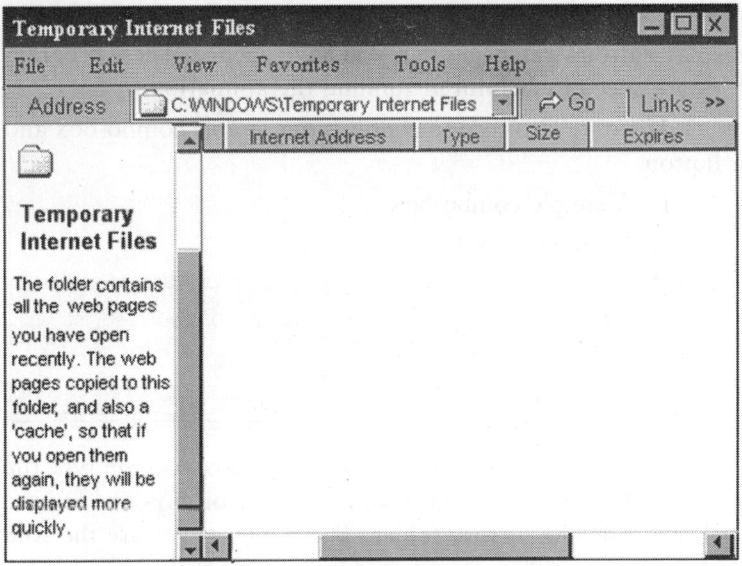

3. View Objects: These are the downloaded program files, which resides in the downloaded program files folder.

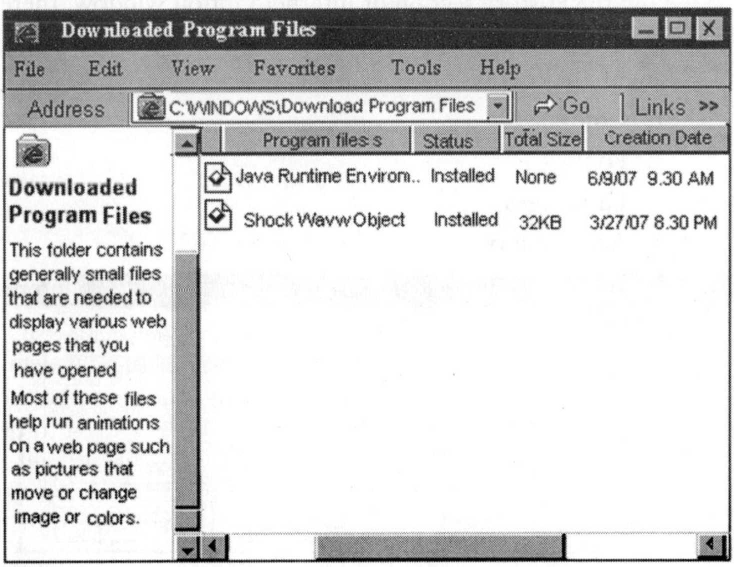

This folder contains generally small files that are needed to display various web pages that you have opened. These program files are specially helpful in running the animation.

3. History. This section contains one simple combo-box and a button.

1. A simple combo-box
2. Clear History Button

1. A simple combo-box: In this combo-box you can type the number. This number indicates the number of days to keep the web pages in the history folder. These web pages are the web pages which you have accessed during surfing.

2. Clear History Button: If you click on this button, all the web pages of history folder will be deleted.

Below the History section of Internet Option window, there are four buttons shown below in the picture.

They are as follows:

1. Colors
2. Fonts
3. Languages
4. Accessibility

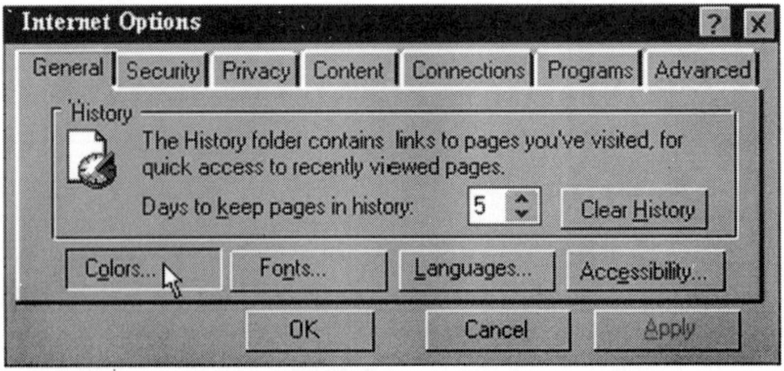

1. Colors: If you click on this button, the following "Colors" window will appear on the screen.

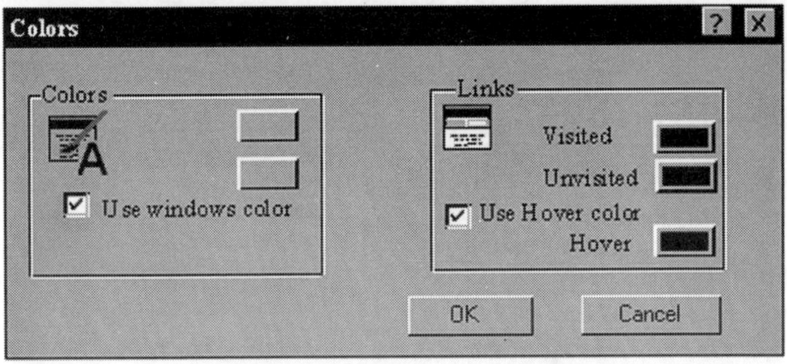

If you want to use the windows color, then you need not to do any thing. Suppose you want to change the background color and text color, then click on the check box and remove the tick mark. You will get the following change in color window.

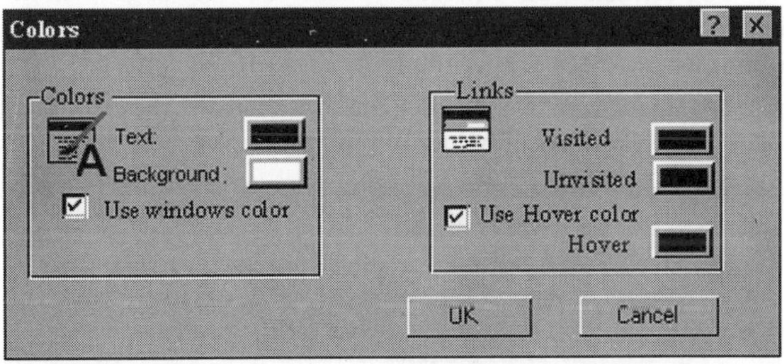

Now if you want to change the text color and background color, you can use the two buttons and can set the text color and background color to your choice. Similarly links page color can be set by using the links section button of the color's window.

2. Fonts: If you click on this button, the following "Fonts" window will appear on the screen.

All the fonts of web page are set to Latin based by default. If you want to set the font to any other base, you can click the arrow, in front of language script, in the font window. There are two list boxes provided below the Language script.

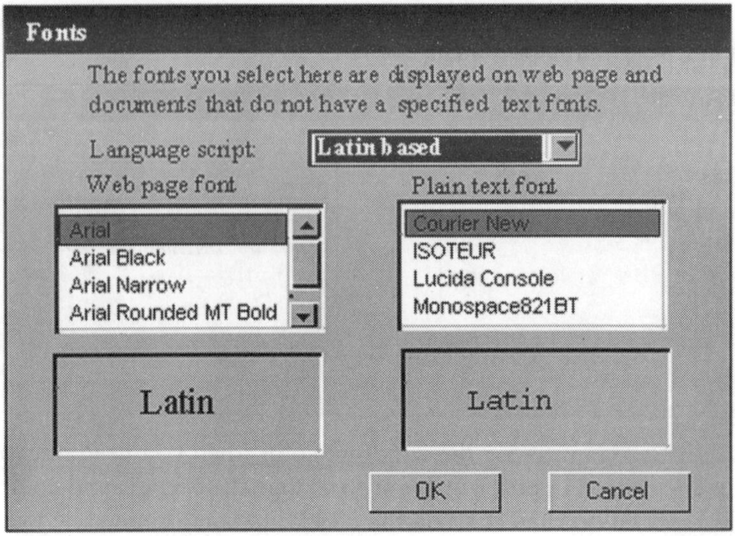

You can select the any font type for your web page from the left side list box and plane text font you can select from the right side list box. After setting the font, click on OK button.

3. Languages: If you click on this button, the following "Language Preference" window will appear on the screen.

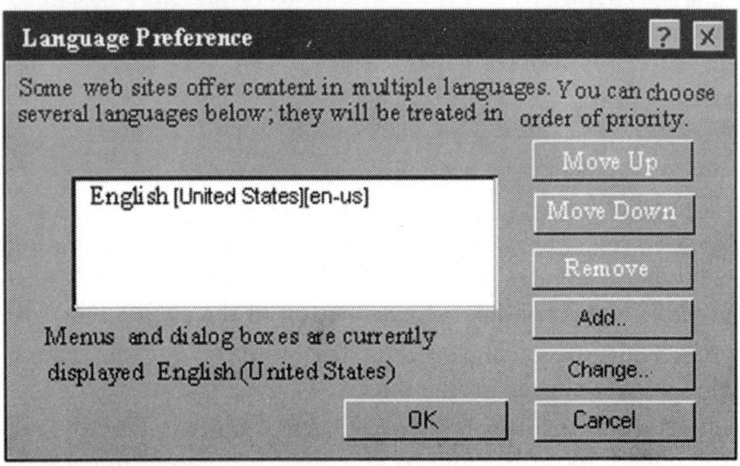

English [United States][en-us] is the default language used by the Internet Explorer. If you want to add some more language then click on the Add button in the Language Preference window. A list of language will appear. You can add as many language as you like. Remove button will remove the language you choose.

4. Accessibility: If you click on this button, the following "Accessibility" window will appear on the screen.

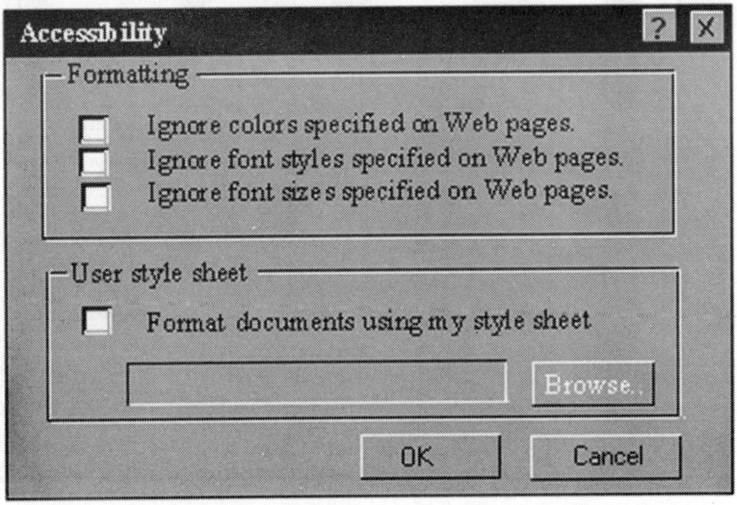

Accessibility window can do the formatting of the web page by ignoring specified color setting, specified font style and font size and can use your own style sheet. You can set the style sheet by clicking in the check box of "User Style Sheet" section of the "Accessibility" window. As soon you click on the Check box, "Browse" button will become active. Click on the Browse button and select the style sheet from the window system.

Security: This is the second button of Internet Options window.

If you click on Security button the following window will appear.

Internet is the web content zone. General button is active as shown above in the Internet Option window.

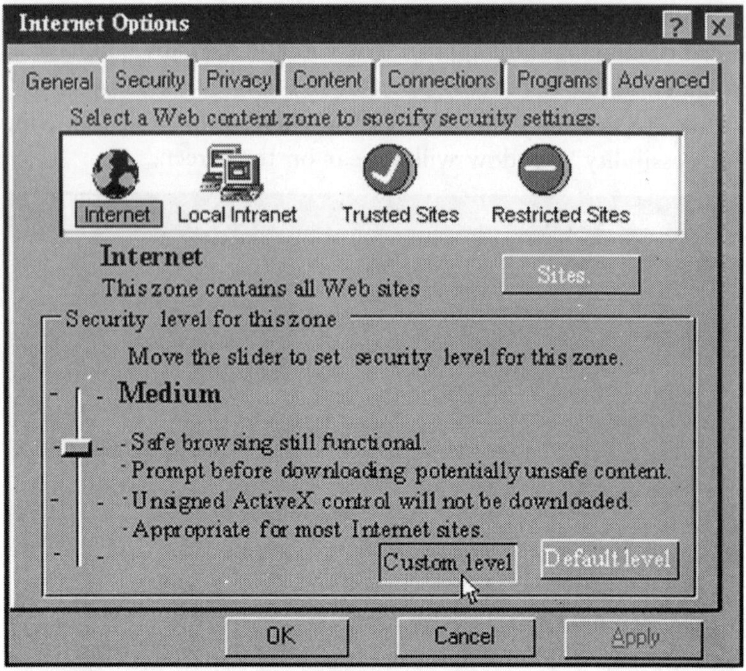

Security level set for this zone is Default level.

Medium Level Security Setting: This is the default level security setting, that has the following characteristics:

1. Browsing is safe with this setting.
2. Internet Explorer will prompt before you download any unsafe content.
3. With medium setting unsigned ActiveX control are not allowed to download.
4. This is the most suitable setting for most of the Internet sites.

Custom Level Security Setting: For setting the custom level security, click on the Custom level button:

You will get the following window:

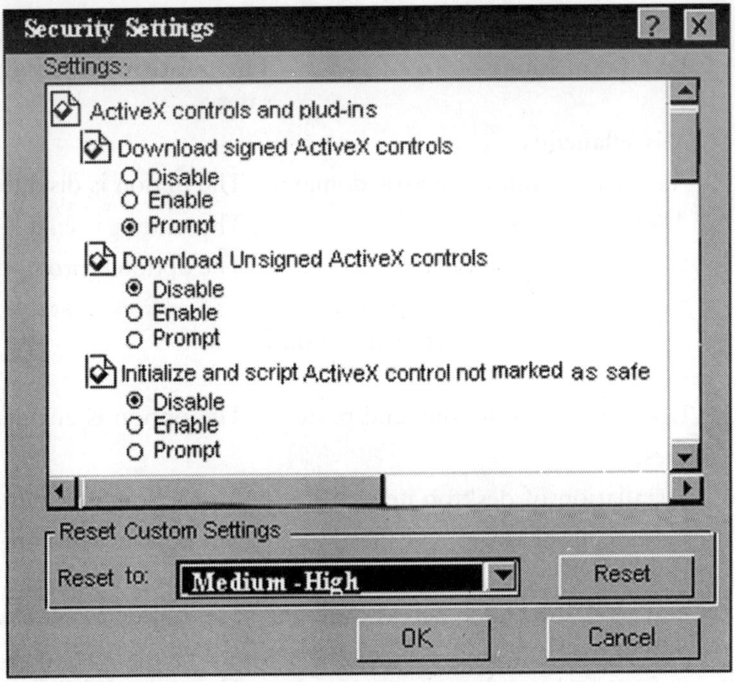

Security Setting windows contains the following items with options:

ActiveX controls and the plug-ins

1. Download signed ActiveX controls. The option is prompt.
2. Download unsigned ActiveX controls. The option is disable.
3. Initialized and script ActiveX controls not marked as safe. The option is disable.
4. Run ActiveX control and plug-ins. The option is enable.
5. Script ActiveX controls not marked safe for scripting. The option is enable.

Downloads

1. File download. The option is enable.
2. Font download. The option is enable.

Java

	Setting	Option
1.	Java permissions	The option is High safety.

Miscellaneous

	Setting	Option
1.	Access data sources across domain.	The option is disable.
2.	Allow META REFRESH.	The option is enable.
3.	Display mixed content.	The option is prompt.
4.	Don't prompt for client certificate selection when no certificate or only one certificate exists.	The option is disable.
5.	Drag and drop or copy and paste files.	The option is enable.
6.	Installation of desktop items.	The option is prompt.
7.	Launching program and files in an IFRAME.	The option is prompt.
8.	Navigate sub-frame across different domains.	The option is enable.
9.	Software channel permissions.	The option is Medium safety.
10.	Submit non-encrypted form data.	The option is prompt.
11.	User data persistence.	The option is enable.

Scripting

	Setting	Option
1.	Active scripting.	The option is enable.
2.	Allow paste operations via script.	The option is enable.
3	Scripting of Java applets.	The option is enable.

User Authentication

1. Logon.

The option is Automatic logon only in Internet zone.

Select the Local Intranet the following window will appear.

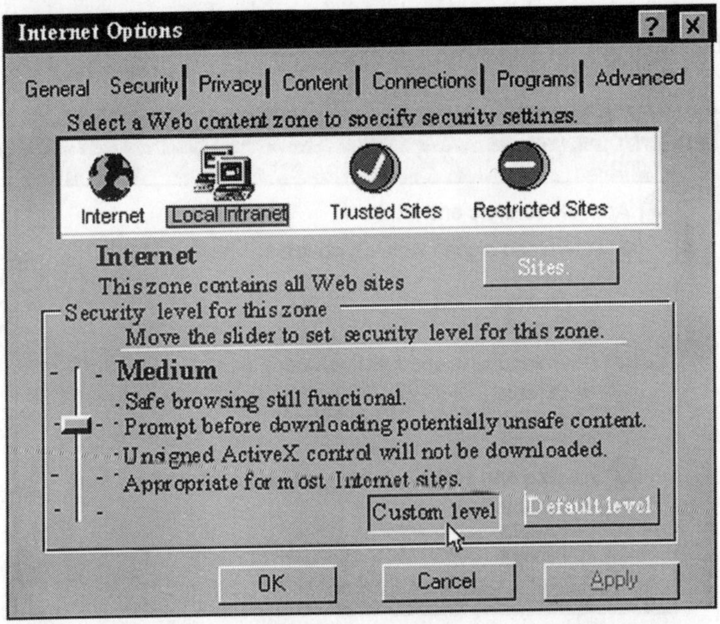

If you click on the Custom Level button, you will get again the same security setting window.

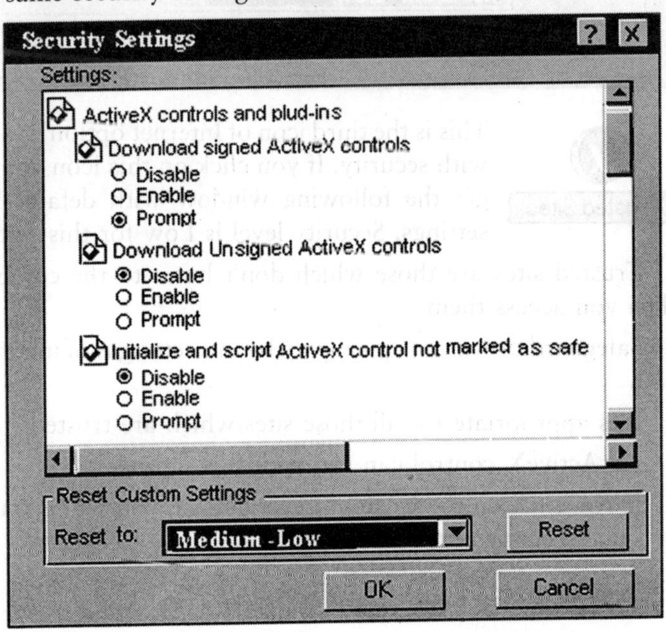

Which you have seen by clicking the Internet icon in the Internet option window. The Reset Custom Setting will be reset to Medium-Low.

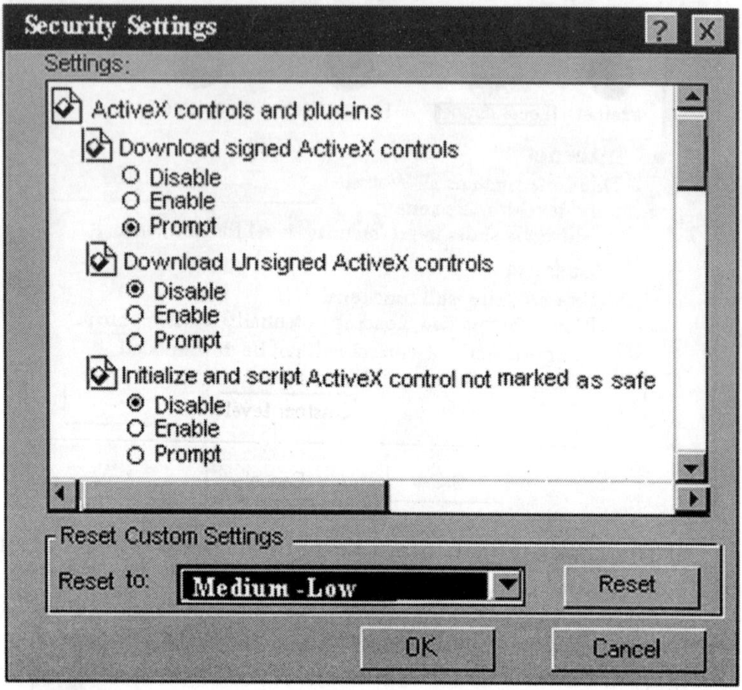

This is the third icon of Internet option window with security. If you click on this icon you will get the following window with default level settings. Security level is Low for this setting.

Trusted sites are those which don't harm to the computer when you access them.

Safeguard or warning prompted by this setting is of minimum level.

It is appropriate for all those sites which are trusted.

All ActiveX control can run with this setting.

If you click on the Custom Level button, you will get again the same security setting window.

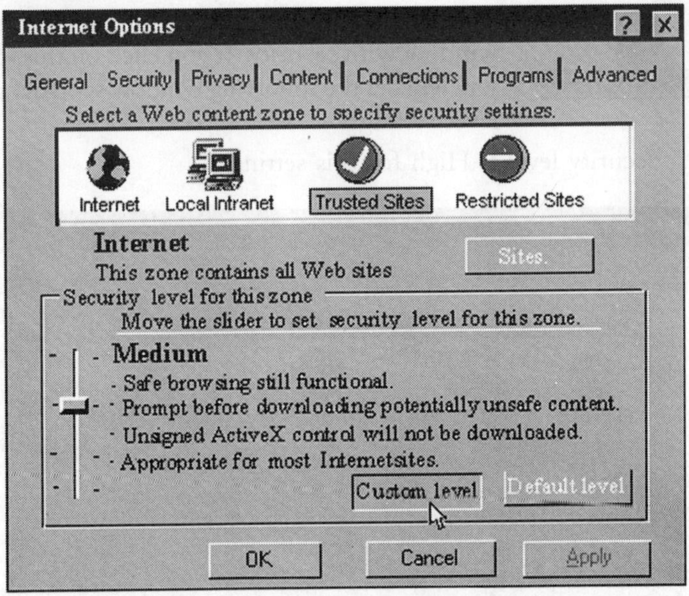

Which you have seen by clicking the Internet icon in the Internet option window. The Reset Custom Setting will be reset to Low.

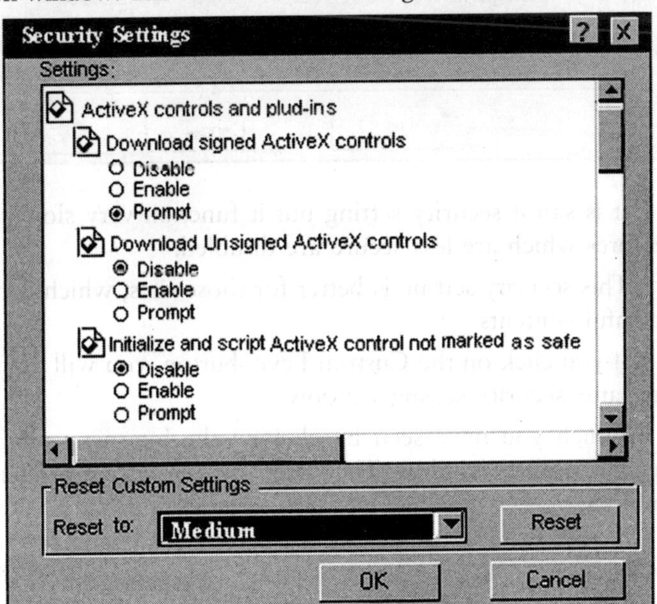

This is the fourth icon of Internet options window with security. If you click on this icon you will get the following window with default level settings.

Security level is High for this setting.

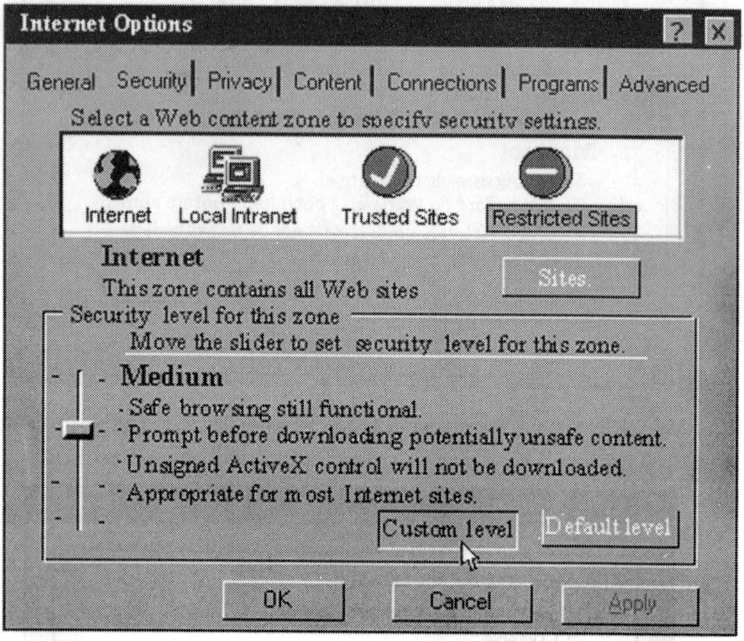

It is safest security setting but it function very slowly. The features which are less secure are disabled.

This security setting is better for those sites, which contains harmful contents.

If you click on the Custom Level button, you will get again the same security setting window.

Which you have seen by clicking the Internet icon in the Internet options window. The Reset Custom Setting will be reset to High.

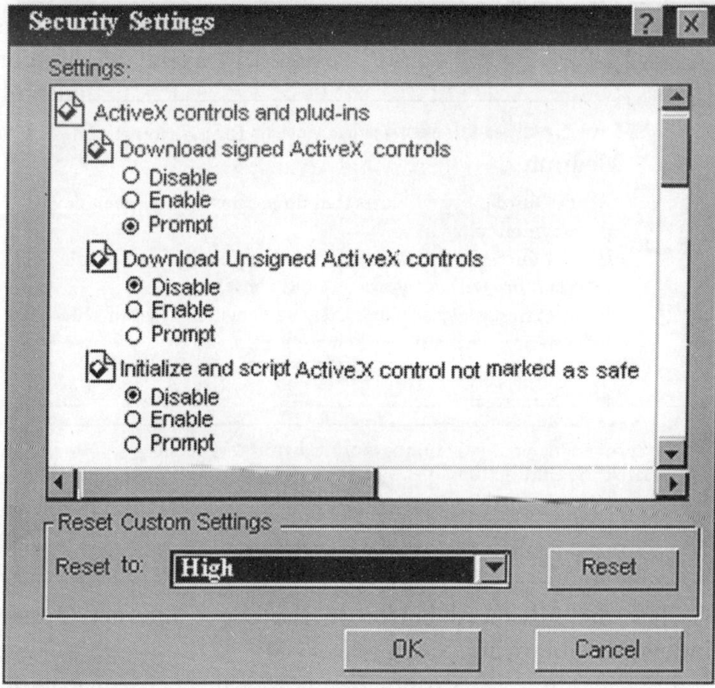

Privacy

This is the third button on Internet Operation window.

Click the Privacy button, you will get the following window on screen.

By default Privacy for the Internet zone is Medium.

Under this privacy policy third-party cookies are blocked and first-party cookies are restricted. Without your permission neither the third-party cookies nor first party-cookies that use personally identifiable information are allowed to use the Internet sites.

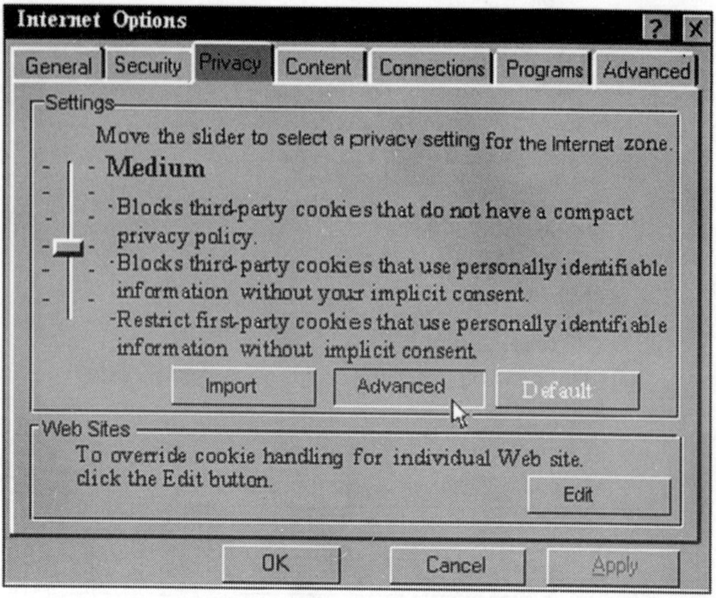

Click the Advanced button in the above Internet Option window, the following.

Advanced Privacy Setting window will appear. Click the check box for overriding automatic cookies handling.

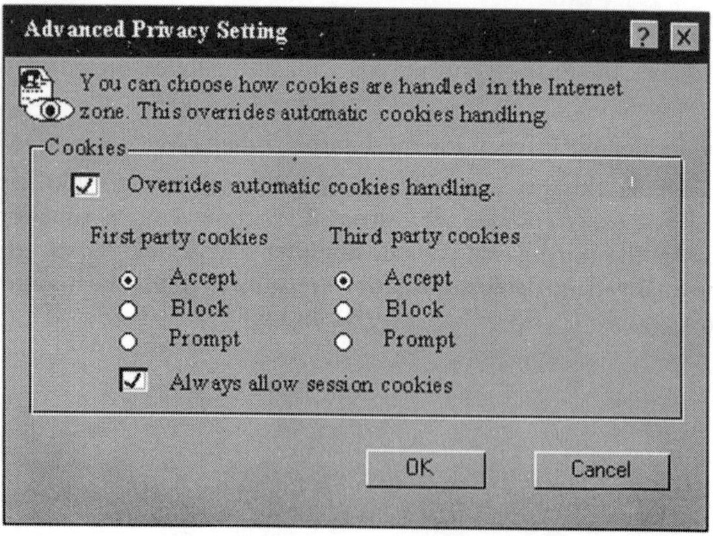

There are two types of cookies first party cookies and third party cookies. First party cookies has three options for each and Third party cookies also have three options. You can override the default setting of cookies by choosing these options.

If you want to allow the session cookies, then click the second check box.

To override cookies handling for individual website, click on the Edit button in website section of the above Internet Options window. You will get the following window.

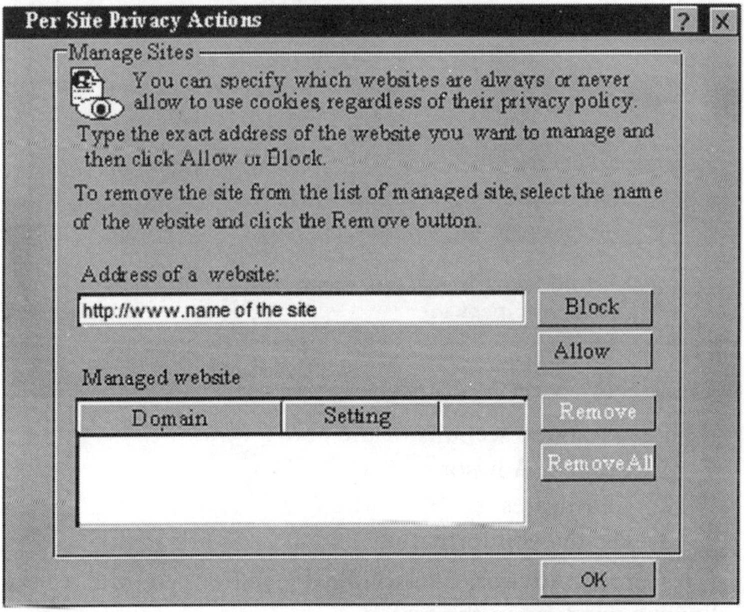

Enter the address of the websites which you either always allow or never allow to use regardless of their privacy policy. After typing address of website, click the Block button to restrict the use cookies by the addressed website.

Click the Allow button to allow the use of cookies by the addressed website.

You can remove the website or sites by using the Remove or Remove All buttons.

Content

This is the fourth button on Internet Operation window. Click the button and you will get the following window.

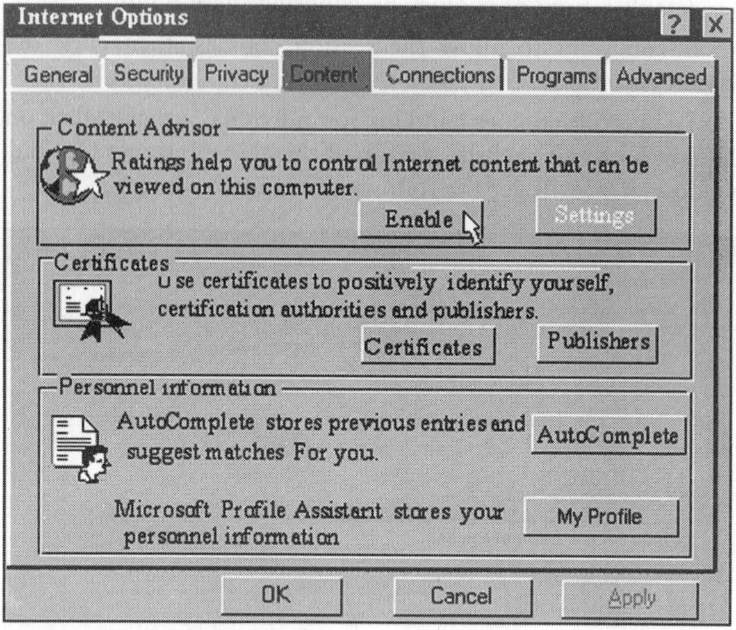

There are three sections of the above window:

1. Content Advisor
2. Certificates
3. Personnel information

1. Content Advisor: Click on Enable button, you will see the following window on the screen.

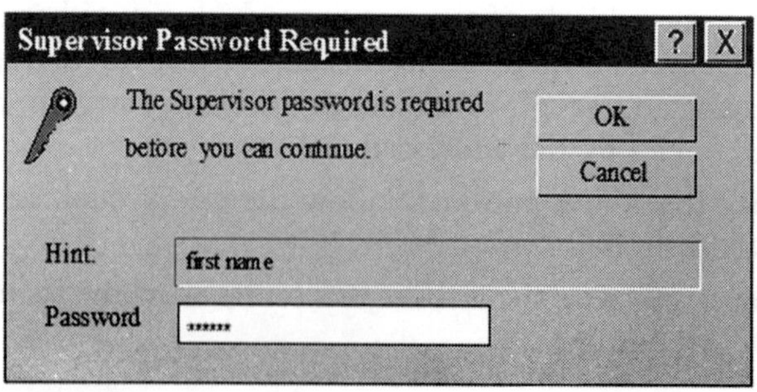

Enter the password in the above window and then click OK button.

Now you are able to control the Internet content that can be seen in your browser.

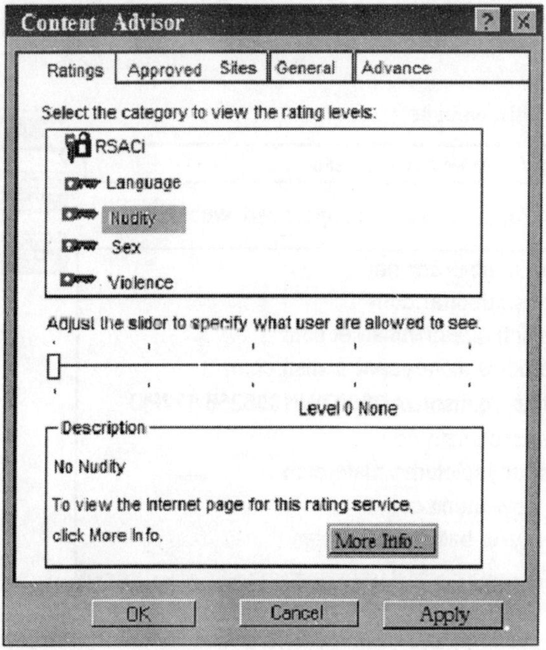

Description is the second section of the Content Advisor. It describes the web page ratings.

You can see the details of web page rating by clicking on More Info button on Internet.

Approve sites is the second button of Content Advisor. A list of approved and disapproved websites can be seen in the window at the page no. 340.

You can add as many websites as you like to open in your browser by typing the address of website and then click OK button. By using Always or Never button you can set the site that can always or never used without considering its ratings. If the site is not required to view in your browser you can removed it.

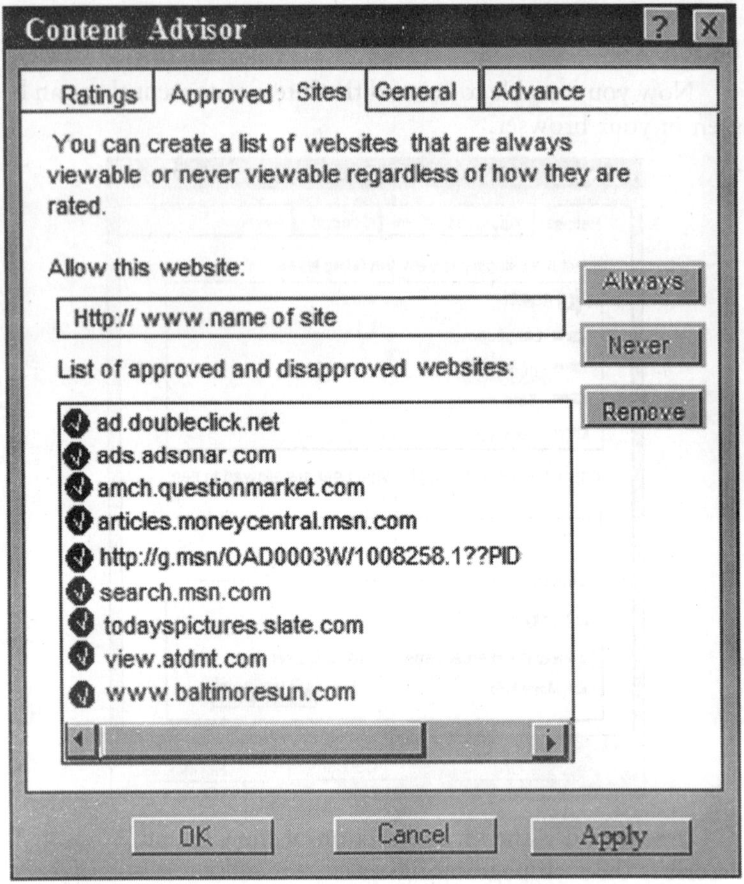

General is the third button of content advisor. Click on it, you will get the following content in the window.

There are three sections of this window:

1. User Options.
2. Supervisor Password.
3. Rating Systems.

1. User Options: User option contains two check boxes.

First check box can be used to see any site that has no ratings while second check box can be used to see restricted content by using supervisor password.

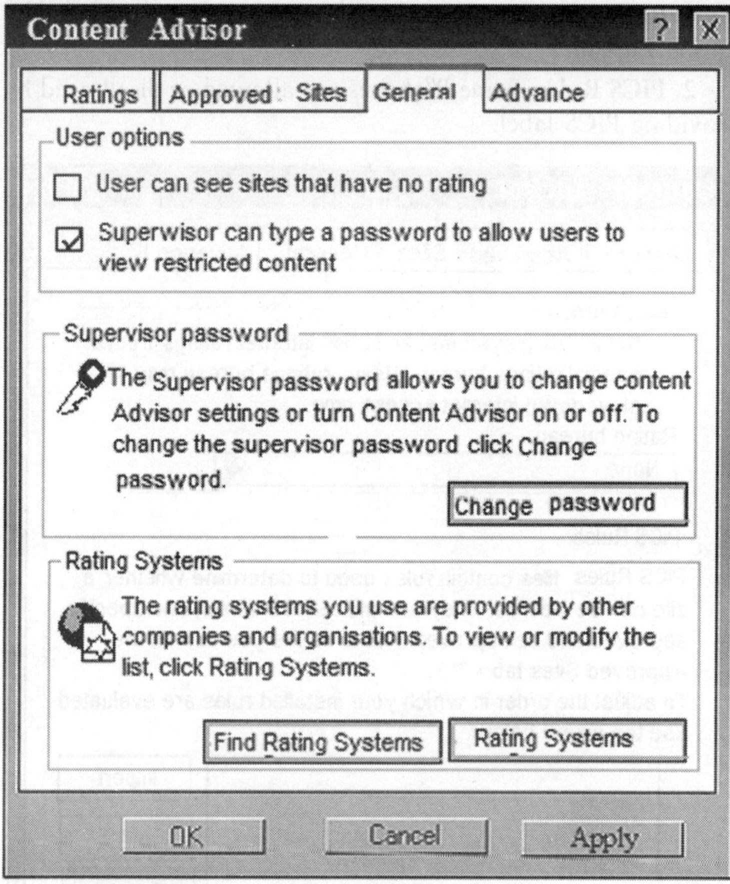

2. Supervisor Password: By clicking on Change Password button you can change the content advisor setting. You can even on and off the content advisor.

3. Rating Systems: You can see any change carried out in rating system by clicking on the Rating System button.

Fourth button on the Content Rating window is Advanced. Click on Advance button, the content of the Content Advisor window will change as shown below.

This window has two sections:

1. Rating Bureau
2. PICS Rules

1. Rating Bureau: Some special site's ratings are provided by Rating Bureau.

2. PICS Rules: Some Websites are allowed or disallowed by providing PICS label.

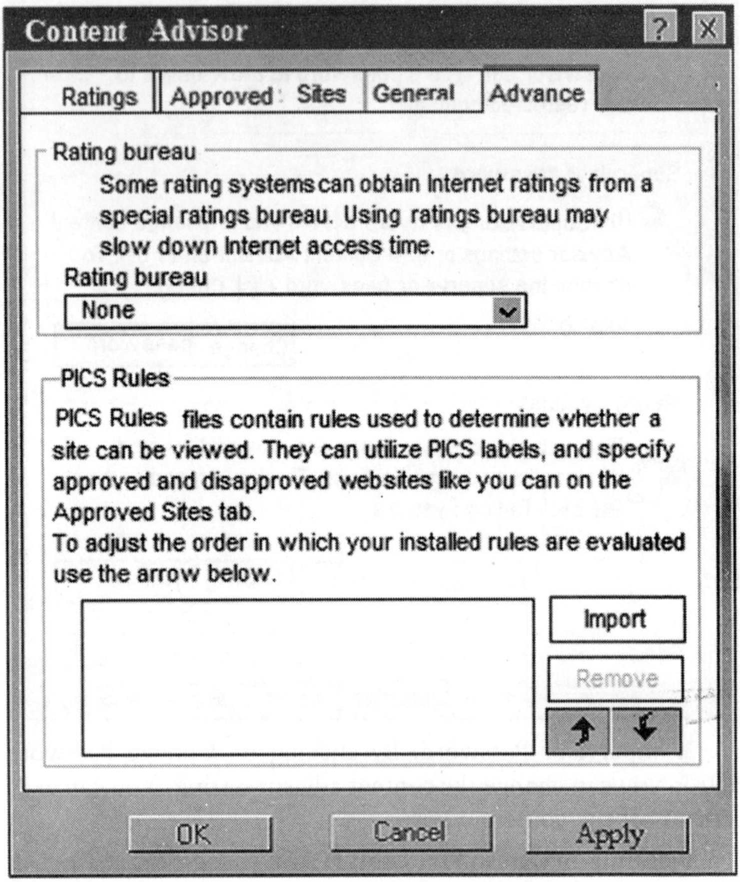

Connections

This is the fifth button on Internet Operation window. There are six buttons used for different functions. The buttons are Set-Up, Add, Remove, Settings, Set-Default and LAN Settings.

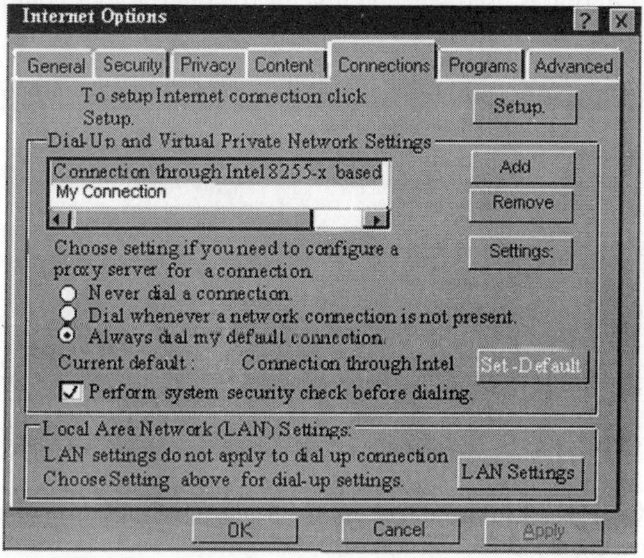

Set-Up Button

If you click on Set-Up button, it will open Connection Wizard window as follows.

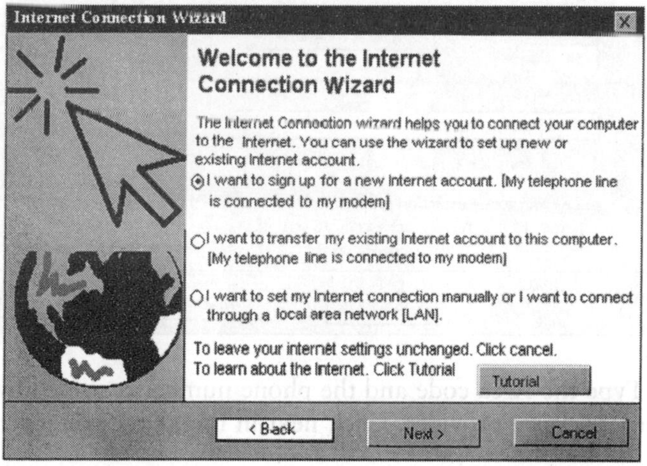

There are three options to connect your computer with the Internet. If you are making Internet connection first time then choose the first option by clicking it. If you want to transfer my existing Internet account to the computer use second option. Third option is used when you want to connect your computer with LAN manually.

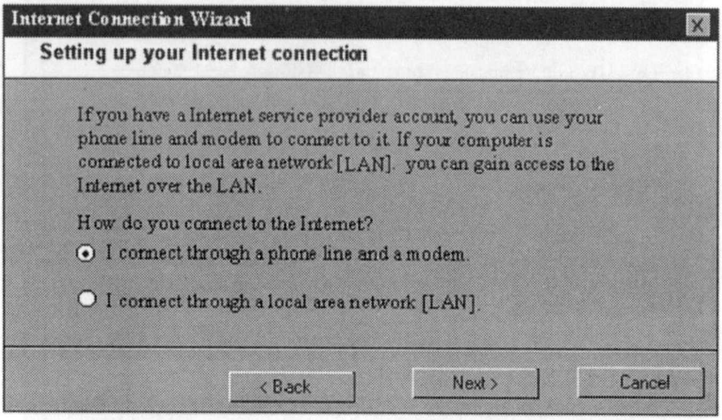

Click Next in the above Internet connection wizard window. Following window will appear.

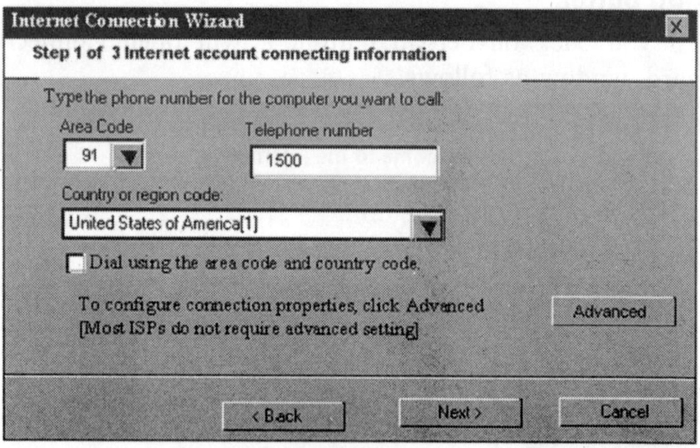

Type the Area code and the phone number provided by the Internet service provider. Click next in the above window.

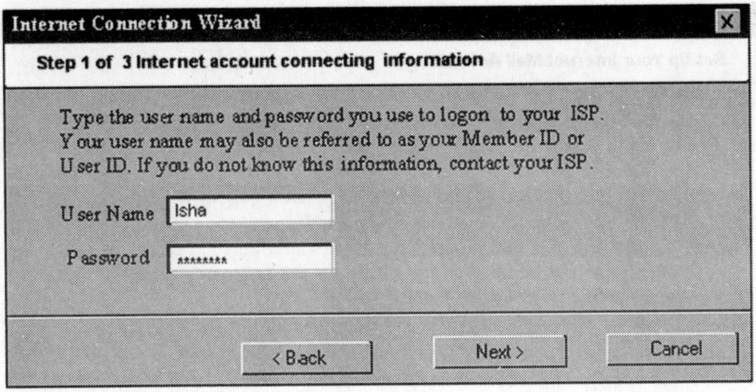

Enter the name and the password provided by your ISP, and then click next. Following window will appear.

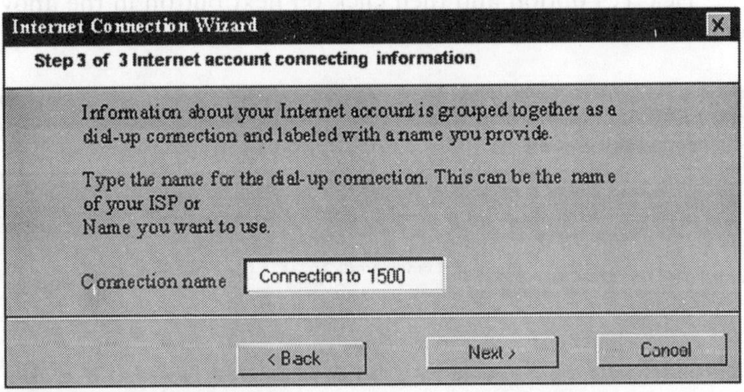

Click the Next Button in the above window. Following window will appear.

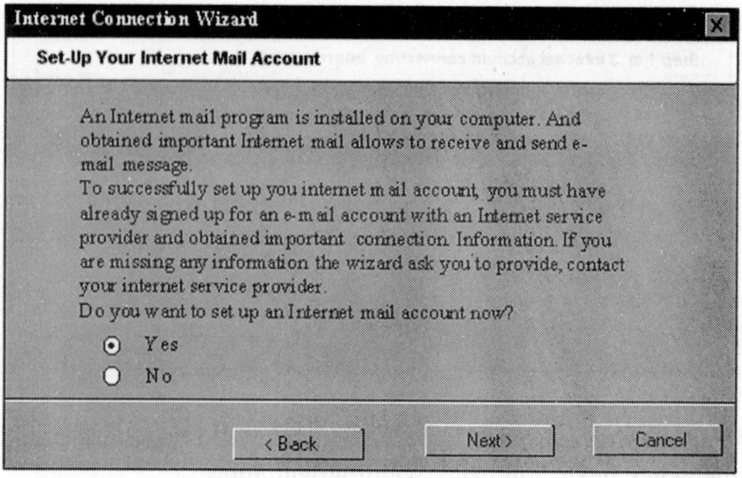

Tick Yes option and then click on next button in the above window.

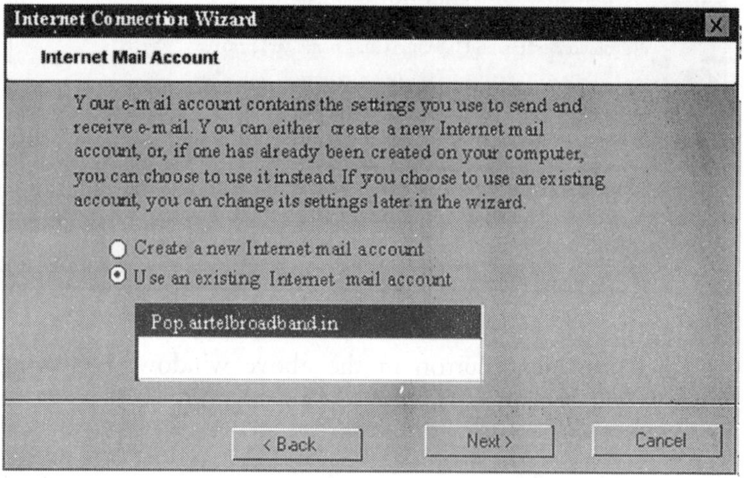

Tick "Use an existing mail account". Then click on next button in the above window. Following window will appear.

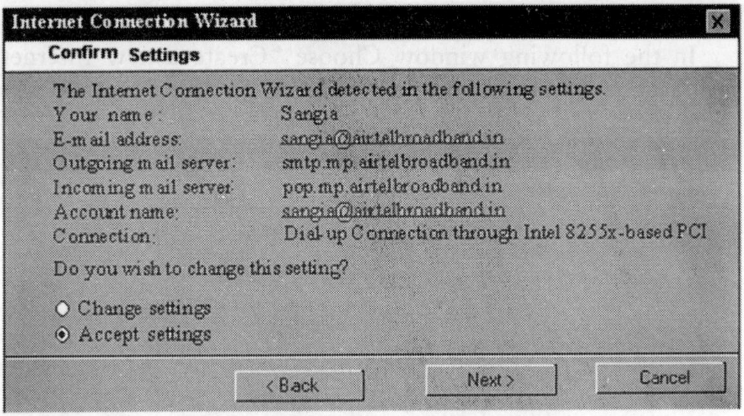

Select the Accept Settings and then click Next in the above window.

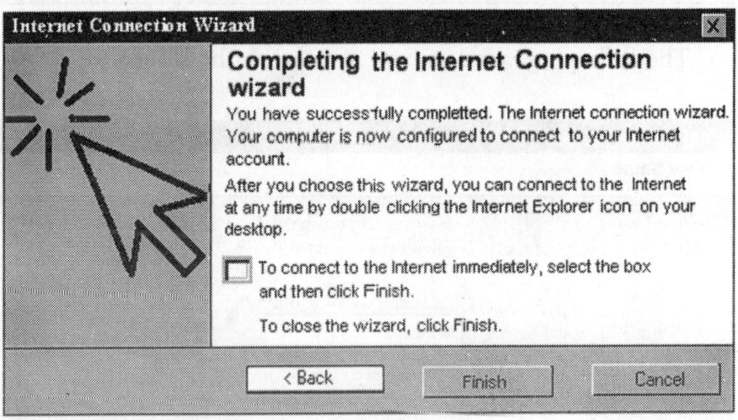

Click Finish in the above window.

Create a new Internet mail account

In the following window Choose "Create a new Internet mail account" option, and then click Next.

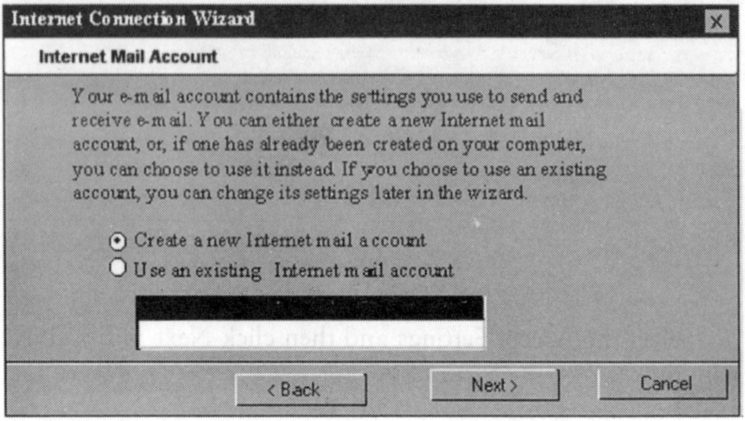

The following window will appear on the screen.

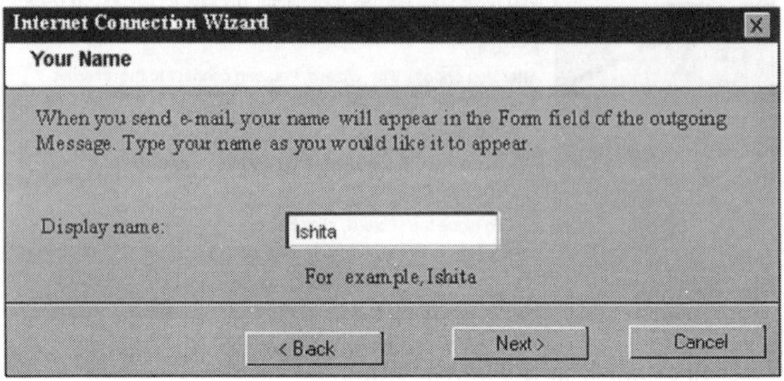

Enter the name in the Display name Text Box. Click Next the following window will appear with "Internet E-mail Address".

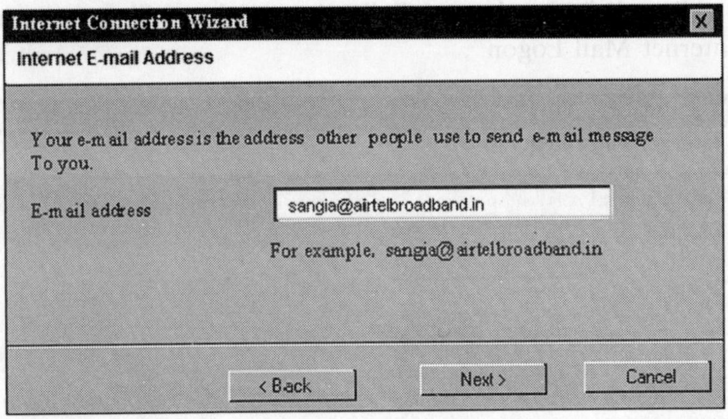

Enter the e-mail address provided by your ISP and then click Next, in the above window. Following window will appear with "E-mail Server Names".

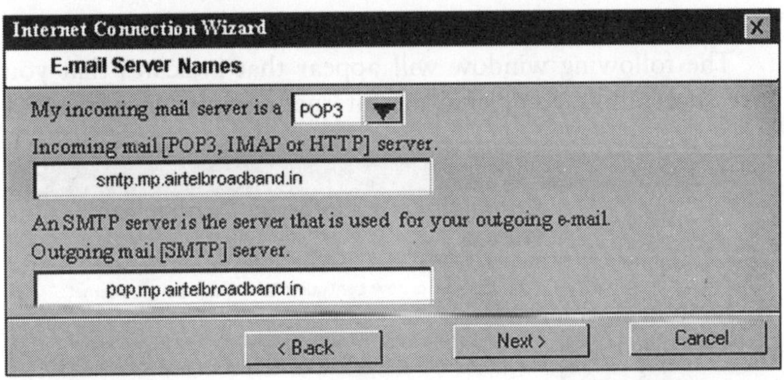

Take three steps as follows.

Choose POP3 in combo box, in front of "my incoming mail server".

Enter the POP incoming mail server address for example smtp.mp.airtelbroadband.in

Enter the smtp incoming mail server address for example smtp.mp.airtelbroadband.in

Now click Next button. Following window will appear with "Internet Mail Logon".

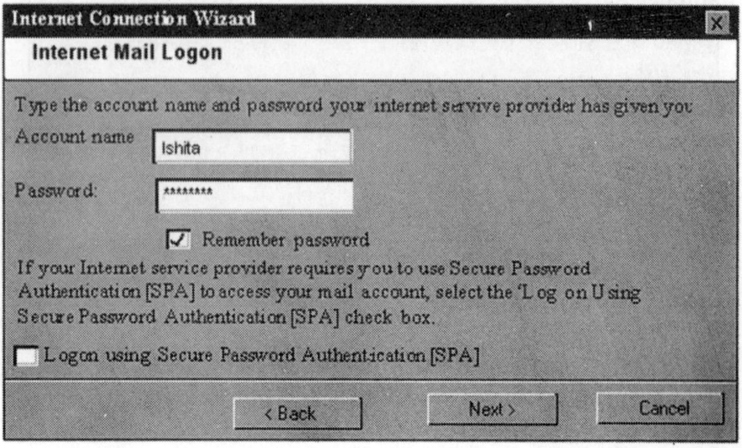

Enter the Account name and Password click Next.

The following window will appear that indicates that you have successfully completed the Internet completion wizard.

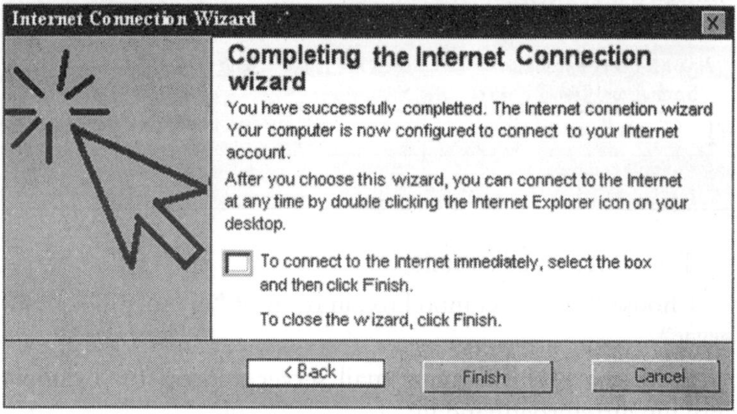

Click Finish, your internet connection is completed. You have created the new Internet account successfully.

Make your LAN connection

Choose the option three "I want to set my Internet connection manually or I want to connect through local area network [LAN] from the Internet Connection Wizard.

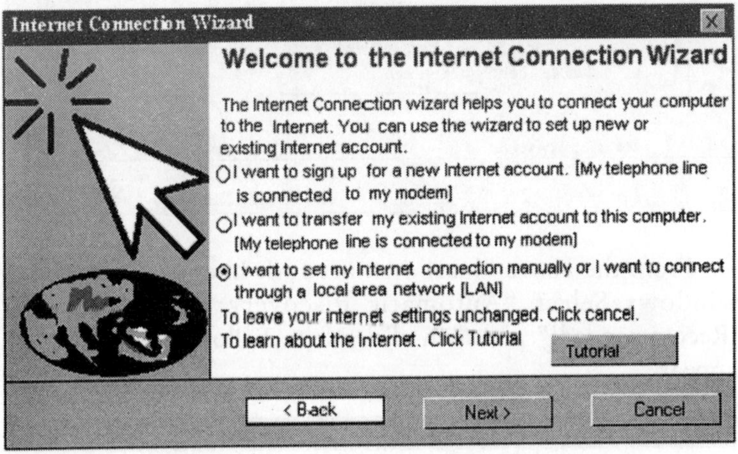

Click the Next. The following "Setting up tour Internet connection window" with two options will appear.

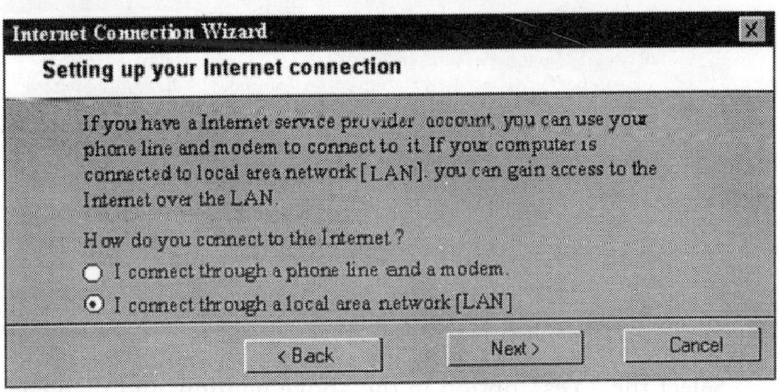

Select the option two "I connect through a local area network [LAN]". Now click Next.

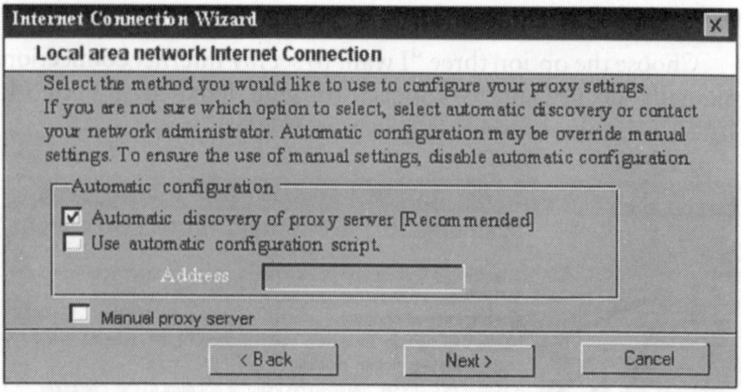

From the above "local area network Internet Connection" windows Select "Automatic discovery of proxy server [Recommended]" and then click Next. Following window will appear.

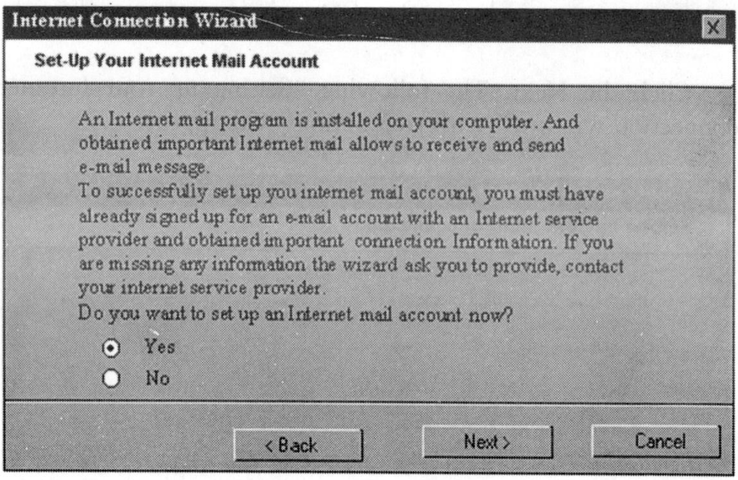

Select the "Yes" option in the above window and then click Next Button. Following window with "Internet mail Account" will appear.

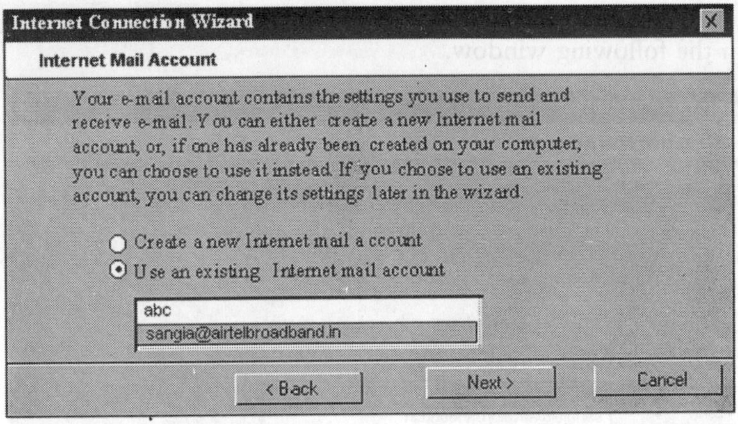

There are two options, Option "Create a new Internet mail Account" already explained.

Choose the second option "Use an existing Internet mail Account" and click Next.

The following "Confirm Setting" wizard will appear.

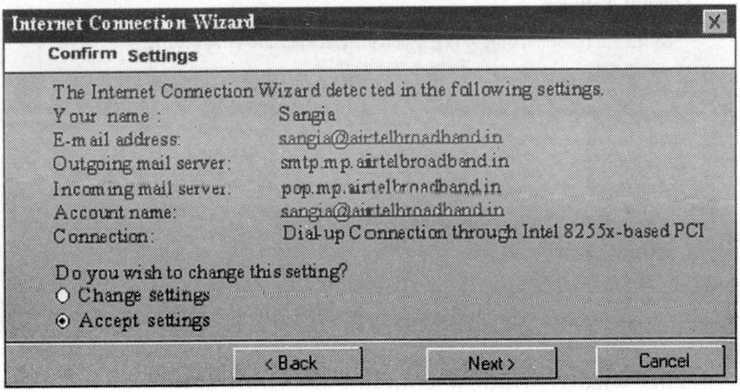

If you select the another existing Internet mail "abc" account in the following window.

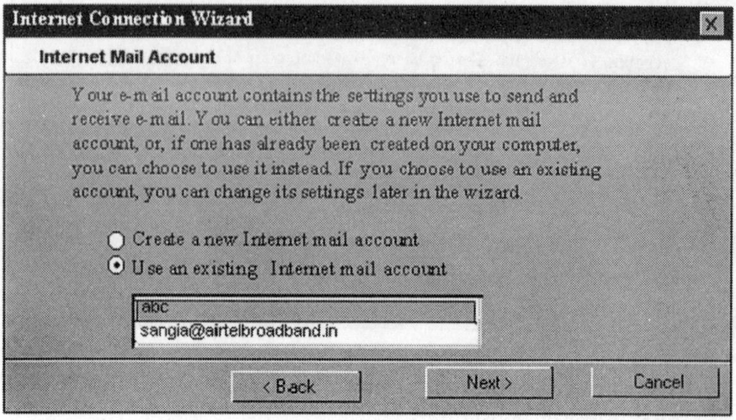

Click Next. Following window with details about the existing Internet mail account "abc" settings will appear.

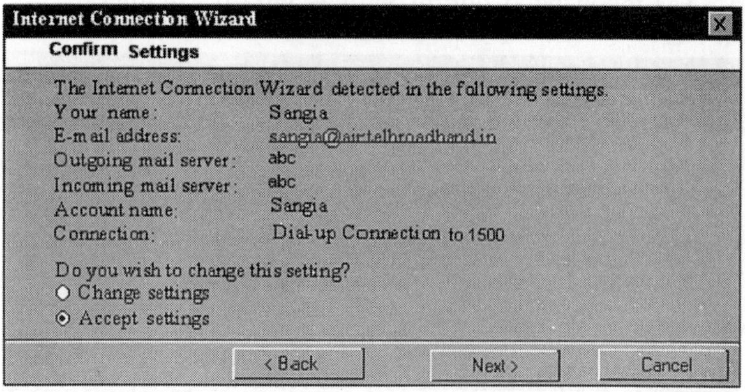

This wizard window contains the information about, your name, e-mail address, outgoing mail server, incoming mail server, account name and connection.

There are two options shown at the bottom of wizard.

1. Change settings.
2. Accept settings.

If you want to change the settings then choose the first option and click next. Internet connection wizard will again open for you where you can change the following information:

1. Your Name
2. E-mail address
3. Outgoing mail server
4. Incoming mail server
5. Account name
6. Connection

You can again see the "Confirm Settings" window in the end of the connection wizard. Select the second option "Accept Setting" and click the Next button.

The following window will appear that indicates that you have successfully completed the Internet completion wizard.

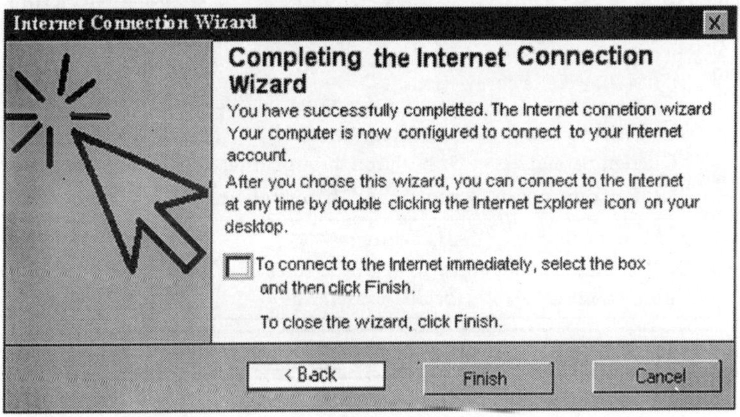

Check the box in the above window, if you want to test your Internet connection immediately.

We have discussed the Setup operation in detail. Below there are Dial-up and Virtual Private network Settings. It contains four buttons.

1. Add
2. Remove
3. Settings
4. Set Default

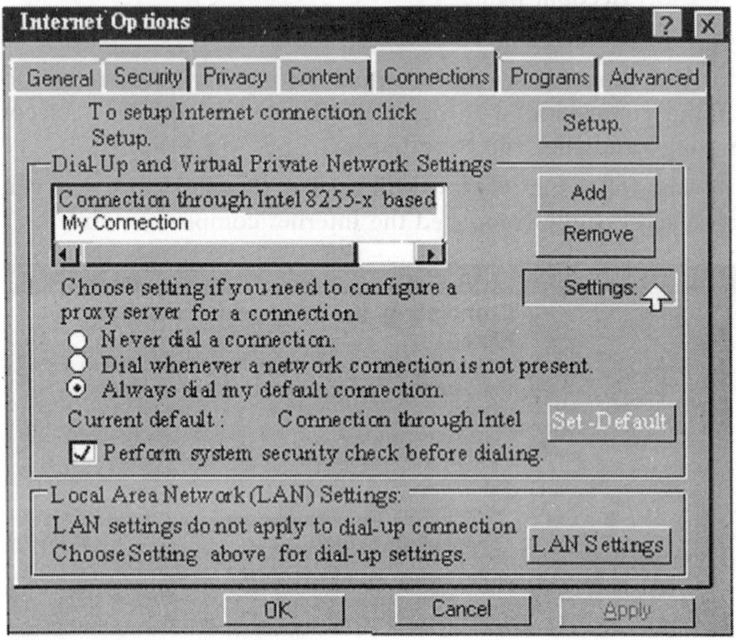

1. Add Button

If you click on Add button, it will open the "Make New Connection" Window wizard. It will guide you to make new connection.

Make New Connection window has a text boxes and a combo box.

1. Type a name for the computer you are dialing.
2. Select a device.

You may see the text "My Connection" in the text box. If you want to change the text you can type your own text.

Select a device combo box displays the specification of the Ethernet Adapter.

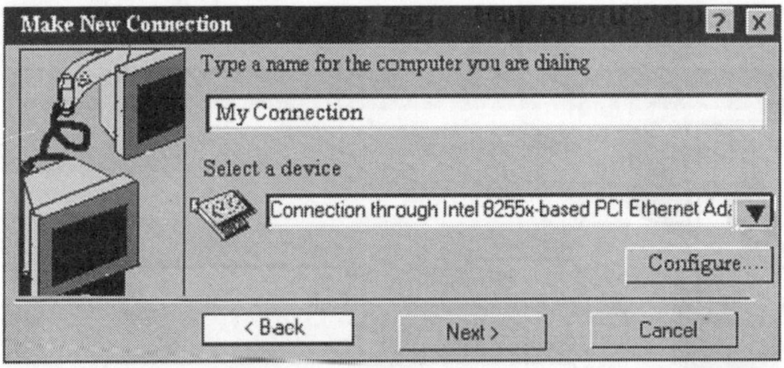

Click the Next button in the above Make Connection Window.

The following window will appear on the screen.

The window requires three information.

1. Area Code which is the country code.
2. Telephone number of the service providing agency.
3. Name of the country from where you make this Internet connection.

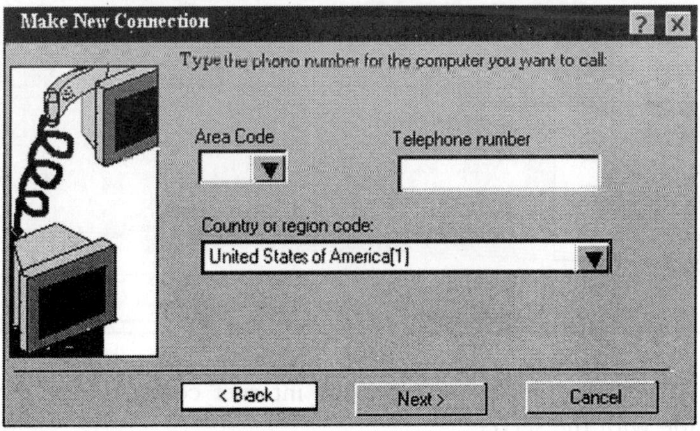

Now type the following in the above window.

1. Inside the Area Code type 91 the code of country India.

2. Type the telephone number of the internet service providing agency here for example 1500.
3. Click the Country or region code. Select India (91) from the list by

Clicking on the arrow button of the combo box.

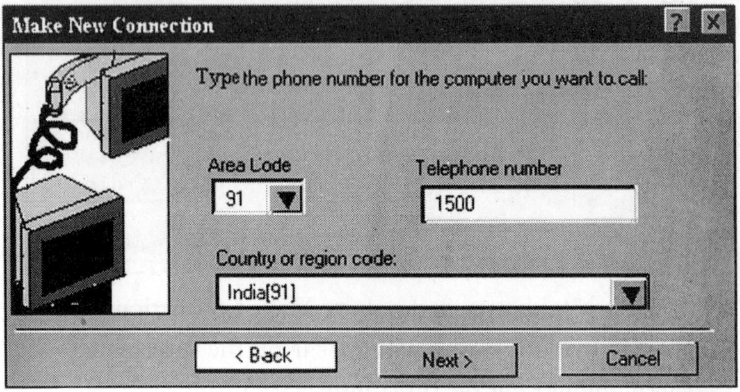

Click the Next button in the above window, you will see the following window.

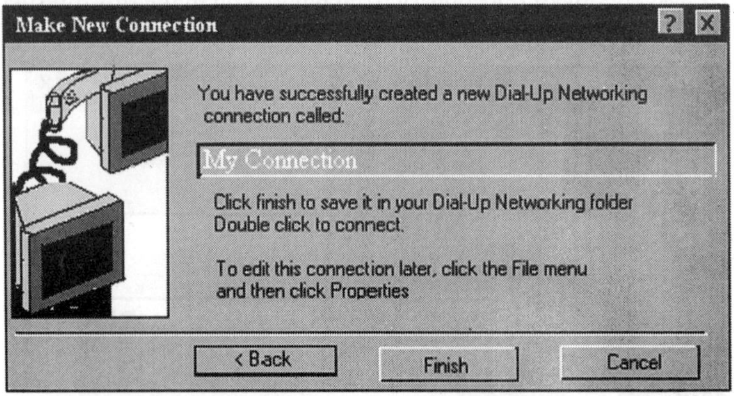

Click the Finish button. Your internet connection is now made with the server.

2. Remove Button

This button is used for removal of the Internet connection.

In the above Internet Option window under connection tab, you see two connections:

1. Connection through Intel 8255-x based Ethernet .
2. My Connection.

In front of Add and Remove button. Select the unwanted connection inside the list box and then click Remove button. The connection will disappear from the list. Suppose you select "My connection" in the following window and click "remove button".

"My Connection" from the list will be deleted.

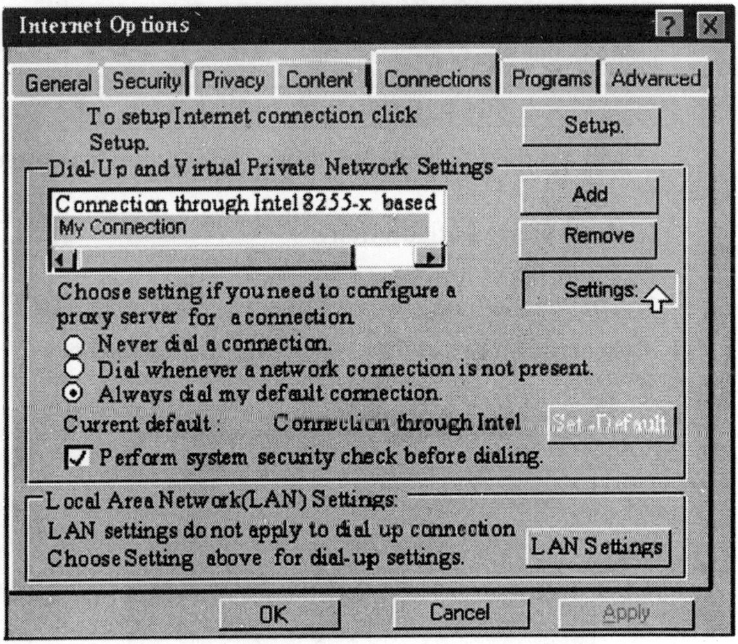

Settings

In the Internet Option window fourth button is Settings. Selecting the "Connection through Intel 8255-x based" from the list and click the Settings button in the following Internet Option window.

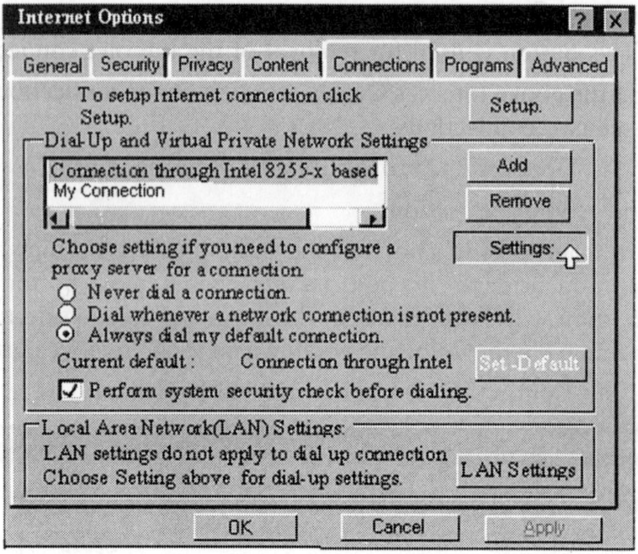

You will get the following window. This window has three sections:

1. Automatic configuration
2. Proxy Server
3. Dial-Up Setting

1. Automatic configuration: There are two check boxes.

1. Automatic detect settings

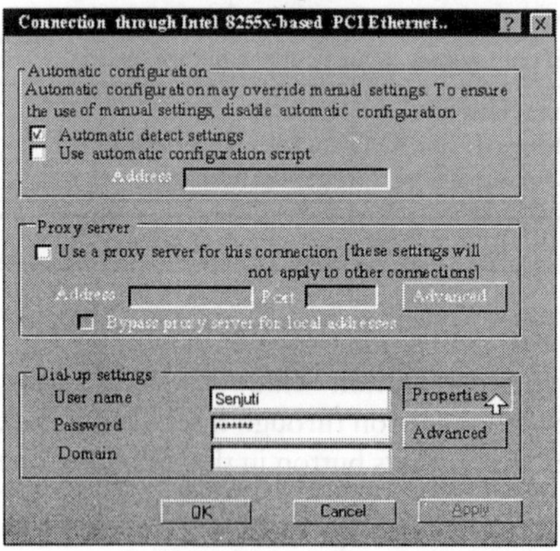

2. Use automatic configuration script.

Tick the "Automatic detect settings". If you select the Automatic configuration then it will override your manual settings.

2. Proxy Server: This section has one check box. If you click on this check box, it means you are going to use the proxy server for your connection. You have to provide the Address of proxy server and its port number.

3. Dial-Up Setting: This section is useful for our present connection. We have to type the user name and password provided by our ISP. Property and Advance are two buttons which we can use for further configuration of our internet connection.

Click on Properties button in the above window. You will see the following window. This window contains four tabs or buttons.

1. General
2. Server Type
3. Scripting
4. Multilink

Following figure describes General button. It shows the type of adapter used in our Internet connection.

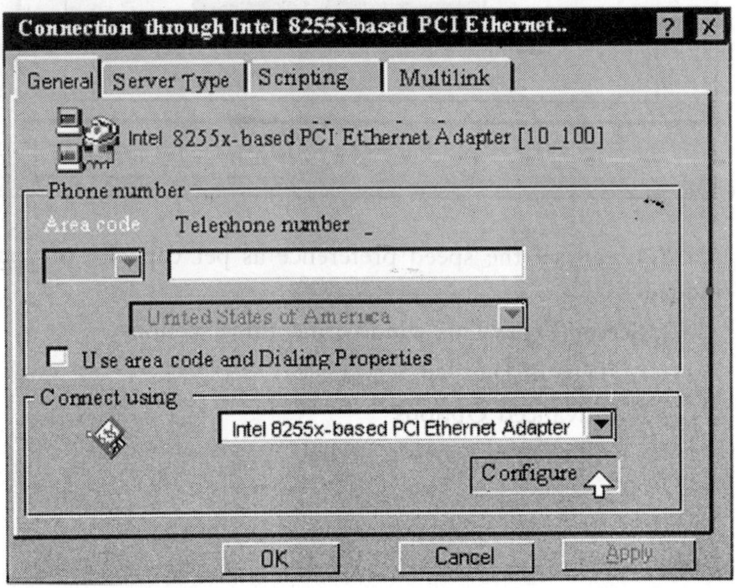

1. General: This wizard window has three sections:

(i) At the top, it indicates the name of the adapter.

(ii) Phone Number: This is the phone number provided by your ISP to which you are connected by dialing.

(iii) This is the description or the name of adapter through which you are going to connect with Internet and which can be configured by using "Configure button".

Click Configure button in the above window, you will get the following "PPP over Ethernet Protocol connection Properties" window. It describes that all the channels are connected through this Ethernet connection.

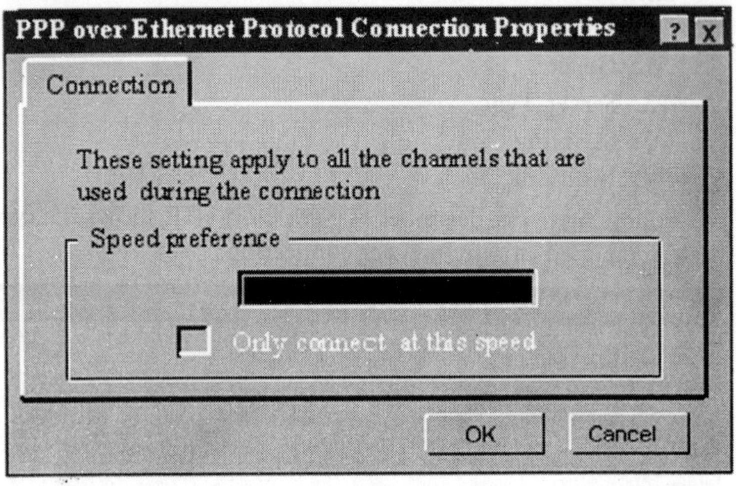

You can set the speed preference as per capacity of your modem.

2. Server Type: This window has three sections:

1. Type of Dial-Up Server
2. Advanced Options
3. Allowed network protocol

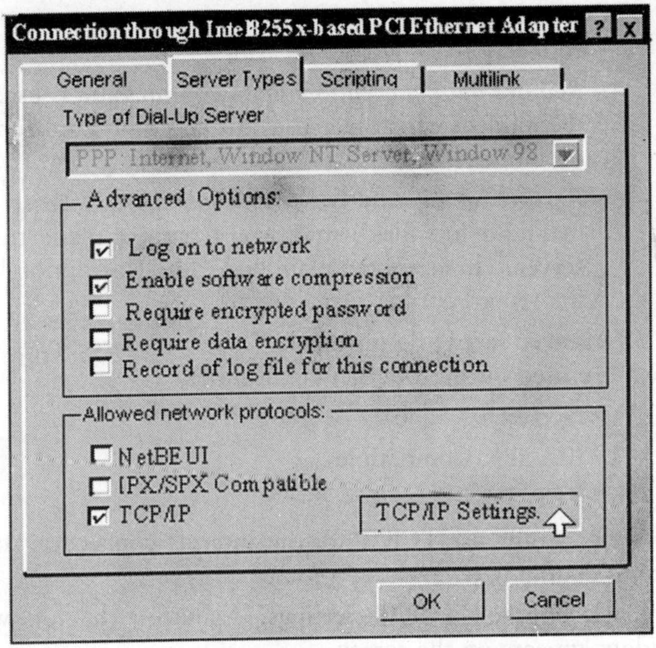

1. Type of Dial-Up Server: In this particular case your type of dial-up server is "PPP, Internet, Window NT Server, Window 98".

2. Advanced Option: There are five options in this section.

1. Log on to network
2. Enable software compression
3. Required encrypted password
4. Requirc data encryption
5. Record of log files for this connection.

1. *Log on to network*: This option is checked for logging on the network connection. Username and password is required.
2. *Enable software compression*: This enable the software compression provided by communication software which increases the speed of data transmission.
3. *Required encrypted password*: This option provide encrypted password which cannot be red by anybody

so that no unauthorized person can use your internet connection.

4. *Require data encryption*: Data compression is used by the modem which increases the speed of data transfer on internet.
5. *Record of log files for this connection*: Web servers maintain log files listing every request made to the server. These are the plain text files. This option keep the records of log file.

3. Allowed network protocol. There are three protocols which are used during Internet connections.

1. NetBEUI
2. IPX/SPX Compatible
3. TCP/IP

We generally use TCP/IP for our internet connection so we have to configure it.

Click on the "TCP/IP Settings..." button the following window appears on the screen.

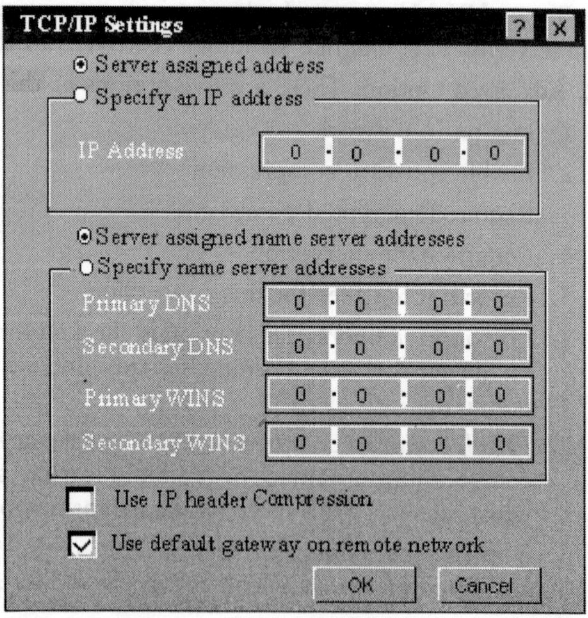

There are two default options in each section of TCP/IP setting window:

1. Server assigned address
2. Server assign name and server addresses

When you select the second option, the TCP/IP window looks like this. First option is to specify an IP address of your computer in the box.

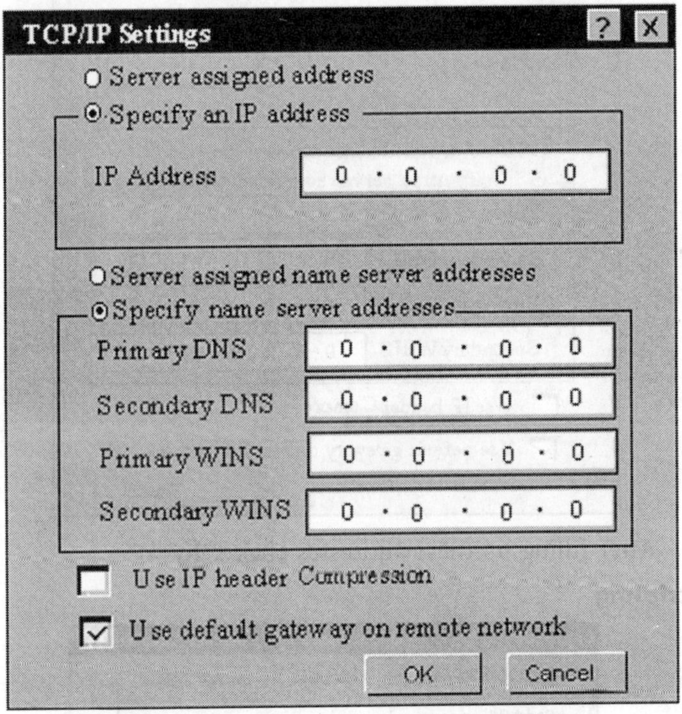

Second section is for specifying the name and server addresses Here you can provide three addresses as follows:

1. IP Address
2. Primary DNS
3. Secondary DNS

The following is the example to fill up the above TCP/IP settings for IP address and DNS server.

These addresses are provided by a particular Internet Service Provider to a particular computer on the network.

IP Address.......................192.168.1.2

Primary DNS Server 202.56.230.6

Secondary DNS Server.........202.56.224.153

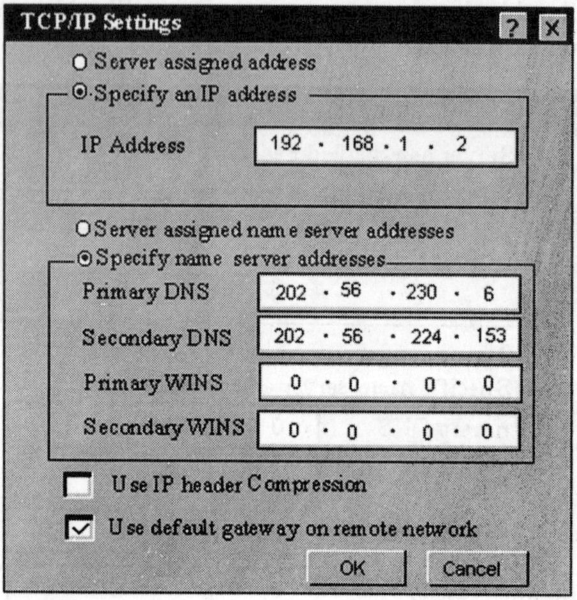

After filling up these addresses click OK.

Scripting

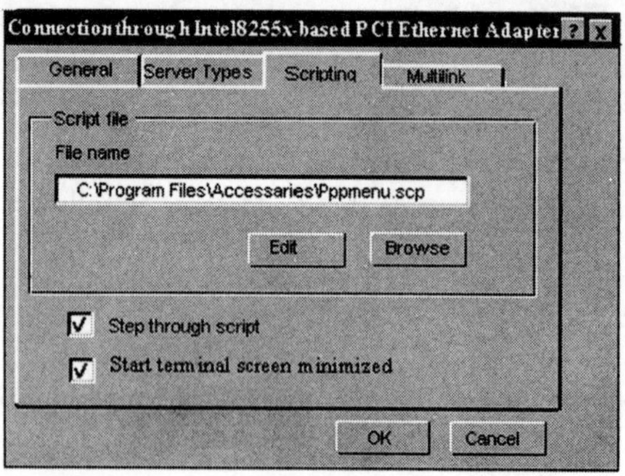

Click Browse button in the above window. You will get the following window.

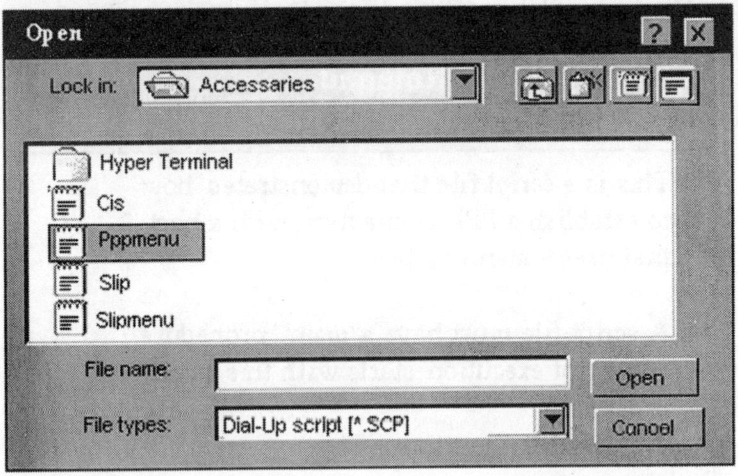

Select the item Pppmenu from the above window and then click on Open button

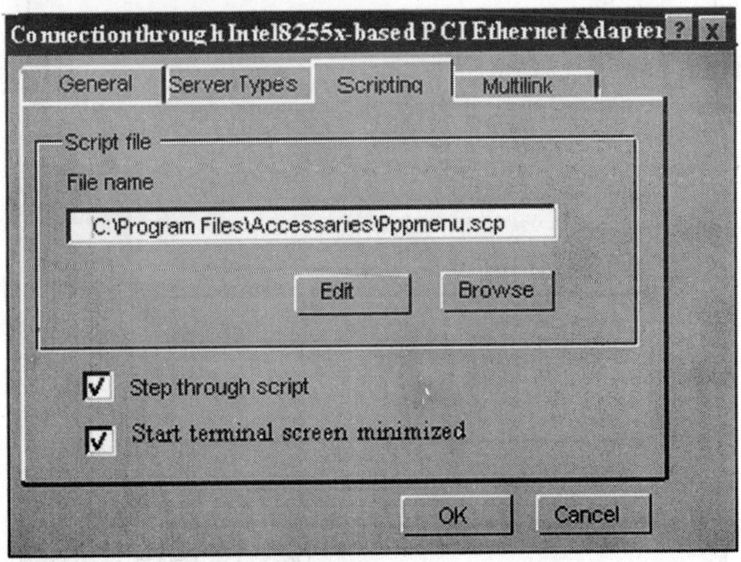

Click Edit Button you will get the following Notepad on the screen.

You can read the script and can edit as per your requirement.

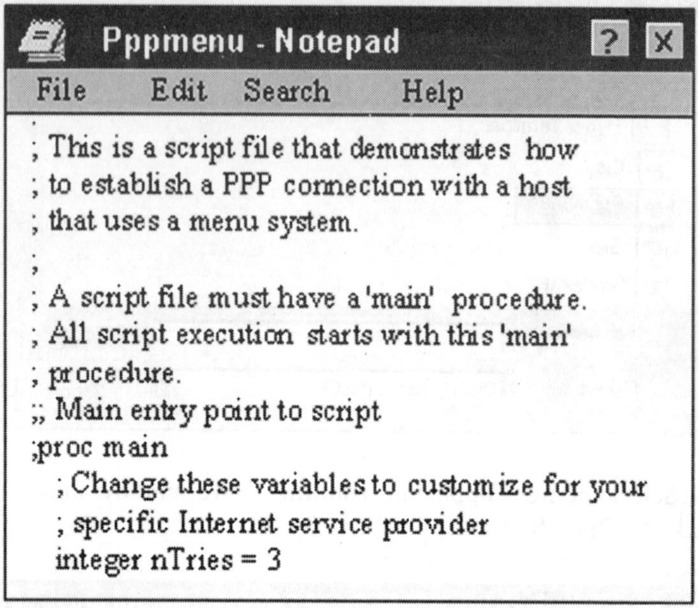

Multi-link

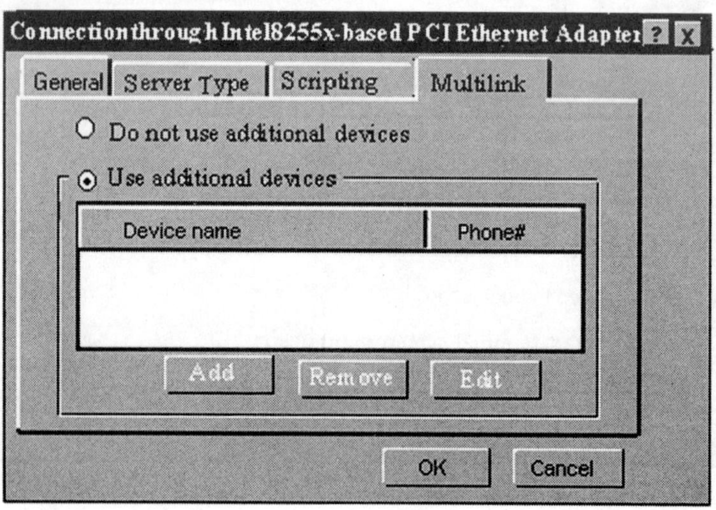

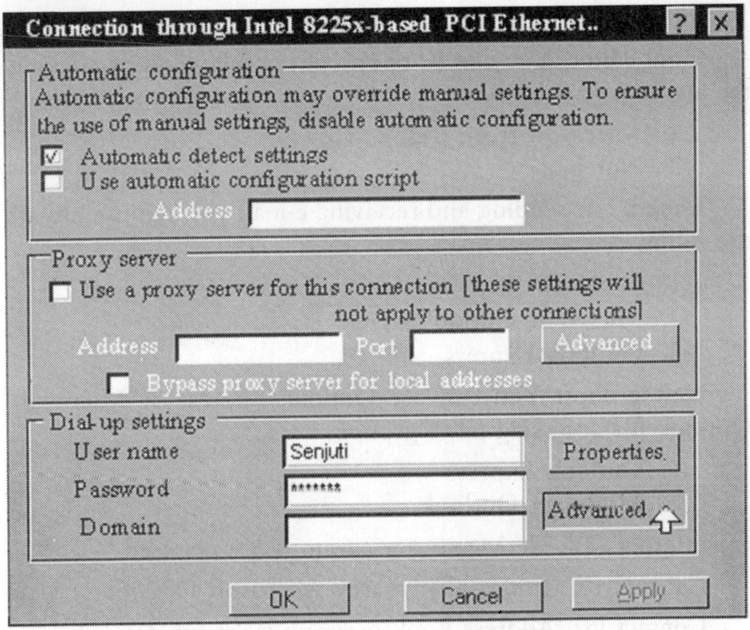

Click Advanced button in the above window. You will get the following window.

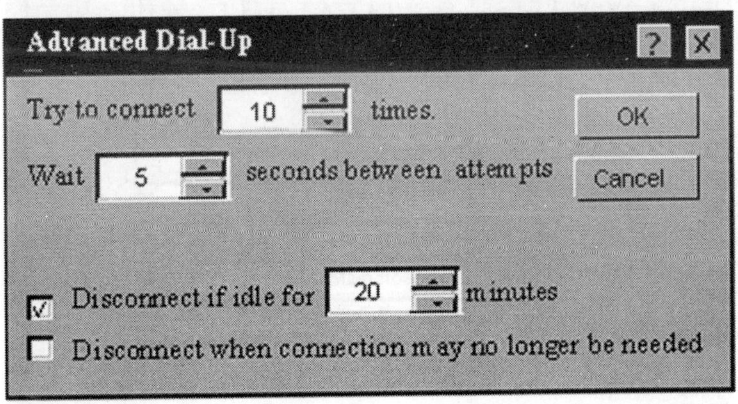

Programs

Programs is the sixth button of Internet Options.

If you click on the Program button on Internet Option, the following window will appear on the screen.

Internet program uses six program as follows:

Html editor: You can be to any of the following by clicking the arrow of combo box.

1. Microsoft front page
2. Notepad

E-mail: For sending and receiving e-mail you can use any of the following:

1. Hotmail
2. Microsoft Outlook
3. Outlook Express

Newsgroups: You can use Outlook Express or Microsoft Outlook for accessing news group:

1. Outlook Express
2. Microsoft Outlook

Internet call: NetMeeting program is always used.

Calendar: Calendar always uses Microsoft Outlook.

Contact list: Address Book program is set for it.

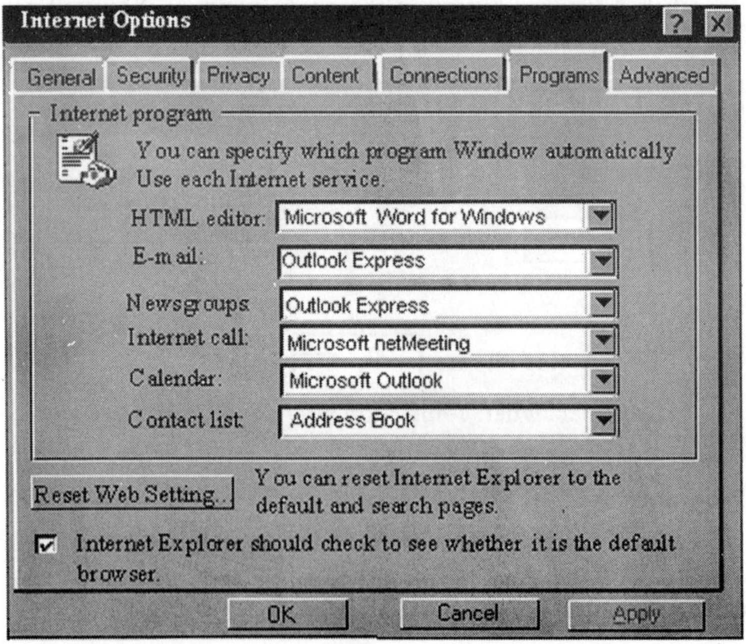

Click the Reset Web Setting Button, you will get the following window.

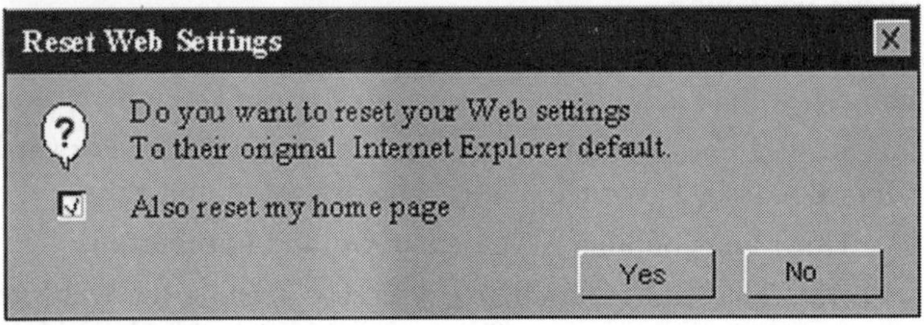

Click "Yes" to reset Web setting or No to exit from the program.

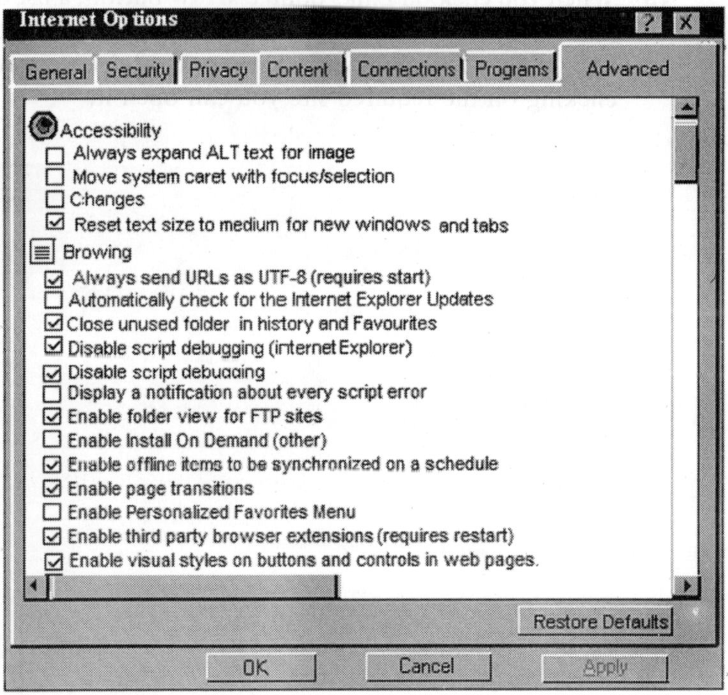

Advance: Advance is the seventh button of the of the Internet options window. If you click on this button you will get the above window.

This window contains the setting of many programs. You can restore the defaults by clicking on Restore Defaults button.

Second line contains the standard buttons Back, Forward, Home, Search, Favorites Media, History, Mail and Print.

Third line contains Address bar Go and link buttons:

(a) The Address toolbar is used for opening the web site. When you type a Web page address inside the address tool bar and then click on Go button or press enter the requested site opens synchronize.

(b) When you click on Links double arrow button, a list of the web sites like, Best of the web, Microsoft, Channel Guide, Customize link etc., appears on the screen. By clicking on the required site you can open it.

Outlook Express

16

Outlook express is a very powerful, economical and efficient tool that is used for sending and receiving e-mails. The most important feature of outlook express is to draft any number of messages offline and can store in draft or outbox folder. If you are not having the dedicated internet connection then you can send the stored e-mails at any time after connecting your computer to internet through dial-up connection. If you are provided internet connection then ask the ISP to configure your outlook express, or get the name of SMTP and POP server from them. If you know the name of SMTP and POP server, you yourself can configure the outlook express as follows:

Configuration of Outlook Express

Click on the "Outlook Express icon" on the desktop. The following "Outlook Express" window will appear.

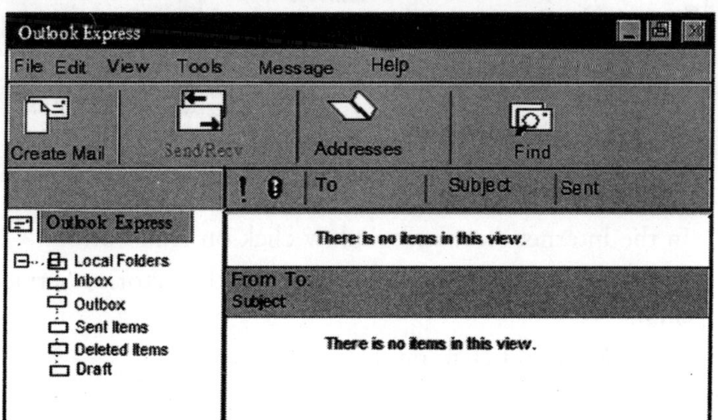

Click on the Tool item on the menu bar. A drop down list of items will appear.

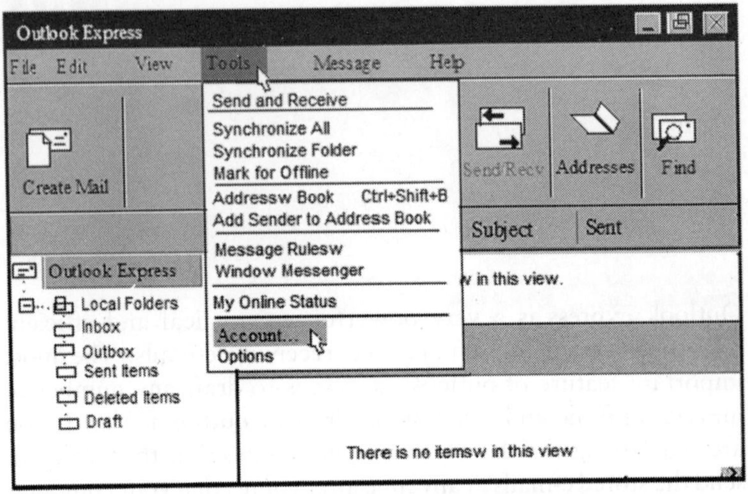

From this list select "Account" and click on it. Following "Internet Account" window will appear.

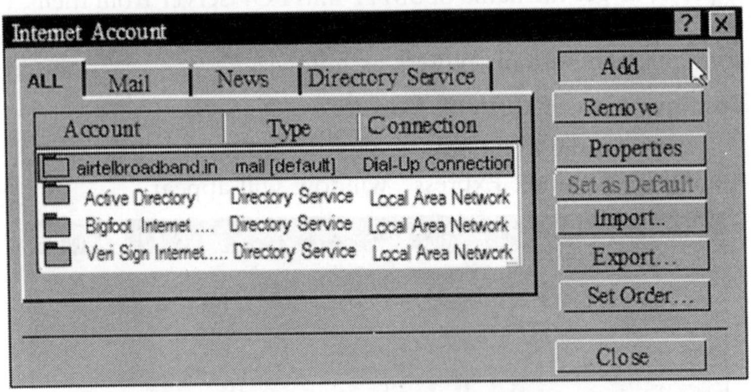

In the Internet Account window click on Add button.

A list of three items Mail, News and Directories Services appears.

Select Mail and click on it.

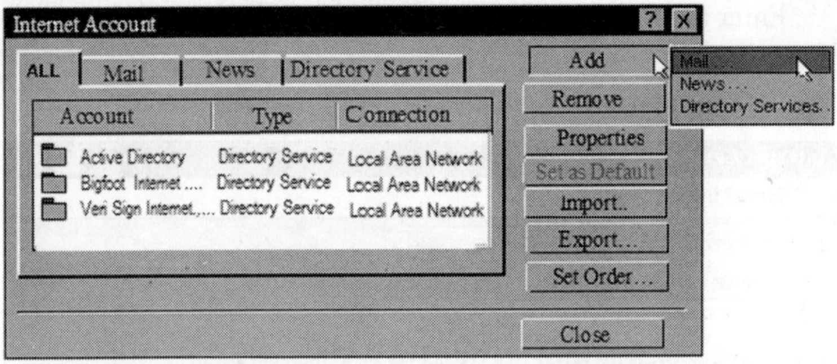

The following Internet connection wizard window will appear.

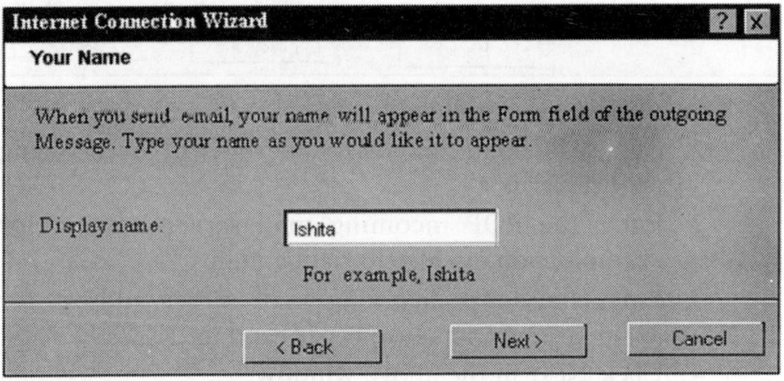

Enter the name in the "Display name" textbox. For example, Ishita.

Click "Next" button.

The following window will appear with "Internet E-mail Address".

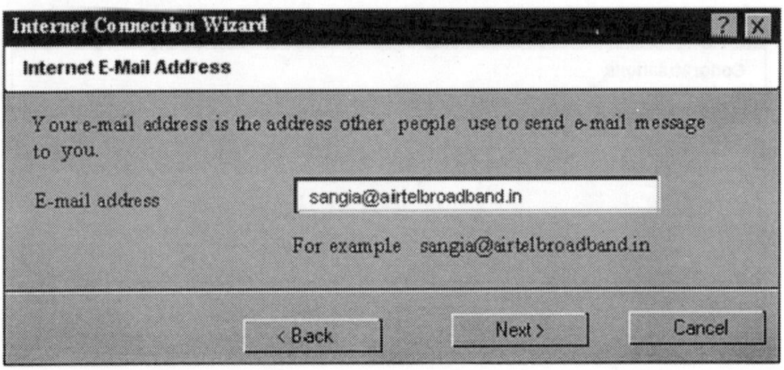

Enter the e-mail address provided by your ISP and then click Next, in the above window.

Following window will appear with "E-mail Server Names".

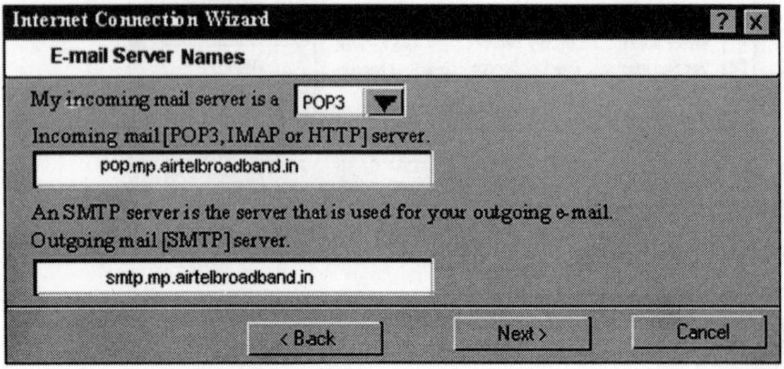

Take three steps as follows:

1. Choose POP3 in combo-box, in front of "My incoming mail server is a".
2. Enter the POP incoming mail server address for example, pop.mp.airtelbroadband.in
3. Enter the smtp incoming mail server address for example, smtp.mp.airtelbroadband.in
4. Click Next in the above window.

The POP incoming mail server address pop.mp. airtelbroadband.in and smtp incoming mail server address smtp.mp.airtelbroadband.in are the examples.

You have to enter the POP and SMTP server addresses which are provided by your "Internet Service Provider Agent".

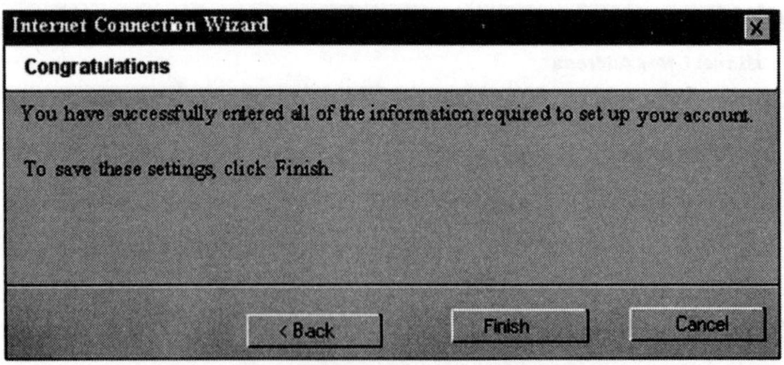

The congratulation window will appear, which will indicate that you have successfully set up your account.

Click on Finish button to save the setting.

Setting Outlook Express account as default.

Open Internet Account window again and Click on the Mail tab.

Server name under Account section will be displayed in the list box which you have just enter as server name in Internet Connection wizard.

If you want to set the Dial-Up connection as a mail default then click on "Set as Default" button.

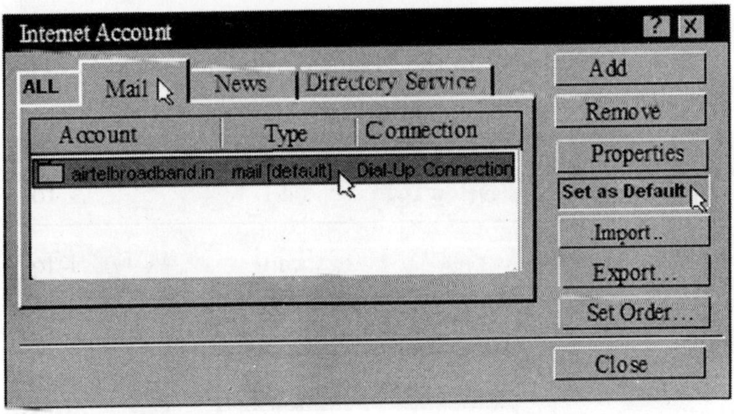

Now you can connect your Outlook Express with the ISP server, if you have completed all necessary formalities of Internet service Provider Agency.

Outlook Express Troubleshooting

Problem 1: Outlook express does not open and the following message is displayed on screen, "MSIMN caused an Invalid page fault in module WAB32.dll".

Solution 1: For rectification of the problem follow the steps below:

Step-1: Click on "Start", go to "Search" and then move the mouse to "Others file and folder" and click on it as given in the following picture.

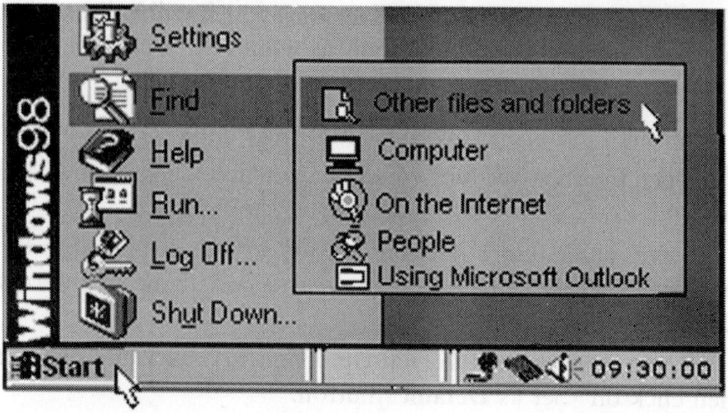

Find all Files window will appear.

2. Type Outloo~1 in the "Named" box and click on "Find Now" button.

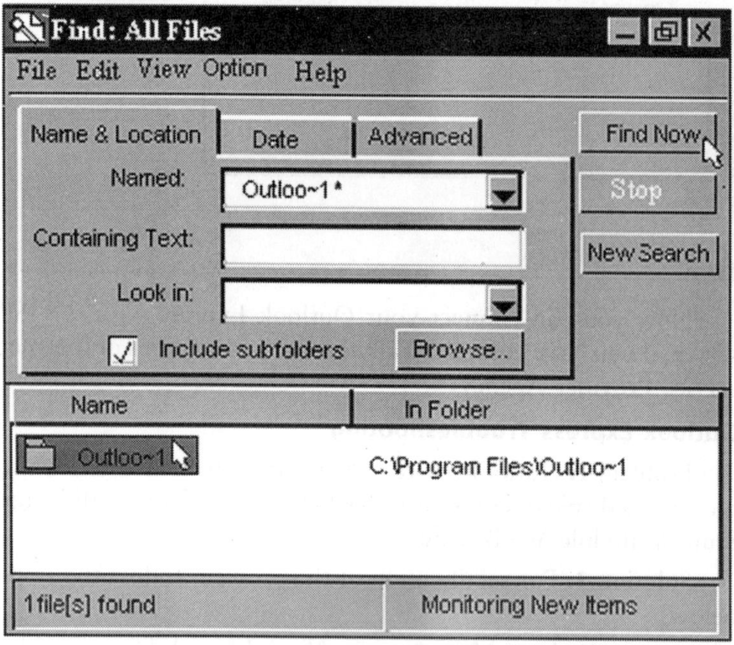

If you will see the folder Outloo~1 in the list box under the "Name" column.

3. Select Outloo~1 and right click on it and rename the folder as "Outlook Express".

4. Click OK. Now restart Outlook Express.

Problem 2: Outlook Express start, but does not connect with ISP server.

Solution 2: Open "Outlook Express", you will see a "Dial-Up Connection" window.

Click on "Connect" button.

You may get the following message in the box, if the problem is related with modem.

"No dial tone. Make sure the modem is correctly connected to the computer and phone line."

There may be following reasons:

1. Telephone line is dead or disconnected.
2. Power of modem may be off in case of external modem.
3. The modem is unsuitable for the system.

1. Check the telephone line connections and hear the dial tone of your phone. If your phone is dead take the help of telephone agency to make it OK. If telephone is OK keep the telephone on the cradle properly.

2. If you are using external modem, check the power is on by checking the power indicator of the modem.

3. You may be using unsuitable modem.

Replace it after consulting with the Internet Service Provider.

Problem 3: Problem in sending and receiving e-mail through Outlook Express.

Solution 3: When you send or receive e-mail through outlook express your computer is to be connected with the SMTP and POP server. The name of the server is provided by the ISP. You can check the name of the server by going through the following steps:

1. Open Outlook Express. Click on the Tool item on the menu bar.

A drop down list of items will appear.

2. From this list select "Account" and click on it.

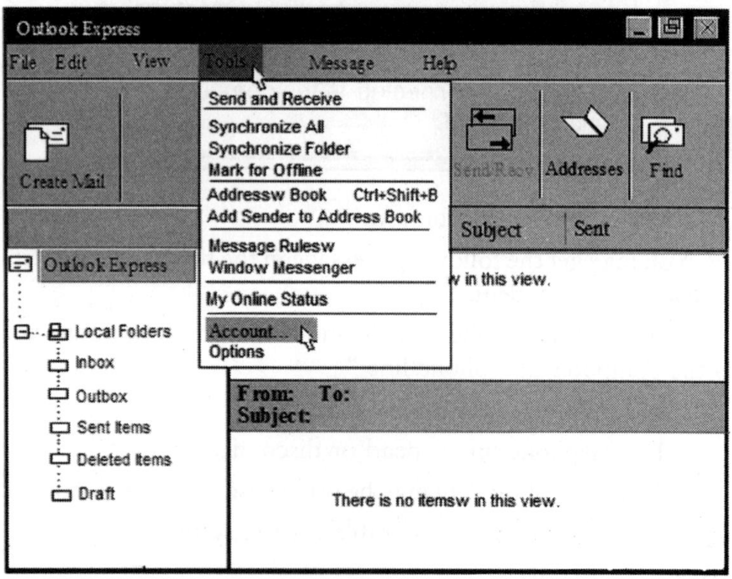

Following "Internet Account" window will appear:

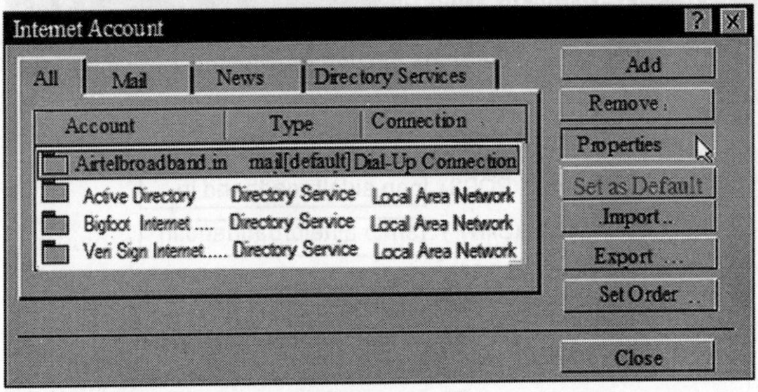

3. Click on "Properties" button.

Following window under "General" tab will appear that is configured for server name, name of the user. Organisation, e-mail address and reply address.

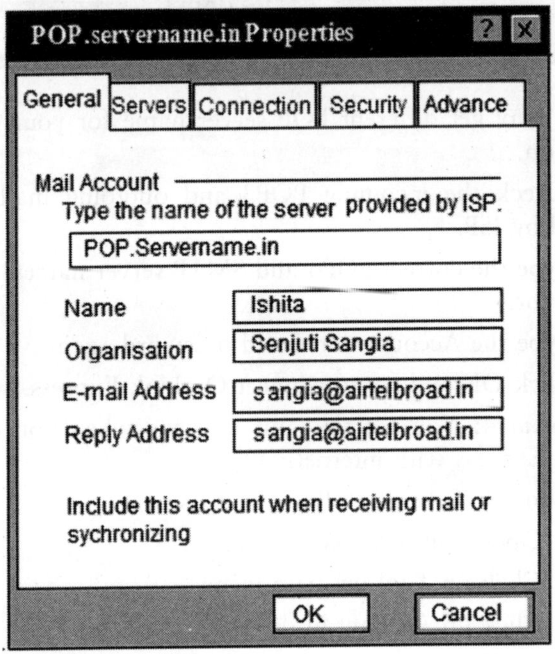

4. Click on Server tab.

Following "POP server-name.in Properties" window appears.

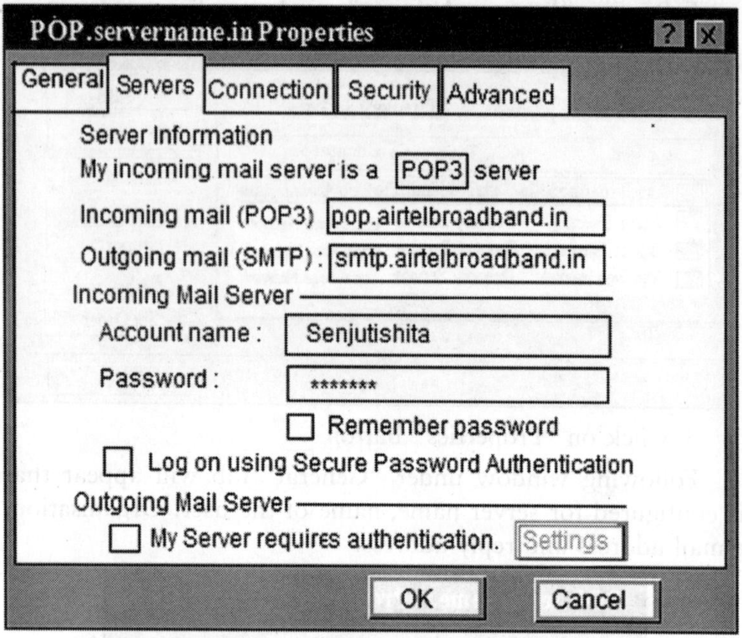

You may get different POP server name for your internet connection.

5. Check the incoming POP3 and outgoing mail SMTP provided by ISP.

6. Type the correct POP3 and SMTP server names. If there is any error.

7. Type the Account name and password again.

8. Click OK and try to connect Outlook Express.

Problem 4: You get time-out message when you connect Outlook Express with internet.

Solution 4: Take the following steps:

1. Open Outlook Express.
2. Click on Tool on main menu.
3. Click on Account in drop down menu.

Internet Account window opens:

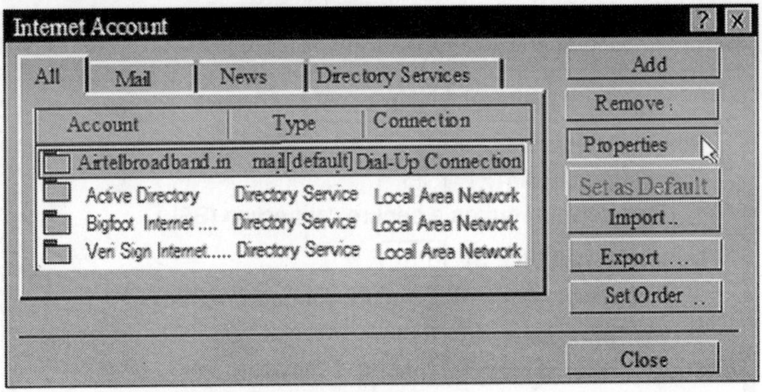

4. Click on Properties in Internet Account window.

POP.servername.in Properties window opens:

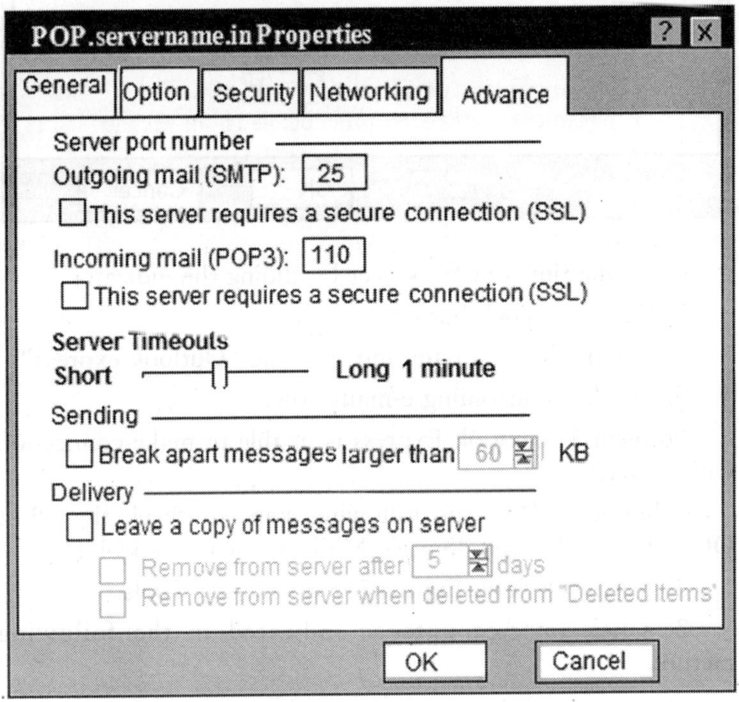

5. Click on Advanced tab.

Following change will occur POP.servername.in Properties windows:

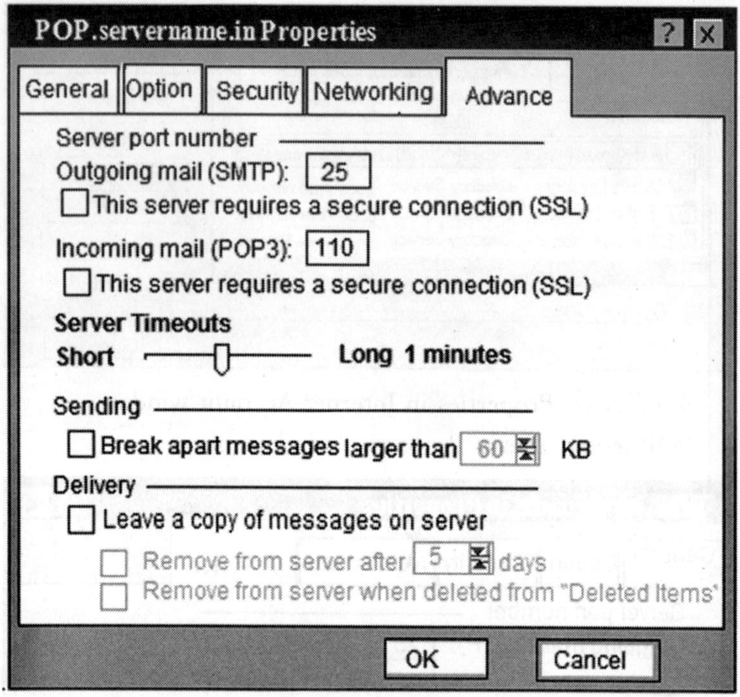

6. Set the time-out for server by sliding the indicator.
7. Click on "OK" button.
8. Restart the computer and start the "Outlook express".
9. Check the incoming e-mails now.

Problem 5: Outlook Express is unable to make connection with server.

Solution 5: Take the following steps to check the "Post Office Protocol 3 and "Simple Mail Transfer Protocol":

1. Open "Outlook Express" and Click on Tools.
2. Click on Accounts as indicated in the following picture:

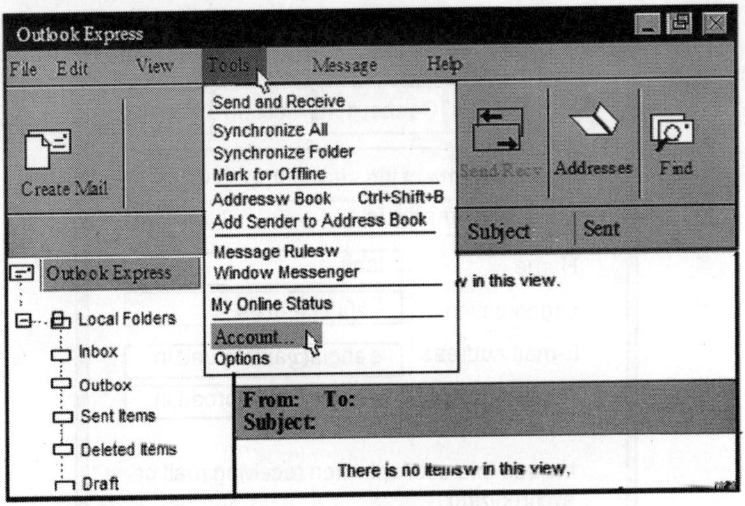

The following window appears.

3. Select your mail "Account" from the list.

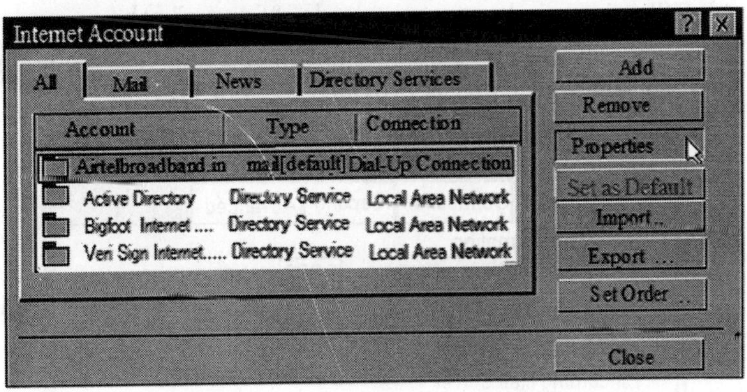

4. Click on "Properties" button.

Following window appears under "General" tab:

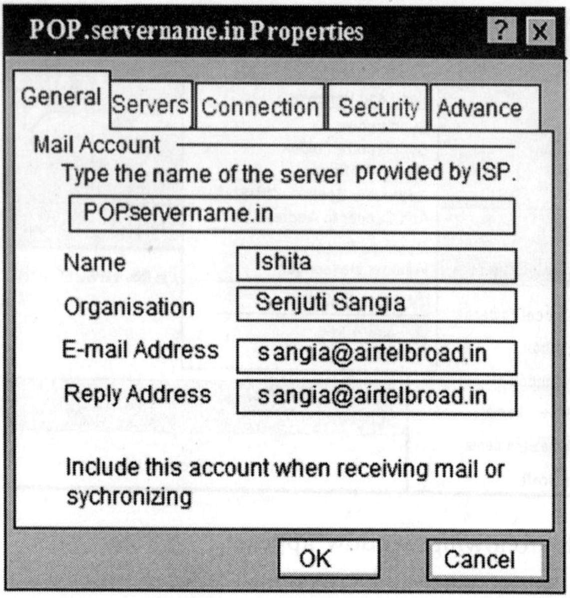

Following window appears under "Servers" tab:

5. Check the spelling of incoming mail (POP3) and outgoing mail (SMTP) server that is provided by your ISP.

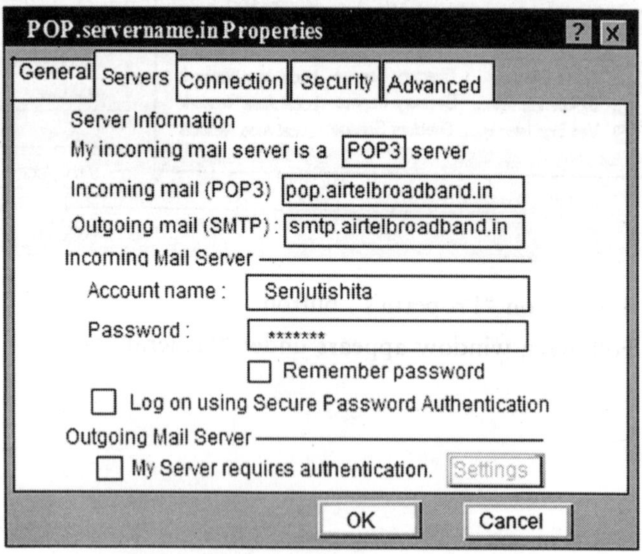

Check specially the dot(.) provided in between text. Still problem exists contact your ISP agent.

6. Check the account name and the password that is provided you by ISP.

7. There is a check box with text as "Log-on using secured password authentication", if you want to use.

"Log-on using secured password authentication" then click on the check box. If you do not want to log-on the server, clear the check box by clicking on it.

8. Next click on the "Advance" tab in "POP.servername.in Properties" window.

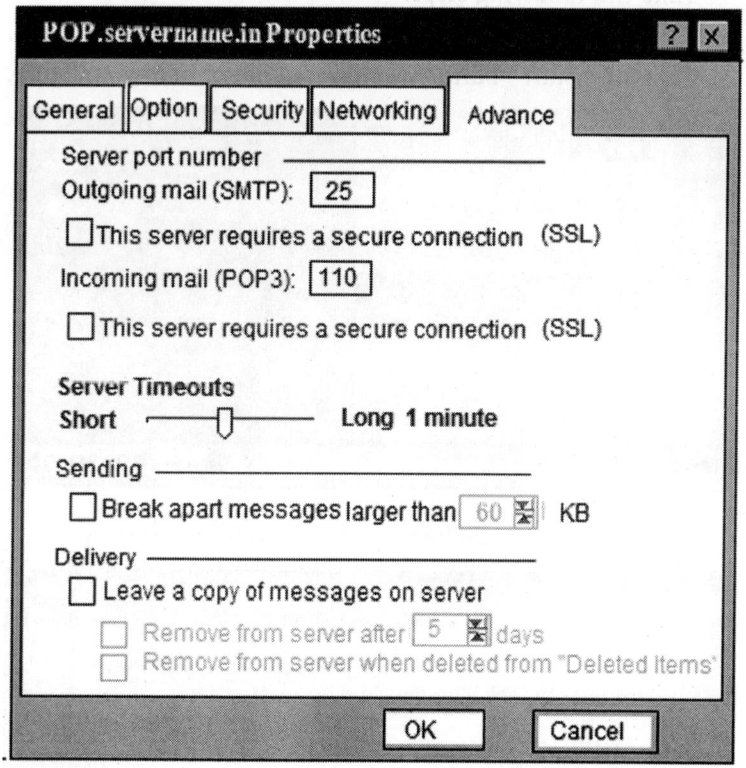

Check the Server Port Number provided by ISP.

Incoming mail (POP3) port number is indicated as-110

Outgoing (SMTP) port number is indicated as-25

It may be different for your connection. You can confirm them from your ISP agent.

9. Finally click on OK button.

10. Start Outlook Express and check the performance.

Problem 6: You are not able to access "Address Book".

Solution 6: In this case your "Address Book" file wab32.dll may be corrupted or missing.

You have to reinstall this file from Window's CD.

Take the following steps:

1. Start your computer and insert "Windows CD" in CD-ROM.

Click on "Start" button as indicated in the following figure.

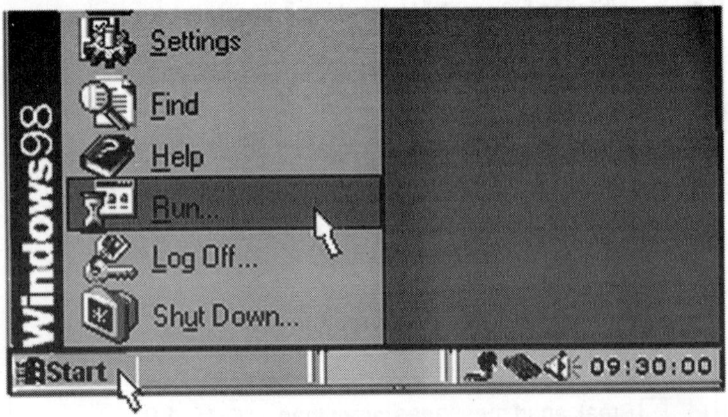

Click on "Run". Following "Run" window appears.

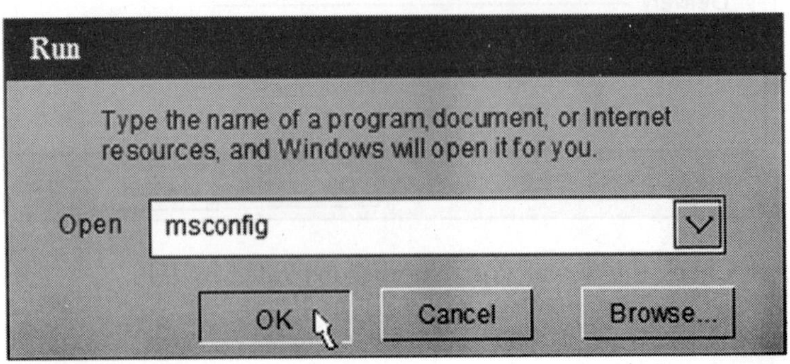

Type "msconfig" inside the "open" textbox.

Click on "OK" button on "Run" window.

Following "System Configuration Utility" windows appears.

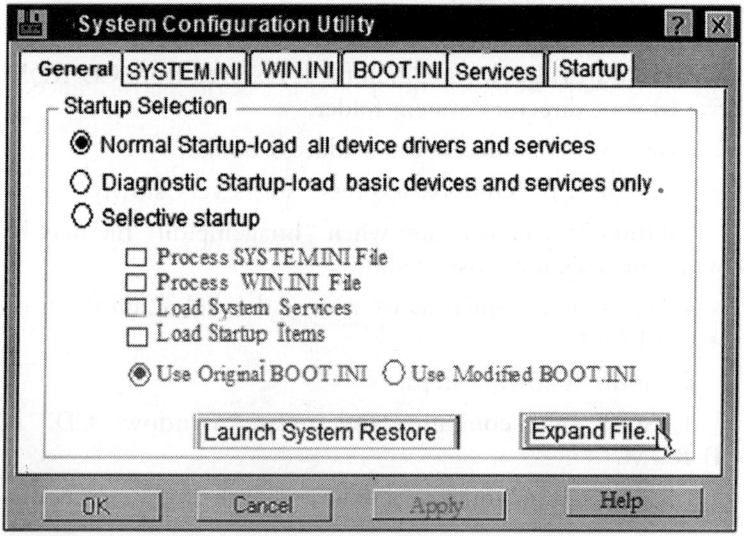

Click on "Expand File". Following "Expand One File from Installation Source" window will appear.

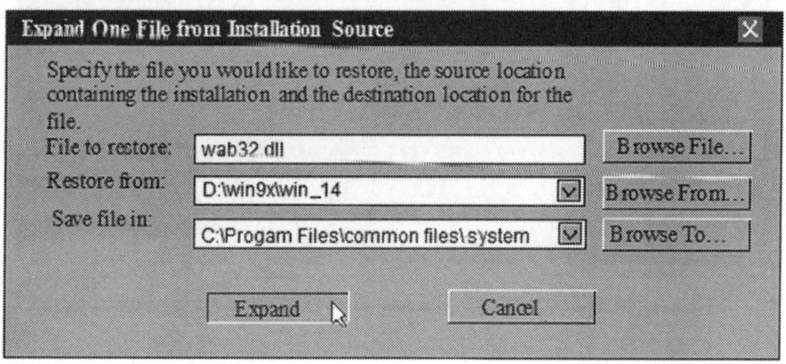

Do the following:

1. Type "wab32.dll" in File to restore textbox.
2. Enter the text "D:\win9x\win_14" in the "Restore from" textbox. Here "D" is the CD-ROM drive.

3. Enter the path "C:\Program Files\common files\system" in "Save file in" textbox.
4. Here C is the root drive where you want to save the file in system folder.
5. Click on "Expand" button.

The Address Book wab32.dll file is restored from CD-ROM drive to root directory system folder.

Now you try to access the "Address Book".

Problem 7: If "Outlook Express" starts very slowly.

Solution 7: This is a case when "Imagehlp.dll" file may be corrupt or does not exist at all.

The process is similar as we restore the wab32.dll file from the CD-ROM.

Take the following steps:

1. Start your computer and insert "Windows CD" in CD-ROM.

Click on "Start" button as indicated in the following figure.

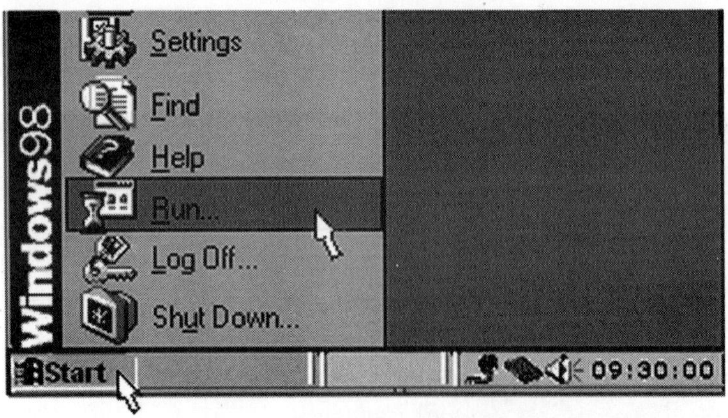

Click on "Run". Following "Run" window appears.

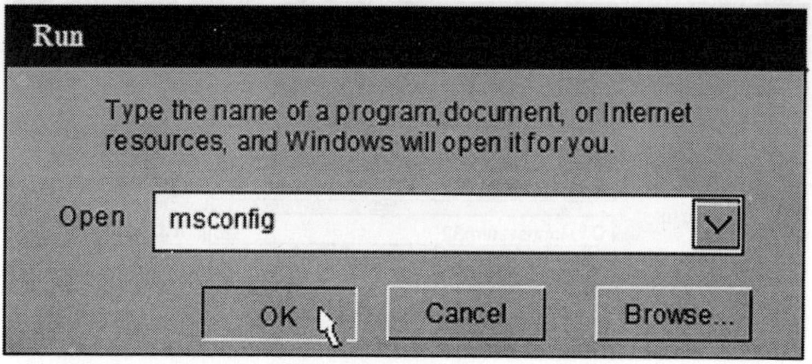

Type "msconfig" inside the "open" textbox.

Click on "OK" button on "Run" window.

Following "System Configuration Utility" windows appears.

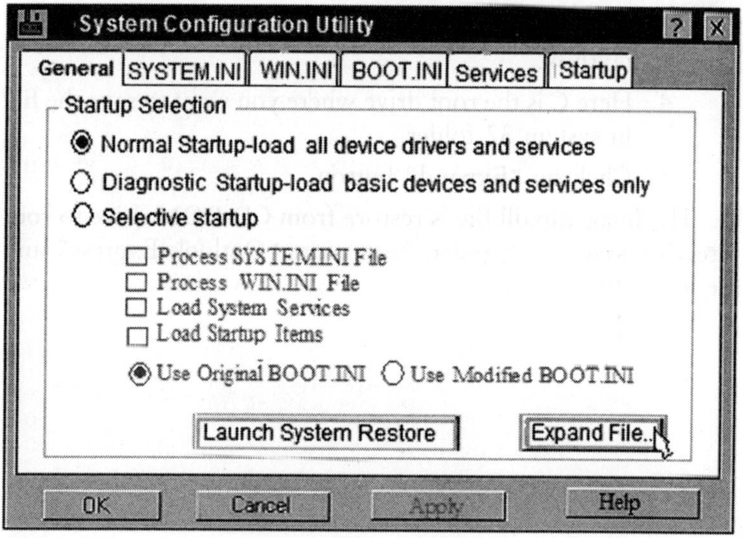

Click on "Expand File". Following "Expand One File from Installation Source" window will appear.

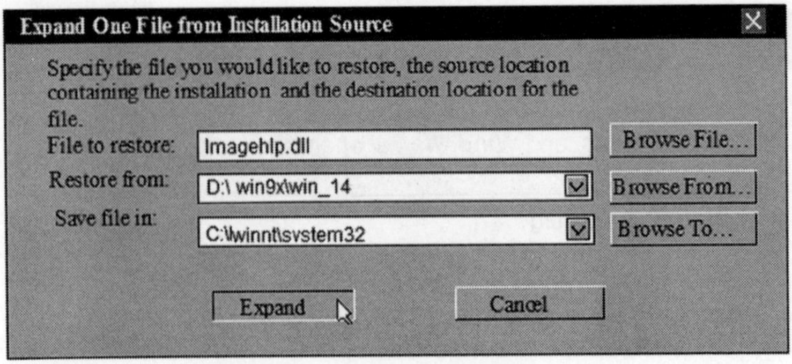

Do the following:

1. Type "Imagehlp.dll" in File to restore textbox.
2. Enter the text "D:\win9x\win_14" in the "Restore from" textbox. Here "D" is the CD-ROM drive.
3. Enter the path "C:\winnt\system32" in "Save file in" textbox.
4. Here C is the root drive where you want to save the file in system 32 folder.
5. Click on "Expand" button.

The Imagehlp.dll file is restore from CD-ROM drive to root directory system 32 folder. Now start "Outlook Express" and see its performance.

Virus and Antivirus

17

About Virus

Virus is a program generally written in high level language. It reproduces its own codes and attaches itself with the executing files. Sometimes it sends the original file to another place on the hard disk and take over its position. Thus, it can replace the complete program. Virus does not require any permission and without the knowledge of the user it acts.

All viruses are used to steal system resources and create bugs to damage the system. Some viruses have the characteristics to hide themselves. Many viruses delete files or change random data on the hard disk, or merely slowing down the PC. Some viruses are less harmful. They play music, create messages or animation on the screen. Some viruses activate on some defined trigger and take time to establish.

Viruses have many different forms, but they execute themselves in two phases. The two phases are infection phase and the attack phase.

1. Infection Phase

When the virus executes it infects a program, but you are not sure when it will infect the other programs. It is very difficult to know when the virus will trigger its infection phase. Many viruses enter into the PC memory and stay there as terminate and stay resident (TSR). These resident viruses consequently take over a portions of the system software on the PC memory. They hide their existence. This technique of hiding is called stealth.

2. Attack Phase

Viruses do not reveal their presence. They launch their attack only when they have ample opportunity to spread. Their attack could be delayed for days, weeks, months, or even years after the initial infection.

Some virus infects other programs each time it is executed; other virus may infect only upon a certain trigger.

This trigger may be anything. It may be a day or time, an external event on your PC, or a counter within the virus, etc. Viruses need time to infect the program.

Some normal consideration about viruses.

Sl. No.	About virus	Description
1.	Virus behavior	The common behavior of all viruses are first infect the files and then attack the program.
2.	Number of viruses	There are lots of known and unknown viruses existing in computer world. There are more than 100000 known viruses.
3.	Name of virus	Virus names are not standardized.
4.	Seriousness about viruses	Our inattention is the serious threat to our computer system.
5.	Is there good viruses also?	Till now there is none.
6.	Why viruses are created?	There are many reasons. One of them is to get money.
7.	Hardware and software threat	Viruses are not only threat to our computer, but there is a threat from Hardware and software also.

Type of Viruses

Following are the types of viruses that choose the particular area of the system to infect and attack:

1. System sector virus
2. File virus
3. Macro viruses
4. Companion files virus
5. Cluster viruses or Directories viruses
6. Batch files virus
7. Source code virus
8. Visual basic worms
9. Spacefiller virus
10. Screen savers virus.

1. System sector virus. There are two types of system sectors on the hard disk. They are DOS Boot Sector and partition Sector (Master Boot Record).

This virus attacks and modifies the program file in either DOS Boot Sector or in the Master Boot Record.

The DOS boot sector is executed every time whenever we start our PC. It is always easy for virus to attack and infect the boot sector. This can make our disk unreadable. If the boot sector is infected, you have to format the hard disk and all the data on the disk will be lost. It is always better to keep the back up of all the important files.

A non-bootable floppy may also contain a virus in the boot sector. If this infected floppy is left inside the floppy drive and when the PC is restarted it will infect the hard disk, even though the PC won't successfully boot from this floppy.

Many system sector viruses spread themselves by infecting files. Viruses of this type are called multipartite viruses. Since they can infect both files and system sectors they have more opportunities to spread.

Some of the known viruses that infect the boot sector are Alameda, Asher, Brain, Clone, Dark Avenger, DBase, Devil

Dance, Den Zuk.Disk Killer, EDV, Joker, Joshi, Korea, Lehigh, Microbe Typo/Fumble, Yale/Alameda, Yankee Doodle, etc.

2. File virus. There are executing files that run and control the program. These executing files use the COM, EXE, overlay or dll.files. This virus attacks the COM, EXE and overlay files and infects them.

The file viruses first locate a type of file. Usually a file name ending in COM or EXE are located by them.

These viruses infect these file by overwriting the part of the program. When this program is executed, the virus code is also executed and more files are infected. These overwriting viruses cannot hide themselves for a long time and almost immediately discovered.

The other sophisticated file viruses do not overwrite but insert their code in the program file and save with the program. This allows the viruses to execute the original program and everything appears normal. Like system sector viruses they can remain resident in memory and use stealth techniques to hide their presence.

If you see the directory listing, you will not find any change in the length of the file and if you try to read the file, the virus will attend your request and return your uninfected program to you.

Some file viruses infect overlay files. Overlay files have various extensions but OVR and OVL are common, Files with the extension. DLL are also venerable to virus attack.

Some of the known viruses Amoeba, Anthrax, Eight, Piere, Jacques, Fish, Ten Bytes Sunday and Saturday 14th infect the com and exe files.

3. Macro viruses. Macro viruses cause more infections than the file virus. They have probably overtaken file viruses in numbers by now. The data files are not the executable files so they cannot be infected by virus.

Virus can only infect a file or a program when they are executed. For opening, manipulating, and closing the data files, macro language is attached. These macro viruses attach themselves with the executable micro programs and run automatically, whenever the data file is loaded.

These data files that contain macro portion are attacked and infected by the micro virus.

There are several triggers that viral code can use to infect these macros.

Generally Antivirus scanners have default settings that scan the most common executable files and data files from programs that contain macro language. So, it is always better to use those programs with their default extension so Antivirus scanners can find the files they need to scan.

4. Companion files virus. This virus adds file to the disk and infects the other program files.

It infects the file without adding a single byte.

Companion virus first locates all the EXE files on the disk. Then this virus creates a matching file name with COM extension. This matching file with COM extension contains the viral code.

Generally this infected COM file which resides in the same directory with the matching EXE file.

Suppose the virus locate a PCM.EXE file, then it creates a PCM.COM file in the same directory, where PCM.EXE resides. Now when you try to open PCM.EXE file on the DOS path, the PCM.COM file will open in place of PCM.EXE. This infected PCM.COM file infects more files and then loads and executes PCM.EXE. The user may not notice anything abnormal.

This type of virus can easily be detected by the presence of additional COM files.

A good integrity map of directory can be used to easily detect and clean companion viruses.

5. Cluster viruses or Directories viruses. The cluster virus changes the directory in such manner so that the virus is run first, before the actual program.

Cluster viruses do not infects the files by changing the size of the file or planting additional files but they change the DOS directory. When you execute a program, DOS first loads and executes the virus code and after that the actual program is executed. Dir-2 is an example of this type of virus.

This type of virus are known as fast infector. When you open any file, the complete current directory will be infected and if you make a search for a file on the DOS path, all directories on the path will be infected.

6. Batch file viruses. In most cases the batch file is used to drop disk virus. The batch file with virus codes takes over when the computer is next started. Some batch file virus when executed, they change Window's registry.

There are several batch file viruses. Each uses the binary codes to infect the batch files.

The labels and batch file instructions may differ; but the method of operation is similar.

7. Source code viruses. Trojan is the virus that adds code to the source code of the program and infects the system. There are several types of compilers and languages used, therefore source code are used in many forms. Due to this source code viruses are not generally common. Because of different programing style and designs, it is difficult for an individuals to write a virus that actually spreads via source code.

Generally a source code viruses will not infect through the source code but they simply add Trojan codes to existing source code so that when it is compiled and run it does something different than expected.

Die hard is a file virus that actually spreads by infecting COM and EXE files but it accompanies the Trojan code virus that infects the ASM (assembly language).

8. Visual basic worms. A worm is a self-reproducing program that does not infect other programs, but it creates copies of itself, and these created copies create even more copies. Worms are usually seen on networks and on multi-processing operating systems, where the worm will create copies of itself that are also executed. Each new copy will create more copies quickly clogging the system.

VBS script is a language that is widely used as active server page or it can be as stand alone file with the VBS extension. Internet explorer is a Microsoft's browser that is generally used by system to access the VBS scripts files.

VBS script is quite capable and can be used to connect to Microsoft's Outlook for receiving and sending e-mails.

It sends files to anyone in the address book. This exposed the VBS script to be attacked by worms, that spread themselves. This visual basic worms spread from one system to another by e-mails.

9. Spacefiller virus. Most viruses attach themselves to the end of the file to infect them.

There are some program files that leave space in between program codes. A spacefiller virus attempts to install itself in this empty space without damaging the actual file.

The Lehigh virus is an example of a spacefiller virus.

10. Screen saver virus. Screen saver is a script and an executable code. It may either contain a virus or be used to house a worm or Trojan. When you start your computer and do not do any thing for few minutes, then as per the time setting the screen saver starts. If the screen saver files are infected, then before starting the screen saver the virus codes are executed and then the screen saver starts.

Following are the symptoms of infected system:

1. Computer hangs frequently.
2. Computer works very slowly.
3. Computer does not boot.
4. Internet connection does not work.
5. Change in file numbers in file system.
6. Change in the directory.
7. Malfunctioning of keyboard and mouse.
8. Changing of the capacity of RAM automatically.
9. Changing of number of bytes in an executing file automatically.

10. Change in the number of system files.
11. Difficulty in opening a program.
12. Getting unwanted error message frequently.

Antivirus

Many Antivirus programs are developed to encounter the virus threat.

Antivirus programs allow you to check programs before execution. You should know the symptoms of viruses that indicates their presence in your system. You should be able to recognize the type of virus so that you can choose the appropriate Antivirus.

Antivirus program need to be regularly updated. Don't use the old scanner.

Do not try to run two Antivirus programs simultaneously otherwise you may find "ghost" positives.

Some viruses try to change their code on the fly. Current scanners are able to analyze code and detect the virus.

It is important to detect and identify specific virus that attacks to your computer. There are three methods in general use. Each has some advantages and disadvantage. Generally an antivirus software program uses a combination of the following techniques for detection and removal of viruses:

1. Scanning
2. Integrity checking
3. Interception

1. Scanning. A virus contains telltale code that is also called signature strings or characteristic of the virus.

Once the programmer of the scanner extracts the characteristics (code) of the virus he uses these codes to search them in the memory, files, and system sectors. If the scanner encounter with this virus code, it declares that it has found a virus. This detection is only applicable on known viruses.

2. Integrity checking. When you run an integrity checking program on your system, it collects the information about your system.

The information is used for later comparison in order to detect changes. But detecting changes is not the solution. Integrity checking software read entire disk and record integrity of data for the files and system sectors. An integrity check program that comes with built-in intelligence is the best solution that can handle all the threats to your data as well as viruses.

3. Interception. Interception program is the method of virus detection. Interceptors are also called resident monitors. They are specially useful for deflecting logic bombs and Trojans. This program works in the background and signifies the presence of a virus.

The virus has a tendency to install itself behind the interception programs. Interception antivirus programs detect such viruses and reinstall themselves under the viruses. This action causes problems on your system.

You cannot fully rely upon interceptor because they can easily be bypassed.

There are some antivirus software described below that you can download from the internet.

Some antivirus program you can download free and some are paid programs.

1. McAfee Free Scan

It scan the latest viruses and displays the list of the infected files. You can delete the infected file from your system and make your system virus free.

2. AVG Antivirus

This antivirus program is available on internet and you can download it free as a trial version. This antivirus provides security to your computer. It finds out the virus and kill it.

3. Panda Active Scan

This antivirus is used for scanning the hard disk and fix the error.

4. PC-cillin

It protect your computer from hackers, viruses and spams. You can download it from internet.

5. Norton

It protect the computer from internet-borne viruses, Spyware and other threats.

6. House Call

You can download this antivirus program free from internet. You can scan and remove the virus.

It provides security to your PC.

7. The Cleaner

This software is registered under antivirus category. It blocks the Trojan and worms.

8. Symantec W32.Blaster

Worm Removal Tool. This antivirus program is useful to remove W32.Blaster.Worm.

9. Ad-Aware Anniversary Edition Pro

This antivirus program removes malicious software and protect your privacy.

Safe Computing Practices

There are some simple things you can do, to help to protect your PC from viruses and worms:

1. Do not share, copy or download a file from virus infected PC.
2. Scan the floppy or pen-drive through antivirus program before using it on your PC.
3. Bootable files, System files and program files are stored inside the C drive. Virus generally infects the C drive therefore do not keep your important data file in C drive, which is also called root directory. Store the important data in D or E directory.

   Suppose your C drive is infected by virus, then you can format the C drive and reload the system and bootable file and required program on it. Your data on the D or E drive remains intact.

4. It is always better to keep the back up of all important data files, because if your bootable sector is infected, you will not be able to start the computer.
5. **Update antivirus software:** You must keep your antivirus software up-to-date. Update it at least weekly; more often if there are news reports of a new fast-spreading virus or worm.
6. **Safe boot disk:** Most antivirus software has an option for creating a safe boot disk, which can be used to clean-boot the computer and, perhaps, also scan for viruses. This safe boot disk should be recreated and can be used for virus scanning. It's important that it contains the latest virus database.
7. **Hard disk boot:** Generally we leave a floppy disk in the drive and if that disk is infected with a boot sector virus then the next time you start the computer the hard disk will become infected. Change your boot sequence so that the hard disk is the first boot disk instead of the floppy disk. If the floppy is not accessed then, the infection won't take place.

Changing the Boot Sequence

1. Start the computer and keep the delete button pressed.

The following CMOS UTILITY window will appear.

CMOS SETUP UTILITY
COMPANY_NAME

STANDARD CMOS SETUP BIOS FEATURE SETUP CHIPSET FEATURE SETUP POWER MANAGEMENT SETUP PNP/PCICOGIGURATION LOAD BIOS DEFAULTS LOAD SETUP DEFAULTS	INTEGRATED PERIPHERALS PASSWORD SETTING IDE HDD AUTO DETECTION SAVE & EXIT SETUP EXIT WITHOUT SAVING
Esc : QUIT F10 Save & Exit Setup	↑ ↓ ← → : Select items by arrow key (Shift) F2 : Change Color

2. By arrow key select the STANDARD CMOS SETUP and press enter.

The following BIOS FEATURE SETUP window will appear:

BIOS FEATURE SETUP

Virus Warning	Disabled
CPU Internal Catch	Enabled
External Catch	Enabled
CPU L2 Catch ECC Checking	Enabled
Quick Power On Self Test	Enabled
Boot Sequence	A,C.SCSI
Swap Floppy Drive	Disabled
Boot Up Floopy Seek	Enabled
Boot Up Numlock Status	On
Gate A20 Option	Fast
Memory Parity/BCC Check	Enabled
Typematic Rate Setting	Disabled
Typematic Rate (Chars/Sec)	6
Typematic Rate Delay (Msec)	250
Security Option	Setup
IDE Second Channel Control	Enabled
PCI/VGA Pallet Snoop	Disabled
OS Select For DRAM>64MB	Non-OS2
HDD S.M.A.R.T. Capability	Disabled
Report No FDD For WIN 95	Yes

Video Bios Shadow	Enabled
C8000-CBFFF Shadow	Disabled
CC000-CFFFF Shadow	Disabled
D0000-D3FFF Shadow	Disabled
D8000-D8FFF Shadow	Disabled
DC000-DFFFF Shadow	Disabled

Esc : Quit ↑↓ →← : Select items
F1 : Help Pu/Pd/+/- : Modify
F5 : Old Values (Shift) F2 : Color
F6 : Load BIOS Defaults
F7 : Load Setup Defaults

3. Select the Boot Sequence from the list by an arrow key.

4. Use <Pg Dn> or <Pg Up> keys to change the boot sequence.

Boot Sequence: There are following options:

C, A, SCSI

C, CDROM, A

CDROM, C, A

D, A, SCSI

E, A, SCSI

F, A, SCSI

A, C, SCSI

C, A

C only

LS/ZIP, C.

5. Change the boot sequence from A, C, SCSI To C, CD-ROM, A.

6. Press F10 key following popup edit window will appear.

SAVE to CMOS and EXIT (Y/N) ? Y

Type Y and press enter.

7. The booting sequence of the computer is set to C, CD-ROM, A now.

When you start the computer, it is booted by C drive first. If drive C does not contain bootable files, the computer will search the CD-ROM and if the bootable files are not found in CD-ROM also, then BIOS will search the floppy and if it is a bootable floppy, the computer will start booting.

You can avoid the booting through infected CD-ROM or floppy by changing the boot sequence.

8. Use **RTF not DOC:** Don't accept any Word. DOC or Excel XLS files from anyone.

There are macro viruses that intercept the request to save to RTF and save the file in DOC format with an RTF extension. Word will unfortunately ignore the RTF extension and open the file as a DOC file.

It is also possible to embed objects into RTF files.

9. **Consider alternate software:** Switch to the software that is not affected by viruses/worms. For many offices a switch away from Word, Excel, and Outlook/Outlook Express would be difficult as these programs came as standard software on many systems. But, it's worth consideration.

10. **Don't open attachments:** Do open any unsolicited attachments to E-mail. This may seem a bit extreme but in today's world where worms send themselves out via personal address books you can't really trust anything coming from anyone; even if you know them.

11. **Turn off preview:** Turn off the preview function. Most of the preview formatted messages use internet explorer components that are less secure.

12. **Disable scripting:** Turn off the windows scripting host if you don't need it. Scripts are macros that are venerable to worms.

13. **Show extensions:** Set all programs to show you the full file name, particularly e-mail programs.

If your program drops the extension you don't really know if the attachment is executable or not.

14. **Protect floppies:** Write-protect any floppy disk you place into another person's computer. If their computer is infected with a boot sector virus at least yours won't be.

When your computer is infected and not booting at all, then scan cannot be carried by any antivirus program because antivirus program can only be applied if your system opens the desk top. Now removal of the virus from your system is only possible by removing all the data stored on your system along with virus codes. Formatting of the C drive is the only remedy.

Suppose your boot system and C drive is infected by virus, then format the hard disk.

Follow the steps:

1. Insert the bootable floppy in floppy drive.

2. Start the computer.

3. After booting, you will see the following DOS command. prompt A:\>.

4. Type FORMAT C: in front of prompt A:\> as follows:

A:\> FORMAT C: Press<Enter>

You will see the following message:

WARNING, ALL DATA ON NON-REMOVABLE DISK

DRIVE C: WILL BE LOST!

5. Proceed with Format (Y/N)? Type Y. and press enter.

You will see the following message:

Checking existing disk format.

Verifying 454.93M

After verification of drive C formatting of drive C will start.

It will take few minutes as per the capacity and condition of hard disk.

Follow the same procedure to format drive D and E by writing command as follows:

A:\> FORMAT D:

A:\> FORMAT E:

This way all the drives C, D and E will be formatted.

Installation of Window 98, Window 2000 or Windows Xp on your computer through CD-ROM.

1. Now switch off the power of computer.

For installation of any program through CD-ROM it is better to change the Boot Sequence.

2. Restart the computer and press the delete button continuously till the following window appears:

CMOS SETUP UTILITY
NAME OF COMPANY

STANDARD CMOS SETUP	INTEGRATED PERIPHERALS
BIOS FEATURE SETUP	PASSWORD SETTING
CHIPSET FEATURE SETUP	IDE HDD AUTO DETECTION
POWER MANAGEMENT SETUP	SAVE & EXIT SETUP
PNP/PCI COGIGURATION	EXIT WITHOUT SAVING
LOAD BIOS DEFAULTS	
LOAD SETUP DEFAULTS	
Esc . QUIT ↑ ↓ ← →	: Select items by arrow key
F10 Save & Exit Setup (Shift) F2	: Change Color

3. By using arrow key select the BIOS FEATURE SETUP option from the above menu.

4. Press <Enter>. You see the following window on screen:

BIOS FEATURE SETUP

Virus Warning	Disabled
CPU Internal Catch	Enabled
External Catch	Enabled
CPU L2 Catch ECC Checking	Enabled
Quick Power On Self Test	Enabled
Boot Sequence	CDROM,C,A
Swap Floppy Drive	Disabled
Boot Up Floopy Seek	Enabled
Boot Up Numlock Status	On
Gate A20 Option	Fast
Memory Parity/BCC Check	Enabled
Typematic Rate Setting	Disabled
Typematic Rate (Chars/Sec)	6
Typematic Rate Delay (Msec)	250
Security Option	Setup
IDE Second Channel Control	Enabled
PCI/VGA Pallet Snoop	Disabled
OS Select For DRAM>64MB	Non-OS2
HDD S.M.A.R.T. Capability	Disabled
Report No FDD For WIN 95	Yes

Video Bios Shadow	: Enabled
C8000-CBFFF Shadow	: Disabled
CC000-CFFFF Shadow	: Disabled
D0000-D3FFF Shadow	: Disabled
D8000-D8FFF Shadow	: Disabled
DC000-DFFFF Shadow	: Disabled

Esc : Quit	↑↓→← : Select items
F1 : Help	Pu/Pd/+/- : Modify
F5 : Old Values	(Shift) F2 : Color
F6 : Load BIOS Defaults	
F7 : Load Setup Defaults	

5. In the above table of BIOS FEATURE SETUP window, go to item boot sequence by using arrow key.

When you reach boot sequence, change the boot sequence by using <PgUp> or <PgDn> keys.

Set boot sequence CD-ROM, C, A.

6. Press the function button F10. Following message appears on screen.

7. Save the BIOS FEATURE SETUP (Y/N) Y Type Y and press <Enter>.

You will come out of BIOS FEATURE SETUP.

8. Switch off the computer.

9. Now restart the computer.

10. INSERT CD of window 98 in CD-ROM drive.

Computer will boot through CD-ROM and prompt C:\> will appear on the screen.

11. Type the following command. Here F is the CD-ROM drive.

12. C:\> F: Press <Enter>. Following prompt will be displayed.

F:\>

13. Type SETUP.exe in front of prompt F:\> as follows:

F:\> SETUP.exe and Press <Enter>

Window setup wizard will appear on screen. Follow the instruction of the wizard.

Window setup will take about half an hour to one hour.

You must have a key of windowS which is required during setup.

Following are the keys:

Key for window98SE WQMR3-XWV6C-8627G-2H4MB-XWBXB

Key for Window 2000 GC6J3-GTQ62-FP876-94FBR-D3DX8

Key for Window Xp BRDDY-R8CGM-R7982-2T4V7-KHP8T

Alternative Method of formatting and loading Window 2000 or Window Xp.

If your computer is infected by virus, but it can boot and open the desk top.

1. Start the computer.

2. Change the boot sequence to CD-ROM, C, A as described above.

3. Insert the window 2000 or window Xp CD in CD-ROM drive.

4. Click the Run on your start menu as follows:

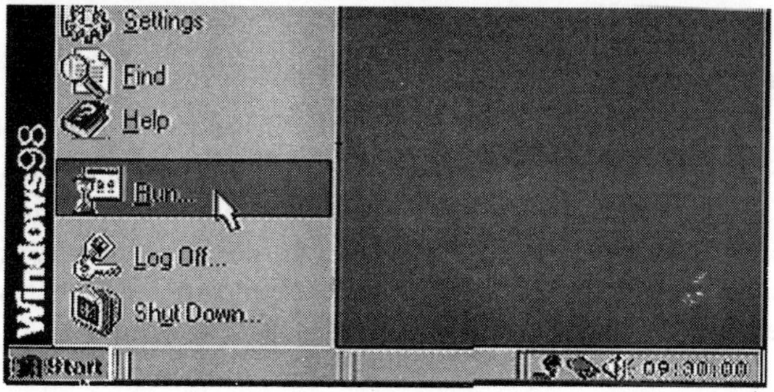

You will see the following window:

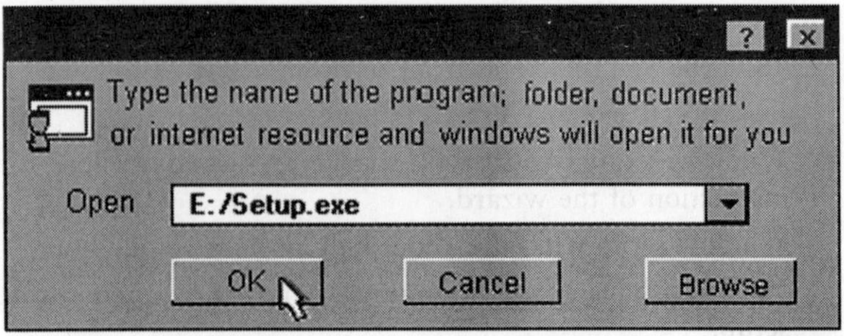

5. Type E://Setup.exe in front of open text strip.

Here E is the CD-ROM drive and Setup.exe is the executable command.

The Window's 2000 CD will execute that the Setup.exe command and welcome message will appear on the screen.

6. There are many steps you have to follow as per the instruction.

7. You will be asked to select the drive to be used for loading window 2000.

Select the C drive and click OK or press enter.

8. You will be asked for provide the key after checking the integrity of C drive.

Provide the Key for Window 2000 as GC6J3 - GTQ62 - FP876 - 94FBR - D3DX8 and press Next button.

9. Follow the instructions and within 45 minutes window 2000 will be loaded.

10. Restart the computer. Now it is free of viruses.

File Extensions

You will like to know that, what extensions file you should scan for, in E-mail attachments?

Extension of file generally shows the nature of content of a file. But there may be double extension file. For example, a file name ending in .DOC, but it can be a template file. When you open this DOC file, template (.DOT) file will open.

Though TXT is safe extension as it indicates a pure text file. But, with extensions turned off if someone sends you a file named BAD.TXT.VBS. You can see BAD.TXT extension and VBS part will not be visible. By considering the BAD.TXT as you open, a file with VBS extension will open. It is, therefore, requested to keep the extensions turned on.

There are some file extensions that are shown with their characteristics. It is to be scanned by a suitable scanner if you feel they are infected by virus.

Extension	Full Form	Characteristics
.386	Windows Enhanced Mode Driver	It is an executable code.
.ADP	Microsoft Access Project	It has macros and exposed to virus.
.ADT	Abstract Data Type	These database and files are executable and can be infected.
APP	Application File	Application files are program and used to interact with database and other program and exposed to virus.
.ASP	Active Server Page	ASP are VB script pages and are exposed to virus.
BAS	Microsoft Visual Basic Class Module	VB script pages are exposed to virus.
BAT	Batch File	There are few viruses that can infect batch file.
BIN	Binary File	Binary files are attached with many program and can be infected.
BTM	4DOS Batch To Memory Batch File	DOS based batch file that could be infected.
CBT	Computer Based Training	These files are used in training program exposed to virus during the application.
CHM	Compiled HTML Help File	Scripting expose them, to be infected.

(Contd...)

Extension	Full Form	Characteristics
CLASS	Java Class File	This file generally not exposed to virus.
CMD	Windows NT Command Script	A batch file exposed to viruses.
COM	Command (Executable File)	They are executable files and can be infected by many ways.
CPL	Control Panel Extension	They are executable files and should be scanned.
CRT	Security Certificate	They have codes and so they are also exposed to viruses.
CSC	Corel Script File	They are script files and should be scanned.
CSS	Hypertext Cascading Sheet	Style sheets can contain code and exposed to viruses.
DLL	Dynamic Link Library	Can be used for a variety of tasks associated with a program.
DOC	MS Word Document	Word documents can contain macros that are powerful enough to be used for viruses and worms.
DOT	MS Word Document Template	Word templates can contain macros so they are exposed to viruses and worms.
DRV	Device Driver	A device driver is executable code file so they can be infected.
E-mail	MS Outlook Express	E-mail messages can contain HTML and scripts. Many viruses and worms use this vector.
EXE	Executable File	Any executable file can be infected in a variety of ways.
FON	Font	Font file are executable file, therefore can be infected.

(*Contd...*)

Extension	Full Form	Characteristics
HLP	Help File	Help files can contain macros, so they are venerable to virus.
HTML	Hypertext Mark-up Language	Contains scripts so.
INF	Setup Information	Setup scripts can be changed to do unexpected things.
INI	Initialization File	Contains program options.
INS	Internet Naming Service	Can be changed to point unexpected places.
ISP	Internet Communication Settings	Can be changed to point unexpected things.
JS	JavaScript	They are rarely infected.
LIB	Library	They are also rarely infected.
LNK	Link	Can be changed to point to unexpected places.
MDB	MS Access Database	Access files can contain macros that are powerful enough to be used for viruses and worms.
MDE	Microsoft Access MDE database	Macros and scripts make venerable to virus.
MHTML	Hypertext Mark-up Language Page	Web page file always venerable to virus.
MP3	Media Player 3	Music files cannot be infected.
MSO	Math Script Object	According to Symantec these are database-related program files.
MSC	Microsoft Common Console	Can be changed to point to unexpected places for virus attack.
MSI	Microsoft Windows Installer	Contains codes and may contain virus.
MSP	Microsoft Windows Installer Patch	Contains codes and may contain virus.
MST	Microsoft Visual Test Source Files	Source can be changed.

(*Contd...*)

Extension	Full Form	Characteristics
OBJ	Relocatable Object Code	Files associated with programs.
OCX	Object Control Extension	A program that can be downloaded from a web page may be infected.
OV	Overlay File	Can be used for a variety of tasks associated with a program.
PCD	Photo CD	MS Compiled script. Scripts are venerable to virus.
PGM	Program File	Associated with a variety of programs; these files interact with such things as database programs to make them look like stand alone programs.
PIF	MS-DOS Short cut	If changed can run unexpected programs.
PPT	MS PowerPoint Presentation	PowerPoint presentations can contain macros that are powerful enough to be used for viruses and worms.
PRC	Palmpilot Resource File	A PDA program (yes, there are rare PDA viruses).
REG	Registry Entries	If run these change the registry.
RTF	Rich Text Format	A format for transmitting formatted text usually assumed to be safe. Binary (and infected) objects can be embedded within RTF files, however, so, to be safe, they should be scanned. RTF files can also be DOC files renamed and Word will open them as DOC files.

(Contd...)

Extension	Full Form	Characteristics
SCR	Screen Saver	Screen savers and scripts files may contain a virus.
SCT	Windows Script Component	Scripts can be infected.
SHS	Ami Pro Macro Shell	Do not open them if they are sent as attachment.
SMM	Scrap Object File	Rare, but can be infected.
ASM, .C, .CPP, .PAS, .BAS, .FOR	Source Code	These are program files that could be infected by a source code.
SYS	System Device Driver	An executable code file should be scanned.
URL	Uniform Resource Locator	Infected file can spread virus.
VBS	Visual Basic Script	A script file may contain a virus.
VXD	Virtual Device Driver	An executable code file should be scanned.
WSC	Windows Script Component	Scripts file exposed to infection.
WSF	Windows Script File	Scripts file exposed to infection.
WSH	Windows Script Host Settings File	Settings can be changed to do unexpected things.

Firewalls

18

Firewall is used in between Internet and the network. Function of firewalls is to protect the network from the hackers and miscreants. They cannot access your network if firewall is properly provided in between internet and your network. Outsiders are kept away from gaining secret information to damage the computer systems. Firewalls are also used to limit the access of individuals on the internal network.

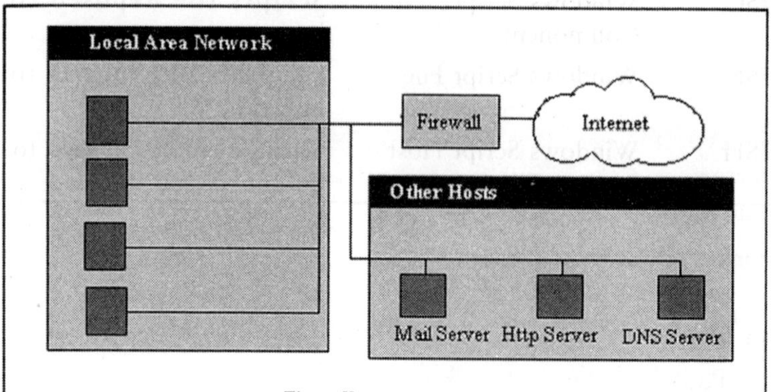

Firewall

Firewall in between Internet and the network + Other Host.

Types of Firewalls:

1. Packet Filtering.
2. Application Proxy Gateway.

1. Packet filtering: Blocks are used to select data packets of the network.

An example of this kind of firewall is Circuit Level Relay—SOCKS. It does not aware of applications but just cross links your connection to another outside connection. It can log activity partially. It is suitable for TCP connections. It does not provide user authentication.

2. Application proxy gateway: The users access the outside internet, using the proxy. The proxy receives the message and returns back to the user. It can record every activity that is carried out by source and destination. User has to log-in for accessing the internet. Rules are set for the functions of an application. Some functions of the application may be accepted while some may be rejected. For example, "get" function may be accepted in the FTP application, but the "put" function may be rejected.

Proxy Servers perform the following functions:

1. Control outbound connections and data.
2. Monitor outbound connections and data.
3. Provide user authentication.
4. Allow and deny application specific functions.
5. Apply stronger authentication mechanisms to some applications.

Application of cache can enhance system bandwidth performance and decrease the time it takes for other users to read the same data.

Packet Filtering Firewall

Packet filtering firewall filtered the data according to some set of rules. It works at the network level.

Packet contains their type, source and destination address and port information.

Firewall filters these packets by type, source address, destination address, and port information.

Packet filter firewall works quite fast but does not allow access to an individual user because it is not programmed to identify the user.

User need not to configure any software to use a packet filtering firewall.

User need not to set a web browser to use a proxy for access to the web.

The firewall is transparent to the client because user is unaware of it.

Circuit Level Relay Firewall

Circuit level relay firewall listens at port 80 for http requests and redirects the request to a proxy server. Redirect function uses ipchains which filters the package at the port, circuit level relay firewall is also transparent to the client.

Configuring a Proxy Server

The following packages are available in Linux:

SOCKS—Circuit Switching firewall. Normally doesn't come with Linux, but is free.

Squid—A circuit switching proxy. Normally comes with Linux.

Juniper Firewall Toolkit—A firewall toolkit product used to build a firewall. It uses transparent filtering, and circuit switching. It is available as open source.

The TIS Firewall Toolkit (FWTK)—A toolkit that comes with application level proxies.

The applications include Telnet, Rlogin, SMTP mail, FTP, http, and windows.

It can also be applied as a transparent proxy for other services.

Data packet management are administered and controlled by the kernel. Kernel supports IP masquerading, packet forwarding, and port redirects. The support is compiled into kernel. The A series of tables information is stored in kernel. The table is called chain. Each chain contains a sequence of rules. Each rule possess two items:

1. Characteristics
2. Instructions

1. Characteristics: Source and destination address, protocols like UDP, TCP, ICMP, and port numbers are called characteristics.

2. Instructions: Instructions are carried out if the rule characteristics match the data packet. Each data packet is filtered by kernel for a particular chain. For example, when a data packet is received, the "input" chain rules are implemented to determine that the data packets are acceptable or not.

First of all rule 1 is applied to check the characteristics of data packet. In case the characteristics of data packet match with the rule 1, instruction is carried out. If they don't match, the rule 2 is applied to check the characteristics of data packet. In this way the data packets are passed through all the rules to match the characteristics. If the characteristics are not matched with any rule data packets are not accepted.

There are three chains as follows:

Input—Regulates acceptance of incoming data packets.

Forward—Defines permissions to forward packets that have another host as a destination.

Output—Permissions for sending packets.

Each rule has a branch name or policy. There are following policies:

Policy	Description
ACCEPT	Accept the data packet.
REJECT	Drop and the packet but send a ICMP message indicating the packet was refused.
DENY	Drop and ignore the packet.
REDIRECT	Redirect to a local socket with input rules only even if the packet is for a remote host.
MASQ	This applies to TCP or UDP packets. Sets up IP masquerading. Works on TCP or UDP packets.
RETURN	The next rule in the previous calling chain is examined.

You can create more chains, then add rules to them. The commands used to modify chains are as follows:

Command	Description
-N	Create a new chain.
-X	Delete an empty chain.
-L	List the rules in the chain.
-P	Change the policy for a chain.
-F	Flush=Delete all the rules in a chain.
-Z	Zero the packet and byte counters in all chains.

Commands to manipulate rules inside the chain are:

-A	Append a new rule to a chain.
-I	Insert a new rule at some position in a chain.
-R	Replace a rule at some position in a chain.
-D	Delete a rule at some position in a chain.

Options for masquerading:

-M with -L to list the currently masqueraded connection.

-M with -S to set the masquerading timeout values.

IPchains Options for setting rule specifications:

-s Source.

-d Destination.

-p Protocol=tcp, upd, icmp, all or a name from /etc./protocols.

-j Jump target, specifies the target of the rule. The target can be a user defined chain, but not the one this rule is in.

-i Interface=Name of the interface the packet is received on or the interface where the packet will be sent.

-t Mask used to modify the type of service (TOS) field in the IP header. This option is followed by two values, the first one is and 'ed with the TOS field, and the second is exclusive or 'ed. The masks are eight bit hexadecimal values.

-f Fragment.

When making changes to firewall rules, it is a good idea to deny all packages prior to making changes with the following three commands:

ipchains -I input 1 -j DENY

ipchains -I output 1 -j DENY

ipchains -I forward 1 -j DENY

These commands inserts a rule at location 1 that denies all packages for input, output, or forwarding. This is done so no unauthorized packets are let through while doing the changes. When your changes have been completed, you need to remove the rules at position 1 with the following commands:

ipchains -D input 1

ipchains -D output 1

ipchains -D forward 1

Examples of the use of ipchains to allow various services.

Create a new chain:

ipchains -N chainame

The option "-N" creates the chain.

Add the chain to the input chain:

ipchains -A input -j chainame.

Allow connections to outside http servers from inside our network:

ipchains commands

-A chainame

-s 10.1.0.0/16 1024

-d 0.0.0.0/0 www

-j ACCEPT

The "-A chainame" adds a rule to the chain called "chainame".

The "-s 10.1.0.0/16 1024:" indicates any traffic on network 10.1.0.0 at port 1024 or above.

The "-d 0.0.0.0/0 www" indicates any destination for www service in the /etc/services file.

The "-j ACCEPT" sets the rule to accept the traffic.

Allow connections from the internet to connect with your http server:

ipchains commands

-A chainame

-s 0.0.0.0/0 www

-d 10.1.1.36 1024:

-j ACCEPT

The "-A chainame" adds a rule to the chain called "chainame".

The "-s 0.0.0.0/0 www" indicates traffic from any source for www service.

The "-d 10.1.1.36 1024:" indicates the http server at IP address 10.1.1.36 at ports above 1024.

The "-j ACCEPT" sets the rule to accept the traffic.

Allow DNS to go through the firewall:

Ipchains

-A chainame

-p UDP -s 0/0 dns

-d 10.1.0.0/16

-j ACCEPT

The "-A chainame" adds a rule to the chain called "chainame".

The "-p UDP" indicates UDP protocol.

The "-s 0/0 dns" indicates any dns traffic from any location.

The "-d 10.1.0.0/16" indicates our network.

The "-j ACCEPT" sets the rule to accept the traffic.

This allows DNS queries from computers inside our network to be received.

Allow e-mail to go from our internal mail server to mailservers outside the network.

ipchains

-A chainame

-s 10.1.1.24

-d 0/0 smtp

-j ACCEPT

The "-A chainame" adds a rule to the chain called "chainame".

The "-s 10.1.1.24" indicates any traffic from 10.1.1.24 IP address.

The "-d 0/0 smtp" indicates any smtp type of service going anywhere on the network.

The "-j ACCEPT" sets the rule to accept the traffic.

Allow e-mail to come from any location to our mail server.

Ipchains has the following four command to allow e-mail:

-A chainame

-s 0/0 smtp

-d 10.1.1.24 smtp

-j ACCEPT

The -A chainame adds a rule to the chain called "chainame".

The -s 0/0 smtp indicates mail traffic from anywhere on the network.

The -d 10.1.1.24 smtp indicates the mail server's traffic.

The -j ACCEPT sets the rule to accept the traffic.

Perform a HTTP port redirect for a transparent proxy server.

ipchains commands for transparent proxy server:

-A input

-p tcp

-s 10.1.0.0/16

-d 0/0 80

-j REDIRECT 8080

The -A input adds a rule to the input chain.

The -p tcp indicates the TCP.

The -s 10.1.0.0/16 indicates the source as a network with netmask 255.255.0.0.

The -d 0/0 indicates a destination anywhere on the network.

The -j REDIRECT 8080 redirects the traffic to port 8080.

The number 80 is the HTTP port number.

Give telnet transmissions a higher priority.

Ipchains

-A output

-p tcp -d 0.0.0.0/0 telnet

-t 0×01 0×10"

The -t 0×01 0×10" indicates hexadecimal format that is used to set the priority of the IP message on the network.

The first value is and 'ed with the TOS field in the IP message header, and the second value is exclusive or 'ed.

The "ipchains-save" and "ipchains-restore" are used to make rules permanent.

After setting ipchains rules, use following method to make them permanent:

Type the command "ipchains-save> /etc/iprules.save".

Type the following script named "packetfw":

```
#! /bin/sh
# Packet filtering firewall script to be used turn the firewall on or off
if [-f /etc/iprules.save]
then
case "$1" in
start)
echo -n "Turning on packet filtering firewall:"
/sbin/ipchains-restore < /etc/iprules.save
echo 1 > /proc/sys/net/ipv4/ip_forward
echo "."
;;
stop)
echo -n "Turning off packet filtering:"
echo 0 > /proc/sys/net/ipv4/ip_forward
```

```
/sbin/ipchains -X
/sbin/ipchains -F
/sbin/ipchains -P input ACCEPT
/sbin/ipchains -P output ACCEPT
/sbin/ipchains -P forward ACCEPT
echo "."
;;
*)
echo "Usage: /etc/init.d/packetfw {start|stop}"
exit 1
;;
esac
exit 0
else
echo the /etc/iprules.save file does not exist.
exit 1
fi
```

Save the file in the /etc/rc.d/init.d directory.

In the /etc/rc.d/rc3.d and the /etc/rc.d/rc5.d directories make a symbolic link called S07packetfw to the /etc/rc.d/init.d/packetfw file with the command "ln -s /etc/rc.d/rc3/S07packetfw /etc/rc.d/init.d/packetfw".

This applies to runlevel 3. Same may be applied to the runlevel 5 initialization directory.

You may use a different number than the "S07" string to number your link file.

See the /etc/rc.d/rc3.d and /etc/rc.d/rc5.d directories to determine what number is available to give this file.

You may provide it a number just below your network number file. You may use the S10network file to start your network.

Hardware and Software Threats

19

Viruses are not the only things that can cause damage to your system. There is a major threat from some hardware and software that damage the data on the disk.

Hardware Threats

There are the following types of hardware threats to your PC that may damage data of the hard disk:

1. Power faults
   - A. Power goes out
   - B. Voltage spikes
   - C. Frequency shifts
2. Age
3. Incompatible device
4. User mistake
5. Unauthorized use of PC
6. Repairing agent
7. Magnetic fields devices

1. Power faults. The following power faults are responsible for data loss on the disk:

A. Power goes out: Your are working on PC and suddenly power goes out. This may create bad sectors and loss of data on the hard disk that increase with the frequent power cut. It is always better to use UPS (Uninterrupted Power Supply) to avoid this problem.

B. **Voltage spikes:** Temporary voltage variations are fairly common that may cause the corruption of data files. Protection devices like CVT or UPS must be used to protect your computer.

C. **Frequency shifts:** Frequency variation from normal 60 Hertz to any other level value may cause data loss on the hard disk. To protect the computer from this problem UPS with inbuilt frequency stabilizer should be used.

2. Age. Electronics components of the computer are stressed frequently. They heat up and cool down several times with the age. Aging of electronics components may cause their failure and data loss on the computer. It is better to replace the computer, if it is more than six years old. Generally the age of an electronics components is five years.

3. Incompatible device. Though your computer is new and perfectly healthy, but due to the incompatible devices on your PC that do not properly share interrupts and cause several problems. Replace the incompatible device immediately by the suitable one.

4. User mistake. By mistake you delete or replace an executable or a programmable file. This is an unintentional loss of data that interrupt the program execution. Suppose you restore the program files, but they are not placed in the same place, where their associated files resides. You have to reinstall the complete program.

5. Unauthorized use. Somebody may use your computer in your absence and accidentally or deliberately delete or change a file on your PC. It is better to power off the computer when it is not used by you. Use security password for starting your computer.

6. Repairing agent. Computer Repairing Agent will almost always run a diagnostic program from diskette. It is possible that these diskettes may be infected and spread the infection to your computer. It is better to scan these diskettes after inserting into the drive.

7. Magnetic fields devices. Do not keep floppy taps and any other storage device near magnetic field generating equipments like freezer, telephone, CVT, UPS or Monitor, otherwise the data storage on the device may get corrupted.

Software Threats

1. Malicious program
2. Software conflicts
3. Utilities software

1. Malicious program. When you start your PC, it is booted first and then start menu appear on the desk top. Many software programs run in the background and interact with each other. Our PC runs in a very complex environment.

There are many resident programs like antivirus, video drivers, etc. running simultaneously with various versions of Windows, DOS, BIOS, and device drivers. These programs that are executed simultaneously and at the same time, share data, are vulnerable to unforeseen interactions between each other. If there is any malicious program, it interacts with the other programs and corrupt their data.

2. Software conflicts. Software conflict accounts for more damage to programs and data than any other.

They are more dangerous to your PC than virus attacks. Virus can be treated by antivirus, but if there is a conflict between two software, it becomes very difficult to run them on the same machine.

3. Hard disk problem. If you are facing the power cut problem frequently, it may generate the bad sectors on your hard drive. When you want to retrieve the file or data from the hard disk and your data are stored in the bad sector on the hard disk, so the sensor head of hard disk is unable to read these data.

You will encounter with the following message:

Data Error Reading Drive C:

Solution

To rectify this problem you have to run surface scandisk .exe program. Scandisk .exe program will remove the data from the bad sector and place these data in a safe or good sector on the hard disk.

Following are the three methods to scan the hard disk:

1. Scan the disks at booting stage.
2. Scanning by MS-DOS Window command.
3. Scanning by window's operating system.

Scan the disk at booting stage:

1. Start the computer.
2. Press <F8> function button.

Following window will appear:

```
Microsoft window 98 startup menu
1.Normal
2.Logged (\BOOTLOG.TXT)
3.Safe mode
4.Step-by-step confirmation
5.Command prompt only
6.Safe mode command prompt only
7.Previous version of MS-DOS
Enter a choice:
F5=Safe Mode  Shift+F5=Command prompt  Shift+F8=step-by-step confirmation [N]
```

3. Select choice 5 command prompt only from the above window.
4. Press <Enter>

   C:\> prompt will appear on screen.
5. Type the scandisk command in front of C:\> as follows:

   C:\>SCANDISK
6. Press <Enter> to start scandisk operation.

You can see the scandisk operation on the progress bar in Microsoft Scandisk window.

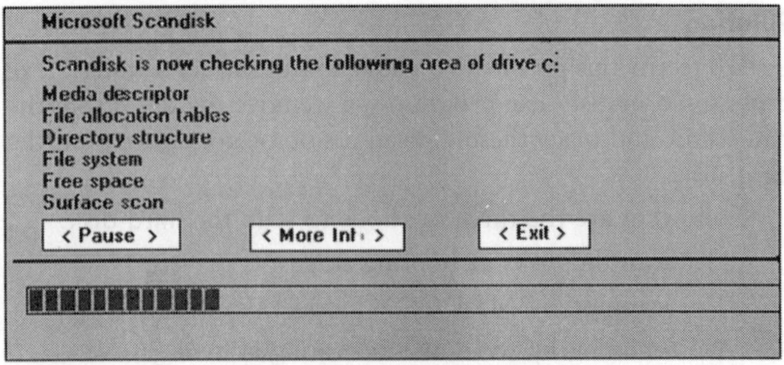

There are three options of the above Microsoft scandisk window:

1. Pause option will halt the scanning.
2. Exit option will skip the scanning operation.
3. More Info will provide you the current position of scanning.

When scandisk checking is completed the following window appears on screen:

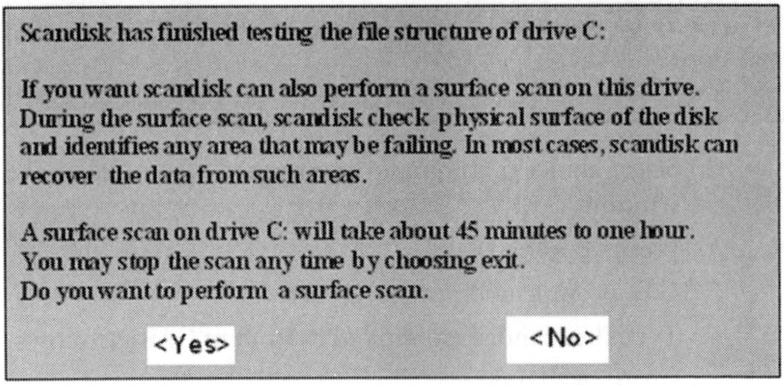

Select Yes 'Surface scanning window' will appear on screen and surface scanning of C: drive will start.

Surface Scanning Window

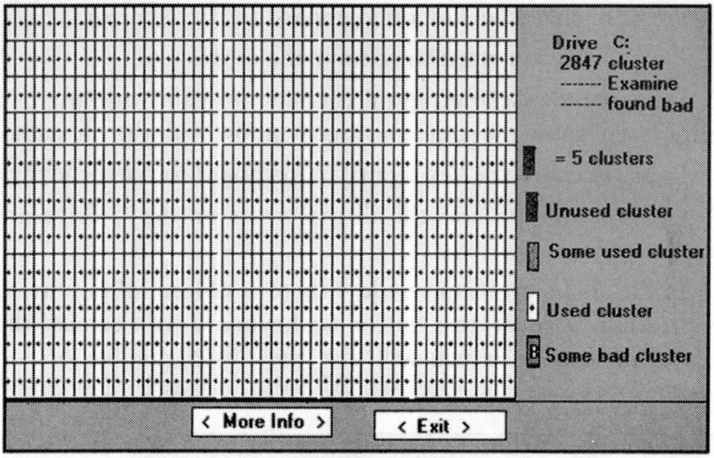

During surface scanning program you can see the scanning details of drive C:.

Total number of cluster in drive C:	5847 Clusters	Figure remains constant.
Number of cluster examined	334 Examine	Figure changes from 0 to 2847.
Number of bad cluster found	53 Found bad	Figure changes from 0 to max bad clusters.

If the scandisk .exe program encounters with any bad sector it will show the following message window:

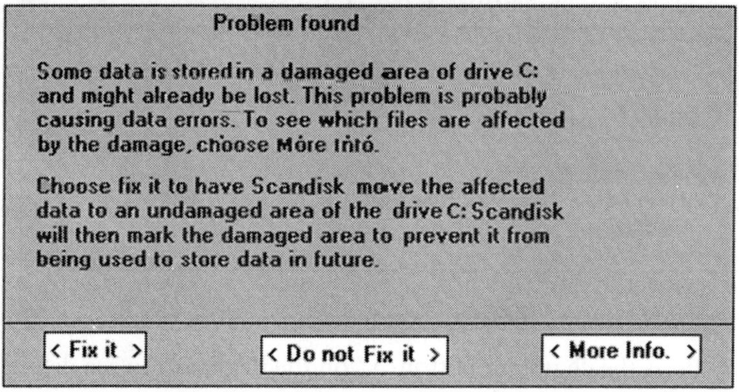

Press 'F' character key on keyboard to fix the error.

Press 'X' if you want to remove the error.

If the scandisk.exe program encounters again with any bad sector it will show the same message window with the file name.

Press 'F' character key again on keyboard to fix the error.

Continue the process till all the errors on the C drive are fixed.

In the above problem window there is <More Info> button. By pressing 'M' character button on keyboard, you can see the following window, which will give the cluster number of bad cluster.

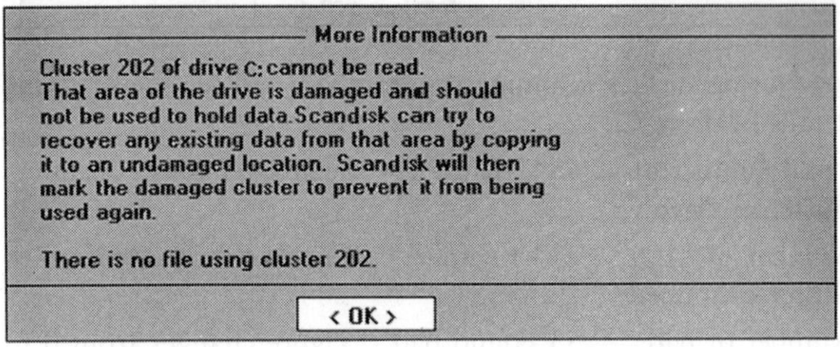

After completion of the surface scanning of drive C: you will get the following message window on screen:

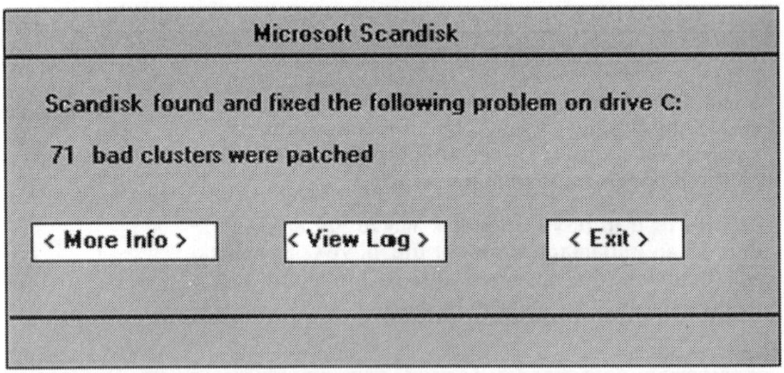

Press the character button 'V' on the keyboard to see details of bad cluster, View Log window.

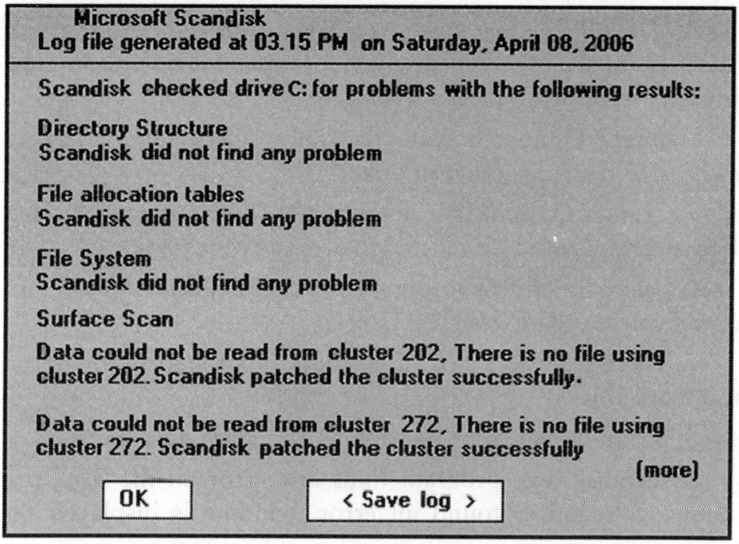

SCANDISK command using Window's DOS Version:

1. Open command prompt from window program by clicking on MS-DOS icon.

2. Type the following command:

C:\>scandiskw

3. Press <Enter>. You will see the following Microsoft Scandisk window:

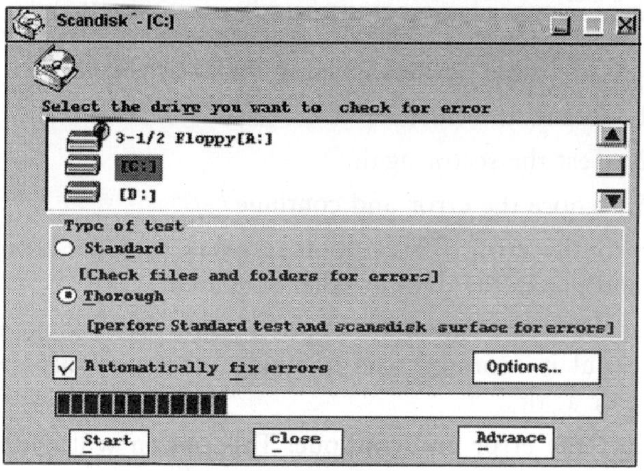

4. Select drive 'C'.

5. There are two options given for type of test standard and thorough. Select any one of them.

Standard Option: It scans files and folders only and takes lesser time than thorough option.

Thorough Option: It scans files and folders as well surface data area and takes more time than standard option.

6. Select the thorough option for scanning files and folders as well surface data area.

7. There is a check box. Tick check box for fixing the error automatically.

8. Scanning will start as soon as you click start button.

If scandisk .exe program finds any error on the disk, the following 'scandisk found an error' window is displayed on screen.

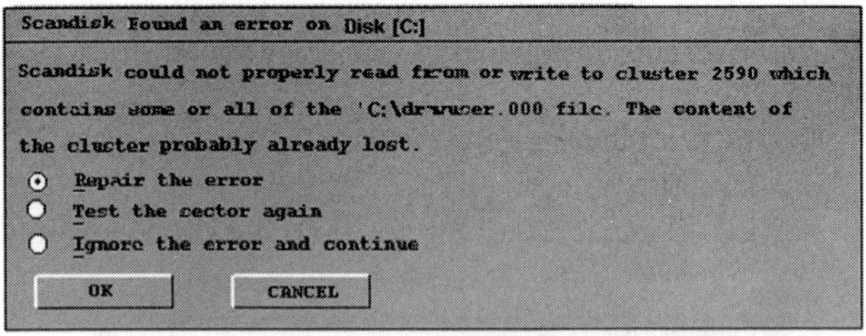

There are three options given in the above window:

1. Repair the cluster.
2. Test the sector again.
3. Ignore the error and continue.

Repair the error: This option recovers the data from bad sector and places the data in other safe area.

Test the sector again: This option scans the disk again and if successful it continues the scanning otherwise displays the same error again.

Ignore the error and continue: This option will ignore the error.

Scanning the Hard Disk using Window Program:

1. For opening the scandisk program follow the path as given below:

Start->Programs. Programs Accessories System Tools Scandisk

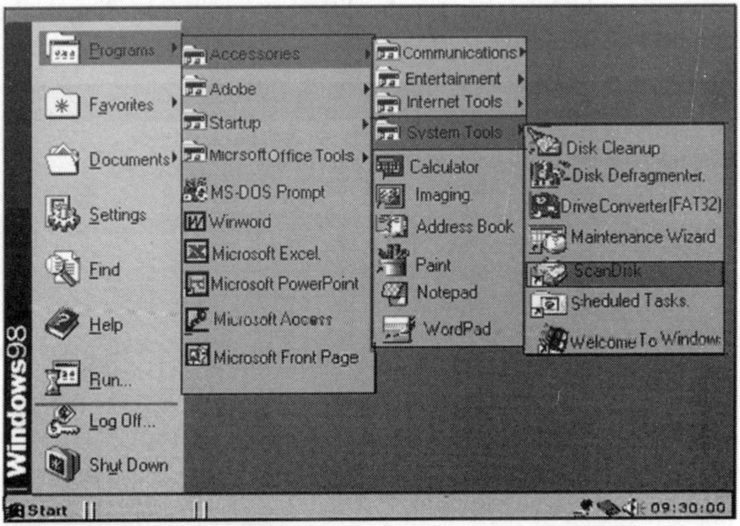

2. Click on Scandisk.

3. Select drive C, D or E.

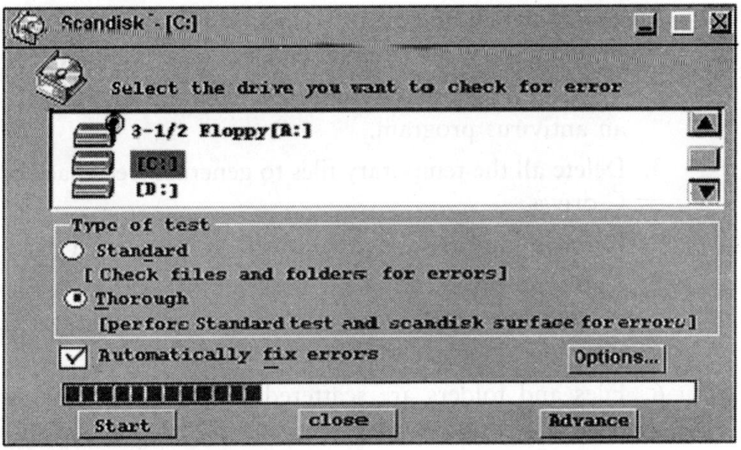

4. Select the thorough option in the wizard window.
5. Press Start button.

Scanning of drive C: It may take 40 to 45 minutes or more according to the capacity of C: drive after completion of scanning you get result. You may get the different result according to the condition of C: drive.

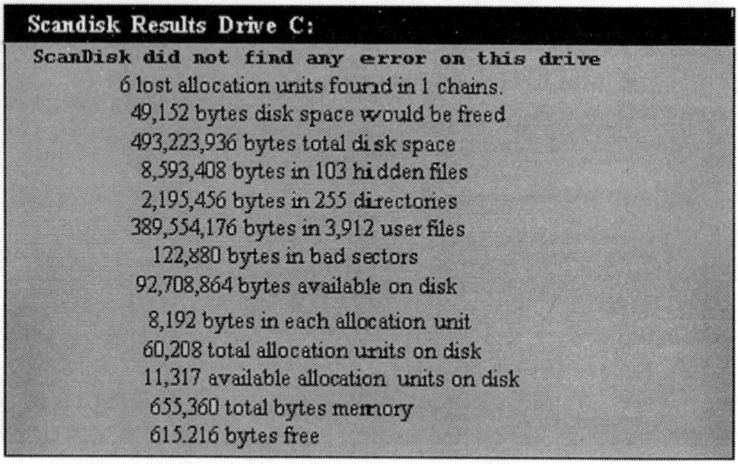

Computer is working very slow.

There may be following reason:

1. Turbo switch may be off. Turn on the turbo switch if provided on your computer.
2. Your hard disk may be infected. Scan the hard disk by an antivirus program.
3. Delete all the temporary files to generate free space on C drives.
4. Remove unnecessary programs from your hard disk.
5. Antivirus program which uses lot of executive files during their application, also causes the computer to run slow. Increase the capacity of SDRAM.
6. Files and folders are scattered on the surface of the disk. To arrange these files and folders on the disk properly, we have to de-fragment the drives.

Defragmentation of Hard Disk

Follow the method to de-fragment the drives:

1. For opening the de-fragmentation program follow the path as given below:

Start->Programs, Accessories, System Tools, Disk Defragmenter

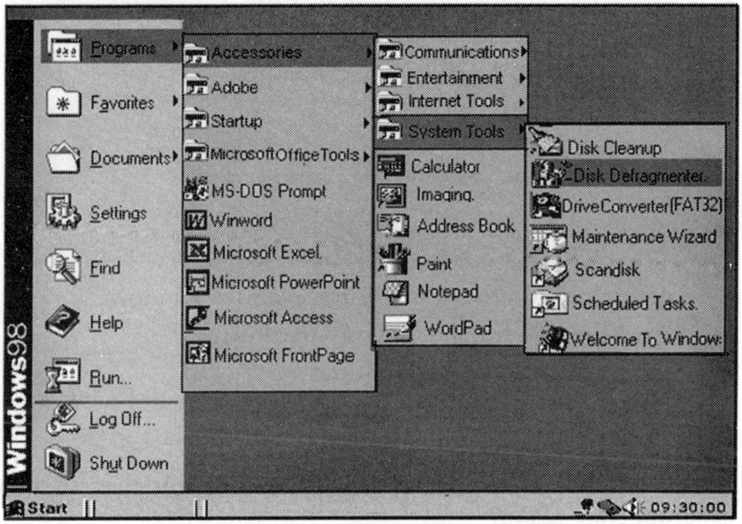

2. Click on Disk Defragmenter.

You will see the following window on the screen.

If you click the arrow pointer near physical drive, you can see the other drives.

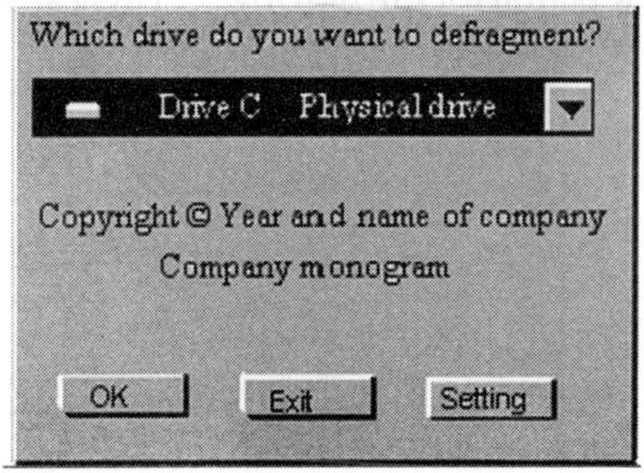

3. Select drive C:.
4. Click on setting button.

Disk defragmenter Setting window appears on the screen.

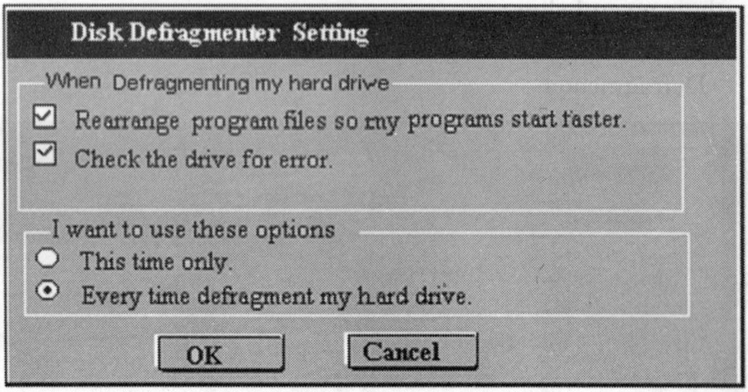

There are two groups given in the above window:

1. When de-fragmenting my hard drive.
2. I want to use these options.

1. When de-fragmenting my hard drive

Tick both the check boxes.

First check box will rearrange the program files so that program start faster.

Second check box will check the error on drive C:

2. I want to use these options

There are two options in this group.

Select the option according to your requirement.

Clock OK button back to the Drive C: Physical drive window.

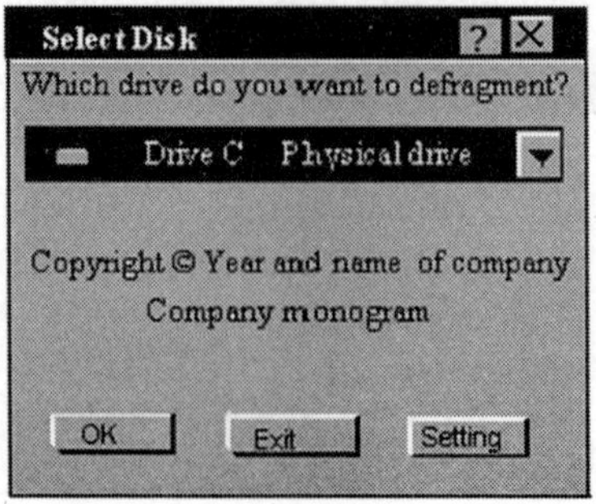

Click on OK. De-fragmenting of Drive C: will start and displayed by the following window:

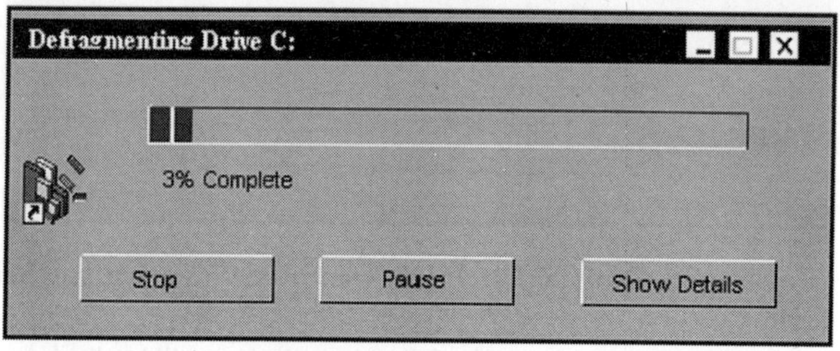

If you click on show details button the following window will be displayed on the screen.

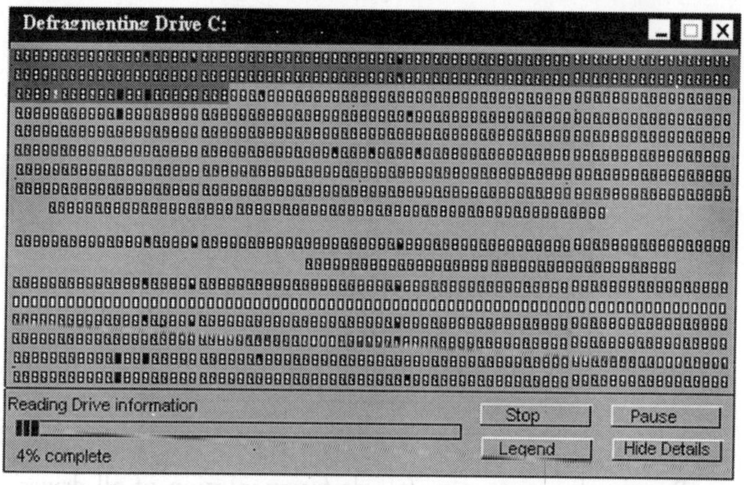

De-fragmenting of the hard disk should be carried out when the computer is idle.

Close all the programs when you de-fragment the disk.

When your de-fragmenting program is completed following window appears on the screen:

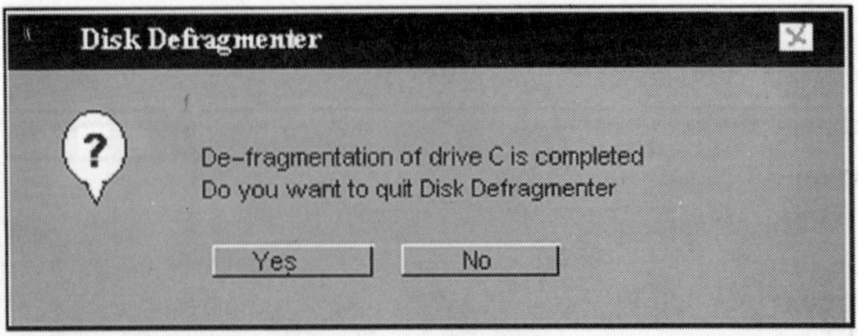

Click on "No" button. If you want to de-fragment another drive.

Click on "No" button the following window will be displayed on the screen.

Select the next drive for de-fragmentation.

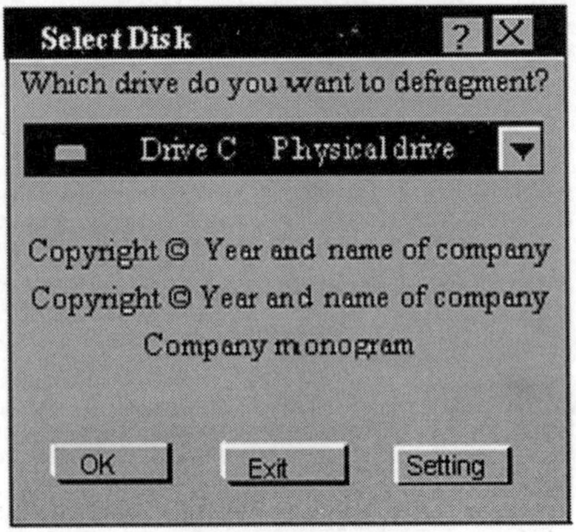

Restart the computer after de-fragmentation of all drives.

General Failure? Message on Screen

Data are stored in the form of magnetic pulse. When you format a disk File Allocation Table are formed on the disk. File Allocation Table is the area where the data are stored.

When these File Allocation Tables are damaged, then you have to format the drive again.

In case the formatting of such drive is not possible, the drive becomes corrupt and cannot be used. In this case you have to change the hard disk.

Invalid Drive Specification? Message on Screen

This message indicates that the (FAT) File Allocation Table on the hard disk becomes unreadable. In this case you have to format the disk. But before formatting the hard disk, we have to delete the partition for making new partition on the hard disk.